# THE GROUNDS OF REFUGEE PROTECTION IN THE CONTEXT OF INTERNATIONAL HUMAN RIGHTS AND HUMANITARIAN LAW

# Refugees and Human Rights

Volume 5



The *Refugees and Human Rights* Series aims to meet the increasing need for literature which probes the nature and causes of forced migration, the modalities and procedures employed when refugees present themselves, and the manner in which the human rights of refugees are, or should be, promoted and protected.

# THE GROUNDS OF REFUGEE PROTECTION IN THE CONTEXT OF INTERNATIONAL HUMAN RIGHTS AND HUMANITARIAN LAW

## Canadian and United States Case Law Compared

By

Mark R. von Sternberg

MARTINUS NIJHOFF PUBLISHERS
THE HAGUE / LONDON / NEW YORK

A C.I.P. Catalogue record for this book is available from the Library of Congress

ISBN 90-411-1726-1

Published by Martinus Nijhoff Publishers,
P.O. Box 85889, 2508 CN The Hague, The Netherlands.

Sold and distributed in North, Central and South America
by Kluwer Law International,
101 Philip Drive, Norwell, MA 02061, U.S.A.

In all other countries, sold and distributed
by Kluwer Law International, Distribution Centre,
P.O. Box 322, 3300 AH Dordrecht, The Netherlands.

*Printed on acid-free paper*



Printed in the Netherlands.

# TABLE OF CONTENTS

# I. INTRODUCTION: THE EMERGING CRITERIA FOR REFUGEE STATUS

## § I.1. The Convention Refugee Definition in the Context of Human Rights and Humanitarian Norms

This is a study of the grounds of refugee protection under the 1951 Convention on the Status of Refugees[1] as these are developed in Canadian and United States case law. Generally, the 1951 Convention, as modified by the 1967 Protocol,[2] establishes an international regime to safeguard the human rights of those fleeing their homelands in fear for their lives or freedom, provided that they can meet certain definitional criteria. Implementing statutory law in Canada and the United States mirrors the substantive provisions of the Convention and Protocol by conferring protection on those individuals who can demonstrate a well-founded fear of being persecuted arising out of one of five enumerated grounds: race, religion, nationality, membership in a particular social group or political opinion.

Canada's Immigration Act,[3] for instance, adopts the exclusively forward-looking test contained in Article 1A(2) of the Convention, defining the term "refugee" as any person who:

> (a) by reason of a well-founded fear of persecution for reasons of race, religion, nationality, membership in a particular social group or political opinion,
>
> (i) is outside the country of the person's nationality and is unable or, by reason of that fear, is unwilling to avail himself of the protection of that country, or
>
> (ii) not having a country of nationality, is outside the country of the person's former habitual residence and is unable or, by reason of that fear, is unwilling to return to that country, and
>
> (b) has not ceased to be a refugee.

---

1 Convention Relating to the Status of Refugees, *signed* 28 July 1951, *entered into force* 22 April 1954, 189 UNTS 150.

2 Protocol Relating to the Status of Refugees, *opened for signature* 31 Jan. 1967, *entered into force* 4 Oct. 1967, 606 UNTS 267, *reprinted in* 6 ILM 78 (1967), Art. 2.

3 R.S.C. 1985 (4th Supp.), c. 28, s.1 and s.2(1.1) enacted by S.C. 1992, c.49, s.1 [hereinafter Immigration Act], s. 2(1).

Section 208(a) of the U.S. Immigration and Nationality Act,[4] on the other hand, empowers the Attorney General to establish a procedure for discretionary grants of asylum with respect to individuals conforming to the statute's definition of "refugee".[5] The political asylum remedy in the U.S. thus tracks the definition of "refugee" contained in Article 1A(2) of the Convention, with the singular exception that the U.S. refugee definition sets forth past persecution as a qualifying basis.[6]

Protection against serious harm in the asylum seeker's home country is thus not unlimited. There must be some connection to a refugee ground for a claim of asylum or refugee status to be viable.[7] The restrictions imposed, particularly under modern jurisprudence, by the five "categories" circumscribing "persecution" have proved to be among the most substantial barriers to relief.

This study explores the ways in which contemporary human rights and humanitarian law (the rules and customs applicable during armed conflict) can serve to clarify the scope of the Convention grounds. The 1951 Convention on Refugees which was adopted under the auspices of the United Nations and is deeply informed with the seminal objectives of the World

---

4 Immigration and Nationality Act of 1952, Pub. L. No. 82-414, 66 Stat. 163 (codified and amended at 8 USC § 1101 *et seq.*) [hereinafter INA], § 208(a), 8 USC § 1158(a).

5 *Id.*, § 101(a)(42), 8 USC § 1101(a)(42).

6 A companion remedy, intended to reflect the *non-refoulement* provisions of Article 33 of the 1951 Convention, is provided for in INA § 241(b)(3) which sets forth that the Attorney General may withhold the removal of any alien who can show that her life or freedom would be threatened on account of any one of the enumerated grounds *See generally* Cardoza-Fonseca v. INS, 480 U.S. 421 (1987).

7 James Hathaway, The Law of Refugee Status 136-37 (1991):

> Under the Convention, then, if the peril the claimant faces—however wrongful it may be—cannot somehow be linked to her socio-political situation and subsequent marginalization, the claim to refugee status must fail. Put succinctly, refugee law requires that there be a nexus between who the claimant is or what she believes and the risk of serious harm in her own state.

*See also,* 1 Atle Grahl-Madsen, The Status of Refugees in International Law 217 (1966):

> The fact that a person has a 'well-founded fear of being persecuted' upon his eventual return to his country does not constitute him a 'refugee', unless he fears persecution for one of the reasons set forth in Article 1A(2) of the Convention; to wit:
>
> (1) race;
> (2) religion;
> (3) nationality;
> (4) membership in a particular social group; or
> (5) political opinion.

Organization. Accordingly, it is essential to interpret the Convention refugee definition in light of the purposes and principles of the United Nations Charter[8] which include the full realization of individual human rights on a non-discriminatory basis.[9]

Atle Grahl-Madsen has made explicit the view that punishment which is related to the asylum seeker's attachment to a fundamental human right constitutes political opinion persecution within the meaning of the refugee definition.[10] The direct relationship between the political opinion category and international human rights shows clearly the dependence of the refugee standard on evolving human rights developments.[11] The refugee definition's essential components, therefore, must be interpreted with a view to offering enhanced consideration, as a matter of public policy, to individuals who promote seminal human rights goals in the face of coercive governmental or third-party action. Of equal concern are those groups which the international community has found to merit special attention in light of their historic vulnerability (e.g., classes defined by intrinsic characteristics such as race, gender, age, social and economic status, etc.) and for which special measures of protection are needed in order to assure their enjoyment of human rights on an equal basis.

---

8 *See* UN Charter, Preamble, identifying the purposes and principles of the United Nations with

> (a) elimination of the "scourge of war";
> (b) reaffirmation of human rights as an organizing social principle;
> (c) the integrity of international law and institutions; and
> (d) working toward a "larger freedom" through social progress.

9 Convention on the Status of Refugees, *supra* this section, note 1, Preamble. The 1951 Convention was clearly adopted in the historical context of the world community's commitment to the realization of human rights as set forth in the Universal Declaration of Human Rights and, most critically, to the proposition contained in Article 2 of UDHR that human rights be enjoyed without discrimination as to any status.

10 1 Grahl-Madsen, *supra* this section, note 7, at 217, noting that individuals may qualify under the Convention refugee definition if they fear persecutory measures flowing from their exercise or insistence upon certain rights set down in the Universal Declaration of Human Rights.

11 Guy S. Goodwin-Gill, The Refugee in International Law 48-49 (2d ed. 1996):

> Finally, the Convention adduces the fear of persecution for reasons of political opinion. Article 19 of the Universal Declaration of Human Rights provides that: 'Everyone has the right to freedom of opinion and expression'; the right includes the freedom to hold opinions without interference and to seek, receive and impart information and ideas through any media and regardless of frontiers.

Relevant, therefore, to the law of refugee status are the Universal Declaration of Human Rights[12] (the matrix of modern human rights doctrine)[13] as well as the implementing Covenants which make applicable the Universal Declaration's normative standards as a matter of treaty law to States parties: the Covenant on Civil and Political Rights[14] and the Covenant on Economic, Social and Cultural Rights.[15] The rights set forth in UDHR, receiving their mature expression in the ICCPR and the ICESR, clearly constitute customary international law and, in the opinion of some commentators, are in the course of becoming *jus cogens*.[16]

Also germane, where the asylum claim arises out of a situation of internal or international armed conflict, is that wide corpus of principles contained in the Geneva Conventions of 1949 and Protocols I and II thereto.[17] These

---

12 Universal Declaration of Human Rights, *adopted* 10 Dec. 1948, G.A. Res. 217A(III), U.N. Doc. A/810 (1948) [hereinafter UDHR].

13 Those rights codified in the International Covenant on Civil and Political Rights and the International Covenant on Economic, Social and Cultural Rights derive from the Universal Declaration of Human Rights, itself a United Nations initiative which was designed to sketch in broad outline the essential rights for eventual inclusion in treaties which would elaborate upon these rights and give them specificity:

> The plan to use the Universal Declaration as a springboard to treaties triumphed, but not as quickly as anticipated. The two principal treaties [the ICCPR and the ICSECR] made their ways through the drafting and amendment process in the Commission, the Third Committee and the General Assembly, where they were approved only in 1966. Another decade passed before the two Conventions achieved the number of ratifications necessary to enter into force.

Henry J. Steiner and Philip Alston, International Human Rights in Context 120 (1996).

14 International Covenant on Civil and Political Rights, *adopted* 16 Dec. 1966,, *entered into force* 23 March 1976, G.A. Res. 2200A (XXI), U.N. Doc. A/6316 (1966), 999 UNTS 171, *reprinted in* 6 ILM 368 (1967) [hereinafter ICCPR].

15 International Covenant on Economic, Social and Cultural Rights, *adopted* 16 Dec. 1966, *entered into force* 3 Jan. 1976, G.A. Res. 2200A (XXI), UN Doc. A/6316 (1966), 993 UNTS 3, *reprinted in* 6 ILM 360 (1967) [hereinafter ICESCR], Art. 11.

16 *See generally* Karen Parker and Lyn Beth Neylon, Jus Cogens: *Forcing the Law of Human Rights,* 12 Hastings Int'l & Comp. L. Rev. 411, 422 (1989).

> The Universal Declaration of Human Rights is the authoritative interpretation of human rights provisions in the United Nations Charter. The Universal Declaration as a whole is customary international law, and is rapidly establishing itself as *jus cogens*.

17 The Geneva Conventions of August 1949, *in force* Oct. 21, 1950, 6 U.S.T. 3114, T.I.A.S. No. 3362, 75 U.N.T.S. 31 (armed forces in the field); 6 U.S.T. 3217, T.I.A.S. No. 3363, 75 U.N.T.S. 85 (sick, wounded and shipwrecked at sea); 6 U.S.T. 3316, T.I.A.S. No. 3364, 75 U.N.T.S. 135 (prisoners of war); 6 U.S.T. 3516, T.I.A.S. No. 3365, 75 U.N.T.S. 267 (civilians); Protocol Additional I to the Geneva Conventions of 1949 (relating to protection of victims of international armed conflict), *in force* Dec. 7, 1978, U.N. Doc.

instruments incorporate human rights norms and make them applicable during wartime.[18] Of paramount importance with respect to groups deserving of enhanced protection are the Apartheid Convention,[19] the Convention on the Elimination of All Forms of Racial Discrimination,[20] the Convention on the Rights of the Child;[21] the Convention on the Elimination of All Forms of Discrimination Against Women;[22] and the Declaration on the Rights of Persons Belonging to National or Ethnic, Religious or Linguistic Minorities.[23]

---

A/32/144/Annex I (1977), *reprinted in* 16 I.L.M. 1391 (1977) [hereinafter Protocol I]; Protocol Additional II to the Geneva Conventions of 1949 (relating to the protection of victims of non-international armed conflict), *in force* Dec. 7, 1978, U.N. Doc. A/32/144/Annex II (1977), *reprinted in* 16 I.L.M. 1442 (1977) [hereinafter Protocol II].

18 *See generally Respect for Human Rights in Armed Conflict, Report of the Secretary General*, U.N. Doc. A/7120 (1969). Significantly, Jean Pictet, perhaps the most celebrated of the commentators on the texts of the Geneva Conventions, sought to combine human rights law and humanitarian law into a common jurisprudence. To that end, Pictet developed a number of principles which synthesize the relationship between humanitarian law and human rights and which work a fusion between these two bodies of jurisprudence. Pictet calls this new jurisprudence Human Law, and he lists its underlying principles as Inviolability, Non-Discrimination and Security. These axioms are important in that they reflect the emerging philosophy of the Geneva Conventions as informed by human rights principles. *See generally* Jean Pictet, Development and Principles of International Humanitarian Law 63-68 (1985).

19 International Convention on the Suppression and Punishment of the Crime of Apartheid, *adopted* 30 Nov. 1973, *entered into force* 18 July 1976, G.A. Res. 3068 (XXVIII), *reprinted in* 13 ILM 50 (1974) [hereinafter Apartheid Convention].

20 International Convention for the Elimination of All Forms of Racial Discrimination, *adopted* 21 Dec. 1965, *entered into force* 4 Jan. 1969, 660 UNTS 195, *reprinted in* 5 ILM 352 (1966) [hereinafter Convention on the Elimination of All Forms of Racial Discrimination].

21 Convention on the Rights of the Child, *adopted* 20 November 1989, entered into force 2 September 1990, G.A. Res. 44/25, 44 UN GAOR, Supp. (No. 49), UN Doc. A/44/49 at 166 (1989), *reprinted in* 28 ILM 1448 (1989) [hereinafter Convention on the Rights of the Child].

22 Convention on the Elimination of All Forms of Discrimination Against Women, *adopted* 18 Dec. 1979, *entered into force* 3 Sept. 1981, G.A. Res. 34/180, 34 UN GAOR, Supp. (No. 46), U.N. Doc. A/34/46, at 193, *reprinted in* 19 ILM 33 (1980) [hereinafter CEDAW].

23 Declaration on the Rights of Persons Belonging to National or Ethnic, Religious or Linguistic Minorities, *adopted* 18 Dec. 1992, G.A. Res. 47/135, *reprinted in* 32 ILM 191 (1993) [hereinafter Declaration on the Rights of National, Ethnic, Religious or Linguistic Minorities]. For an article anticipating many developments in this field, *see* Arthur Helton, *Persecution on Account of Membership in a Social Group as a Basis for Refugee Status,* 15 Columbia Hum. Rts. L. Rev. 39 (1983).

United States jurisprudence has tended to emphasize the asylum seeker's "intrinsic" characteristics in developing the law of refugee status, particularly where social group persecution is involved. It has been argued, for instance, that an examination which rests too heavily on "external" characteristics (i.e., which looks to the persecutor's perceptions) runs the risk of becoming circular.[24] It is the submission of this study that an approach which avoids the "external" features of the claimant's persona does disservice to development of the Convention refugee definition. Seminal treatise law establishes that whether an act can be characterized as "persecutory" (and the related question of whether that act can be connected to a protected ground) can best be determined by examining the perceptions and motivations of the persecutor.[25] And the Immigration and Naturalization Service's *Basic Law Manual*[26] accepts that attribution principles relate to all five "reasons" for serious harm (including the "particular social group" category). These considerations lend substantial support to the view that what constitutes persecution based on a protected ground is context-dependent and is often compellingly related to the will and imagination of the persecutor. Attributed characteristics and beliefs also go far to demonstrate that the refugee grounds are potentially open-ended and rely for their interpretation on the social environment giving rise to the claim for international protection.[27]

It has often been remarked that the 1951 Convention was drawn up with a view to the individual in mind. Notwithstanding this broad (and unchallengeable) proposition, the protected grounds themselves do not refer to individualized characteristics, but to group traits. Hence, while the asylum seeker is under a burden to make out an objectively reasonable possibility of individual persecution, it is absolutely incorrect to identify this individualization with the protected grounds.[28] Race, religion, nationality, membership in a social group constitute, on their face, collective human aggregates.

---

[24] *See, e.g.*, Deborah Anker, *Defining "Particular Social Group" in Terms of Gender: The* Shah *Decision and U.S. Law*, 76 Interpreter Releases 1005, 1010 (July 2, 1999). Such a methodology seems most to be avoided where the results of persecution are looked at (common victimization) rather than the incentives for imposing serious harm.

[25] 1 Grahl-Madsen, *supra* this section, note 7, at 175. *See also* Goodwin-Gill, *supra* this section, note 11, at 362.

[26] U.S. Immigration and Naturalization Service, Basic Law Manual: U.S. Law and INS Asylum/Refugee Adjudications 36, n. 9 (1994) [hereinafter Basic Law Manual].

[27] Goodwin-Gill, *supra* this section, note 11, at 312.

[28] The applicant must show a possibility of future persecution, either alone or as the member of a group. Kotasz v. INS, 31 F.3d 847 (9th Cir. 1994); Salibian v. M.E.I. (1990), 113 N.R. 123 (F.C.A.).

Moreover, although the political opinion ground may formally embrace situations of highly individualized beliefs, it hardly ever does so: political adversaries do not fear isolated individuals but reserve their anxieties (and animosities) for those beliefs which can be identified with broad collective movements.[29] Here again, the protected grounds track nicely the developing law of "persecution" which, it has been long recognized, is essentially "non-comparative" in nature, and includes serious harm applied to human collectivities as well as to individuals.[30]

## § I.2. Unifying Elements of the Grounds of Refugee Protection

Are there common attributes that these collective descriptions have in common which would help explain their application as well as identify the parameters of the social group basis of refugee protection? Standards establishing the outer limits of protection have not been systematically set forth either by scholars or in the case law. The most comprehensive effort to bring the grounds of persecution within a common framework was made by James Hathaway in his influential study, *The Law of Refugee Status*.[31] There the author sought to identify the Convention grounds with serious harm connected in some way to the claimant's "civil or political status".

Hathaway's analysis of the "reasons" for persecution was closely related to his understanding of "persecution" which was determined to consist of the "sustained or systemic violation of basic human rights resulting from a

---

[29] As was noted in *Kotasz* v. *INS*, 31 F.3d 847 (9th Cir. 1994):

> While it is not inconceivable that a person would be individually persecuted on the basis of his uniquely abhorrent (in the persecutor's view) political beliefs, such occurrences would be rare. Political parties, factions, ideologies and movements are group phenomena. Moreover, it is generally the existence of a group of opponents that concerns the governments or other persecutor sufficient to provoke oppression.

*Id.* at 853, n. 9.

[30] *Cf.* United Nations High Commissioner for Refugees, Handbook on Procedures and Criteria for Determining Refugee Status Under the 1951 Convention and the 1967 Protocol Relating to the Status of Refugees ¶ 44 (Geneva 1992) [hereinafter Handbook]. The *Handbook* is viewed by national authorities as an authoritative guide (although not formally binding) with respect to refugee status/asylum determinations. *Compare* INS v. Cardoza-Fonseca, 480 U.S. 421 (1987) and Zolfagharkani v. M.E.I. (1993), 155 N.R. 311, 317 (F.C.A.).

[31] *See* Hathaway, *supra* § I.1, note 7, chapter 4.

failure of State protection".[32] Juxtaposed to this concept of "persecution", the enumerated grounds are identified with the claimant's "membership rights in her community". These "membership rights" clearly constitute the normative content of "civil or political status" as a litmus test for the types of serious harm embraced by the refugee definition. Hathaway writes:[33]

> These early refugees were not merely suffering persons, but were moreover persons whose position was fundamentally at odds with the power structure in their home state. It was the lack of a meaningful stake in the governance of their own society which distinguished them from others, and which gave legitimacy to their desire to seek protection abroad.
>
> The modern refugee definition gave voice to this premise by moving away from protection on the basis of named marginalized groups, and toward a more generic formulation of the membership principle. Given the prevailing primacy of the civil and political paradigm of human rights, it was contextually logical that marginalization should be defined by reference to norms of non-discrimination: a refugee was defined as a person at risk of serious harm *for reasons of* race, religion, nationality, membership of a particular social group or political opinion. The rationale for this limitation was not that other persons were less at risk, but rather that, at least in the context of the historical moment, persons affected by these forms of socio-political disfranchisement were less likely to be in a position to seek effective assistance within the state.

This study resists the "civil or political status" test as a unifying basis of the protected grounds on the principle that "persecution" (which the refugee grounds clearly track) is not limited to human rights violations which are caused by State inaction or ineffectiveness.[34] Persecution in the Convention sense can be imposed either by the State or by "agents" of persecution which the State is unable or unwilling to control.[35] The protected grounds seek, among other things, to identify a causative relationship between the persecutor's incentive and a "reason" for persecution which is recognized under the Convention refugee definition. It is clear that such motivation on

---

[32] *Id.* at 101. The Hathaway analysis has been largely accepted by Deborah Anker in the most recent edition of her treatment of U.S. asylum law. *See* Deborah Anker, The Law of Asylum in the United States 191-199 (3d ed. 1999) [hereinafter cited as Anker 99].

[33] Hathaway, *supra* § I.1, note 7, at 136.

[34] *See, e.g.*, Goodwin-Gill, *supra* § I.1, note 11, at 73-74, cautioning against a requirement that there be institutions of State protection present in the country of claimed persecution in order for a refugee claim to be made out.

[35] *See generally* Handbook, *supra* § I.1, note 30, ¶ 65.

the part of a private party cannot be characterized solely by reference to the claimant's relationship to the State and its protective apparatus.[36]

All this is not to ignore situations in which the State's failure to protect specific groups lies at the heart of the mistreatment and so can constitute serious harm within the meaning of the 1951 Convention. It is rather to suggest that such an approach is not an exclusive methodology for discerning the existence of a protected ground; the unavoidable conclusion remains that it is often the claimant's relationship to a powerful group threatening injury which is material to the analysis. An asylum applicant who seeks to avoid retaliation by guerillas for openly defying them in some way fears persecution "on account of" a political opinion which will be attributed to the claimant by the insurgents (disloyalty to the rebel cause). This "reason" for persecution[37] is entirely unrelated to any standard of State protection.[38]

It is a central theme of this study that the refugee definition has been expanding to include those reasons for serious harm which describe not only the claimant's position with respect to State authority, but also to "private" groups which, by virtue of their importance or social dominance, can act with comparative impunity. Phrased alternatively, it is the claimant's relationship to powerful interests seeking to impose their will which often establishes the existence of a protected ground, not necessarily her relationship to a standard of State protection.

The approach followed here has been to view the refugee grounds as essentially "open-ended" and to be shaped by actual discriminatory State, social or cultural practices. For its foundations, the present view draws, in part, upon the standard of international penal law which holds individuals criminally accountable for grave violations of internationally protected

---

36 The conclusion that serious harm can result from mistreatment by "private parties" in civil war situations is supported by parallel developments in human rights and humanitarian law. Among the most significant of these developments are substantive principles still evolving in the customs and regulations applicable during armed conflict which establish a right/duty relationship between non-State (private) belligerents and protected persons in internal armed wars. *See, e.g.*, Sylvie-Stoyanka Junod, *Commentary on the Protocol Additional to the Geneva Conventions of 12 August 1949, and relating to the Protection of Victims of Non-International Armed Conflicts in* Commentary on the Additional Protocols of 9 June 1977 to the Geneva Conventions of 12 August 1949, 1345 (Y. Sandoz *et al.* eds.) [hereinafter *Commentary to Protocol II*].

37 *Cf.* Matter of Maldonado-Cruz, 19 I&N Dec. 509 (BIA 1989), *rev'd,* Maldonado-Cruz v. INS, 883 F.2d 788 (9th Cir. 1990).

38 State protection addresses specifically the "well-founded fear" component of the refugee definition, not the "persecution" element. *See* Goodwin-Gill, *supra* § I.1, note 11, at 73-74.

human rights.[39] Secondly, international humanitarian law, postulating "elementary dictates of humanity" and protecting rights in armed conflict, has established that, in internal wars, obligations run not merely to State parties but also to private individuals so as to govern the latter's rights and duties.[40] Finally, the position adopted here also enjoys broad support in the still developing doctrine under regional human rights regimes that human rights can be enforced both "vertically" (i.e., against the State and its agents) and "horizontally" (i.e., by and between private parties [*Drittwirkung der Grundrechte*]).[41]

## § I.3. Proposed Test for Establishing the Existence of a Refugee Ground

Modern jurisprudence has emphasized the non-discrimination foundations of international human rights law as providing an appropriate framework within which to examine the relationship between serious harm and a protected ground. Accordingly, in *Islam (A.P.)* v. *Secretary of State for the Home Department, Regina* v. *Immigration Appeal Tribunal and Another Ex Parte Shah (A.P.),*[42] the British House of Lords issued a decision of extraordinary scope finding eligible for asylum two Pakistani women largely on the basis that they feared domestic violence if returned to their homeland. In setting forth the principles upon which the Lords were prepared to view the parameters of the social group ground of refugee protection (and implicitly the parameters of the refugee definition itself), the opinion of Lord Hoffman referred to the preamble to the 1951 Convention (incorporating the non-discrimination mandate of UDHR Art. 2) and concluded:

> In my opinion, the concept of discrimination in matters affecting human rights and freedoms is central to an understanding of the Convention. It is concerned not with all cases of persecution, even if they involve denials of human rights, but with persecution which is based on discrimination. And in the context of a human rights instrument, discrimination means making distinctions which principles of fundamental human rights regard as inconsistent with the right of every human being to equal treatment and respect. The obvious examples based on experience of persecution in Europe which would have been in the

---

[39] *See, e.g.*, Kenneth Randall, *Universal Jurisdiction Under International Law,* 66 Tex. L. Rev. 785, 838 (1988).

[40] *Cf.* Commentary: I Geneva Convention for Amelioration of the Condition of the Wounded and Sick in the Armed Forces in the Field 51 (Jean Pictet ed. 1952) [hereinafter Commentary to Geneva Convention I].

[41] Andrew Clapham, Human Rights in the Private Sphere 89-133 (1993).

[42] [1999], 2 All ER 545 (House of Lords).

> minds of the delegates in 1951, were race, religion, nationality and political opinion. But the inclusion of 'particular social group' recognized that there might be different criteria for discrimination, in *pari materiae* with discrimination on the other grounds, which would be equally offensive to principles of human rights. [...] [T]he concept of social group is a general one and its meaning cannot be confined to those social groups which the framers of the Convention may have had in mind. In choosing to use the general term 'particular social group' rather than the enumeration of specific groups, the framers of the Convention were, in my opinion, intending to include whatever groups might be regarded as coming within the anti-discrimination objectives of the Convention.[43]

The Human Rights Committee has consistently maintained that the grounds of discrimination are not limited but can be found whenever the rights of a discernable class have been made the subject of nullification or impairment on an objective basis. Obviously included are not only those forms of status which relate to innate characteristics (race, ethnicity, gender), but also those which flow from economic and social criteria (e.g., the poor, the unfed, the unhoused). The objective criteria for discriminatory treatment have their source in contemporary human rights standards with their emphasis on the fundamental right to equal treatment and respect.[44] Accordingly, wherever a collectivity having discrete characteristics has been the victim of generalized practices (governmental or social) which have the effect of curtailing internationally respected rights or freedoms, the requirements of discrimination will have been met.[45]

The analysis which follows locates a unifying factor of overriding importance in an implicit or explicit policy of discrimination on the part of the claimant's oppressor. The proposed test, however, would not limit the

---

[43] *Id.* at 562 (Hoffman, L.).

[44] The outlook of the Human Rights Committee tracks thus the reasoning of the (U.K.) House of Lords' decision in *Islam (A.P.)* v. *Secretary of State for the Home Department, Regina* v. *Immigration Appeal Tribunal and Another Ex Parte Shah (A.P.)* [1999], 2 All ER 545 (House of Lords).

[45] *See, e.g.*, General Comment 18(37), UN Doc. A/45/40, at 174, ¶¶ 7, 8, 45 UN GAOR, Supp. (No. 40) (1990), *quoted in* Dominic McGoldrick, The Human Rights Committee 276 (1994):

> While these Conventions [CEDAW, Convention on the Rights of the Child] deal only with discrimination on specific grounds, the *Committee believes that the term "discrimination" as used in the Covenant should be understood to imply any distinction, exclusion, restriction or preference which is based on any ground such as race, colour, sex, language, religion, political or other opinion, national or social origin, property, birth or other status, and which has the purpose or effect of nullifying or impairing the recognition, enjoyment or exercise by all persons on an equal footing, of all rights and freedoms.* [Emphasis supplied].

grounds to objective bases for discrimination, but would include those reasons which might be attributed to the claimant by her persecutor. Following the broad principle of refugee analysis that the asylum seeker may have a political, racial, religious or social persona imputed to her by her persecutor and suffer serious harm on that basis, the test would seek to incorporate the full scope of attribution principles, including attributed membership in a particular social group. Such an approach finds support in Lord Hope of Craighead's separate opinion in *Islam (A.P.)* v. *Secretary of State for the Home Department, Regina* v. *Immigration Appeal Tribunal and Another Ex Parte Shah (A.P.)*:[46]

> The rule that the group must exist independently of the persecutor is useful because persecution alone cannot be used to define the group. But it must not be applied outside its proper context. The point has been well made by *Guy S. Goodwin-Gill, The Refugee in International Law*, 2d ed. (1996). [Goodwin-Gill] observes that that the importance and therefore the identity of a social group may well be in direct proportion of the notice taken of it by others. Thus, the notion of a social group is an open-ended one, which can be expanded in favor of a variety of different classes susceptible of persecution. [...] [H]e notes that the 'grouping' will often be independent of will, so that the requirement of voluntary association relationship, if adopted in all cases, would introduce an additional, unjustified evidential burden on the person who seeks protection under the Convention. [A]fter further discussion, he concludes that to treat persecution as the sole factor which results in identification of the social group may be too simple. Persecution may be but one facet of broader policies and perspectives, all of which contribute to the group and add to its preexisting characteristics.[47]

The foregoing represents the prevailing view of the relationship between social group and discriminatory animus put forward by leading commentators and is consistent with the views of UNHCR[48] on social group formation. The analysis makes clear that in determining whether a group exists for Convention purposes, the policies, perceptions and programs of the persecutor must be examined. As a paramount criterion, the persecutor's motivation in pursuing the group must flow from an "external preference" rather than a merely "personal" one.[49] Objectively conceived, the discriminatory motive giving rise to harm or suffering must relate to a "public" feature of the claimant's persona, i.e., to a characteristic or belief which defines the applicant's relationship either to the whole of her community

---

[46] The decision is reprinted and analyzed in 11 Int'l J. Refugee L. 496, *et seq*. (1999).

[47] *Id.* at 519.

[48] *See* Handbook, *supra* § I.1, note 30, ¶ 78.

[49] For fundamental guidance in shaping this principle, critical reliance has been placed on Ronald Dworkin, Taking Rights Seriously 235-245 (1977).

(i.e., to the State) or to an important sub-group within that community. Such an approach hopes to retain the "open-ended" aspect of the refugee definition, while at the same time incorporating the implicit limitations on recognition which the framers of the Convention obviously intended to apply.[50]

The emerging refugee analysis brings the protected grounds into conformity with the prevailing definition of persecution by emphasizing a position of intolerance in the persecutor toward a characteristic or belief in the claimant which the persecutor seeks to "overcome".[51] Where attributed characteristics and beliefs form the basis of the analysis, objective violations are material to establishing persecutory intent. Such situations, however, should be distinguished from those in which "intrinsic" opinions or group characteristics constitute the basis for the claim. In such cases, all that may have to be established is that the persecutor's actions have had an adverse effect on the claimant which approaches serious harm. This will particularly be the case where the claimant is exercising a right or belongs to a group which commands an enhanced level of protection under international law and policy.

Reference must be made here to an emerging form of refugee analysis as it relates to particular classes to which international law affords special protection (e.g., women in given circumstances) or to activity which international law renders comparatively privileged (e.g., the right not to be associated with violations of the rights of others). Here, refugee jurisprudence is less concerned with the discriminatory incentive of the persecutor so much as it is with the *discriminatory effect* of the persecutor's actions in an individualized setting. Violations of enumerated rights which international law protects as to specific classes (e.g., the right of women not to undergo FGM) will often be deemed persecutory irrespective of a lack of discriminatory animus in the agent of persecution, particularly where the right protected enjoys relative primacy within the hierarchy of modern international human rights.[52]

---

[50] Goodwin-Gill, *supra* § I.1, note 11, at 43:

> The Convention identifies five relevant grounds of persecution, all of which, to varying degrees, have been correspondingly developed in the field of non-discrimination.

[51] *Cf.* Hernandez-Ortiz v. INS, 777 F.2d 509, 516 (1985). Persecution will occur:

> only when there is a difference between the persecutor's views or status and those of the victim; it is oppression which is inflicted on groups or individuals because of a difference that the persecutor will not tolerate.

[52] *Cf.* Matter of Kasinga, 21 I&N Dec. 357 (BIA 1996).

The proposed test (nexus to an explicit or implicit policy of discrimination) will help explain that the refugee definition can be applied in contexts other than those involving "politics" in the conventional sense. It should be clear that conflicts giving rise to serious harm in the social and cultural sphere are clearly cognizable under the Convention if the persecutor views the asylum seeker as constituting a principled opponent to his or her goals. The proposed test also seeks to restore the concept of attributed characteristics and beliefs to its rightful role, not as a revolutionary and novel method of interpreting the refugee definition, but as constituting what seminal treatise law has long accepted as appropriate refugee analysis.

## § I.4. Outline of Thematic Study

This study seeks to analyze the grounds of international protection not so much by emphasizing those forms of serious harm which the framers sought to include within the law of refugee status, but by looking at those kinds of mistreatment which they obviously intended to exclude. The Convention refugee definition was never intended to embrace, for instance, acts of lawful prosecution supported by legitimate governmental interests and accompanied by measured sanctions.[53] This fundamental limitation of the law of refugee protection is examined in the discussion of insurrection against preemptively authoritarian States, resistance to conscription, coercive family-planning programs, and gender-based claims involving opposition to cultural and religious norms.[54] Similarly not recognized under the Convention are those types of harm arising from conditions of generalized violence or upheaval caused by man-made or human calamity which is not directed against specific individuals and groups.[55] The nature of this condition on the refugee definition is fleshed out in the sections dealing with civil war determinations and with refugee flows caused by the State's arbitrary refusal to accept international relief consignments.[56] Finally, the framers clearly did not seek to offer protection against mistreatment flowing from a purely personal dispute.[57] This limitation is analyzed in the discussion of the case law

---

53 Handbook, *supra* § I.1, note 30, ¶¶ 57, 58.

54 *See infra* §§ IV.5(a), IV.5(c); IV.7, III.8 and V.5(b)(2).

55 Handbook, *supra* § I.1, note 30, ¶ 164.

56 *See infra* §§ IV.4 and V.5(c).

57 Handbook, *supra* § I.1, note 30, ¶ 62.

surrounding one of the most controversial areas of modern asylum jurisprudence, claims based on domestic violence.[58]

In the comparative study which follows, a common thematic situation will often be presented (e.g., coercive family planning) in which the U.S. and Canada have chosen differing protected grounds as the basis for relief. These results, however, should not be understood as indications of the "arbitrariness" of the grounds themselves but rather as evidence of the continuing dominance of the term persecution (understood as a "difference between persecutor's views and status and those of the victim" which the "persecutor will not tolerate"[59]) in the development of refugee jurisprudence. Attributed characteristics and beliefs focus largely on the discriminatory animus inherent in the "persecution" definition and allow for doctrinal growth consistent with the framers' obvious intent to incorporate into the law of refugee status the clear mandate of UDHR that human rights be enjoyed by all without discrimination as to any form of status.

## § 1.5. A Note on the Jurisdictions

The vehicle by which this thematic study is to be developed is a comparative analysis of Canadian refugee jurisprudence and the law of asylum in the United States. Generally, comparative asylum law seeks to identify methodologies in different jurisdictions for interpreting the criteria for refugee status with a view to exploring contrasting methods of analysis.[60] Ultimately, the comparative method may urge the adoption of an interpretation arrived at in one of the jurisdictions under study as being most consistent with the social objectives of the 1951 Convention on the Status of Refugees.[61]

---

58 *See infra* § V.5(b)(4).

59 Hernandez-Ortiz v. INS, 777 F.2d 509, 516 (1985).

60 On the use of the comparative method in modern asylum adjudications, *see* Maryellen Fullerton, *A Comparative Look at Refugee Status Based on Persecution Due to Membership in a Particular Social Group,* 26 *Cornell Int'l L.J.* 505 (1993). On the purposes of comparative law generally, *see* Rudolf Schlesinger, Comparative Law 1-37 (3d ed. 1970).

61 Canadian initiatives have already influenced United States treatment of gender-based and children's asylum claims. *See Considerations for Asylum Officers Adjudicating Asylum Claims From Women* (Memorandum from Phyllis Coven, Office of International Affairs, U.S. INS, to All INS Asylum Officers, HQASM Coordinators, and Asylum Directors dated May 26, 1995) [hereinafter *United States Gender Guidelines*]; *Guidelines for Children's Asylum Claims* (Memorandum from Jeff Weiss, Office of International Affairs, U.S. INS, to All INS Asylum Officers, Immigration Officers and Headquarters Coordinators (Asylum and Refugees), dated December 10, 1998).

The case law of both Canada and the United States analyzing the refugee definition is prolific. In part, this is due to the fact that multiple jurisdictional levels are involved in the process. In the United States, for instance, administrative decisions (involving claimants who seek asylum in removal proceedings) are made by the Board of Immigration Appeals.[62] These adjudications (where designated by the Board as precedent) are controlling at the national level. Often, however, such determinations are reversed by the U.S. Court of Appeals having jurisdiction over the immigration court which initially heard the asylum claim.[63]

There are twelve circuit courts of appeal altogether and there can be considerable diversity between circuits as concerns discrete questions of asylum law. Moreover, even where an administrative decision is overturned by a circuit court, the Board will often continue to adhere to the decision in question in other circuits as reflecting the "philosophy" of the Board.[64] This entire process is subject to review by the U.S. Supreme Court, which is the Court of last resort. However, even where the Supreme Court purports to act with finality, its own decisions will often spawn interpretations of scope, both at the court of appeals level and within the administrative decision-making process.[65]

This rich diversity of interpretation is also characteristic of Canadian refugee law. A highly elaborate body of case law has been developed by the Immigration and Refugee Board (IRB) acting through the Convention Refugee Determination Division (CRDD). A decision of the CRDD may be reviewed by the Federal Court-Trial Division (FCTD), provided that a judge of the FCTD grants leave.[66] An appeal from the FCTD to the Federal Court of Appeal is possible where the FCTD has certified that a question of general importance is involved.[67] As in the United States, review by the Supreme Court is final as concerns all questions decided.

The jurisprudence of both Canada and the United States constitutes a conscientious effort to develop the refugee definition within the broader

---

62 8 CFR § 208.2.

63 INA, *supra* § I.1, note 4, § 242(a)(1), 8 USC § 1252(a)(1). As will be noted throughout, decisions by U.S. immigration judges, although clearly not of precedential weight, are often recognized as advancing valid principles of U.S. asylum law.

64 *See, e.g.,* Matter of Maldonado-Cruz, 19 I&N Dec. 509 (BIA 1988), *rev'd,* Maldonado-Cruz v. INS, 883 F.2d 788 (9th Cir. 1990).

65 *See. e.g.*, Matter of S-P-, 21 I&N Dec. 486 (BIA 1996), *interpreting* the Supreme Court's decision in INS v. Elias-Zacarias, 502 U.S. 478 (1992).

66 Immigration Act, *supra* § I.1, note 3, s. 82.2.

67 *Id.*, s. 83(4).

framework of human rights and humanitarian concerns that the framers obviously intended. Both nations are countries of immigration and both have active refugee resettlement programs.[68] Most importantly, Canada and the U.S. enjoy a compelling human rights heritage which deeply informs their respective interpretations of the refugee definition. This feature of the adjudicative process has caused both jurisdictions to turn substantially to human rights and humanitarian law principles in determining the scope of the protected grounds.

The influence of human rights and humanitarian law on the growth of the refugee definition has been most evident in gender-based persecution claims[69] and in civil war cases.[70] Canada's Immigration and Refugee Board has established *Guidelines* for adjudicating both types of case, while formulating directives which look respectively to international human rights and humanitarian law as providing a contextual framework for decision. The United States has followed the Canadian example of adopting *Guidelines* in the case of women's asylum claims while its case law has incorporated humanitarian law standards in deciding asylum claims arising in situations of internal armed conflict. In both instances, international law has had the effect of broadening and deepening the law of refugee status. The methodologies followed by the U.S. and Canada in this respect are highly indicative of the future course of refugee jurisprudence, as they point the way to application of the refugee definition which is most consistent with the framers' concern for the universal enjoyment of human rights without discrimination as to status or beliefs.

---

68 Goodwin-Gill, *supra* § I.1, note 11, at 279.

69 Discussed *infra*, § IV.5(b).

70 Discussed *infra*, § IV.4.

# II. RACE, NATIONALITY, RELIGION: THE MODEL OF "INTERNAL" CHARACTERISTICS AND BELIEFS

## § II.1. Race

Race unquestionably occupies a position of centrality in the hierarchy of those interests which are protected against discrimination by public international law. As Guy Goodwin-Gill has pointed out, race as a protected ground has as its foundation the Convention for the Elimination of All Forms of Racial Discrimination.[1] Of equal, if not more importance, however, in assessing the prominence of race as a protected ground is the close analogy existing between the concept of persecution in refugee law and activity which is specifically prohibited and made the basis of universal criminal jurisdiction by the Apartheid Convention.[2] That Convention makes it unlawful to engage in "inhuman acts" for the purpose of achieving the racial hegemony of one racial group over another.[3] Included among the acts which are rendered unlawful if undertaken for that purpose are the following: denying members of a racial group the "right to life and liberty of person"; measures designed to prevent members of a racial group from participating in the political, social, economic or cultural life of the country; measures undertaken with a view to separating members of a given racial group such as placing them into ghetto areas or adopting miscegenation laws; exploiting the labor of an ethnic or racial group (for instance by policies of forced labor); and persecution of individuals and groups because they oppose the practice of *apartheid*.[4]

The special status of race as a protected ground is fully recognized by the *Handbook*. Because race enjoys an enhanced position within the grounds of refugee protection, the *Handbook* makes clear that discrimination alone may constitute persecution where race is the characteristic giving rise to serious harm. By way of explanation, the *Handbook* sets forth that discrimination

---

1 Goodwin-Gill, *supra* § I.1, note 11, at 43, *citing* Convention for the Elimination of All Forms Racial Discrimination, *supra* § I.1, note 20.

2 *Id.* at 78-79, *citing* Apartheid Convention, *supra* § I.1, note 19.

3 Apartheid Convention, *supra* § I.1, note 19, Art. I.

4 *Id.*, Arts. II(a) through (f).

against individuals and groups on account of race has been internationally condemned as a fundamental assault on human dignity.[5] Importantly "race" is to be understood in its widest context so as to embrace "all kinds of ethnic groups" and minorities enjoying a common heritage.[6]

By maintaining that discrimination alone may constitute a basis for finding racial persecution, the *Handbook* places "race" on a unique footing with respect to the law of refugee status. Generally, acts of discrimination not leading to more serious forms of harm do not constitute persecution within the meaning of the refugee definition.[7] In viewing racial discrimina-

---

5 *See, e.g.*, Handbook, *supra* § I.1, note 30, ¶¶ 68, 69:

> Race, in the present connection, has to be understood in its widest sense to include all kinds of ethnic groups that are referred to as race in common usage. Frequently it will also entail membership in a specific social group of common descent forming a minority within a larger population. *Discrimination for reasons of race has found world-wide condemnation as one of the most striking violations of human rights. Racial discrimination, therefore, represents an important element in determining the existence of persecution.*
>
> * * *
>
> *Discrimination on racial grounds will frequently amount to persecution in the sense of the 1951 Convention. This will be the case if, as a result of racial discrimination, a person's human dignity is affected to such an extent that as to be incompatible with the most elementary and inalienable human rights, or where the disregard of racial barriers is subject to serious consequences.* [Emphasis supplied].

6 *Id.*, ¶ 68.

7 *Cf. id.*, ¶ 54. Ordinarily, a finding of discrimination will support the definition of "persecution" only where it entails restrictions on fundamental liberties, e.g., the right to earn a livelihood, the right to practice one's religion, and access to normally available educational facilities. *See, e.g.*, Handbook, *supra* § I.1, note 30, ¶¶ 54-55:

> Differences in the treatment of various groups do indeed exist to a greater or lesser extent in many societies. Persons who receive less favorable treatment as a result of such differences are not necessarily victims of persecution. It is only in certain circumstances that discrimination will amount to persecution. This would be so if measures of discrimination lead to consequences of a substantially prejudicial nature for the person concerned, e.g., serious restrictions on his right to earn a livelihood, his right to practice his religion, or his access to normally available educational facilities.
>
> * * *
>
> Where measures of discrimination are, in themselves, not of a serious character, they may nevertheless give rise to a reasonable fear in the mind of the person concerned, a feeling of apprehension and insecurity as regards his future existence.... A claim to fear persecution will of course be stronger where a person has been the victim of a number of discriminatory measures of this type and where there is thus a cumulative element involved.

tion potentially as serious harm, the *Handbook* is drawing upon the subjective feature of persecution: even mild acts of discrimination may satisfy the Convention standard where they produce in the mind of the asylum seeker "a feeling of apprehension and insecurity as regards his future existence."[8] The fact that racial discrimination will "often" entail persecution, whereas discrimination toward the other enumerated classes will not, can only be explained by the relative primacy which the elimination of racial discrimination enjoys by virtue of international law (the public policy foundations) as well as by a recognition of the intense relationship between the individual's subjective sense of security and worth on the one hand, and, on the other, a developed standard of human dignity.

The broad interpretation of "race" as a protected ground is generally supported by U.S. and Canadian jurisprudence. The *Basic Law Manual*, for instance, defines "race" in the following context:

> Race includes all kinds of ethnic groups that are referred to as "races" in common usage. It can entail membership in a specific social group of common descent forming a minority within a larger population.[9]

Despite the generally clear policy underlying both the *Handbook* and historical solicitude for suffering based on racial discrimination, cases awarding refugee status based on the race category have been sparse. Lack of relief in such cases, at least in the United States, can generally be attributed to the fact that the Board and the courts have not focused on the emotional harm which flows from racial discrimination, but have demanded a showing of "objective" persecution based on grave or significant human rights violations.

Accordingly, in *Limsico* v. *USINS*,[10] a Philippine national was denied asylum because he was unable to demonstrate that violence against him was occasioned by his Chinese nationality. In *DeSouza* v. *INS*,[11] a national of Kenya who was of Indian descent was unable to make out a showing of persecution based on:

> (i) refusal to grant the applicant citizenship flowing exclusively from her ethnic origins;
>
> (ii) refusal to provide her public education in high school—again because of her ethnic origins; and

---

8 *Id.*, ¶ 55.

9 Basic Law Manual, *supra* § I.1, note 26, at 37.

10 951 F.2d 210 (9th Cir. 1991).

11 999 F.2d 1156 (7th Cir. 1991).

(iii) police harassment.[12]

In a similar vein, in *Kotasz* v. *INS*,[13] an appeals court ruled that a Gypsy from Hungary was unable to meet the refugee standard. The applicant had urged race as a protected ground based on general discrimination toward the Gypsy minority within Hungary, alleging that she was "ashamed to admit" that she was a Gypsy. The denial of the claim rests on the insufficiency of the alleged serious harm and the fact that the Hungarian government was engaged in widespread efforts to improve the lot of Gypsies economically. Again, little attention was paid to the emotional suffering clearly evident in the applicant's claim and its relationship to social conditions which, at least arguably, constituted a deliberate assault on the asylum seeker's legitimate demand for equal treatment and human respect.[14]

Despite the case law, the *Basic Law Manual* (although it does not embrace the subjective component of persecution which is put forward by the *Handbook*) appears on its face to offer a more generous statutory standard for claims relating to harm or suffering based on the first protected ground. The *Basic Law Manual* provides:

> [R]acial discrimination may amount to persecution where a person's human dignity is affected to such an extent as to be incompatible with the most elementary and inalienable human rights, or where the disregard of racial barriers is subject to serious consequences.[15]

Recent jurisprudence in the United States and Canada suggests that the adjudicative patterns may be changing. One recent decision which appears to give at least partial realization to the *Handbook*'s and the *Basic Law Manual's* liberal approach to persecution on account of race is *Matter of O-Z- and M-Z-*.[16] In that case, the Board acknowledged that cumulative acts of discrimination against Ukrainian Jews by private groups had become so

---

[12] A surprising aspect of the decision in light of the *Basic Law Manual's* position that "exclusion from institutions of higher learning may constitute persecution". *See* Basic Law Manual, *supra* § I.1, note 26, at 25.

[13] 31 F.3d 847 (9th Cir. 1994).

[14] On the status of Gypsies generally, *see* Stephen Berman, *Gypsies: A National Group or a Social Group*, 13(4) Refugee Survey Quarterly 51 (1994). The author criticizes discriminatory legislation in Europe aimed at Gypsies and purporting to rest on rational grounds, strongly suggesting that such legislation may well constitute persecution with respect to affected individuals.

[15] Basic Law Manual, *supra* § I.1, note 26, at 27.

[16] Interim Decision 3346 (BIA 1998). Although the case is predicated on persecution related to "nationality", it is clear that claims based on "nationality" and those based on "race" are interrelated and that these two grounds of persecution substantially overlap. *See* Anker 99, *supra* § I.2, note 32, at 408, n. 801.

overwhelming as to amount to persecution. These acts, committed by private, non-State parties, included (i) repeated beatings of applicant's son; (ii) the burglary of applicant's apartment and the theft of his valuables; (iii) the receipt by applicant of anti-Semitic fliers in his home; and (iv) applicant's son being forced to undress by his classmates.[17] The Board found that these repeated acts could not be considered as random, but had to be seen as tied together by a relentless policy of discrimination which, in the aggregate, constituted past persecution.[18]

Moreover, in *Singh* v. *INS*,[19] the Ninth Circuit ruled that ethnic Indian Fijians constituted a group which had been the object of historical harassment and violence.[20] Accordingly, such asylum seekers were relieved of the normally applicable statutory standard of showing individualized persecution. In *Singh*, the applicant had been made the object of death threats and his family had experienced assaults. An attempt had been made against claimant's life when he refused to quit his job as the manager of a shipping company. And he was threatened with a knife and with having his house burned down when he chose to retain his employment. These acts of third party intimidation against claimant were sufficient to meet the statutory standard in light of the severity with which the Indian population treated Indo-Fijians as a whole.

Finally, a similar approach was adopted in *Avetova-Elisseva* v. *INS*,[21] where the Ninth Circuit overturned the Board of Immigration Appeals to grant asylum to an Armenian native fearing ethnic persecution in Russia. The reviewing court apparently conceded that the asylum seeker could not establish her claim exclusively on a "pattern or practice" of serious harm against Armenians in Russia, standing alone. It found, however, that Ms Avetova-Elisseva had made out an individualized showing of persecution based on (1) her having been harassed and pushed by Russian officers because of her Armenian ethnicity; (2) impediments she experienced in finding employment; and (3) the rape and beating of a friend's daughter by Russian police officers. These facts were coupled with strong background evidence showing systematic discrimination against the Armenian minority consisting of racial and ethnic harassment. The generalized discrimination against Armenians in Russia, taken in conjunction with the individualized

---

17 Interim Decision 3346, at 4.

18 *Id.*

19 94 F.3d 1353 (9th Cir. 1996).

20 *Cf.* 8 CFR § 208.16(b)(1)(3).

21 No. 98-70547, 2000 WL 575243 (9th Cir. May 15, 2000). The case is digested in 77 Interpreter Releases 762 (June 12, 2000).

facts of the case, were sufficient to demonstrate that the well-founded fear of being persecuted standard had been met.

A comparatively liberal test for establishing racial persecution had been earlier adopted in Canada by the Immigration Appeals Board.[22] Under the Board's prior rulings, "Ibos from Nigeria, the Mohajirs of Pakistan, the Baganda from Uganda, Guyanese of East Indian descent, Tamils from Sri Lanka, the Baluba from Zaire, and Gypsies of Polish origin" satisfied the refugee definition of "race."[23] Under the Board's doctrine, the refugee definition is met where a ruling minority effectively disenfranchises an ethnic majority with respect to the latter's exercise of its fundamental human rights.[24]

The modern jurisprudence of the Federal Court-Trial Division clarifies that configurations of violence which target a specific ethnic group will be sufficient to meet the well-founded fear test without the need for additional showings. In *Veeravagu* v. *M.E.I.*,[25] the claimant had shown a "real and oppressive risk of substantial violence" flowing from State-sponsored persecution in Sri Lanka. The court concluded that the prevalence of such violence against "young Tamil males" was enough to show that the claimant was objectively at risk.

Several recent decisions by the Federal Court-Trial Division, moreover, have applied an essentially liberal test for persecution based on "race" employing similar reasoning to that adopted in *Matter of O-Z- and M-Z-*.[26] In *Bobrik* v. *M.C.I.*,[27] the claimants were a Jewish couple residing in Russia

---

22 Pierre Katanku Tshiabu Tshibola, Immigration Appeals Board Decision M84-1074, May 30, 1985.

23 Hathaway, *supra*, at 143, *citing* Jones Adeniji Adeluyi, Immigration Appeal Board Decision 79-9057 (March 5, 1979); Owais Uddin Ahmad, Immigration Appeal Board Decision 79-1197 (November 21, 1979); Joseph Maria Mpagi, Immigration Appeal Board Decision V80-6254 (August 13, 1980); Benaiserie Mangra, Immigration Appeal Board Decision T83-10491 (January 5, 1984); Krishnapillai Easwararamoorthy, Immigration Appeal Board Decision T82-9736 (June 18, 1984); Pierre Katanku Tshiabu Tshibola, Immigration Appeal Board Decision M84-1074 (May 30, 1985); Boleslaw Dytlow, Immigration Appeal Board Decision V87-6040X (July 7, 1987, *aff'd*, Federal Court of Appeal Decision A-569-87 (April 13, 1988).

24 Pierre Katanku Tshiabu Tshibola, Immigration Appeals Board Decision M84-1074, May 30, 1985.

25 (F.C.A., no. A-630-89), May 27, 1992.

26 Interim Decision 3346 (BIA 1998).

27 (F.C.T.D., no. IMM-5519-93), September 16, 1994. Technically, *Bobrik* and the case discussed next (*Kraitman* v. *S.S.C.* (1994), 27 Imm. L.R. (2d) 283 (F.C.T.D.), are "religious" persecution cases. For the reasons discussed earlier, however, there is substantial overlap between the cases based on religion as a protected ground on the one

who had been the victims of religiously motivated harassment. After the couple's daughter had fled Russia, the male claimant was fired from his job and a note was left on his car telling him to follow his daughter to Israel or take the consequences. The female claimant was assaulted on Passover, and anti-Semitic slurs were found painted on the door to the family apartment. Finally, the male claimant was twice physically attacked, requiring him to be hospitalized on one occasion. The court found that these acts had been "systematically" imposed over a two-and-a-half year period. In the aggregate they were sufficient to establish a well-founded fear of persecution.

In *Kraitman* v. *S.S.C.*,[28] claimants were Jewish citizens of the Ukraine. The male claimant had been the victim of anti-Semitic harassment during his school years. He was denied admission to medical school because of his Jewish background and was able to pursue his education in engineering only by paying a bribe. After graduation, claimant was the only member of his class not to be "assigned" employment, again because of his ethnic and religious identity. The door of his home was painted with anti-Semitic slogans and the gravestones of his parents were similarly defiled. The applicant was beaten up by four men as he was leaving synagogue and required eye surgery as a result. Efforts to involve the police were not responded to, the claimant being informed that there were too many such complaints by Jews to be acted upon.

The Immigration and Refugee Board had determined that the mistreatment to which claimant had been subject did not meet the Convention standard in light of the Ukraine's formal policy of being non-racist. This determination was overturned as "capricious and perverse" by the Federal Court Trial Division. The IRB, the court ruled, did not take into account that there was an organization in the Ukraine (Pamyat) which persecuted Jews openly despite the government's position. The Federal Court Trial Division concluded that the acts complained of gave rise to a well-founded fear of persecution in light of the country background of widespread social discrimination against Jews in the Ukraine.

Despite the new direction of the case law and its own expansive interpretation of the first Convention ground, the *Basic Law Manual* provides examples of racial persecution tending to equate serious harm with extreme

---

hand, and those based on ethnicity or race on the other. *See* Anker 99, *supra* § I.2, note 32, at 408, n. 801. Such similarities are enhanced where the claimant's religion *per se* serves as the motive of serious harm (i.e., without the claimant's attracting persecution by actively engaging in his or her faith).

28 27 Imm. L.R. (2d) 283 (F.C.T.D.).

violations of human rights.[29] Two of the case studies set forth (slavery in the United States and the Holocaust in Europe) are linked to enslavement and genocide respectively. Such punishment would entail "persecution" under even the most conservative of definitions. The *Basic Law Manual's* mention of *apartheid* as constituting persecution clearly comes closer to the mark, but the implications of such inclusion remain unexplored.[30] It is not clear from the *Basic Law Manual's* discussion that the crime of *apartheid* can include such acts as placing members of a particular race in ghetto areas or excluding them from the cultural and social life of the country. A detailed analysis of the crime itself would have made mention of *apartheid* in the *Basic Law Manual*'s list of acts constituting racial persecution more meaningful from the viewpoint of practitioners and adjudicators.

In light of the relative primacy of "race" as a protected interest under international law and the *Handbook's* position that discrimination alone may, in given instances, constitute racial persecution, a less egregious form of punishment (e.g. than genocide) should satisfy the refugee definition. It would have been more suitable to emphasize other forms of "persecution" which could support a determination of refugee status on the first Convention ground and which do not require the more extreme violations of human rights norms manifested by genocide and institutional slavery.[31]

The *Handbook's* selection of "race", however, for apparently special treatment, should not result in a conclusion that other groups with fixed characteristics may not be persecuted through policies of discrimination. "Racial discrimination" is a prevalent social and political device for denying human rights on a collective basis. Where societies are "stratified" on other grounds (class, gender, religious affiliation, clan, etc.), a similar disposition on the part of the adjudicator can be adopted, applying the *Handbook*'s passages on "race" by analogy.[32] In such instances, the distinction normally maintained between discrimination on the one hand and persecution on the

---

29 Basic Law Manual, *supra* § I.1, note 26, at 37.

30 *Id.*

31 *Cf. id.* at 25. Importantly for this purpose the *Basic Law Manual* has defined "persecution" in the context of discrimination to embrace lesser violations of internationally respected human rights including: arbitrary interference with privacy; deprivation of means of maintaining a livelihood; relegation to substandard dwellings; and exclusion from educational, civic or social institutions. *Id.*

32 *Cf.* Handbook, *supra* § I.1, note 30, ¶ 72: Serious measures of discrimination imposed on individuals because they practice their faith or belong to a particular religious community may constitute persecution.

other should be deemed to have been breached, at least where the resulting denial of equal protection[33] has been comprehensive and sustained.

## § II.2. Nationality

Nationality is appropriately discussed along with race since these are the two protected grounds which transparently relate exclusively to "immutable characteristics" as the predicate for persecution. In fact, nationality shares many of the attributes which have been identified with race. The *Handbook* indicates, for instance, that the term is not limited to "citizenship," but refers also to membership in ethnic or linguistic groups.[34] Like the *Handbook's* analysis with respect to "race," persecution on account of "nationality" may embrace acts of collective mistreatment.

In this respect, "adverse attitudes and measures" directed against an ethnic or religious minority can constitute persecution so that the mere fact of belonging to such an identifiable group may, in appropriate circumstances, support a fear of persecution in the Convention sense.[35] Moreover, the mere fact that the ethnic group to which the refugee claimant belongs happens to be in the majority does not undermine his or her claim to refugee status: a majority may be quite helpless at the hands of a controlling minority.[36]

There are few precedent decisions of moment in either Canada or the United States concerning "nationality"[37] as a protected ground.[38] The Board of Immigration Appeals' decision in *Matter of O-Z- and I-Z-*[39] has already been digested in the discussion of the "race" ground. Canada's Federal Court

---

33 UDHR, *supra* § I.1, note 12, Art. 2.

34 Handbook, *supra* § I.1, note 30, ¶ 74:

> It [nationality] refers also to membership of an ethnic or linguistic group and may occasionally overlap with the term "race."

35 *Id.*

36 *Id.*, ¶ 76.

37 *But see* § II.1, *supra*, for a discussion of decisions involving the first Convention ground which may apply to cases based on "nationality" by analogy.

38 This may change dramatically, however, as the break-up of former communist States and the ensuing displacement of persons previously considered nationals gives rise to claims for asylum. For an interesting discussion, *see* Bohdan Nahajlo, *Forcible Population Transfers, Deportation and Ethnic Cleansing in the CIS: Problems in Search of Responses,* 16 Refugee Survey Quarterly 26 (1997).

39 Interim Decision 3346 (BIA 1998). Persecution for reassons of "race", "religion", and "nationality"involve a common method of analysis based on immutable characteristics; these grounds overlap. *See* Anker 99, *supra* § I.2, note 32, at 408, n. 801.

Trial-Division has ruled on persecution on account of "nationality" in *Baffoe* v. *M.C.I.*[40] In *Baffoe*, the claimant was able to show that a land dispute, which had resulted in the murder of his parents, three brothers and four sisters, had its origins in the fact that the claimant and his family were not "nationals" of Ghana. (The family's lack of Ghanaian nationality was traced, in turn, to the fact that claimant's paternal grandfather had not been born there). The court identified the source of the harm and suffering involved in claimant's nationality. The court's conclusion that the claimant had suffered past persecution on account of "nationality" under these facts reveals how the clear existence of a refugee ground can transform what appears to be a case involving a "private" dispute into one warranting refugee protection.

The U.N. Declaration on the Rights of Persons Belonging to National or Ethnic, Religious and Linguistic Minorities[41] is certainly relevant to determining whether persecution has occurred based on the third refugee ground (nationality). It is imperative to remark in this respect that the Declaration sets out not only restrictions on the exercise of State power where minorities are concerned, but also establishes affirmative duties on the part of States to protect minorities against non-State actors.[42]

Included among the rights protected are the right to national or ethnic, cultural, religious and linguistic identities;[43] the right of such groups to practice their own religion and use their own language;[44] the right to participate in national and regional decision-making;[45] the right of association within the relevant group and with other groups;[46] and the right to exercise these rights without adverse consequences.[47] States, on the other hand, are required to "take measures" to ensure that minorities may exercise their rights effectively, including the right to develop their own culture, language, religion, traditions and customs.[48] States are also called upon to

---

40 (F.C.T.D., no. IMM-3216-93), September 28, 1994.

41 Declaration on the Rights of National, Ethnic, Religious or Linguistic Minorities, *supra* § I.1, note 23.

42 In this sense, the Declaration may be considered as representative of the affirmative or "social" interpretation of human rights. *See, e.g.*, McGoldrick, *supra* § I.2, note 45, at 274.

43 Declaration on the Rights of National, Ethnic, Religious or Linguistic Minorities, *supra* § I.1, note 23, Art. 1.

44 *Id.*, Art. 2(1).

45 *Id.*, Art. 2(3).

46 *Id.*, Art. 2(5).

47 *Id.*, Art. 3(2).

48 *Id.*, Art. 4(1).

undertake affirmative measures in the field of education so as to encourage minorities in the understanding of their own history, traditions, language and culture and to assure that "persons belonging to minorities may participate fully in the economic progress and development in their country".[49] These "affirmative" obligations of States under the U.N. Declaration on the Rights of Persons Belonging to National or Ethnic Religious or Linguistic Minorities are in conformity with the position taken by both the Human Rights Committee and the Committee on Economic, Social and Cultural Rights:

> More significantly, however, and following the example of the HRC, the Committee has recognized the existence of certain positive obligations with respect to minorities. In its concluding observations on the report of Mexico, the Committee expressly referred to the need for resources to be made available to indigenous groups 'to enable them to preserve their language culture, and traditional way of life'. The significance of this obligation is not so much that the States have undertaken a resource commitment, but rather the implicit assumption that the disposal of those resources should be in the hands of the groups concerned.[50]

Under principles of refugee law, therefore, when the State (or a dominant group within the State) deliberately infringes rights closely connected with a group's linguistic, cultural or religious identity, a claim of persecution may, in appropriate circumstances, be made out.[51] What, however, of the State's affirmative duty to involve minorities, for instance, in the economic progress of the country? Can a deliberate neglect of an abandoned minority give rise to refugee status where the State has merely failed to exercise affirmative duties and has allowed "natural" economic deprivation to take its toll? The view that such neglect may constitute "persecution" has received some scholarly support:

> In countries which are more stratified socially or in societies segmented through ethnic or religious cleavage, economic oppression and deprivation may strike a specific group—whether through active measures or resulting from a policy of neglect. In such circumstances, any member of that group may individually qualify for refugee status, particularly if the economic oppression and deprivation are tantamount to destitution or otherwise of a serious nature.[52]

---

49 *Id.*, Art. 4(4).

50 Matthew Craven, The International Covenant on Economic, Social and Cultural Rights 190 (1995).

51 *Cf.* Basic Law Manual, *supra* § I.1, 26, at 24.

52 G. Jaeger, *The Definition of 'Refugee': Restrictive Versus Expanding Trends*, (1983) World Refugee Survey 5, at 7, *quoted in* Hathaway, *supra* § I.1, note 7, at 94. *See also*

Failure to observe affirmative obligations toward specific individuals within defined national, ethnic, religious or linguistic groups may give rise to a claim that serious harm has been imposed on account of a protected ground, at least where it is clear that aid has been withheld systematically. In this way, the failure of a State to extend necessary assistance to ethnic minorities which results in placing those minorities significantly at risk of life-threatening consequences (e.g., of starvation) should result in a finding of serious harm on a Convention ground for those affected. As in the case of racially motivated injury, however, such an approach to determining group persecution should not be limited to aggregates identified by ethnicity or nationality, but should be made applicable to all collectivities which are defined by fixed characteristics, either objectively or in the perception of the persecutor. The denial of famine relief, for instance, with respect to those belonging to organized groups which are opposed to government policies should be viewed as persecution based on the fourth Convention ground (membership in a particular social group).[53]

## § II.3. Religion

"Religion" as a protected ground, draws upon both the voluntary exercise of human rights connected with freedom of thought, conscience and religion on the one hand, and, on the other, immutable status similar to that protected in the refugee grounds of "race", and "nationality."[54] The *Handbook* recognizes that religion as a basis for refugee status may include the right to change one's religion, and the right to manifest one's religion in public and private through teaching, practice or observance.[55]

Accordingly, "religious" persecution may include a variety of guises. Prohibiting the members of a religious community from practicing their religion or barring them from teaching their religion may constitute serious

---

James Hathaway, *Reconceiving Refugee Law as Human Rights Protection*, 4 Journal of Refugee Studies 122, 123 (1991):

> [T]he State which ignores or is unable to respond to legitimate expectations in international human rights fails to comply with its most basic duty, thereby giving rise to the prospect of legitimate disengagement from that community in favor of surrogate protection elsewhere.

[53] *See generally* Note: *From Definition to Exploration: Social Groups and Political Asylum Eligibility*, 26 San Diego L. Rev. 740, 814 (1992). The doctrine of imputed characteristics or beliefs which can serve to establish such identity is discussed in Part IV, *infra*.

[54] *See, e.g.*, 1 Grahl-Madsen, *supra* § I.1, note 7, at 217.

[55] Handbook, *supra* § I.1, note 30, ¶ 71.

harm within the meaning of the refugee standard.[56] Acts of discrimination based on individual or group religious affiliation or attachment may also rise to the requisite degree of suffering to constitute persecution.[57]

There are instances wherein mere membership in the religious community without more will suffice to establish a claim of persecution, i.e., where "special circumstances" exist. As with all of the statutory grounds which are predicated on status, however, membership alone will normally not be enough to provide a basis for determining that the well-founded fear component of the definition has been met.[58] Some further showing of individualized harm must normally be made out by the claimant.[59]

Canadian case law accepts that laws which compel citizens to refrain from an element of religious practice which is central to their faith may constitute persecution in the Convention sense, provided that the religious practice is "not unreasonable". Canada's initial jurisprudence on this subject was developed by the former Immigration Appeals Board. In *Matter of Tomasz Gozdalski*, a Polish Catholic claimed to have been the victim of economic persecution as the result of his having refused to join a State union. Claimant's reasons for not joining were based on the union's requirement that claimant attend meetings on Sunday morning, a time when he would have been obliged to forego mass. As summarized by the Canadian Law Information Council:

> Applicant is determined to be a Convention refugee. The interference with the practices of his religion was a disguised way of limiting freedom of religion. For a deeply religious person this would amount to persecution. The Board accepts the applicant's claim to economic discrimination. Although the applicant will not be physically abused if he is sent back to his country, he will be deprived of his most basic rights: freedom of thought, conscience and religion. The discrimination experienced by the applicant amounted to persecution in the case of this applicant.[60]

Modern case law developed by the Federal Court-Trial Division has followed the essential reasoning of *Tomasz Gozdalski.* In a recent decision,

---

[56] *Id.*, ¶ 72.

[57] *Id.*

[58] *Id.*, ¶ 73.

[59] *Compare* Handbook, *supra* § I.1, note 30, ¶¶ 73 and 79. As concerns both a religious community and a particular social group, mere membership normally will not be sufficient to ground a claim. In both cases, however, special circumstances may be present to render "mere membership" a sufficient basis for refugee status.

[60] Matter of Tomasz Gozdalski, Immigration Appeal Board Decision M87-1027X, April 23, 1987, *abstracted in* 106 Canadian Law Information Council, *Notes of Recent Decisions Rendered by the Immigration Appeals Board* ¶ 106.14 (January 1988).

for instance, the F.C.T.D. ruled, in connection with a general law against proselytizing:

> A law which requires a minority of citizens to breach the principles of their religion ... is patently persecutory. One might add, so long as these religious tenets are not unreasonable as, for example, exacting human sacrifice or the taking of prohibited drugs as a sacrament.[61]

Canadian jurisprudence accepts that restrictions on the right to practice one's faith may amount to persecution in appropriate cases. In *Fosu* v. *M.E.I.*,[62] the claimant was a member of the Jehovah's Witnesses whose right of assembly in order to practice their religion had been prohibited. The court determined that religious persecution could assume many guises, including prohibitions on the providing or the receiving of religious instruction as well as bars against public and private worship. Under the instant facts, the court ruled that the prohibition against assembling for religious purposes could very well amount to persecution.

On the other hand, Canadian law views membership in the religious community standing alone as normally insufficient to support a finding of persecution.[63] For instance, in Pakistan, legislation specifically directed against the Ahmadi sect and subjecting those practicing the Ahmadi faith to severe sanctions (Ordinance XX) was held by the Federal Court-Trial Division not to give rise to a claim to persecution in the Convention sense as to all individuals potentially affected.[64] The basis for the decision appears to be that the law was perceived as sporadically enforced.[65] An ensuing case involving the Ahmadi sect, however, may reveal the inherent strictures which apply to qualifying for refugee status on the "religion" ground. In *Thathaal* v. *S.S.C.*,[66] the Federal Court-Trial Division had before it the case of an Ahmadi whose children had been precluded from attending public schools because of their faith (although they were permitted to attend their own "private" schools). In light of the alternative education available, the court concluded that bar against attending public schools did not arise to the level of persecution.

---

61 Kassatkine v. M.C.I. (F.C.T.D., no. IMM-978-95), August 20, 1996, at 4.

62 (1994), 27 Imm. L. R. (2d) 75 (F.C.T.D.).

63 *See generally* Immigration and Refugee Board, Interpretation of the Convention Refugee Definition in the Case Law § 9.3.8.2 (December 31, 1999) [hereinafter Interpretation of the Convention Refugee Definition in the Case Law] and cases cited therein.

64 Butt v. S.G.C., (F.C.T.D., no. IMM-1224-93), September 8, 1993.

65 *Id.*

66 (F.C.T.D. A-1644-92), December 15, 1993, *aff'd,* (F.C.A. A-724-93), April 16, 1996.

A similar result was reached in another case involving Ordinance XX, but which is perhaps somewhat more questionable. In *Rehan* v. *M.C.I.*,[67] the claimant showed that he had suffered grave discrimination as the result of adhering to his faith. His mistreatment (which did not rise to the level of persecution in the view of the court) included several beatings by private individuals; difficulties in obtaining an education; and bars against the public practice of the Ahmadi faith. The court viewed this treatment as consisting of harassment only, concluding that claimant could effectively accommodate himself to the strictures of Ordinance XX by practicing his religion in private in a neighboring township. The court implied that only through open defiance of Ordinance XX could the claimant establish refugee status.

Where more serious consequences are at stake, courts have been more inclined to find persecution by reason of the second Convention ground. In *Chabira* v. *M.E.I.*,[68] an Algerian claimant had impregnated a young woman and, as a result, was confronted with serious threats by the young woman's (orthodox) family. The family had in fact gone to the length of having the claimant's photograph placed in mosques together with exhortations that claimant be extrajudicially murdered. The F.C.T.D. overturned the determination of the Immigration and Refugee Board that a Convention ground was not involved, noting that the claimant was an atheist and was coming into conflict with the staunch values of a highly fundamentalist religious community. The court concluded that there were at least some religious implications to this conflict and that the Board was wrong to disregard these. The case reveals convincingly that religious persecution cases must be viewed in context and that the viability of a religious claim must usually be determined by analyzing the viewpoint of the persecutor.

The foregoing doctrine received explicit recognition in *Daghigi* v. *M.C.I.*[69] The claimant in *Daghigi* was a non-observant Moslem from Iran who had been harassed by the Revolutionary Guards as the result of his playing Western music in his hotel room. The guards beat the applicant, invaded his hotel room, and destroyed his musical instruments and tapes. He was subsequently ordered to report to the Revolutionary Guards on a daily basis and to attend mosque and undergo religious instruction. The court found the Immigration and Refugee Board's conclusion that the foregoing abuse was not related to a Convention ground to be "not sustainable".

---

67 (F.C.T.D. A-580-92), October 18, 1996.

68 (1994), 27 Imm. L. R. (2d) 75 (F.C.T.D.).

69 (F.C.T.D., no. A-64-93), November 16, 1995.

United States case law is in general conformity with the foregoing holdings. Accordingly, in *Refahivat* v. *DOJ INS*,[70] the Tenth Circuit Court of Appeals held that mere membership in a religious community will not ordinarily be enough to make out asylum eligibility. However, where the State goes beyond punishing broad groups and selects out affirmative religious choice, a targeted individual may establish a claim. Accordingly, in *Bastanipour* v. *INS*,[71] an Iranian convert to Christianity was held to have met the refugee standard since Iran punishes conversion from Islam by death.

The applicant in *Bastanipour* had lived in the U.S. for about five years and was arrested for heroin possession upon returning from Iran. He requested asylum and withholding of removal, arguing that he had converted from Islam to Christianity, and that such conversion is punishable in Iran by death. The Board rejected the claim, ruling that applicant's conversion had not been a "formal" one; that "apostasy" was not an offense under Islamic law; and that applicant's "new" religion would not come to the attention of the authorities. The Seventh Circuit overturned this finding, ruling that the question of how applicant's conversion would be viewed in Iran was to be examined from the perspective of an Iranian judge, not from the viewpoint of the Board. With respect to the Board's skepticism concerning the genuineness of Bastanipour's conversion and the effectiveness thereof, the Seventh Circuit ruled as follows:

> This is poorly reasoned, and not only because Bastanipour requested the pork-free prison diet before he turned to Christianity. The opinion does not consider what would count as conversion in the eyes of an Iranian religious judge which is the only thing which would count as far as the danger to Bastanipour is concerned. ... [Bastanipour] renounced Islam for Christianity. He has not been baptized or joined a church but he has made it clear that ... he believes in Christianity rather than in Islam—and *that* is the apostasy, not compliance with the formalities of affiliation. Whether Bastanipour believes the tenets of Christianity in his heart of hearts or, as hinted but not found by the Board, is acting opportunistically (though at great risk to himself) in the hope of staving off deportation would not, we imagine, matter to an Iranian judge.[72]

The Circuit Court thus considered the applicant's motives as secondary to the consequences which would flow from an objective manifestation of belief. Moreover, the only way in which applicant could avoid his religion coming to the attention of his persecutors was to stop practicing it, an independent form of persecution.

---

[70] 29 F.3d 553 (10th Cir. 1994).

[71] 980 F.2d 1129 (7th Cir. 1992).

[72] *Id.* at 1132.

Finally, in *Bucar* v. *INS*,[73] the Seventh Circuit ruled that it is the very definition of religious persecution to preclude those espousing a religion from practicing it. Hence, it is irrelevant that an asylum seeker has not been imprisoned and tortured or forbidden to attend school, if he in fact has been barred from practicing his faith.

Recent jurisprudence has confirmed this trend while illustrating the applicability of the second refugee ground (religion) to highly nuanced situations. In *Maini* v. *INS*,[74] for instance, the Ninth Circuit granted asylum to a family from India based on their having been harassed by an extremist group (the Communist Party Marxist or CPM) which had (i) threatened the mother and father; (ii) attacked the son; and (iii) forced the father to resign from his job. The court determined that the CPM's motivation for its attacks derived predominantly from the fact that asylum seekers comprised an interfaith family consisting of Hindus and Sikhs. The court concluded that the asylum seekers' evidence showing that the CPM may have had incentives besides their interfaith relationship to molest them was not sufficient to preclude a finding that the applicants were persecuted "on account of" their religion.

*Maini* was followed in *Bandari* v. *INS*[75] where the Ninth Circuit, again reversing the Board, granted asylum to an Armenian Christian who had been tortured because of his relationship to a Muslim girl. The couple had been reprimanded by police for publicly embracing. When it was discovered that Mr. Bandiri was an Armenian, however, he was told he had no right to date a "Persian girl" and was taken to a police station. There, police officials whipped him with a rubber hose, often until he lost consciousness, and demanded that he sign a confession to the effect that he had raped his companion. The asylum seeker was later taken before a court, told that non-Muslim men could not marry Muslim women, and that he would have to convert to Islam on pain of being stoned to death. (Mr. Bandiri refused to convert but the court reduced the sanction to 75 lashes and a year's confinement in light of his youth). The applicant was released when his father paid a bribe to a prison guard and he returned home to recover from the wounds he had received at the hands on the police.

The immigration judge had determined that the applicant had suffered "prosecution" and not "persecution" as the result of publicly embracing, a

---

[73] 109 F.3d 399 (7th Cir. 1997).

[74] 212 F.3d 1167 (9th Cir. 2000). The case is digested in 77 Interpreter Releases 1448 (October 9, 2000).

[75] No. 98-71189, 2000 WL 1376245 (9th Cir. Sept. 26, 2000). The case is digested in 77 Interpreter Releases 1484 (October 16, 2000).

finding implicitly adopted by the Board when it affirmed the decision. Following established precedent in the political opinion cases, the Ninth Circuit ruled that the acts of the police were disproportionate to a measured enforcement of Iran's criminal laws and were directed instead to punishing Mr. Bandiri on account of a protected ground.

Claims of "persecution" which urge religion as their basis have come to overlap to some extent with gender-based asylum cases. It is accepted in this respect by both United States and Canadian refugee doctrine that religious norms which are discriminatory in nature (e.g., are gender-specific) or which infringe upon the individual's right to human dignity and cultural independence, may give rise to a claim of persecution either where these norms are transgressed (inviting punishment) or where, because of their severity, they can reasonably be expected to inflict extreme emotional distress on someone deeply opposed to them.[76] *Interpretation of the Convention Refugee Definition in the Case Law* provides a contextual framework of analysis for adjudicating such claims:

> Every society has limits on what it regards as acceptable behavior. In some countries the norms of the society (or the norms laid down by some ruling group) may be more constraining than elsewhere. The norms may interfere with the exercise of human rights, and may impose limitations on certain categories of people—categories which may be defined by Convention-protected characteristics. These restrictions may be entrenched in law, and may be backed up by coercive action and penalties. A claimant who transgresses the conventions of his or her homeland (and perhaps at the same time violates the law) may be at risk of serious harm.[77]

Important to analyzing this genre of claim is the subjective component of persecution espoused by the *Handbook*,[78] and now largely accepted by Canadian and U.S. law Accordingly, in *Fisher* v. *INS*,[79] the appeals court held that:

> [W]hen a person with religious views different from those espoused by a religious regime is required to conform to, or is punished for failing to comply with, laws which are fundamentally abhorrent to that person's deeply held religious convictions, *the resulting anguish should be considered in deter-*

---

[76] Interpretation of the Convention Refugee Definition in the Case Law, *supra* this section, note 63, § 9.3.8.1 and cases cited therein; *Basic Law Manual, supra* § I.1, note 26, at 37-38.

[77] Interpretation of the Convention Refugee Definition in the Case Law, *supra* this section, note 63, § 9.3.8.

[78] Handbook, *supra* § I.1, note 30, ¶ 32.

[79] 37 F.3d 1371 (9th Cir, 1994), *redecided en banc,* 79 F.3d 976 (9th Cir. 1996).

> *mining whether the authorities have engaged in 'extreme conduct' that is 'tantamount to persecution.'*[80]

Canadian law also adopts the view that forced conformity with unusually restrictive cultural standards may rise to the level of persecution in an asylum seeker who is adversely affected by such restraints. For instance, the Federal Court Trial Division has considered, as an aspect of persecution, the claimant's being forced to enter into a pre-arranged marriage without her consent.[81] The effect of repressive laws *vis-à-vis* the individual psychological proclivities of the asylum seeker thus play a direct role in both gender-based claims and those involving the free exercise of religion. Both lines of cases, however, must be understood as involving discriminatory effects on select classes who are seeking to pursue deeply held beliefs. Moreover, the restrictions on fundamental liberties in these cases are not supported by any showing of State necessity. Perhaps, the complete absence of any interest on the part of the State in regulating the activity in question can be gleaned in the judicial finding that the religious practice in question is "not unreasonable".[82]

The cases dealing with restrictive social and cultural practices giving rise to claims of persecution draw, at least in part, their rationales from the general proposition that cultural standards enforced on a discriminatory basis against particular groups (notably women) violate the fundamental principle of international human rights law that liberties are to be enjoyed on an equal basis and without discrimination.[83] Beyond this, however, norms which are facially non-discriminatory may be enforced in such a way as to frustrate the exercise of individual human rights, including the right to thought,

---

80 *Id.* at 1375 (emphasis supplied), *quoted with approval in* Basic Law Manual, *supra* § I.1, note 26, at 37. Although *Fisher* was later overturned (*see* Fisher v. INS, 79 F.3d 976 (9th Cir. 1996)), the decision's broad statement of principle in this respect remains beyond question. *See generally* Fatin v. INS, 12 F. 3d 1233 (3d Cir. 1992) which provided the original rationale for *Fisher* as well as its operative language. *See also* Bacur v. INS, 109 F.3d 405 (7th Cir. 1997): Denial of one's right to practice one's faith is "virtually the definition of religious persecution".

81 Vidhani v. M.C.I., [1994] 3 F.C. 60 (T.D.).

82 Interpretation of the Convention Refugee Definition in the Case Law, *supra*, this section, note 63 § 4.4.

83 UDHR, *supra* note 12, art 2:

> Everyone is entitled to all of the rights and freedoms which are set forth in this Declaration, without distinction of any kind, such as race, color, sex, language, religion, political or other opinion, national or social origin, property, birth or other status.

conscience and religion.[84] The view that forced compliance with such practices may constitute persecution *per se* for purposes of the refugee definition can only be explained by the thrust of modern asylum law which takes into account the subjective viewpoint of the asylum seeker and asks, not on an objective basis, but rather through the eyes of the victim and accepting her psychological makeup, whether serious harm can be said to flow from the involuntary strictures thus imposed.[85] As noted by Guy Goodwin-Gill:

> It is increasingly accepted in a variety of different contexts that it may be unconscionable to require the individual to change, or to exercise their freedom of choice differently. The question is how to distinguish between those opponents of State authority who do, and those who do not, require international protection. For sincerely held reasons of conscience may motivate the individual who refuses to pay such proportion of income tax as is destined for military expenditures; or the shopkeeper who wishes to trade on Sundays; or the parents who, on grounds of religious conviction, refuse to send their children to public schools.[86]

Perhaps illustrative of the foregoing doctrine is the case presented by those seeking exemption from military service on account of religious principle (conscientious objection). The *Basic Law Manual*[87] severely delimits a decision of the Ninth Circuit Court of Appeal's[88] dealing with the problems raised under the refugee definition by conscientious objectors who decline military service on purely religious grounds.[89] The *Basic Law Manual* essentially adopts the position that States have the right to proscribe certain forms of conduct, and that where an otherwise neutral regulatory scheme is violated by the applicant because of religious principle, any resulting punishment is "prosecution", not persecution. As noted in the *Basic Law Manual*:

> A Supreme Court decision outside the asylum context ... held that it is not a denial of religious freedom for a government to refuse to grant a person an exemption from the effect of a valid or neutral law of general applicability on the ground that the law proscribes (or prescribes) conduct that his religion prescribes (or proscribes). In accord with this decision, the Court held persecution is not established when the alien's government merely seeks to punish conduct it may lawfully forbid and is not using its criminal laws as a

84 ICCPR, *supra* § I.1, note 14, Art. 18.

85 *Cf.* Handbook, *supra* § I.1, note 30, ¶ 40.

86 Goodwin-Gill, *supra* § I.1, note 11, at 56.

87 Basic Law Manual, *supra* § I.1, note 26, at 38.

88 Canas-Segovia v. INS, 902 F.2d 717 (9th Cir. 1989), *remanded* 112 U.S. 1152, *decision on remand,* 970 F.2d 599 (9th Cir. 1992).

89 This problem is dealt with in greater detail *infra* this section.

> pretext for punishing persons because of their religious beliefs. INS v. Zacarias-Elias, 502 U.S. 478, 112 S.Ct. 812 (1992); Canas-Segovia v. INS, 970 F.2d 599 (9th Cir. 1992).[90]

The principle embraced by the Immigration and Naturalization Service on religiously-inspired conscientious objection raises many complex questions regarding the relationship between individual human rights and the refugee standard which it fails to explore. In this respect, it is far from clear that the analysis adopted in the *Basic Law Manual* can be taken at face value as a correct restatement of United States asylum law on this subject. Among other things, the position of the Immigration and Naturalization Service seems to offer strong deference to the "intent to persecute" criterion which itself has been rejected by the United Nations High Commissioner for Refugees as a requirement of refugee status and which is now in a state of comparative decline in U.S. asylum law.[91] Moreover, it leaves entirely unexamined the legal implications for the refugee definition of situations in which non-derogable human rights are brought into conflict with an otherwise neutral law or regulation.[92]

Special issues may arise where an asylum seeker or refugee claimant seeks to interpose his or her faith to otherwise legitimate interests of the government in enforcing its criminal laws. Such questions tend to arise with regard to the second Convention ground under circumstances where religion is engaged in the "active" sense, that is, where the claimant is predicating his or her claim to refugee status on the internationally respected right to freedom of thought, conscience and religion.

In order to fully develop the relationship between international human rights and the refugee standard in such cases, it is essential to look to general principles adopted by the UNHCR, as these principles have been clarified through the agency's intervention in U.S. litigation.[93] In *Canas-Segovia* v. *INS*,[94] the Ninth Circuit originally held that two Jehovah's Witnesses who were opposed to war on account of their faith, and who would be prosecuted under a draft law which did not contain a "conscientious objection"

---

90 Basic Law Manual, *supra* § I.1, note 26, at 38.

91 *See generally* Matter of Kasinga, 21 I&N Dec. 357 (BIA 1996).

92 *Cf.* Matter of Izatula, 20 I&N Dec. 149 (BIA 1990); Zolfagharkhani v. M.E.I. (1993), 155 N.R. 311 (F. C.A.).

93 G. Goodwin-Gill, S. Timberlake and R. Steinhardt, *Canas-Segovia* v. *Immigration and Naturalization Service: Brief Amicus Curiae of the Office of the High Commissioner for Refugees, reprinted in* 2 Int'l J. Refugee L. 390 (1990) [hereinafter *Brief Amicus Curiae of UNHCR in Canas-Segovia*].

94 Canas-Segovia v. INS, 902 F.2d 717 (9th Cir. 1989), *remanded* 112 U.S. 1152, *decision on remand,* 970 F.2d 599 (9th Cir. 1992).

exemption, had a well-founded fear of persecution within the meaning of the refugee definition.

This decision was vacated by the Supreme Court on the basis of its earlier opinion in *Elias-Zacarias* v. *INS* [95] and, on remand, the Ninth Circuit determined that the applicants had made out a claim based on the principles of attributed political opinion.[96] The Ninth Circuit's second decision was predicated on the clearly excessive punishment which would be visited on draft resisters in El Salvador, even those whose opposition to the military was not based on ideological grounds, but on religious principle. In determining that the petitioners would fall subject to serious harm if they refused to serve in the military irrespective of their reasons, the appeals court ruled:

> The Board of Immigration Appeals rejected the Canas-Segovias' contention that they qualify for relief under [the ground of religion]. It reasoned that the two petitioners could simply tell their persecutors that they were refusing to serve for religious rather than political reasons. This analysis assumes, however, that the persecutors would believe them and that the Canas-Segovia could communicate the information before any harm befell them.[97]

The final decision of the Ninth Circuit, therefore, rests not on the second refugee ground (religion), but on the basis of attributed political opinion. In the course of the original litigation, however, the UNHCR filed a *Brief Amicus Curiae*[98] which set out the agency's formal position on the Canas' entitlement to political asylum. The norm-setting character of the UNHCR's interpretation of the refugee definition, particularly as that interpretation relates to a doctrinally central question of law, makes its analysis of the questions involved in the *Canas-Segovia* litigation obligatory.[99]

---

95 INS v. Elias-Zacarias, 502 U.S. 478 (1992). In this decision, which is discussed at length in § IV.2(b), *infra*, the Supreme Court determined that the applicant is required to show that he fears persecution "on account of" one of the five statutory grounds. Accordingly, the asylum seeker must adduce evidence, either direct or circumstantial, regarding the motive of his persecutor.

96 Canas-Segovia v. INS, 970 F.2d 599 (9th Cir. 1992).

97 *Id.* at 602: Under the *Handbook*, examination of a claim to refugee status should never look only to the law in question, but rather at whether the law is being applied in a pretextual way so as to reach a protected ground. *See, e.g.,* Handbook, *supra* § I.1, note 30, ¶ 59.

98 *See Brief Amicus Curiae of UNHCR in Canas-Segovia, supra* this section, note 93, at 402.

99 *See, e.g.*, Goodwin-Gill, *supra* § I.1, note 11, at 216:

> UNHCR is not only a forum in which the views of States may be represented; it is also a subject of international law; an actor in the relevant field whose actions count in the process of law formation.

UNHCR adopted the broad position that, since conscientious objection was itself a human right, the

> State's legitimate right to self-defense must accommodate the individual's corresponding right to conscientious objection.[100]

The right itself (to conscientious objection) is an "emerging" and derivative right, although the right to freedom of conscience, the anchor right involved, is firmly established in international law.[101] The *Brief* concludes that, if the right to "conscientious objection" is an internationally respected human right, then an absence of alternative service coupled with forcing the asylum seeker to choose between imprisonment and violating his conscience would constitute persecution in the Convention sense, *irrespective of the government's intention either in adopting or in implementing the law*:

> In the refugee context also, particular weight must be attached to what happens in fact. Governments and laws can have a variety of aims: a law restraining and punishing the expression of political opinions may seek merely to preserve order and good government, enhance welfare and development. A law on segregation or forbidding inter-marriage may be "intended" to promote separate development or racial harmony; and a law on conscription, to raise a defence force on the basis of treating equally all members of the community. In practice, however, in each case, the law itself singles out and penalizes whoever exercises freedom of speech; or struggles for racial equality; or whose ties of affection know no racial barrier; or whose convictions compel them to refuse to be coerced into military service. Each has a fear of prosecution, shared in common with other violators of the same generic class; each is persecuted in application of the law, because the law itself, necessarily in its own terms, fails to accommodate, either wholly or in part, the fundamental rights of its subjects—to freedom of expression, to equality, to freedom to marry, to freedom of conscience.[102]

In the alternative, the *UNHCR Brief* posits that (assuming *arguendo* conscientious objection not to be a "right") the State's efforts to regulate those who seek to exempt themselves from active military service on grounds of conscience is subject to the limitations inherent in the doctrine of proportionality.[103] The ends of State defense must be balanced against the

---

[100] *See Brief Amicus Curiae of UNHCR in Canas-Segovia, supra* This section, note 93, at 402.

[101] *See, e.g.*, Goodwin-Gill, *supra* § I.1, note 11, at 56, *citing Conscientious Objection to Military Service,* UN Doc. E/CN.4/Sub. 2/1983/30/Rev. 1

[102] *See Brief Amicus Curiae of UNHCR in Canas-Segovia, supra* this section, note 93, at 401-402.

[103] UDHR, *supra* note 12, Art. 29-1 (requiring that any "limitations" on human rights be solely for the purpose of securing the rights and freedoms of others and of meeting certain "just requirements" of a democratic society).

need of the individual to exercise his or her human rights so that the least onerous means of enforcing the State's interest should be adopted:

> If conscientious objection were accepted as a basic human right, then the degree of punishment would be irrelevant. The absence of choice, of exemption, of alternative service, the constraint to act and the threat of imprisonment in default, are themselves the incidents of persecution. On the other hand, if conscientious objection is a more relative claim, then the precise nature of its consequences count in the assessment of a claim to refugee status. The State and community have a recognized interest in defence, but the measures taken to that end should at least be 'reasonably necessary in a democratic society'; specifically, there ought to exist a relationship of proportionality between the ends and the means. At this juncture, alternative service is a potential means for reconciling competing duties in a manner which best promotes community interests in defence and equality of treatment, and the individual's interest in his or her conscience.[104]

The *UNHCR Brief* thus points to an emerging method of analysis in modern refugee law whereby the animus of the persecutor becomes of less concern to the adjudicator, and the focus becomes instead *the discriminatory effect of applying the restrictive law in question.*[105]

The *UNHCR Brief* adopts broad principles with respect to interpretation of the Convention refugee definition which will become of increasing importance in the course of this study. The first of these is the core notion of proportionality. States are obligated, in pursuing legitimate national concerns, to conform their measures to a standard of strict necessity and not to exceed that standard where to do so would affect the claimant's basic human rights. The State is responsible, in other words, to pursue the least restrictive alternative.

The second principle (which is actually a correlative of the first) is that it is not always necessary to demonstrate an intention on the part of the persecutor to punish the asylum seeker "on account of" a ground of refugee protection. Where the claimant is asserting a right which enjoys relative primacy within the more general field of international law, it may well be sufficient that the State (or powerful non-State agent) has adopted a course which infringes upon the enjoyment of that right. Such actions are not discriminatory in purpose, but they are discriminatory in effect. Under

---

[104] *See Brief Amicus Curiae of UNHCR*, *supra* this section, note 93, at 407.

[105] This methodology is consistent with the (U.S.) Religious Freedom and Restoration Act, 42 USC §§ 2000 (bb), declared unconstitutional by the Supreme Court in *City of Boerne* v. *Flores*, 117 S. Ct. 2157 (1997). For an interesting analysis of religious persecution claims in a modern context, *see* Arthur Helton and Jochen Munker, *Religion and Persecution: Should the U.S. Provide Refuge to German Scientologists*, 11 Int'l. J. Refugee L. 310 (1999).

appropriate conditions acts undertaken for otherwise legitimate purposes, although undirected and not aimed at punishing the applicant on account of a Convention ground, may well satisfy the requirements for refugee status if they unnecessarily restrict or compromise the exercise of a fundamental human right.

# III. THE APPLICANT'S PERSONA IN A POLITICAL AND SOCIAL SETTING: THE REFUGEE DEFINITION AS AN EVOLVING INTERNATIONAL NORM

## § III.1. The Refugee Definition and "External" Perceptions of the Persecutor

The framers of the Refugee Convention sought to protect refugees against only specific forms of harm as represented by the "reasons" for persecution.[1] The scope of international protection lies at the heart of much litigation surrounding the Convention refugee definition. The two protected interests which remain to be discussed, political opinion and social group, have proven to be the most elastic of the Convention grounds and, therefore, the most fertile sources of the refugee definition's future development. Among other things, the fourth and fifth Convention grounds (political opinion and social group) lend themselves to analysis based on attributed characteristics and beliefs, and to the principle of refugee analysis that, in determining whether persecution is related to a protected ground, it is the perception of the persecutor which is the dominant criterion.

The importance of the notion of imputation (or attribution) to refugee law cannot be underestimated. Its centrality to determinations of the refugee standard is not something novel, but a feature of refugee jurisprudence which is of long-standing. Hence, with respect to attributed political opinion, Atle Grahl-Madsen maintains that any "real, alleged or implied" opinion which leads to a violation of UDHR will qualify as a "political" opinion within the meaning of the fifth Convention ground. The character of the opinion is irrelevant: it may relate to matters of purely administrative convenience (a preference for construction of a road on the right bank of a river as opposed to the left); a local political choice (preference for one candidate over another in municipal elections); or to the aesthetics of a national symbol (preference for a blue as opposed to a green flag).

The fact that the individual is threatened with serious harm because of his choice indicates that the authorities of his country view his decision as a political one and are prepared to punish him for it. This is an aspect of the

---

1 Hathaway, *supra* § I.1, note 7, at 159.

more general proposition, Grahl-Madsen maintains, that it is the behavior of the persecutor that "determines what persons shall be considered refugees".[2] Hence, under the international standard, what constitutes a "political opinion" will often be context dependent. Moreover, although Grahl-Madsen's comments seem confined to the political opinion ground, they could easily be extended to the other grounds of refugee protection.

The "liberal" view that the grounds of international protection were not meant to "freeze" the growth of refugee jurisprudence finds support in the Convention's inclusion of the "social group" category which, it has been saliently noted, is potentially "open-ended" in scope.[3] Differences remain, however, as to the latitude in signatory States with respect to construing social group persecution in light of the specific enumeration made in Article 1A(2) of the Convention. James Hathaway, for instance, in expressing approval for the definition of "social group" put forward in the (U.S.) *Acosta* case, placed considerable stress on the protected grounds as constituting absolute limitations on the Convention's scope of protection:

> By basing the definition of "membership of a particular social group" on application of the *ejusdem generis* principle, we respect both the specific situation known to the drafters—concern for the plight of persons whose social origins put them at comparable risk to those in other enumerated categories—and the more general commitment to grounding refugee claims in civil or political status. Beyond that, the linkage between this standard and fundamental norms of human rights correlates well with the human rights-based definition of persecution. Most importantly, the standard is sufficiently open-ended to allow for evolution in much the same way as has occurred with the other four grounds, but not so vague as to admit persons without a serious basis to claim international protection.[4]

Those seeking an enlarged interpretation of the term "refugee" generally attribute critical importance to the notion of persecution and only derivative consideration to the protected grounds.[5] However, an interpretation which emphasizes the concept of "persecution" itself (rather than precise conformity with the refugee grounds) must stress not merely its serious harm aspect, but also the animus (real or implied) with which that harm is threatened or imposed. Generally, the case law captures this analysis through the formulation that persecution is the product of a difference between the

---

2 1 Grahl-Madsen, *supra* § I.1, note 7, at 250.

3 Goodwin-Gill, *supra* § I.1, note 11, at 47-48.

4 Hathaway, *supra* note 7, at 161, commenting on *Matter of Acosta,* 19 I&N Dec. 211 (BIA 1985).

5 *Cf.* Deborah Anker, The Law of Asylum in the United States: A Guide to Administrative Practice and Case Law 147-148 (1991) [hereinafter cited as Anker 91].

persecutor's views or status and those of the victim which the persecutor will not tolerate.[6]

The emphasis in this study is on the term "persecution" with a corresponding de-emphasis on the protected grounds as delimiting factors in the scope of refugee protection. Accordingly, the concept of attribution, most clearly identified with political opinion persecution, seeks to explain the relationship between serious harm and a refugee ground by examining the will and imagination of the persecutor: an asylum seeker who belongs to a group which is perceived as a political threat and fears punishment as a result is clearly entitled to relief under the Convention irrespective of what the constituent elements of the group happen to be. The persecutor has focused on a human aggregate whose objectives are opposed in principle (which has characteristics or beliefs which the persecutor wishes to "overcome"). In this case, the "reason" for persecution is really one-sided; it flows exclusively from the persecutor's conception of a political, racial, national, or social group as being inimical or otherwise in need of suppression. It is this persecutory animus which both establishes the existence of a protected ground and connects it, in a material way, with serious harm.

Reliance on attributed characteristics and beliefs has often been criticized as being "circular" (with respect to social group persecution) or as excessively vague and undefined (as concerns the political opinion ground). The "circularity" argument has most recently served as the basis for criticizing interpretations of the "social group" ground in terms of "external" perceptions. As Deborah Anker cautions:

> An excessively externalist approach [...] can result in groups being circularly defined by common victimization.[7]

It is important to note, however, that the circularity argument closely resembles those made earlier in connection with attribution principles as applied to the now accepted doctrine of imputed political opinion. In the words of one widely noted law review article:

> Essentially, the *Hernandez-Ortiz* court dispensed with political opinion as a category for meeting the statutory definition of a refugee, at least insofar as an alien's legitimate fear of persecution is based on prior persecutorial acts perpetrated against her family. While the result is agreeable, the court's reasoning is dubious. It is unwise to presume that persecution practiced by a government is necessarily political and based on disagreement. Moreover, it is probably incorrect to apply this reasoning to the particular situation of El Salvador. It is not unheard of for a government attempting to suppress internal

---

6 Hernandez-Ortiz v. INS, 777 F.2d 509 (9th Cir. 1985).

7 Anker 99, *supra* § I.2, note 32, at 378.

> dissent to proceed with a purposefully overinclusive program of oppression, especially where the government is unable to distinguish dissenters from the surrounding populace adequately. These governments commit seemingly random violence without often discovering, or even caring, whether the victim is really a dissenter.[8]

Those who contend that an approach based on the "external" features of the claimant's persona is "circular" or "excessively open-ended" refer generally to a relaxed interpretation of "persecution" which would eliminate the implicit requirement that the persecutor act with discriminatory animus. Obviously, if such an interpretation were to be combined with a diminished view of the protected grounds persecution could arguably be defined in a circular manner so as to afford protection to those who were merely objects of undirected victimization. Some form of political or social targeting aimed at the asylum seeker must be made out in cases involving attributed characteristics or beliefs: a discriminatory animus is absolutely essential in such cases if the refugee definition is to retain its integrity and to provide the basis for formal analysis.

The risks involved in emphasizing purely "internal" characteristics of the asylum seeker were made apparent in *Matter of Acosta*,[9] dealing with "social group" persecution. In *Acosta*, the Board found that the remaining four grounds of persecution enumerated in the Act and in the Protocol "restrict refugee status to individuals who are either unable by their own actions, or as a matter of conscience should not be required to avoid persecution." The Board utilized this characterization of the remaining classes of protected interests to find that those seeking asylum under the fourth ground of refugee protection (social group) must in general be able to demonstrate inclusion within one of the broad unifying elements of the refugee definition (i.e., immutable characteristics or conscientiously held beliefs).

The anomalies of this result are self-evident when "social group" and "political opinion" persecution are compared. Under modern jurisprudence, the political opinion category does not require that the opinion be held as a matter of conscience, and asylum seekers can often have characteristics and beliefs ascribed to them which they do not possess or entertain.[10] The Board's analysis, although it touches upon this aspect of the refugee definition, fails to develop it thereby leaving asylum law in the U.S. (and

---

8 D.P. Gagliardi, *The Inadequacy of Cognizable Grounds of Persecution as a Criterion for According Refugee Status*, 24 Stanford J. Int'l L. 259, 279 (1987).

9 19 I&N Dec. 211, 233 (BIA 1985).

10 *See, e.g.*, Matter of S-P-, 21 I&N Dec. 486 (BIA 1996).

indirectly in Canada) open to a more stringent evolution than would otherwise have been the case.

## § III.2. Intrinsic Features of the Applicant's Persona: The Exercise of Fundamental Human Rights and Specifically Protected Groups

On the other hand, refugee doctrine must take account of groups and belief-oriented activities which are granted special protection under international law and policy. A refugee claimant who engages in non-violent political protest, or who refuses to be inducted into an army which is committing war-time atrocities, has undertaken an action which refugee policy views as comparatively privileged. In a similar way, the claimant may be a member of a socially vulnerable group (e.g., women[11] and children[12]) towards which precise duties exist under treaty law, pursuant to customary law, or by virtue of both. State action (or the action of powerful groups) which derogates from the specific rights protected under international law may well be persecutory if it entails serious harm. Where certain vulnerable groups and specific belief-oriented activities enjoy such protection, refugee analysis can and should adopt an effects-based interpretation of "persecution" which is not dependent on the discriminatory animus of the persecutor. A pattern of conduct having serious adverse consequences for protected classes can be said to flow from an actual or an implied policy which is discriminatory in effect.[13]

The analysis suggested here is to the effect that the "nexus" requirement is essentially flexible and should be given a fluid interpretation which will depend on the weight of the protected ground being asserted. Hence, where an "external" characteristic or belief is being asserted (i.e., the analysis depends on attributed characteristics or beliefs), some causative nexus tied to the discriminatory intent of the persecutor will have to be made out. Where on the other hand, internationally protected activity or status is specifically

---

[11] *See, e.g.*, CEDAW, *supra* § I.1, note 22.

[12] *See, e.g.*, Convention on the Rights of the Child, *supra* § I.1, note 21.

[13] The "nexus" requirement (i.e., connection between serious harm and a protected ground) has never been finally settled in refugee doctrine. Article 1A(2) of the 1951 Convention refers to persecution "for reasons of" a protected ground. Canada had adopted a "but for" rule, largely following the Hathaway formulation which asks whether the "claimant would be similarly at risk of serious harm but for her civil or political status". Hathaway, *supra* § I.1, note 7, at 140. U.S. law, like that of the majority of signatory States, follows Grahl-Madsen in requiring, in the majority of instances, some causative connection between persecution and a protected ground. 1 Grahl-Madsen, *supra* § I.1, note 7, at 192.

involved, analysis can turn to the effect which the persecutor's actions will produce. In this connection, the Convention refugee definition specifically allows for an examination which rests not so much on the intent of the persecutor to "punish" individuals because they have a particular characteristic or viewpoint, as it does in identifying serious forms of harm which have the effect of prejudicing specific groups held together by common status or shared beliefs.[14]

Within this broader framework of discussion, formal analysis, insofar as it deals with "internal" attributes, tends to view the protected grounds as based on two conceptual parameters. Certain of the protected grounds are predicated on characteristics which the asylum seeker is powerless to change (e.g., race, nationality and, in some cases, religion); the remaining grounds pertain to the free exercise of fundamental rights (e.g., political opinion and, where it is active, religion) which can be viewed as fundamental to the individual human personality.[15] The "particular social group" rubric has been held to occupy a middle ground between these two categories, on the one hand drawing upon immutable characteristics, and, on the other, comprising those beliefs and associations which the asylum seeker should not be required to relinquish because they are fundamental to his/her dignity, conscience or identity.[16]

Often analysis will adopt a hybrid of these two strains (immutable status and conscientious beliefs) to show that fundamental human rights have been denied to groups sharing immutable characteristics on a discriminatory basis so that conscientious opponents of such a practice will qualify for refugee status.[17] Human rights law plays a role not merely in establishing which

---

14 *Cf.* Goodwin-Gill, *supra* § I.1, note 11, at 192.

15 It may be of moment that Grahl-Madsen treats the "particular social group" classification as falling under the broad category of reasons which are beyond the power of the individual to change. *See, e.g.*, 1 Grahl-Madsen, *supra* § I.1, note 7, at 217:

> It is apparent that the above-mentioned five reasons fall under two main headings. Firstly, we have the reasons which are beyond the control of the individual, namely race, nationality, membership in a particular social group, and—in certain respects—religion. Secondly, we have reasons of an individual character: political opinion and active religion.

*But see* Matter of Acosta, 19 I&N Dec. 211, 233 (1985), discussed below.

16 *See, e.g.*, Matter of Acosta, 19 I&N Dec. 211, 233 (1985). For Canadian jurisprudence following the *Acosta* criteria, *see* Canada (Attorney General) v. Ward, [1993] 2 S.C.R. 689.

17 Fatin v. INS, 12 F.3d 1233, 1241 (3d Cir. 1993):

> Limited in this way, the "particular social group" identified by petitioner ["Iranian women who refuse to conform to the government's gender-specific laws and

voluntary associations are worthy of international protection (in the sense of specifying those human rights which are regarded as so "fundamental" that the claimant should not be obligated to retreat from them),[18] but also in identifying which groups with fixed characteristics have been made the subject of unacceptable discrimination so as to benefit from a form of special solicitude on the part of the international community.[19]

For a belief or an association to form the basis for a protected ground, however, it is not enough that the claimant maintain a conscientious attachment to it: the belief or association must enjoy some foundation in general international law. The bar against constraining individuals to betray their fundamental loyalties, to fight compatriots or give evidence against them, or to take life against genuinely maintained principles of conscience has compelling underpinnings in international human rights and humanitarian law.[20] In the law of refugee status, such coercion may constitute serious harm

---

> norms"] may well satisfy the BIA's definition of that concept, for if a woman's opposition to the Iranian laws in question is so profound that she would choose to suffer severe consequences of noncompliance, her beliefs may well be characterized as "so fundamental to [her] identity or conscience that [they] ought not be required to be changed."

18 1 Grahl-Madsen, *supra* § I.1, note 7, at 217, *citing* UDHR, *supra* § I.1, note 12.

19 Examples of such specific protections based on class membership can be found in CEDAW; in the Convention on the Rights of the Child; the Convention for the Elimination of All Forms of Racial Discrimination; the Apartheid Convention; and the Declaration on the Rights of National, Ethnic, Religious or Linguistic Minorities, *supra* § I.1, notes 22, 21, 20, 19 and 23. For an article anticipating many developments in this field, *see* Helton, *supra* § I.1, note 23.

20 *See generally Brief Amicus Curiae of UNHCR in Canas-Segovia, supra* § II.3, note 93. *See also* Matter of A-G-, 19 I&N Dec. 502 (BIA 1987); Matter of Salim, 18 I&N Dec. 311 (BIA 1982). Article 18 of the Universal Declaration of Human Rights lays down the foundation for asserting the right to conscientious objection:

> Everyone has the right to freedom of thought, conscience and religion; this right includes freedom to change religion or belief, and freedom either alone or in community with others and in public or private, to manifest his religion or belief in teaching, practice, worship or observance.

UDHR, *supra* § I.1, note 12, Art. 18. However, it is important to note that the right against betraying one's fundamental loyalties has older recognition in international humanitarian law. *See generally* Pictet, *supra* § I.1, note 18, at 64:

> Amongst the practices which are condemned, that of torture to extract information appears to be the most reprehensible and dangerous. For the individual, it is the source of unspeakable suffering. It is also a serious affront to the dignity of man, forcing him to perform acts and make statements against his will, obliging him to betray his comrades, and even his family, degrading him to the level of a slave in the barbaric ages, or one might say that of a beast, a subhuman.

on a protected ground where the claimant's genuinely held beliefs will cause her pronounced psychological suffering if restricted or suppressed.[21]

## § III.3. Trends in the Evolution of Modern Refugee Law

Critical in this respect is the situation of those asylum seekers who have conscientiously opposed a law (or cultural norm) of general application, urging either discriminatory treatment or infringement of a fundamental human right: civil disobedience in the face of China's family planning program;[22] rebellion against authoritarian regimes;[23] conscientious objection to becoming involved in a national army's execution of atrocities;[24] resistance to cultural standards requiring bodily mutilation;[25] and refusal to conform to political or social practices which have the effect of subordinating the status of women to that of men in such matters as equality before the law, inheritance rights, custody disputes, health care, political participation and matters affecting family life.[26]

In the past, case law had shown a marked proclivity to view individuals who challenge generally applicable statutory standards (or similar cultural or religious norms) as not being eligible refugees.[27] A variety of rationales accompanied such denials, ranging from the broad "prosecution versus persecution" bar[28] to the more generalized insistence that mandatory cultural

---

21 *Cf.* Basic Law Manual, *supra* § I.1, note 26, at 25, noting that pressure to become an informer may constitute an act of persecution.

22 *See, e.g.*, [1993] Cheung v. M.E.I., 153 N.R. 145 (C.A.); Matter of X-P-T-, Interim Decision 3299 (BIA 1997).

23 *Compare* Matter of Izatula, 20 I&N Dec. 149 (BIA 1990) *and* Gil v. M.E.I.(1994), 174 N.R. 292 (F.C.A. 1994).

24 *Compare* Matter of A-G-, 19 I&N Dec. 502 (BIA 1987), *rev'd sub nom.* M.A. v. INS (I), 899 F.2d 304 (4th Cir. 1990), *vacated,* M.A. A26 851 062 v. INS (II), 899 F.2d 304 (1990) *and* Zolfagharkhani v. M.E.I. (1993), 155 N.R. 311 (F.C.A.).

25 *Compare* Matter of Kasinga, 21 I&N Dec. 357 (BIA 1996) *and* Annan v. M.C.I., [1994] 3 F.C. 25 (T.D. 1993).

26 Nancy Kelley, Deborah Anker and Michele Beasley, *Guidelines For Women's Asylum Claims,* 72 Interpreter Releases 812, 821 (1994), and cases cited therein.

27 The original definitions of persecution were largely responsible for limiting the criteria for refugee status in this regard. For instance, in *Matter of Acosta,* the Board of Immigration Appeals defined persecution as being limited to those situations where the persecutor had the disposition and the power to "punish" the alien exclusively for reasons relating to a specific ground enumerated in the refugee definition. Matter of Acosta, 18 I&N Dec. 211, 226 (1985).

28 *See, e.g.,* Matter of Chang, 20 I&N Dec. 38 (BIA 1989). *See also* Handbook, *supra* § I.1, note 30, ¶ 56:

or religious conformity did not result from an "intent to punish" the asylum seeker on one of the enumerated grounds.[29]

These rationales have received substantial modification in modern law and, as a result, have undergone considerable decline. In broad outline, it is now appropriate to say that generalized regimes are subject to scrutiny under general international law. The law in itself may not be in conformity with prevailing human rights principles (e.g., a law compelling segregation in violation of the Apartheid Convention). Modern human rights norms must be given a comprehensive application which would include their equal protection component.[30] Accordingly, where a regime is discriminatory (e.g., gender-specific religious codes), it cannot be considered as embracing laws of general application.[31] Alternatively, the law may be applied in such a way that its enforcement is clearly pretextual, enforcement being chiefly directed at a "ground" which is protected under the Convention refugee definition.[32]

Individuals who fear punishment because they have overtly challenged official or customary restraints which offend human rights or humanitarian law principles are eligible refugee claimants—irrespective of whether the State (or other agent of persecution) possesses the "malignant intent" to punish them.[33] The defining limits of "persecution" in such instances must be seen in the discriminatory impact of the persecutor's acts, i.e., in a position

---

> Persecution must be distinguished from prosecution for a common law offence. Persons fleeing from prosecution or punishment for such an offence are not normally refugees. It should be recalled that a refugee is a victim—or a potential victim—of injustice, not a fugitive from justice.

For a vigorous critique of the "intent to persecute" criterion in the context of the "prosecution versus persecution" bar, *see Brief Amicus Curiae of UNHCR in Canas-Segovia, supra* note 163, at 401-402.

29 *Cf.* Brief of the Immigration and Naturalization Service in *Matter of Kasinga,* 21 I&N Dec. 357 (BIA 1996), *abstracted in* 73 Interpreter Releases 577, 578 (April 29, 1996):

> We support the notion that ordinarily any action that constitutes persecution is taken with an intent to do harm to the victim. But in some circumstances, the intention of the actor pales in significance in the face of evidence about the nature of the practice itself.

30 *See, e.g.*, UDHR, *supra* § I.1, note 12, Art. 2.

31 Fathi-Rad v. S.S.C., (F.C.T.D., no. IMM-2438-93), April 13, 1994. *See also* 1 Grahl-Madsen, *supra* § I.1, note 7, at 227.

32 *Compare* Handbook, *supra* § I.1, note 30, ¶ 59 and Basic Law Manual, *supra* § I.1, note 26, at 73-75.

33 *See generally* Matter of Kasinga, 21 I&N Dec. 357 (BIA 1996); Cheung v. MEI (1993), 153 N.R. 145 (F.C.A.).

of intolerance *which has an adverse effect* on the exercise of a human right which is privileged under international or municipal constitutional law.[34]

The grounds of persecution will in many cases overlap.[35] Thus, while the sections which follow concern themselves primarily with political opinion and social group persecution, other grounds of refugee protection will necessarily form a part of the analysis. Moreover, as noted in the *Handbook*, individuals do not necessarily know the exact reason which has induced a persecutor to threaten them with serious harm. It is a fundamental principle of refugee adjudication, however, that asylum seekers are not under a duty to analyze the precise nature of the persecutor's motivation.[36] The *Handbook*'s injunction has received express recognition in the *Basic Law Manual*:

> These grounds should not be considered in a narrow or technical fashion as clear-cut "categories." They are broad categories, and are not meant to exclude from consideration people who can demonstrate persecution or fear of persecution which is targeted and is not only the result of private or personal vengeance or of proximity to civil strife. ... To some extent, these grounds may overlap in a given case. For example, in a given country, persons may be persecuted on both racial and religious grounds. In the same way, if the alien's testimony establishes that the alien is a refugee, the adjudicator should not deny asylum simply because the alien did not specify on which ground he or she feared persecution. The asylum officer is required to be well-versed in United States asylum law. The alien is not.[37]

---

[34] *Cf.* Zolfagharkhani v. M.E.I.(1993), 155 N.R. 311, 319 (F.C.A.): claimant's desertion from military service in Iran occasioned by conscientious refusal to become involved in chemical weapons violations gave rise to persecution, not prosecution, because:

> appellant's refusal to participate in military action against the Kurds would be treated by the Iranian government as an unacceptable political opinion.

[35] Handbook, *supra* § I.1, note 30, ¶ 67:

> It is for the examiner, when investigating the facts of the case, to ascertain the reason or reasons for the persecution feared and to decide whether the definition in the 1951 Convention is met with in this respect. It is evident that the reasons for persecution under the various headings will frequently overlap. Usually there will be more than one element combined in one person, e.g., a political opponent who belongs to a religious or national group, or both, and the combination of such reasons in his person may be relevant in evaluating the well-founded fear.

[36] *Id.*, ¶ 66:

> In order to be considered a refugee, a person must show well-founded fear of persecution for one of the reasons stated above. It is immaterial whether the persecution arises from any single one of these reasons or from a combination of one or more of them. Often the applicant himself may not be aware of the reasons for the persecution feared. It is not, however, his duty to analyze his case to such an extent as to identify the reasons in detail.

[37] Basic Law Manual, *supra* § I.1, note 26, at 36-37.

The asylum seeker's lack of knowledge, however, concerning the basis for his or her persecution has often led to denials of claims on the ground that the "harm or suffering" complained of flows from generalized sources and cannot be traced to a protected ground.[38] The law of refugee status in such instances has undergone a pronounced evolution so that those individuals who in the past might well have been viewed as migrants fleeing general conditions of unrest (i.e., as merely "displaced persons" who have crossed an international frontier) now may claim legitimately that they are Convention refugees.[39]

The notion of attributed characteristics and beliefs has largely made this evolution possible. The concept of attribution really contains two inter-related components. The first of these is the transparent one that an asylum seeker need not demonstrate that she has an actual political opinion (or other characteristic or belief) if the persecutor seeks to punish her for an opinion which the persecutor believes her to possess. On the other hand, and perhaps less obviously, the record may not expressly reveal the existence of a persecutory motive, and the adjudicator may be required to infer one. Where the claimant is unaware of the persecutor's incentives or is unable to explain her dilemma, the adjudicator has a responsibility to examine the claim objectively and to infer nexus to a protected ground where the facts justify such inference. As noted in the *Basic Law Manual*:

> [I]nsofar as the asylum officer has a duty to elicit all relevant and useful information regarding the applicant's claim, ... the asylum officer should probe the connection between applicant's fears and the five grounds. For instance, where forced recruitment is the issue, the applicant should be asked why he thinks the guerillas wanted to recruit him or why he thinks they might have harmed him if he refused to be recruited. The officer may also look to country conditions information on these same issues.[40]

The evolution of modern refugee law, strongly identified with the developing concept of attributed characteristics and beliefs, has been the product of an inferential analysis on the part of adjudicators whereby it is not essential for the victim of persecution to prove the exact motivation of her persecutor. Rather it is enough to present objective evidence "direct or

---

38 A complete lack of knowledge regarding the persecutor's motives is not uncommon in many cases but tends to be emphasized in the area of mass migrations where large groups have been forced to flee because of discriminatory policies.

39 *See generally* Matter of S-P-, 21 I&N Dec. 486 (BIA 1996); Guidelines, *Civilian Non-Combatants Fearing Persecution in Civil War Situations,* Immigration and Refugee Board, Ottawa, Canada, Mar. 1996 [hereinafter *Canadian Civil War Guidelines* or *Civil War Guidelines*].

40 Basic Law Manual, *supra* § I.1, note 26, at 36, n. 9.

circumstantial" showing that persecution on a protected ground is reasonable.[41] Under such an analysis, persecutory motive need not be the subject of an individualized showing which links motivation directly to a characteristic or belief in the victim. Rather, persecution on a protected ground can be established by demonstrating specific configurations of violence involving deliberately targeted groups, i.e., an historical pattern of discriminatory mistreatment on the persecutor's part toward a human aggregate which includes claimant or to which she is perceived to belong.

The analysis, therefore, as to whether a protected interest is involved in the case rests on a pattern or practice of human rights and humanitarian law violations directed at human aggregates with which claimant can be identified on an objective basis.[42] Progressively, moreover, the analysis as to whether a protected ground is involved in the case is becoming coterminous with the issue of whether persecution in the Convention sense has been threatened or imposed. Again, as noted in the *Basic Law Manual*:

> If the adjudicator determines that the alien has a well-founded fear of persecution, the adjudicator must determine if the fear of persecution is based on ("on account of") race, religion, nationality, membership in a particular social group, or political opinion. **The "on account of" requirement should not be narrowly construed against the applicant.**[43]

Finally, a growing body of case law is seeking to explore the limits of the refugee definition in another area, namely, situations in which it is asserted that the claimant is fleeing harm which is based on a "personal" dispute, not involving the grounds for refugee status. Like the adjudications dealing with general conditions of upheaval, Canadian and U.S. decisions grappling with the issues generated by domestic violence have found that, where such mistreatment is the product of an implicit policy of discrimination, and is exercised without adequate State redress, the conditions for refugee status will have been met. As noted in leading commentary contributing to the adoption by the U.S. Immigration and Naturalization Service of *Guidelines* for adjudicating gender-based claims:

> [Eligible asylum seekers include] women whose claims are based past or anticipated battering or other abuse by non-governmental actors and who cannot obtain the protection of the government. Women may face battering and other abuses, including psychological abuse, at the hands of their spouses and other non-governmental actors. In some situations, because of laws, customs, religious practices or government inability or indifference, women

---

41 INS v. Elias-Zacarias, 502 U.S. 478 (1992).

42 1 Grahl-Madsen, *supra* § I.1, note 7, at 250; Hathaway, *supra* § I.1, note 7, at 89.

43 Basic Law Manual, *supra* § I.1, note 26, at 35. [Emphasis in original].

> are subject to severe abuse with no recourse. In such cases, the applicants may be eligible for asylum. To evaluate the claim of a woman seeking asylum on this basis, the adjudicator must evaluate the severity of the harm and the applicant's access to protection from the harm.[44]

The case law in this area has come to rely strongly on both attributed characteristics and beliefs and on the emerging doctrine that affirmative duties are owed to certain vulnerable groups by virtue of international law and policy. The environment of impunity in which serious mistreatment is inflicted in domestic violence cases serves as compelling evidence that the harm feared or endured is not "personal" but flows from a larger context of social discrimination against persons linked together by an immutable characteristic.[45] Conversely, official inaction may lead to the conclusion that the State has failed to observe affirmative obligations owed to a specific class under international treaty or customary law. The State's failure to provide human rights protection to designated groups may well result in a finding of persecution where that failure can be objectively linked to acts of serious harm.[46]

---

44 Kelley, Anker and Beasley, *supra* this section, note 26, at 821.

45 *Id.*, *citing* U.S. and Canadian authorities.

46 *Cf. Islam (A.P.)* v. *Secretary of State for the Home Department, Regina* v. *Immigration Appeal Tribunal and Another Ex Parte Shah (A.P.)* [1999], 2 All ER 545 (House of Lords).

# IV. POLITICAL OPINION AND ITS RELATIONSHIP TO THE OTHER GROUNDS OF REFUGEE PROTECTION: THE RISE OF ATTRIBUTED CHARACTERISTICS AND BELIEFS

## § IV.1. Political Opinion: The Essential Framework

A central question in modern refugee law is the legitimate scope of the fifth Convention ground. Guy Goodwin-Gill has offered perhaps one of the broadest interpretations of the political opinion category by linking this "reason" for persecution any opinion or activity of the claimant which relates to State action or policy. Opinions may be held outright or attributed (rightly or wrongly) to the applicant. With respect to the central question of whether such opinions can give rise to a well-founded fear, it is enough if the applicant (or someone similarly situated to the applicant) has been oppressed or threatened. Goodwin-Gill writes:

> In the 1951 Convention, 'political opinion' should be understood in the broad sense, to incorporate, within substantive limitations now developing generally within the field of human rights, any opinion on any matter in which the machinery of the State, government and policy may be engaged. The typical 'political refugee' is one pursued by the government of a state on account of his or her opinions, which are an actual or a perceived threat to that government or its institutions. Political opinions may or may not be expressed and they may be rightly or wrongly attributed to the applicant for refugee status. If they have been expressed, and if the applicant (or others similarly placed) has suffered or been threatened with oppressive measures, then a well-founded fear may be made out.[1]

Atle Grahl-Madsen, on the other hand, stresses the human rights underpinnings of the 1951 Convention, and the seminal goals of refugee protection which are reflected in the instrument's preamble. The Refugee Convention must be given an interpretation which is consistent with its policy aim of advancing the full enjoyment of human rights without discrimination. Accordingly, a construction is required under which the claimant's attachment to any of the rights set forth in the Universal Declaration of Human Rights will qualify as a political opinion:

---

[1] Goodwin-Gill, *supra* § I.1, note 11, at 49.

> In view of the fact that the first paragraph of the Preamble to the Refugee Convention contains a direct reference to the Universal Declaration and the principle which has thereby been affirmed 'that human beings shall enjoy fundamental rights and freedoms without discrimination', it seems reasonable to infer that a person may justly fear persecution 'for reason of political opinion' in the sense of the Refugee Convention if he is threatened with measures of a persecutory nature because of his exercise of or his insistence on certain of the rights laid down in the Declaration.[2]

Importantly, such freedoms would include not merely those rights which have been reduced to treaty form in the International Covenant on Civil and Political Rights, but also those which are now set forth in the International Covenant on Economic, Social and Cultural Rights.[3]

Commentary to the *U.S. Gender Guidelines* clarifies that political opinion need not be limited to the sovereign State and its activities, but can be an opinion with respect to powerful social aggregates which have actual power to affect the claimant's status. In this respect, political opinion may consist of:

> an opinion regarding the treatment or status of women within her country, culture or social, religious or ethnic group.[4]

The foregoing definition provides clear doctrinal support for the proposition that the political opinion ground of refugee protection has become separated

---

[2] 1 Grahl-Madsen, *supra* § I.1, note 7, at 217.

[3] The UDHR was intended as a basic charter which could serve as a springboard for a single Convention covering both the civil-political and the social-economic dimension of international human rights. The separation of these two broad categories into distinct Covenants (the ICCPR and the ICESCR) undoubtedly reflected underlying political realities, rather than universal legal concerns. The continuing vitality of the UDHR, however, has been well summed up by Philip Alston and Henry Steiner:

> During the 28 years between 1948 and 1976, specialized human rights treaties such as the Genocide Convention entered into force. But not until the two principal Covenants became effective did treaties achieve as broad coverage of human rights topics as the Universal Declaration. It was partly for this reason that the UDHR became so broadly known and frequently invoked. During these intervening years, it was the only broad-based human rights instrument available. *To this day, it retains its symbolism, rhetorical force and significance to the human rights movement. It is the parent document, the initial burst of idealism and enthusiasm, terser, more general and grander than the treaties, in some sense the constitution of the entire movement. It remains the single most invoked human rights instrument.*

Steiner and Alston, *supra* § I.1, note 13, at 120 (1996). (Emphasis supplied).

[4] Kelley, Anker and Beasley, *supra* § III.3, note 26, at 817, *citing* Fatin v. INS, 12 F.3d 1233 (3d Cir. 1993). A refugee can thus base her claim on opposition to racial, religious or cultural norms provided that she will encounter serious harm as a result.

from its historical moorings in State action or policy. Rather, a political belief can now be one which relates to norms advocated by powerful non-State groups founded upon religious, social, cultural or ethnic principle, or upon custom.

The Supreme Court of Canada has expressly adopted the test for political opinion set forth by Guy Goodwin-Gill above, i.e., that political opinion consists of "any opinion on any matter in which the machinery of state, government, and policy may be engaged."[5] The court added two conditions to this formulation: (i) the opinion need not be expressed outright; and (ii) it can be based on actions of the claimant, in which case the relevant opinion is said to be imputed or attributed to claimant.[6]

## § IV.2. The *Ward* and *Elias-Zacarias* Decisions: The "Political Opinion" Ground in a Modern Context

The Supreme Court of the United States and that of Canada have recently articulated the parameters of the political opinion ground. A review of the holdings in these two cases, *Ward* v. *Canada*[7] and *Elias-Zacarias* v. *INS*,[8] provides a necessary background for understanding the evolution of refugee and asylum law in both jurisdictions. While the *Ward* decision purports to carry forward established principles of political opinion persecution in Canada, the *Elias-Zacarias* decision has raised serious questions regarding the future course of U.S. asylum law and, in many instances, has been thought to unduly restrict prior approaches to refugee analysis.

---

5 Canada (Attorney General) v. Ward [1993], 2 SCR 689, 746, *citing* Guy S. Goodwin-Gill, The Refugee in International Law 31 (1st ed. 1983). Importantly, the court rejected Grahl-Madsen's characterization of political opinion claimants ("that they are alleged or known to hold opinions contrary or critical of the policies of the government or ruling party") on the ground that it was too narrow. Attorney-General. *Id., citing* 1 Grahl-Madsen, *supra* § I.1, note 7, at 220.

6 Canadian case law has been more deeply influenced by the internationally accepted method of refugee analysis that nexus to a protected ground must be determined by viewing the actions and perceptions of the persecutor. *See, e.g.*, 1 Grahl-Madsen, *supra* § I.1, note 7, at 175. In this respect, the Federal Court of Appeal has ruled that:

> [T]he crucial test in this regard should not be whether the Board considers that the applicant has engaged in political activity, but whether the ruling government of the country from which [applicant] claims to be a refugee considers his conduct to have been styled as political activity.

Inzunza v. M.E.I. (1979), 103 D.L.R. (3d) 105, 109 (F.C.A.).

7 [ 1993] 2 S.C.R. 689.

8 502 U.S. 478 (1992).

In *Canada (Attorney-General)* v. *Ward*,[9] the claimant had been a member of the Irish National Liberation Army (INLA), a paramilitary group dedicated to the political unification of Northern Ireland with the Republic of Ireland. Claimant had been assigned to guard hostages who were in no way involved in the conflict. When Ward discovered that the hostages were to be executed, he effected their release at great personal risk to himself. INLA members discovered claimant's actions; they confined and tortured him, later sentencing Ward to death following a "court martial". Claimant escaped to the United Kingdom where he was charged with the seizing of the hostages. With the help of the Irish authorities, Ward escaped to Canada where he applied for refugee status.

The primary focus of the *Ward* decision clearly relates to its restatement of attribution principles.[10] The Supreme Court held that international protection under the fifth Convention ground extends not only to those who are viewed as a threat by the government, but also to those who are perceived as a threat by groups which may be wholly unrelated to the government.[11] As indicated earlier, the opinion need not have been expressly articulated, but may have been implicit in the claimant's actions. In the latter instance, a political opinion is said to have been "imputed" to the claimant.[12] Finally, the views actually ascribed to the victim by the persecutor need not conform to the claimant's true beliefs. In this respect, the Court ruled:

> The examination of the circumstances should be approached from the perspective of the persecutor since it is the perspective which is determinative of the persecution. The political opinion that lies at the root of the persecution, therefore, need not necessarily be correctly attributed to the claimant. *Similar considerations would seem to apply to the other bases of persecution.*[13]

The above references in *Ward* clearly evidence that Canadian tribunals will not demand that the exact motivation of the persecutor be supplied but that objective criteria will be examined to determine whether serious harm is feared based on a protected ground.[14] Indeed, an essentially "liberal" methodology was the one which was followed in the Supreme Court's analysis

---

9 Canada (Attorney General) v. Ward, [1993] 2 S.C.R. 689.

10 [1993] 2 S.C.R. 689, 746-47.

11 *Id.* at 746.

12 *Id.* at 746-47.

13 *Id.* at 747. [Emphasis supplied].

14 In the area of civil war, for instance, contemporary Canadian doctrine establishes that a severe violation of international humanitarian law on the part of a belligerent may give rise to an inference that the resulting injury has been "on account of" a Convention ground. *See generally Civil War Guidelines, supra* note 214.

determining that Ward would be persecuted on the political opinion ground.[15]

But, the Court ruled, Ward also had an actual political opinion for which he would be punished by INLA, his act of conscience in releasing the hostages. Both in INLA's perception and in the eyes of the claimant, this act of conscience had significant political implications. Ward clearly believed that the act of killing innocent persons to achieve political change was unacceptable;[16] the act of releasing the hostages was not consistent with any motive other than one which was politically based. The Court ruled:

> This act [refusing to kill the hostages as ordered by INLA] made Ward a political traitor in the eyes of a militant para-military organization, such as INLA, which supports the use of terrorist tactics to achieve its ends. The act was not merely an isolated incident devoid of greater implications. Whether viewed from Ward's or the INLA's perspective, the act is politically significant. The persecution Ward fears stems from his political opinion as manifested by this act.
>
> * * *
>
> In Ward's case, ... his act was inconsistent with any other possible motive. He was already a member of the INLA; any fear of retaliation could have been dispelled simply by executing the order. The rationale underlying his decision was unequivocal, both in his eyes and in those of INLA.[17]

In the Court's final determination, however, attribution principles are blended with Ward's actual political opinion in releasing the hostages. In this respect, Ward's action in refusing to execute hostages (as ordered by INLA) was characterized as a political opinion, "both in [applicant's] eyes and in those of INLA". The Court thus found that the refugee claimant in *Ward* had demonstrated political opinion as the basis for his claim both because a political animus would be attributed to him by INLA, and because of claimant's intrinsic beliefs.[18]

A potential limitation on the court's treatment of the fifth refugee ground must be noted. Under received doctrine, any overt act which causes the refugee claimant to be viewed as politically hostile will be sufficient to satisfy the requirements of attributed political opinion. Nonetheless, the

---

15 [1993] 2 S.C.R. 689, 747-49. The Court took great pains to distinguish the *Elias-Zacarias* decision, noting that in that case the evidence pointed to the conclusion that the asylum seeker had not been motivated by considerations of conscience to decline induction by the guerillas, but by fear that his family may have been molested by his being enlisted. *Id.*

16 *Id.* at 748.

17 *Id.* at 749.

18 *Id.*

Court in *Ward* strongly implied that something more than mere dissent would be required in the applicant's case, namely, a form of "conscientious objection" to INLA's *modus operandi.* Although the Court found that Ward had satisfied this criterion by his release of the hostages, the heightening of attributed political opinion requirements may be troubling in future cases. Specifically, the Court ruled:

> Not just any dissent to any organization will unlock the gates of Canadian asylum; the disagreement must be rooted in political conviction. This approach to Ward's case would preclude a former Mafia member, for example, from invoking it as a precedent.[19]

The last sentence, however, reveals that this heightening of the standard pertains to the fact that INLA had been characterized as a terrorist organization, and Ward had voluntarily been a member. A disagreement over strategy, perhaps, would not have been sufficient in the circumstances. Ward is virtually required to show some act of conscience by which he distinguished himself from INLA's terrorist methods in order to qualify under the refugee definition. It would probably be wrong, however, to give greater scope to the Supreme Court's ruling in this respect (i.e. by requiring an act of conscience in all instances of imputed political opinion where the claim is based on some form of dissent from an insurgent organization).

Imputed political opinion (like its counterpart, the concept of political neutrality) has played a major role in the development of U.S. asylum law relating to the acts of putative persecution arising out of recruitment by the insurgents. This development was thrown into substantial disarray by the Supreme Court's decision in *INS* v. *Elias-Zacarias.*[20] In *Elias-Zacarias*, the Supreme Court ruled that a young Guatemalan who had fled rather than be co-opted by the insurgents in his country had failed to make out a claim of persecution in the statutory sense. The asylum applicant was eighteen years old when he was visited by guerillas seeking to recruit him. The claimant feared that the government would retaliate against him and his family if he joined the insurgents and he subsequently fled. The Court of Appeals had ruled that the attempt to recruit constituted persecution in that:

> [T]he person resisting forced recruitment is expressing a political opinion hostile to the persecutor and because the persecutor's motives in carrying out the kidnapping are political.[21]

---

19 *Id.* at 750.

20 502 U.S. 478 (1992).

21 Elias-Zacarias v. INS, 921 F.2d 844, 850 (9th Cir. 1990).

Prior the *Elias-Zacarias*, there had been a serious division between the Ninth Circuit and the Board regarding the implications for refugee analysis of forced induction of the claimant by the insurgent elements. The Board continually held that neither forced recruitment nor punishment following desertion would support an asylum claim since the rebels were simply acting out of a need to maintain and equip a fighting force.[22] The Ninth Circuit, however, ruled that such individuals would be punished either because of their "neutrality"[23] or because an anti-guerilla animus would be attributed to them.[24] These cases have undoubtedly been impacted by *Elias-Zacarias*, and it is difficult to assess their vitality in the post-*Elias-Zacarias* period.[25]

The Court in *Elias-Zacarias*, reversing the Ninth Circuit, ruled that resistance to forced recruitment does not necessarily manifest a political opinion of neutrality; refusal in such instances might be based on non-political motives, a fear of danger, for instance.[26] The Court stressed that the political opinion of the applicant remains the centerpiece of the analysis, rather than the persecutor's objectives:

> [T]he guerillas seek to fill their ranks in order to carry on their war against their government and to pursue their political goals. ... But that does not render the forced recruitment 'political opinion'. In construing statutes, 'we must, of course, start with the assumption that the legislative purpose is expressed by the ordinary meaning of the words used' ... The ordinary meaning of 'persecution on account of ... political opinion' in § 101(a)(42) is persecution on account of the *victim*'s political opinion, not the persecutor's. If a Nazi regime persecutes Jews, it is not, within the ordinary meaning of the language engaging in persecution on account of political opinion; and if a fundamentalist Moslem regime persecutes democrats, it is not engaging in persecution on account of religion. Thus the mere existence of the guerillas' forced recruitment is inadequate to establish (and, indeed, goes far to refute) the proposition that Elias-Zacarias fears persecution *on account of* political opinion, as § 101(a)(42) requires.[27]

---

22 *See, e.g.*, Matter of Maldonado-Cruz, 19 I&N Dec. 509 (BIA 1988), *rev'd,* Maldonado-Cruz v. INS, 883 F.2d 788 (9th Cir. 1990).

23 Bolanos-Hernandez v. INS, 767 F.2d 1277 (9th Cir. 1984).

24 Arteaga v. INS, 836 F.2d 1227 (9th Cir. 1988).

25 The issues raised by recruitment by the insurgents must be kept separate and distinct from those at play in cases involving putatively lawful recruitment by the government. Recruitment by the insurgents essentially involves an unlawful act of kidnapping while recruitment by the government purports to rest on a legitimate exercise of sovereign authority by the State. For a discussion of the distinction, *see* Alonzo v. INS, 915 F.2d 546 (9th Cir. 1990).

26 Elias-Zacarias v. INS, 502 U.S. 478, 482 (1992).

27 *Id.*

On a helpful note, the Court remarked, in language which would later be taken up to liberalize the "nexus" requirement of the refugee definition, that the claimant was not obligated to supply the exact motivation of his or her persecutor, only to submit some evidence, "direct or circumstantial" that persecution was feared on account of a refugee ground.[28]

*Elias-Zacarias* thus draws upon two distinct methods of analysis which are not necessarily compatible. The accentuation of an internal characteristic or belief in the applicant seems to overshadow (though not to preclude) an analysis based on the persecutor's motive as determined by an examination of objective circumstances. On the other hand, the Court treated the nexus requirement as dependent upon an evidentiary showing. This aspect of the decision definitely points toward a "liberal" method of analysis in which the facts are looked to as the basis for decision, the adjudicator's power to infer the existence of a protected ground being comparatively unrestricted. What remains unclear (so far as civil war cases are concerned) is the precise role of the goals of the combatants in assessing whether an opinion can be "imputed" to a claimant who resists guerilla demands.

Under *Elias-Zacarias*, the fact that those goals may be political does not establish, automatically, such attribution as a matter of law. But in the presence of other, probative factors, the existence of such political goals on the part of the persecutor may serve as important evidence that a claimant who openly resists insurgent demands will be viewed as politically hostile and thus that the harm which the asylum seeker fears is linked to a protected ground.

## § IV.3. Persecution Based on Opinions, Associations, or Advocacy of the Applicant: Intrinsic Beliefs Versus the Perception of the Persecutor Approach

United States asylum law does not contain any explicit guidance on the question of what constitutes a political opinion where the claim of persecution is based on an affirmative body of beliefs in the applicant.[29] The

---

[28] *Id.* The Supreme Court's decision was followed by the Board in *Matter of R-O-*, 20 I&N Dec. 455 (BIA 1992).

[29] Such cases must be distinguished from decisions dealing with imputed or attributed political opinion as established during periods of upheaval, discussed in § IV.4, *infra*. The view of the Board (and of the federal courts) appears to be that the "political" dimension of the claimant's views must be adjudicated on a case by case basis. *See generally Basic Law Manual, supra* § I.1, note 26, at 48 and cases cited therein.

Supreme Court in *Elias-Zacarias* v. *INS*[30] has ruled, somewhat ambiguously, that the opinion involved in asylum cases is that of the applicant, not of his pursuer. This has led United States tribunals to emphasize "internal" features of the asylum claimant in determining whether the refugee definition has been satisfied. This *de facto* retreat from the notion of attributed characteristics or beliefs has produced highly restrictive interpretations of the refugee standard. In Canada, the Supreme Court's decision in *Ward*[31] also refers to "intrinsic" elements of the claimant's persona,[32] but, unlike *Elias-Zacarias*, the *Ward* case expressly invites an analysis which examines the situation from the viewpoint of the persecutor and accepts that political values can be ascribed to the applicant by her pursuers.[33]

An organizing principle of Canadian refugee jurisprudence (which, in terms of emphasis, often distinguishes it from U.S. asylum law) is the proclivity of Canadian adjudicators to accept the internationally recognized standard of refugee analysis that whether an opinion is political is a determination which is made by the refugee claimant's country (and its institutions) and not by the adjudicator.[34] This has resulted in Canadian decision-makers perceiving political implications in the applicant's involvement, actions or speech whereas U.S. tribunals, searching for a nexus to "intrinsic" characteristics or beliefs, often ignore the historical context in which the claim is being developed.

Interpretation of "political opinion" persecution by United States adjudicators has historically suffered from an exceptionally restrictive construction. Limiting interpretations have resulted from, among other things, an austere view of the nexus requirement[35] as well as from a highly limited view of the sort of opinions which could be characterized as political.[36] Recently, how-

---

30 502 U.S. 478 (1992).

31 [1993] 2 S.C.R. 689.

32 *Id.* at 747.

33 The issues raised by *Ward* and *Elias-Zacarias* which relate to establishing a refugee claim during periods of upheaval are expressly covered in § IV.4(a), *infra*.

34 For the seminal case on this point, *see* Inzunza v. M.E.I. (1979), 103 DLR (3d) 105 (F.C.A.).

35 *See, e.g.*, Matter of Acosta, 19 I&N Dec. 211 (BIA 1985) which seems to demand a direct causative nexus between the "characteristic or belief" in the applicant and the serious harm feared or sustained.

36 *Cf.* Matter of McMullen, 19 I&N Dec. 90 (BIA 1989), *aff'd,* McMullen v. INS, 788 F.2d 591 (9th Cir. 1986). In that case, an Irish national who had been a former member of the Provisional Irish Republican Army (PIRA) later cooperated with British and American authorities in an investigation of PIRA. The Board determined that the applicant would not be punished because of his political opinion:

ever, evolution of United States jurisprudence has veered in a discernibly liberal direction.

In *Carranza-Hernandez* v. *INS*,[37] the asylum seeker's claim was based on a warrant for his arrest arising out of his activities in a Honduran labor union. The claimant had been advised that the arrest warrant resulted from his "bad record", and the Board reasoned that applicant had not shown that there was a basis for the warrant other than a lawful criminal investigation. The Second Circuit reversed, however, concluding that the claimant's labor union activities gave rise to persecution on the political opinion ground.[38]

In *Osorio* v. *INS*,[39] the Second Circuit Court developed this premise further, ruling that a conflict between a union leader and the Guatemalan government taking place in the context of an economic dispute constituted a basis for political opinion persecution.[40] Holding that the asylum seeker was not under an obligation to establish the precise motive of his persecutor, the court found that the Guatemalan government clearly viewed the asylum seeker's union activity as political in nature:

> Any attempt to unravel economic from political motives is untenable in this case. No substantial evidence supports the view that Osorio's dispute with the Guatemalan government officials was solely economic. Rather, substantial evidence, as recounted in the background evidence of this opinion, compels the view that Guatemalan authorities persecuted Osorio because he and his union posed a political threat to their authority via their organized opposition activities. Although conflicts between Osorio and his government were in the context of economic disputes, the death threats to him and others were independent of these disputes. Osorio and his colleagues presented grievances to the government but not solely in the form of strikes.[41]

Beyond this, however, and most importantly, the reviewing tribunal found that it was impossible, given the social context in which the claim arose, to segregate political from economic issues:

---

> The record clearly shows that the PIRA uses violence and threats of violence internally to maintain discipline and order within the rank and file of its membership. As such, the PIRA's use of violence against its members is essentially apolitical, representing an indifference to the personal views and opinions of its members who are subject to sanctions. We conclude that this internal use of violence by PIRA does not constitute persecution within the meaning of the Act.

*Id.* at 598.

37 12 F.3d 4 (2d Cir. 1993).

38 *Id.* at 8.

39 18 F.3d 1017 (2d Cir. 1994).

40 *Id.* at 1028-1031.

41 *Id.* at 1029.

> Union leaders such as Osorio also challenge the political status quo in Guatemala by example because they are democratically elected to represent the interests of their constituents. These interests ordinarily include better terms and conditions of employment, or higher wages. These interests also include the attainment of civil liberties, particularly where the employer is the government.[42]

The *Osorio* decision, however, illustrates a fundamental doctrine in refugee law, although this doctrine was not explicitly referred to by the Second Circuit in rendering its opinion. Individuals who are punished for asserting a human right which is recognized under the Universal Declaration of Human Rights will be deemed to be subject to political opinion persecution for purposes of the refugee definition.[43] In this connection, there is now little doubt but that the right to form trade unions[44] together with the right to a living wage and decent working conditions[45] (initially set forth in the Universal Declaration) are now protected by the International Covenant on Economic, Social and Cultural Rights.[46] Those who advance human rights recognized under international law, whether those rights are Convention-based or customary, should be deemed to have a protected political opinion under the refugee definition.[47] A view which seeks to exclude social rights from consideration in determining the scope of refugee protection is contrary to the obvious intention of the drafters of the 1951 Convention that refugee

---

[42] *Id.* at 1038-1030.

[43] 1 Grahl-Madsen, *supra* § I.1, note 7, at 217.

[44] UDHR, *supra* § I.1, note 12, Art. 23-4:

> Everyone has the right to form and join trade unions for the protection of his interests.

[45] ICESCR, *supra* § I.1, note 15, Art. 25-1:

> Everyone has the right to a standard of living adequate for the health and well-being of himself and his family, including food, clothing, housing, and medical care and necessary social services, and the right to security in the event of unemployment, sickness, disability, widowhood, old age or other lack of livelihood in circumstances beyond his control.

[46] *Id.*, Arts. 7 and 8.

[47] On the substantive rights set out in UDHR as *jus cogens, see* Parker and Neylon, *supra* § I.1, note 16, at 442:

> The Universal Declaration as a whole is itself customary international law, and is rapidly establishing itself as *jus cogens.*

As indicated earlier, for purposes of determining whether assertion of a social right constitutes "political opinion", it is not relevant that the State may be without adequate resources to satisfy the right being asserted. Availability of resources becomes relevant only with respect to the question of whether the State's failure to fulfill rights protected under ICESCR is in fact "persecution". Hathaway, *supra* § I.1, note 7, at 111.

status should be determined in the context of international human rights which, under UDHR, include broad social rights as a matrix of public policy.[48]

*Sotelo-Aquije* v. *Slattery*[49] involved another case in which the Board attempted to distinguish between inherently political activities on the one hand, and social advocacy on the other. The applicant, a native and citizen of Peru, had been a member of CUAVES, a municipal organization existing in the City of Villa San Salvador outside the capital city of Lima. CUAVES was dedicated to the political and economic development of Villa San Salvador and the city had received national and international recognition for progress it had made, largely as the result of CUAVES' efforts. Beginning in 1990, Sotelo began receiving threats from the Shinning Path (*Sendero Luminoso*), urging him to resign from CUAVES in that he (Sotelo) was an obstacle to the Shining Path's goals. The threats became more dramatic over time; in 1992, the mayor of Villa El Salvador (with whom applicant had worked) was killed by the Shining Path; a final threat was issued in March of 1992 which prompted Sotelo to leave Peru with his family. By this time, about 30 CUAVES members had been killed by the Shining Path.[50]

The Board had reasoned that, although applicant's membership in CUAVES, and his open opposition to the Shining Path, were political acts, the claimant did not fear persecution for this reason (a protected ground), but rather because he was a community leader (not a protected ground). The Second Circuit found the Board's logic not sustainable: the reviewing court determined that the Board's own findings compelled a conclusion that Sotelo feared persecution on account of the fifth Convention ground:

> It [the Board] concluded that "[t]he record establishes that the Shining Path victim[s] are generally targeted based on their activities or vocalism that opposed the organization or its goals." […] In its own words, based on testimony and information in the record, the BIA acknowledged that Sotelo spoke out against the Shining Path and that only those CUAVES members who had actively opposed the guerilla group became the targets of violence. These findings and the record before us compel the conclusion that Sotelo had a well-founded fear of persecution on account of his acts and expressions of political opposition to the Shining Path.[51]

Even where the applicant is not directly involved in the area of "social rights" advocacy, U.S. law will characterize a seemingly neutral posture on

---

48 *See, e.g.*, UDHR, *supra* § I.1, note 12, Art. 23-4.

49 17 F.3d 33 (2d Cir. 1994).

50 *Id.* at 35-36.

51 *Id.* at 37.

the part of the claimant as political opinion if it entails significant "public" consequences, or at least relates to the manner in which the public interest is safeguarded by the authorities. In *Borca* v. *INS*,[52] for example, the Seventh Circuit overturned a Board finding to the effect that a young Romanian woman who had been interrogated, terminated from her employment as a radiologist, and barred from future government employment did not have a well-founded fear of persecution arising out of her public denunciation of a State "cover-up". The applicant had found evidence that the transitional government in Romania which succeeded the Ceausescu regime in power had made efforts to keep from public view evidence of firearm injuries and deaths occurring during Ceausescu's overthrow. Her making this information public both in speeches and in newspaper articles was considered by the reviewing court to constitute political opinion which would support a claim of asylum.

Similarly, in *Grava* v. *INS*,[53] the Ninth Circuit developed considerably the premise that individuals who denounce corrupt governmental practices have a fear of political opinion persecution if they are threatened with serious harm as a result. In *Grava*, the asylum seeker had been a policeman and customs official in the Philippines. While on assignment to the Port of Macetan in 1977, he uncovered a smuggling scheme involving the collector of customs who was also Grava's supervisor. As a result, administrative charges were brought against the applicant and he was transferred. After being reassigned in 1987 again to the Port of Macetan, applicant sought to expose another smuggling scheme on the part of another collector of customs with strong legislative and administrative ties. As before, applicant was reassigned. Finally, in 1990, applicant brought to light a third smuggling conspiracy against his supervisor and testified in the ensuing investigation against the supervisor's orders. As a result, he was transferred in apparent retaliation, and numerous threats were made against the asylum seeker and members of his family.

The Board of Immigration Appeals had dismissed the claim, holding that Grava was involved in a strictly "personal" dispute with his supervisors. In an opinion which will undoubtedly influence the outcome of future cases, the Ninth Circuit reversed this holding. The court opined that a "refusal to accede to governmental corruption can constitute political opinion" and that "official retaliation against those who expose and prosecute governmental corruption may, in appropriate circumstances, amount to persecution on account of political opinion". Further refining its holding, the *Grava* court

---

52 77 F.3d 210 (7th Cir. 1996).

53 205 F.3d 1177 (9th Cir. 2000). The case is reprinted in 12 Int'l J. Refugee L. 276 (2000).

viewed "whistle-blowing" activity as political where the denounced corruption was intertwined with governmental activity.

The decision is illuminating for a number of reasons. Primarily, it gives clear application to the classic definition of political opinion persecution put forward by Guy Goodwin-Gill ("any opinion on any matter in which the machinery of the State, government or policy may be engaged"). Opinions such as the one Grava advanced clearly are "political" either where the State is hopelessly involved in the corrupt activity (as was the case in *Grava*) or where the State is powerless to curb systematic or widespread official malfeasance. In either case, the asylum seeker has taken up a principled position relevant to the supremacy of neutral and operative law *vis-à-vis* lawless social elements which has caused him/her to become exposed to serious harm. A position of conscience with respect to the integrity of the State's institutions must be characterized as political where that integrity has been cast in doubt.[54]

Atle Grahl-Madsen accentuates the perspective of the victim's oppressor in refugee analysis, maintaining that any real or implied opinion of the applicant which leads to violations of the rights contained in the Universal Declaration of Human Rights will support a claim on the fifth Convention ground. Implicit in Grahl-Madsen's analysis, however, is the broader view that all of the grounds of refugee protection are compellingly related to the viewpoint of the persecutor and that violations of human rights carried out on the basis of a policy of discrimination will satisfy the litmus test for refugee status:

> Any real, alleged or implied opinion which leads to persecution in violation of the Universal Declaration of Human Rights, may qualify as a 'political opinion' in the sense of the Refugee Convention. Thus, if a person is threatened with persecution because he prefers a blue flag to a green flag or because he prefers a construction of a road on the right bank of a river and not on the left bank, or because he wants to vote for candidate A and not for candidate B in a municipal general election, or because he holds any other opinion which is not in conformity with that of the authorities, he may claim a

---

[54] *See also* Reyes-Guerrero v. INS, 192 F.3d 1241 (9th Cir. 1999). In *Guerrero*, the Ninth Circuit determined that a Colombian prosecutor and his wife should be granted asylum and withholding of removal. The asylum seekers had demonstrated that they were at risk by virtue of the husband's having prosecuted 18 defendants who had diverted funds from the public treasury to the Liberal Party. An immigration judge had granted asylum, but the Board reversed, holding that the criminal defendants were motivated solely by a desire to "thwart the criminal process" and not by the claimant's political opinion. According to the appeals court's findings, the Board's reasoning ignored accompanying motives by the defendants who viewed the husband as a member of their political rival, the Conservative Party. The case is digested in 76 Interpreter Releases 47 (January 10, 2000).

> fear of persecution 'for reasons of' political opinion' because the very fact that he is threatened with persecution implies that the persons in power consider his opinion 'political' in the existing circumstances. This is but another facet of what we have pointed out another connection, namely, that the behavior of the persecutor determines what persons shall be considered refugees.[55]

Canadian law clearly orients the question of whether serious harm can be linked to a refugee ground to an examination of the perception of the persecutor. *Interpretation of the Convention Refugee Definition in the Case Law* sets forth the governing test of political opinion persecution in Canada:

> [I]t is the perception of the persecutor which is relevant. The question to be answered is: does the agent of persecution consider the claimant's conduct to be political or does it attribute political activities to him or her?[56]

Canadian refugee jurisprudence thus explicitly adopts attribution principles as the cornerstone of its analysis. The question of "Who is a refugee?" must be seen, under Canadian law, as one which is context dependent and as requiring an inferential analysis in which the persecutor's perceptions are gleaned from a wide spectrum of operative fact. The criteria for examining those perceptions will clearly be objective, and the critical inquiry will be whether systemic violations of human rights have been committed against other similarly situated individuals or groups.

For instance, Canadian law clarifies that neither title nor official status within a political organization is necessary to establish persecution on the fifth Convention ground so long as the persecutor perceives the group and its activities (or the individual and his or her activities) as political in nature, thus making the fear of serious harm objectively reasonable.[57] Under the broad interpretation offered by *Ward,* a claimant is not required to be a member of a political party to be recognized under the political opinion ground.[58] Thus, individuals who are not high-profile members of an opposition party can qualify for refugee status even in the absence of being

---

55 1 Grahl-Madsen, *supra* § I.1, note 7, at 250.

56 Interpretation of the Convention Refugee Definition in the Case Law, *supra* § II.3, note 63, § 4.6, *citing* Inzunza v. M.E.I. (1979), D.L.R. (3d.) 105, 109 (F.C.A.).

57 *See, e.g.,* Hilo v. M.E.I. (1991), 15 Imm. L.R. (2d) 199, 130 N.R. 236 (F.C.A.), granting refugee status to a Syrian where the claimant's activity in joining a charitable organization was thought politically suspect by the authorities; Aranguiz v. M.E.I. (1991), 15 Imm. L. R. (2d) 313, 139 N.R. 79 (F.C.A.), recognizing as a refugee a Chilean claimant whose refusal to cooperate with a State organization gave rise to the authorities' conclusion that he was politically undesirable. *See also* Astudillo v. M.E.I. (1979), 31 N.R. 121 (F.C.A.) where another Chilean was granted refugee status when his membership in a sports club was seen as a mark of political opposition.

58 Armson v. M.E.I. (1989), 9 Imm. L.R. (2d) 150 (F.C.A.).

party leaders or organizers.[59] Accordingly, the Federal Court Trial-Division has overturned a determination by the Immigration and Refugee Board (CRDD) that a Haitian claimant who regularly attended political rallies and helped shelter a political leader in her home was not a refugee because she had no visible political profile.[60] The cases which follow illustrate the ways in which Canadian tribunals have adopted an inferential analysis to identify a political opinion in the claimant based on an analysis of objective facts which reveal the will and imagination of the persecutor.

In *Astudillo* v. *M.E.I.*,[61] the Court of Appeal overturned a determination by the (prior) Immigration Appeal Board that a Chilean claimant was not politically involved, a finding largely based on the claimant's self-assessment. Whereas claimant had testified as to a lack of political involvement, the court ruled, there was abundant evidence in the record to suggest that the Chilean authorities believed applicant to be politically engaged. While in detention, applicant had been accused of advocating socialism by virtue of his presidency of a sports club at his school. The sports club in fact had no political purposes and existed solely for the athletic recreation of its members. Nonetheless, a guard informed applicant during his detention that he was being detained because of his presidency of a "politically active group". In reversing the Board, the appeals court reechoed the axiom that what constitutes political conduct must be determined from the viewpoint of the persecutor.

Similarly, in *Oyarzo* v. *M.E.I.*,[62] Chilean authorities detained the claimant for several weeks because they maintained he was involved in a political

---

59 Butucariu v. M.E.I. (F.C.A., no. A-534-91), February 5, 1992.

60 Aristil v. M.E.I. (F.C.A., no. A-902-90), September 28, 1992. U.S. case law is in agreement that "prominence" within an organization (while it may help to satisfy the well-founded fear component of the refugee definition) is not essential to establishing inclusion within the political opinion category. A case illustrating this feature of U.S. asylum doctrine is *Cordero-Trijo* v. *INS,* 40 F.3d 482 (1st Cir. 1994). There, a Guatemalan doctor had received death threats as the result of his work with *Laicos Comprometidos*, an essentially religious organization committed to relieving the plight of the rural poor through charitable work. The First Circuit rejected the reasoning of the BIA that the applicant had not demonstrated individualized persecution because of the small number of missions he had participated in and because he held no office. The record reflected that both the claimant's brother and priests with whom he had worked had been killed in the course of their missionary work. The appeals court determined that a well-founded fear of persecution had been made out based upon what had transpired to similarly situated persons, namely, "non-prominent lay or volunteer workers … who carried out the missions for social change to which they or their organizations are committed." *Id.* at 490.

61 (1979), 31 N.R. 121 (F.C.A.).

62 [1982] 2 F.C. 779 (C.A.).

organization called "MAPU". Applicant's brother had also been detained for similar reasons. The appeals court again ruled that it is reversible error for the trier of fact to substitute its own judgment for that of the authorities of the persecuting State with respect to the seriousness of the claimant's political involvement.

*Hilo* v. *M.E.I.*,[63] involved a Shiite Muslim who had joined a mosque which had for its purpose the raising of money to help the poor in Lebanon. Syrian secret police had interrupted the meeting and advised the members to discontinue their activities. Claimant, however, and the other members believed they had a religious obligation as Muslims to help the poor, and they continued their efforts. Applicant's brother had been beaten when he attempted to explain the group's activities to the authorities. The brother was arrested and had not reappeared since; the remainder of the members escaped.

The Court of Appeal set down the now accepted interpretive rule that, when evaluating whether conduct is to be considered "political", it is the viewpoint of the authorities belonging to claimant's country which is dispositive of the characterization. Under the facts of the instant case, it was clear that the Syrian authorities viewed the charitable group as politically hostile to the Syrian government. It was irrelevant, in the Court of Appeal's opinion, that the organization was loosely knit, had no official status or title. Nor was it germane (i) that the claimant was a boy of fourteen at the time these events transpired; (ii) that he had not been prominent within the group; or (iii) that he had engaged in no other activities. The governing criterion, according to the tribunal, was the perception of the Syrian authorities that the group and its members had become a political threat:

> [O]ne is impelled to the inescapable conclusion that the members of the appellant's charitable group were persecuted because the Syrian security forces had concluded that the group was politically motivated against the Government and thus politically undesirable. I agree with counsel for the appellant that the Board's comments that the group is 'loosely knit', that it has 'no official title, office or status' is irrelevant. Likewise, the comment that the appellant was a boy of 14 at the time, had no specific role or responsibility within the group, and engaged in no other form of behavior or expression giving rise to a perception of his political opinion, is also irrelevant. The Syrian authorities sought to persecute the appellant because of his perceived political opinion.[64]

---

[63] (1991), 15 Imm. L.R. (2d) 199, 130 N.R. 236 (F.C.A.).

[64] *Id.*

The "seriousness" of the claimant's involvement was also at stake in *Chen* v. *M.E.I.*[65] The claimant had been a male vocalist for a Chinese musical group which had given a performance to raise funds for the Tiennamen Square demonstrations. After flying back to Guangzhou, claimant and two other members were arrested. He was interrogated for 24 hours during which time his mother suffered a heart attack; claimant agreed to sign a confession solely so that he would be permitted to see her. After visiting with his mother, claimant went into hiding. The Immigration and Refugee Board placed great reliance on the fact that claimant had been released from prison and allowed to retain his exit permission. The Court of Appeals found that this approach ignored the salient facts of the claim: applicant was a popular artist who had signed a confession to participating in counter-revolutionary activities.

Whether a close relationship or friendship (as opposed to membership in an association) can serve as the basis for political opinion persecution was explored in *Chen* v. *S.S.C.*[66] In *Chen*, the claimant's family in Shanghai had been visited by the police who advised them that the claimant had committed a crime and had fled in the company of a criminal. The Immigration and Refugee Board (C.R.D.D.) had concluded that the real reason for the Chinese State's interest in the claimant related to his close relationship with a Chinese activist, and that he therefore stood in no better position than would a relative of a prominent politician. Again the Federal Court-Trial Division ruled that the Board was substituting its own judgment for that of the authorities with respect to how claimant's relationship with a known activist would be viewed.

In *Guerassimova* v. *M.E.I.*,[67] the claimant was neither a political leader nor a member in any political organization. She had merely participated in demonstrations. Claimant had been interrogated by the police in a car on four separate occasions and in one instance she was advised that her participation in demonstrations was an act of disloyalty to the country which made her a traitor; and that, if she did not cease her activities, "serious consequences" would follow. Ruling that claimant's political involvement must be assessed from the perspective of the officials of the country from which refugee status is claimed, the Court of Appeal overturned the Immigration and Refugee Board's conclusion that persecution on a protected ground was not involved.

---

65 (F.C.A., no. A-30-91), October 4, 1993.

66 (F.C.T.D., no. IMM-2930-93), December 7, 1993.

67 (1994), 167 N.R. 78 (F.C.A.).

Under Canadian doctrine, political opinion can be manifested by a seemingly neutral act. Accordingly, in *Chen* v. *M.E.I.*,[68] the claimant had experienced a series of difficulties in China, beginning with the "Great Leap Forward" in the late 1950's, carrying over to the "Cultural Revolution" of 1966-76, and extending until claimant was accused of supporting the "pro-democracy" movement which came to fruition in the spring of 1989. Applicant had placed on public display drawings which were intended subtly to satirize the government of China. The Immigration and Refugee Board was unable to glean the political messages which lay hidden in the drawings. The Federal Court-Trial Division reversed, again reminding the Board that the key question was how the drawings would be viewed by officials of the Chinese State, not how the Board believed the drawings should be interpreted.

The degree to which an otherwise neutral act can have "political" implications was further explored in *Bohorquez* v. *M.C.I.*[69] The refugee claimant had established a cooperative in Colombia for the purposes of selling lottery tickets. The cooperative had employed members of M-19, a left-wing political movement dedicated to radical political and social change in Colombia. The claimant's goals were clearly social, to provide better jobs with improved working conditions and social benefits. The cooperative came into competitive conflict with a government-sponsored lottery which evidently wished to act as a monopoly. The ensuing conflict resulted in claimant's receiving numerous death threats. The Federal Court-Trial Division overturned the Board decision finding no well-founded fear, ruling that the cooperative's acting for political and social reform challenged vested interests in Colombia so that a finding of persecution on the fifth Convention ground was proper.

Interesting questions are raised when the claimant maintains a position which is directed toward the integrity of law enforcement. In *Femina* v. *M.C.I.*,[70] claimants maintained that they had "opposed the existence of corrupt police and advocated their removal and prosecution", seeking to establish eligibility for refugee status under the political opinion category. The Federal Court-Trial Division, however, rejected the claim holding that, although the machinery of the State was engaged in providing police services, it was not engaged in the criminal conduct of corrupt police

---

68 (1993), 22 Imm. L.R. (2d) 160 (F.C.T.D.).

69 (F.C.T.D., no. IMM-7078-93), October 6, 1984.

70 (F.C.T.D., no. IMM-3852-94), October 30, 1995.

officers.[71] The case clearly ignores the principle that, whereas the State may not be responsible for supplying corrupt police, it certainly is involved in disciplining them, the very outcome the claimant was advocating and which was advanced as the predicate for persecution.

A more recent case suggests that, under appropriate facts, the result may well be different. In *Berrueta* v. *M.C.I.*,[72] the court overturned the denial of a claim by the CRDD where the claimant had denounced drug kingpins to the authorities in an environment where corruption was widespread. Under these conditions, the court ruled, "[t]o decry corruption … is to strike at the core of governmental authority". Similarly, in *Diamanama* v. *M.C.I.*,[73] the claimant's refusal to produce dresses for a corrupt official served as the basis for a grant of refugee status on the ground that the claimant's act was perceived as a threat to governmental authority. A similar result was reached in *Bohorquez* v. *M.C.I.*[74] (discussed above). In that case, a claimant's opposition to the State lottery resulted in his being threatened by corrupt officials: the court ruled that the claimant had expressed views which were opposed to vested political interests. Moreover, in *Vassiliev* v. *M.C.I.*,[75] the claimant was a Russian national who was employed by a State-operated business. He based his claim of future persecution on the fact that he had refused to cooperate with demands by his superiors that he give bribes and launder money. The Federal Court Trial Division upheld the claim, ruling that corruption was so widespread that refusing to comply with it was virtually identical to voicing opposition to vested authority.

---

[71] Interpretation of the Convention Refugee Definition in the Case Law, *supra* § II.3, note 63, § 4.6, *citing* Femenia v. M.C.I., (F.C.T.D., no. IMM-3852-94), October 30, 1995.

[72] (F.C.T.D., no. IMM-2303-95), March 21, 1996, at 2.

[73] (F.C.T.D., no. IMM-1808-95), January 30, 1996.

[74] (F.C.T.D., no. IMM-7078-93), October 6, 1994.

[75] (F.C.T.D., no. IMM-3443-96), July 4, 1997. *See also* Choo v. S.S.C.(F.C.T.D., no. IMM-1865-93), February 21, 1994. The male claimant in *Choo* had been a known activist in the 1989 pro-democracy demonstrations. In 1991, he was confronted with extortion demands by officials when he attempted to obtain a business license. He subsequently submitted a petition in which he asked that corruption within the police be investigated. Claimant was taken into custody and released on condition that he supply the names of persons who had signed the petition. In the meantime, the female claimant was experiencing discrimination at work. The male claimant feared that the petition would eventually expose him as a pro-democracy activist which would lead to his arrest. The IRB denied the claim since it viewed the case as one involving law enforcement only, claimant's difficulties with the police being resoluble through a civil complaint or ordinary prosecution. The appeals court overturned this decision, ruling that it ignored the nature of claimant's interrogation which focused on the political dimension of submitting the petition as well as claimant's role in the pro-democracy movement.

The jurisprudence in this area has now been clarified to some degree by a recent decision of the Federal Court of Appeal. In *Klinko* v. *MCI*,[76] the claimant was a native and citizen of the Ukraine. He, together with five other businessmen, filed a complaint regarding widespread corruption among officials with a regional authority. When that complaint produced retaliation, the claimant fled with his family to Canada and sought refugee status based on the fifth Convention ground. The Trial Division denied the claim reasoning that, for the political opinion ground to be viable, the government must have "sanctioned, condoned or supported" the corruption complained of.

This interpretation was rejected by the Court of Appeal which ruled that a "political opinion" need not relate specifically to "any matter in which the machinery of state, government and policy may be engaged". Looking to the Supreme Court's decision in *Ward*, the Court of Appeal found that the claimant's opinion in that case was the conscientious belief that innocent hostages should not be executed by a ruthless paramilitary unit, an essentially ethical position which *per se* had no bearing on the State, its policies or its manner of enforcement. Implicitly, under *Klinko*, an opinion conscientiously maintained by the claimant upholding minimum standards *of a public interest nature vis-à-vis* powerful lawless elements may be considered as "political" under the fifth Convention ground.[77]

The Court of Appeal's ruling in *Klinko* clearly brings Canadian law into line with the Ninth Circuit's treatment of the same issues in *Grava*.[78] Case law in both the U.S. and Canada makes clear that the State need not condone or tacitly accept the "official" corruption in question for refugee status to be recognized. It is enough if that corruption is widespread and the State is unable to restrain its influence and effects.

Although it is not as developed as it is in Canada, United States asylum law accepts the notion of attributed characteristics and beliefs, including imputed political opinion.[79] Treatment of ascribed beliefs is largely reserved

---

76 Klinko v. M.C.I. (F.C.A., no. A-321-98), February 22, 2000).

77 *See also* Interpretation of the Convention Refugee Definition in the Case Law, *supra* § II.3, note 63, § 4.7, *quoting with approval* Klinko v. M.C.I. (F.C.A., no. A-321-98), February 22, 2000) and noting that the Court of Appeal has answered affirmatively the following question certified by the Federal Court Trial Division:

> Whether the making of a public complaint about widespread corrupt conduct by customs and police officials to a regional governing authority ... [even where] the corrupt conduct is not officially sanctioned, condoned or supported by the state....

78 205 F.3d 1177 (9th Cir. 2000). The case is reprinted in 12 Int'l J. Refugee L. 276 (2000).

79 Basic Law Manual, *supra* § I.1, note 26, at 36, n. 9, *citing* INS v. Elias-Zacarias, 112 S. Ct. 812 (1992); Matter of S-P-, 21 I&N Dec. 486 (BIA 1996).

for § IV.4, *infra*, which deals with establishing a protected ground during conditions of upheaval. The doctrine of imputed political opinion in United States jurisprudence, however, clearly has its origins in the case law of the Ninth Circuit; a few seminal decisions are analyzed here to provide some indication of its scope.

In *Desir* v. *Ilchert*,[80] a Haitian asylum seeker had been made the subject of serious harm by the Ton Ton Macoutes as the result of his refusal to submit to extortion demands. The Ton Tons, however, treated the applicant's refusal as an act of political insubordination. The Ninth Circuit held:

> We must view Desir as having a political opinion because his persecutors, the Ton Ton Macoutes, both attributed political views to and treated him as a subversive.[81]

The facts and holding of *Desir* are compelling and reveal the full scope of attribution principles, at least where political opinion is concerned. Desir had been arrested, assaulted and threatened by the Macoutes on several occasions as the result of his failure to pay bribes as well as for his competition with Macoutes-approved fishing vessels.[82] The Appeals Court overturned the Board's determination that a political opinion had not been established, concluding instead that the social and political context in which serious harm had been imposed made it clear that applicant's actions caused him to be viewed as someone who was politically hostile. In determining that that applicant would be persecuted on account of a protected ground, the court adopted the following methodology:

> The record contains substantial evidence that the Haitian government under Duvalier operated as a "kleptocracy", or government by thievery from the highest to the lowest level. The Ton Ton Macoutes, an elaborate network of official and semi-official security forces, factions of which were fiercely loyal to the Duvalier family, formed the heart of the system. Because the Macoutes went unpaid except for a few of their highest ranking officers, they depended on their fellow Haitians for their livelihood, a circumstance encouraging wide-scale corruption, extortion and violence. Refusal to comply with extortionate demands resulted in the attribution of anti-government sympathies and also in swift reprisals, including beatings, imprisonment and death.
>
> * * *
>
> Desir's refusal to accede to extortion in a political system founded on extortion resulted in his classification and treatment as a subversive.[83]

---

80 840 F.2d 723 (9th Cir. 1988).

81 *Id.* at 729.

82 *Id.* at 724.

83 *Id.* at 724.

Importantly, the *Desir* court relied for its determination that the Macoutes would view Desir as a political opponent, not on the individualized facts of the case, but on a broad social and historical analysis of country conditions. The court concluded that Desir's refusal to comply with extortion demands in a political system founded on extortion would cause him to be perceived and punished as a subversive.[84]

Similarly, in *Hernandez-Ortiz* v. *INS*,[85] the Ninth Circuit was confronted with the plight of a family which had been made the subject of constant harassment and intimidation by the Salvadoran government. The record contained no specific evidence revealing the government's motivation in inflicting this suffering. The Ninth Circuit held that the unexplained use of excessive force by the government, coupled with the absence of any indication that criminal activity was being pursued, gave rise to a presumption that serious harm was being imposed because of a perceived political animus:

> A government does not under ordinary circumstances engage in political persecution of those whose views and philosophies differ, at least in the government's perception. It is irrelevant whether a victim's political view is neutrality, ... or disapproval of acts or opinions of the government. Moreover, it is irrelevant whether a victim actually possesses any of these opinions as long as the government believes that he does.... In most societies, a failure to take sides, or to articulate a political opinion does not ordinarily trigger retribution. However, when through legally recognizable inferences, an alien establishes a prima facie case that he is likely to be persecuted because of the government's beliefs about his views or loyalties, his actual political conduct, be it silence or affirmative advocacy, and his actual political views, be they neutrality or partisanship, are irrelevant; whatever the circumstances, the persecution is properly characterized as being "on account of ... political opinion."[86]

In this seminal ruling, the Ninth Circuit clearly demonstrates its proclivity to treat serious violations of respected human rights as giving rise to a presumption that the harm imposed has been on account of a protected ground, specifically political opinion.[87] The Board of Immigration Appeals has now adopted without reservation the doctrine of attributed political opinion, holding that extrajudicial punishment imposed on an ethnic Tamil by Sri Lankan authorities was tantamount to persecution based on a

---

84 *Id.*

85 777 F.2d 509 (9th Cir. 1985).

86 *Id.* at 517.

87 *Id.*

perception by the persecutors that the applicant harbored a hostile political animus.[88]

## § IV.4. Civil War Cases: Imputed Political Opinion, Neutrality and Other Grounds; the Growth of Attributed Characteristics and Beliefs[89]

This section deals with the growth of imputed political opinion, particularly as that concept has come to relate to identifying a protected ground where the claim arises from a situation of upheaval. The *Basic Law Manual*, commenting on the *Elias-Zacarias* decision, remarks that the notion of attribution relates not simply to political opinion, but informs all five grounds.[90] The Canadian Supreme Court in *Ward* also adopted this methodology as being consistent with sound refugee analysis.[91] The civil war cases demonstrate the dangers of viewing the protected grounds as fixed categories rather than of focusing on the issue of whether persecution has been threatened or imposed because the persecutor believes the claimant to be a social or political threat. Attribution principles make clear that the grounds themselves are flexible components of the refugee definition which are essentially context-dependent. The actions and views of the persecutor determine whether a protected ground can be inferred by the adjudicator based upon a review of objective circumstances in individual cases.

Many of the cases which follow deal with grounds other than imputed political opinion. They do so, however, in situations where a civil conflict lies at the source of the persecution experienced or feared and which, to some degree, is political in nature. Moreover, the vast majority of the cases analyzed herein rely, to an exceptional degree, on attribution rules. Even where this reliance is not made explicit in the decision in question, attribution can be seen to play a role by virtue of the inferential analysis adopted which relies heavily on the historical origins of the struggle giving rise to the claim. Despite the fact that "intrinsic" characteristics or beliefs may be in question, the existence of a protected ground and of nexus is often determined based upon the social and political context in which the claimant becomes subject to acts of serious harm.

---

88 Matter of S-P-, 21 I&N Dec. 486 (BIA 1996).

89 This section draws upon an earlier essay by the author. *See generally* Mark R. von Sternberg, *The Plight of the Non-Combatant in Civil War and the New Criteria for Refugee Status*, 9 Int'l J. Refugee L. 169 (1997).

90 Basic Law Manual, *supra* § I.1, note 26, at 36, n. 9.

91 Canada (Attorney General) v. Ward, [1993] 2 S.C.R. 689, 747.

In this respect, U.S. asylum law employs almost exclusively the political opinion category in analyzing civil war cases. Canadian refugee law, on the other hand, is not so limited and utilizes the full scope of the protected grounds. However, both U.S. and Canadian cases in this area deal with the same general problem (linkage to a refugee ground). And segregating the Canadian cases based upon the precise ground involved would skew effective comparative analysis. Finally, as scrutiny of the cases will show, the question of whether a protected ground has been made out is practically coterminous with the issue of whether the case involves persecution in the Convention sense.

In short, the civil war cases illustrate a fundamental theme of this study, namely, that excessive reliance on the "categories" of persecution is often misplaced in refugee analysis. The critical inquiry is whether the persecutor is prepared to impose mistreatment based on a difference between the persecutor's views or status and those of the victim (real or perceived) which the persecutor will not tolerate.

### § IV.4(a). Establishing Persecutory Animus during Periods of Upheaval: The New Refugee Analysis

Establishing persecutory motive (i.e., relationship between harm or suffering and a protected ground) during armed conflict constitutes one of the most formidable challenges of refugee protection. The 1951 Convention was framed with a specific view to the individual claimant and under the assumption that the Treaty would not be utilized to accommodate the exigencies of mass influx.[92] This largely procedural observation, however, has been accompanied by a more general (but misplaced) viewpoint, namely, that the Geneva Conventions of August 12, 1949 (setting forth the rules applicable in international and internal armed conflict) provide an exclusive remedy for those fleeing the generalized violence spawned by civil or by interstitial wars:[93] accordingly, those seeking relief from such conditions cannot qualify under the law of refugee status.

---

[92] *See generally* Goodwin-Gill, *supra* § I.1, note 11, at 197.

[93] *See, e.g.*, Handbook, *supra* § I.1, note 30, ¶ 164:

> Persons compelled to leave their country as the result of international or national armed conflict are not normally considered refugees under the 1951 Convention and the 1967 Protocol. They do, however, have the protection provided under other international instruments, e.g., the Geneva Convention of 1949 on the Protection of War Victims and the 1967 Protocol Additional to the Geneva

Too often, however, refugee doctrine as developed by signatory States has overlooked the facts of individualized cases in applying the foregoing doctrine and, more importantly, has ignored general configurations of violence aimed at specific groups. These "patterns or practices"[94] should, under accepted evidentiary principles, give rise to an inference that the harm or suffering complained of is not undirected, but rather is specifically aimed at human aggregates pursuant to an implicit policy of discrimination. Concerted violence against specific groups should provide the basis for finding a "reason" for persecution under the Convention refugee definition.

This section explores the question of "nexus" in United States and Canadian jurisprudence with respect to claims arising out of situations of armed conflict.[95] Both jurisdictions have undergone in this connection a similar form of evolution. An early form of adjudication requiring the claimant to establish that she would be treated distinctly or in some unique manner which distinguishes her from her fellow nationals (or from other members of her group)[96] has come to be rejected. In its place there has

---

Convention of 1949 relating to the Protection of Victims of International Armed Conflicts.

94 *See generally* 8 CFR § 208.13(b)(2)(i) indicating that the asylum seeker need not show that she would be "singled out" for persecution if she can demonstrate a "pattern or practice" of persecution aimed at a larger collectivity of which she is a member, provided that she can also demonstrate inclusion in the group so that persecution upon return to the home country is reasonable.

95 Situations of civil war have proved central in the development of the refugee definition in both United States and Canadian law. For instance, many of the principal decisions of the (U.S.) Board of Immigration Appeals relating to interpretation of the refugee standard have arisen in the context of civil war. *See, e.g.*, Matter of Salim, 18 I&N Dec. 311 (BIA 1982); Matter of Acosta, 19 I&N Dec. 211 (BIA 1985); Matter of Mogharrabi, 19 I&N Dec. 439 (BIA 1987); Matter of A-G-, 19 I&N Dec. 502 (BIA 1987); Matter of Maldonado-Cruz, 19 I&N Dec. 509 (BIA 1988); Matter of Vigil, 19 I&N Dec. 572 (BIA 1988); Matter of Izatula, 20 I&N Dec. 149 (BIA 1990); Matter of T-, 20 I&N Dec. 571 (BIA 1992); Matter of R-, 20 I&N Dec. 621 (BIA 1992); Matter of H-, 21 I&N Dec. 337 (BIA 1996); Matter of S-P-, 21 I&N Dec. 486 (BIA 1996). On the other hand, the importance of civil war cases to the evolution of the refugee standard in Canadian law can be gleaned from the fact that the Immigration and Refugee Board has recently adopted specific guidelines as a frame of reference for the Convention Refugee Determination Division in adjudicating such cases. *See Canadian Civil War Guidelines, supra* § III.3, note 39.

96 Prior jurisprudence in the U.S. must be examined to understand where asylum principles stand today. Under the rationale of prior case law, the Board of Immigration Appeals and the immigration courts would view the persecutor's motivation as essentially driven by the needs of the civil strife in which the conflicting parties found themselves. Hence, excessive mistreatment meted out by the insurgent groups to co-opted individuals who desert their ranks was said to flow from a desire to maintain military discipline, and not

emerged a growing viewpoint that the claimant need establish nothing more than that she would experience serious harm which is linked, directly or indirectly, to a refugee ground.[97]

The model which comes closest to an ideal restatement of appropriate principles for adjudicating civil war cases is contained in the *Canadian Guidelines*. The refugee analysis recommended in the *Canadian Guidelines* clearly reflects the basic approach that an individual asylum seeker can establish a claim to refugee status in civil war situations and that the claimant need not demonstrate that he or she will be "singled out" for persecution. This methodology (which is described as the "non-comparative" approach) has received fundamental support in leading cases decided by the Court of Appeal. The seminal decision in this respect, *Salibian* v. *M.E.I.*,[98] set forth broad criteria to be followed where the claim arises from general conditions of upheaval caused by a situation of internal armed conflict.

*Salibian* holds that, generally, conditions of civil war do not operate to preclude recognition of refugee status, provided that the harm feared is not felt "indiscriminately" by all citizens. The risk may relate to the applicant personally, to a group to which she belongs, or even to all citizens in her country, provided that the risk is linked to a refugee ground.[99] The best

---

because of perceived political hostility. Matter of Maldonado-Cruz, 19 I&N Dec. 509 (BIA 1988), *rev'd,* Maldonado-Cruz v. INS, 883 F.2d 788 (9th Cir. 1990). On the other hand, clearly disproportionate punishment in the form of transparent human rights violations imposed by governmental authorities (and their affiliates) against innocent civilians was held to derive from the government's legitimate need to protect itself against insurgency, and not from a political animus against the victim. Matter of T-, 20 I&N Dec. 571 (BIA 1992); Matter of R-, 20 I&N Dec. 621 (BIA 1992), *rev'd sub nom.* Rana v. Moschorak, No. 93-0274 SVW (SH), slip op. (C.D.Ca. May 24, 1993), *appeal dismissed,* 37 F.3d 1506 (9th Cir. 1994). For a parallel case following the same general methodology in Canadian jurisprudence, *see* Isa v. S.S.C., (F.C.T.D., no. IMM-1760-94), February 16, 1995.

97 For early cases which serve as prototypes of the new analysis, *see, e.g.*, Hernandez-Ortiz v. INS, 777 F.2d 509 (9th Cir. 1985); Blanco-Lopez v. INS, 858 F.2d 531 (9th Cir. 1988); Maldonado-Cruz v. INS, 883 F.2d 788 (9th Cir. 1989); Singh v. Ilchert, 63 F.2d 1501 (9th Cir. 1995).

98 (1990), 113 N.R. 123 (F.C.A.).

99 *Id.* at 132-133:

> It can be said in light of earlier decisions by this Court on claims to Convention refugee status that
>
> (1) the applicant does not have to show that he had himself been persecuted or would himself be persecuted in the future;
>
> (2) the applicant can show that the fear he had resulted not from reprehensible acts committed or likely to be committed directly against him but from reprehensible

evidence that this is indeed the case is the treatment afforded to individuals similarly situated in the claimant's country. The court concluded by quoting Hathaway's treatise to the following effect:

> In sum, while modern refugee law is concerned to recognize the protection needs of particular claimants, the best evidence that an individual faces a serious chance of persecution is usually the treatment afforded similarly situated persons in the country of origin. In the context of claims derived from situations of generalized oppression, therefore, the issue is not whether the claimant is more at risk than anyone else in her country, but rather whether the broadly based harassment or abuse is sufficiently serious to substantiate a claim to refugee status. If persons like the applicant may face serious harm for which the state is accountable, and if the risk is grounded in civil or political status, then she is properly considered to be a Convention refugee.[100]

In *Rizkallah* v. *M.E.I.*,[101] moreover, the Court of Appeal ruled that a refugee claimant seeking protection in the context of civil war need only establish a link between persecution and a Convention reason, or, alternatively phrased, some form of personal or collective targeting.[102] On the facts, however, the court went on to hold that the claimants (Lebanese nationals) had not established that they had been targeted "in some way different" from other victims in the civil war.[103]

The last conclusion by the Court of Appeal has been adopted in several decisions of the Trial Division as authority for the proposition that the claimant's position must be compared to that of other individuals within the country from which asylum is sought, and that if the claimant would not be

---

> acts committed or likely to be committed against members of a group to which he belonged;
>
> (3) a situation of civil war in a given country is not an obstacle to a claim provided that the fear felt is not that felt indiscriminately by all citizens as a consequence of civil war, but that felt by the applicant himself, by a group with which he is associated, or, even by all citizens on account of a risk of persecution based on one of the reasons stated in the definition; and
>
> (4) the fear is that of a reasonable possibility that the applicant will be persecuted.

100 *Id.* at 134, *quoting* Hathaway, *supra* § I.1, note 7, at 97.

101 156 N.R. 1 (F.C.A.).

102 *Id.*:

> To succeed, refugee claimants must establish a link between themselves and persecution for a Convention reason. In other words, they must be targeted for persecution in some way, either personally or collectively.

103 *Id.*:

> [T]he evidence, as presented to us, falls short of establishing that Christians in the claimant's Lebanese village were collectively targeted in some way different from the general victims of the tragic and many-sided civil war.

"differentially treated" refugee status is inappropriate.[104] Accordingly, in *Isa* v. *S.S.C.*,[105] the case which most forcefully illustrates the "comparative" approach, the Trial Division ruled in effect that since many civil wars were racially or ethnically motivated, recognizing as refugees those targeted on racial grounds in such conflicts would have the effect of allowing all individuals on either side of the conflict to qualify. As noted by the *Isa* court:

> Given the totality of the documentary evidence before us, it appears that all clans and subclans are both perpetrators and victims of the ongoing violence. We do not find that the claimant's clan has been differentially targeted for persecution from any other clan nor that he has been targeted any differently from any other Somali.
>
> * * *
>
> Many, if not most civil war situations are racially or ethnically based. If racially motivated attacks in civil war circumstances constitute a ground for Convention refugee status, then, all individuals on either side of the conflict will qualify. The passages quoted by the Board from [paragraph 164 of] the United Nations Handbook ... indicates [sic] that this is not the purpose of the 1951 Convention.[106]

U.S. asylum law has undergone a comparable tension between "comparative" and "non-comparative" approaches.[107] However, until 1996, the doctrinal perspective which governed the Board's approach to civil war cases maintained that an asylum claim could not be established if the harm or suffering complained of originated from the conflict itself.

In one seminal case,[108] the Board acknowledged that the forms such harm might take were myriad. The conscription and disciplining of combatants (whether by the government or by the insurgents); governmental investigation and prosecution of rebels and those resisting lawful induction; attacking enemy positions and supporting military units and property, all these were deemed to be within the province of armed struggle and hence not persecution in the statutory sense.[109] The Board did not discriminate in making its analysis between the uses of force which were in conformity with

---

[104] *See generally* Interpretation of the Convention Refugee Definition in the Case Law, *supra* § II.3, note 63, § 9.2.1 and cases cited therein.

[105] (1995), 28 Imm. L.R. (2d) 68 (F.C.T.D.).

[106] *Id.* at 72.

[107] The terms "comparative" and "non-comparative" are based on terminology in the *Canadian Civil War Guidelines*. These terms are useful, however, in describing parallel developments in United States case law.

[108] Matter of Rodriguez-Majano, 19 I&N Dec. 811 (BIA 1988).

[109] *Id.* at 815.

international humanitarian law, and those which were clearly proscribed by it.[110] The Board specifically opined, for instance, that the burning of cars and other property would not be offensive. And, as will be shown in the discussion which follows, the Board failed entirely to grasp the fundamental principle of all international humanitarian law, that of proportionality, both between the means used and the importance of the military objective, and between the advantages anticipated from a military attack and the collateral effect of that attack on protected classes (e.g., civilians).

The leading case which set the trend for much that was to follow is *Matter of McMullen*.[111] McMullen, an applicant for withholding of deportation under (previous) INA § 243(h), had been a member of the Provisional Irish Republican Army (PIRA) who had deserted after refusing to carry out a kidnapping scheme. The Board concluded that McMullen had himself engaged in a "campaign of violence randomly directed at civilians" so as to be barred from withholding under the preclusion relating to serious non-political crimes.[112] However, with respect to the claimant's contention that he would be punished by PIRA for his act of desertion, the Board reasoned that PIRA's relations with its members were non-political and were governed, for the most part, by the practical need for a paramilitary organization to impose discipline on its members.[113]

The Salvadoran cases, decided by the Board in the late 1980s, followed *McMullen*'s rationale. In *Matter of Maldonado-Cruz*,[114] the Board upheld denial of an asylum claim submitted by a young Salvadoran who had been

---

[110] *Id.*

[111] 19 I&N Dec. 90, 94 (BIA 1984).

[112] *See* (superseded) Immigration and Nationality Act § 243(h)(2)(C), 8 USC § 1253(h)(2)(C).

[113] The Ninth Circuit eventually affirmed the Board's decision denying relief. McMullen v. INS, 788 F.2d 591, 596 (9th Cir. 1986). It should be noted, however, that the "exclusion" clause pertaining to "serious non-political crimes" (which the Board found PIRA and the applicant to have engaged in), and the finding that applicant's relations with PIRA were non-political, are clearly related. The entire scope of the enterprise was non-political, according to the Board as well as to the Ninth Circuit by virtue of the atrocious nature of PIRA's para-military activities. In this respect,

> PIRA's acts of violence against ordinary citizens of Northern Ireland and elsewhere … are not sufficiently linked to political objectives and by virtue of their primary targets, so barbarous, atrocious and disproportionate to their political objectives that they constituted "serious non-political crimes" for purposes of section 243(h)(2)(C) and the Convention.

*Id.* at 598.

[114] *See, e.g.,* Matter of Maldonado-Cruz, 19 I&N Dec. 509 (BIA 1988), *rev'd,* Maldonado-Cruz v. INS, 883 F.2d 788 (9th Cir. 1990).

involuntarily conscripted by the rebels. The claimant had managed to flee from captivity, but only after he had seen a close friend killed in a similar escape attempt.

The Board's reasoning in *Maldonado-Cruz* illustrates how hardened U.S. asylum adjudications can be. The Board viewed extra-judicial killing of an involuntary conscript by insurgents not as targeting on account of a protected ground (attributed political opinion), but as an effort by the rebels to maintain discipline within their ranks. *Matter of Vigil*,[115] virtually a companion case, took a similar tack. The claimant, a Salvadoran youth residing in the capital, had been appalled by guerilla excesses (including acts of decapitation) deployed to bring reluctant recruits into the rebel fold. The Board concluded that "young, male, urban, unenlisted Salvadorans" were not a "particular social group". The excesses of the rebels were, moreover, not aimed at a specific class, but at overthrowing the Salvadoran government. This was held to be a generalized political motive which did not become persecutory even when deliberate (and unlawful) acts of serious harm were inflicted either on those resisting the rebels' will, or on those thought likely to resist.

The Ninth Circuit Court of Appeals struck out in another direction. Claimants seeking to resist coercive action by the rebels were deemed to fall within a protected ground if they faced serious harm as a result. In adopting this analysis, the Ninth Circuit leaned heavily on dual theories which largely overlapped with one another: (i) "neutrality", an affirmative political opinion in the claimant not to become involved with either side;[116] and (ii) imputed political opinion,[117] a set of values or beliefs the rebels would ascribe to the claimant arising out of the applicant's acts of opposition. A combination of these rationales was adopted by the Ninth Circuit in reversing *Maldonado Cruz*.[118] With respect to the argument that the applicant was the mere victim of violence, the appeals court has stressed the difference between the "willing traveler" who cooperated with the insurgents and the individual

---

[115] Matter of Vigil, 19 I&N Dec. 572 (BIA 1988).

[116] *See, e.g.*, Bolanos-Hernandez v. INS, 767 F.2d 1277 (9th Cir. 1985). *Bolanos-Hernandez* is in fact the first in a line of cases finding asylum-eligible those who had resisted pressures from both governmental and insurgent forces in the Salvadoran civil conflict. The court characterized the applicant as having a "principled position" of neutrality. However, its ruling is clearly broader than that and is based, at least in part, on the notion of attributed characteristics and beliefs.

*Id.* at 1286.

[117] *See, e.g.*, Arteaga v. INS, 836 F.2d 1227 (9th Cir. 1988).

[118] *See* Maldonado-Cruz v. INS, 883 F.2d 788 (9th Cir. 1990).

who refused to be swayed by the guerillas' unlawful demands.[119] The Ninth Circuit, unlike the Board, has viewed the political end of the insurgents as relevant to the question of the guerillas' motives in imposing persecution, ruling that "[c]learly forced recruitment into a war against the government is politically motivated".[120] The political motivation of the guerillas, therefore, both in waging the war and in recruiting the applicant was relevant to the ultimate question of whether the applicant's desertion would cause him to be viewed as a political enemy.[121]

While the impact of *Elias-Zacarias* on the evolution of U.S. asylum law cannot be gauged with effectiveness at this time, subsequent developments have made it clear that the doctrine of attributed political opinion survives. Ensuing treatise and decisional law, interpreting *Elias-Zacarias*, has established a methodology pursuant to which the issue of whether the claimant faces persecution on account of a protected ground is treated as a matter of evidence based on an objective test. Where belligerents have engaged in excessive force amounting to serious violations of international humanitarian law against protected classes such as civilians, it is reasonable to infer that such "harm or suffering" is based on a refugee ground. This is especially the case where the conflict in question is being waged for reasons which are themselves related to the recognized reasons for persecution, e.g., race, religion or political opinion.[122]

The Ninth Circuit's "neutrality" cases will undoubtedly continue to be entitled to some weight, although it would appear (i) that their precedential value has been substantially curtailed by *Elias-Zacarias*; and (ii) the usefulness of "neutrality" as a theory of political opinion persecution has been subsumed by the still developing doctrine of attributed characteristics

---

119 *See, e.g.*, Arteaga v. INS, 836 F.2d 1227, 1232 (9th Cir. 1988).

120 *Id.* at 1232.

121 These rationales do not seem entirely precluded by the Supreme Court's decision in *Elias-Zacarias* v. *INS*, 112 S. Ct. 812 (1992). With respect to the motivation of the persecutor, the Court found that the generalized political motive underlying acts necessary to wage the war (raising an army, for instance) does not demonstrate a specific motivation in inflicting "harm or suffering" on the victim, at least with respect to the act of co-opting claimant for the guerilla cause. The *Elias-Zacarias* decision, therefore, seems to reject as individual propositions: (i) that the insurgents' motivations in accomplishing forced recruitment lead to a finding of political opinion persecution; and (ii) that the claimant's act of refusing induction is indicative of political opinion. The Court, however, does not explicitly reject the two propositions combined, i.e., that the guerillas' political animus in "kidnapping" the claimant can constitute *important evidence* of the guerillas' political incentive in retaliating against him because of his desertion.

122 *See generally* Basic Law Manual, *supra* § I.1, note 26, at 36, n. 9; Matter of S-P-, 21 I&N Dec. 486 (BIA 1996).

and beliefs. It is important to note that the concept of "neutrality" as a political opinion was unique to U.S. asylum law and that there is no comparable doctrine in Canadian refugee jurisprudence.

The initial "neutrality" opinion of the Ninth Circuit was *Bolanos-Hernandez* v. *INS*.[123] *Bolanos-Hernandez* involved a Salvadoran whom the guerillas had sought to recruit because of his prior membership in a right-wing Salvadoran political party, hoping to exploit the applicant's contacts and to infiltrate the government. When Bolanos refused this "invitation", the guerillas indicated they would kill him if he did not either join them or leave the country.

The Ninth Circuit overturned the Board's determination that neutrality was not a political choice. One of the chief objectives of the Refugee Act, to protect individuals irrespective of ideology, would be frustrated if applicant were required to join one of the warring sides in the conflict. In a compelling statement of policy the court remarked:

> [I]t is irrelevant why the individual has made his choice. It does not matter to the persecutors what the individual motivation is. The guerillas in El Salvador do not inquire into the reasoning of those who insist on remaining neutral and do not join their cause. They are concerned only with the act that constitutes an overt manifestation of political opinion. Persecution on account of that overt manifestation is persecution because of political opinion.[124]

Several decisions interpreting the scope of neutrality as political opinion followed *Bolanos-Hernandez*. These included: *Del Valle* v. *INS*[125] (Salvadoran national granted asylum who had refused to join the Squadron of Death and was later beaten by men in military attire who charged him with being a member of the Popular Force of Liberation); *Argueta* v. *INS*[126] (claimant granted asylum who had remained conscientiously neutral toward both sides in the conflict); *Turcios* v. *INS*[127] (Salvadoran applicant granted asylum where claimant had been beaten and tortured by the National Police after talking publicly with a professor of known leftist views, the court ruling that, irrespective of applicant's intention, he was punished because of an overt manifestation of political opinion which was deemed sufficient); and *Arteaga* v *INS*[128] (asylum granted to Salvadoran national who had refused to be inducted into the insurgent FMLN and was threatened as a result, the

[123] 767 F.2d 1277 (9th Cir. 1985).

[124] *Id.* at 1286.

[125] 776 F.2d 1407 (9th Cir. 1985).

[126] 759 F.2d 1395 (9th Cir. 1985).

[127] 821 F.2d 1396 (9th Cir. 1987).

[128] 836 F.2d 1227 (9th Cir. 1988).

court ruling that the conscription was illegal and the claimant's deliberate and open refusal was enough to qualify him). The evolving case law, prior to *Elias-Zacarias*, thus evidenced an increasing reliance on attributed political opinion and a progressively reduced dependence on "neutrality" as political opinion.

The case law arising since the Supreme Court's decision in *Elias-Zacarias* reveals that the doctrine of neutrality as political opinion is presently extremely limited. In *Sangha* v. *INS,*[129] an asylum seeker from India based his claim on efforts made to recruit him made by the Bindrawala Tiger Force (BTF), an insurgent force dedicated to the establishment of an independent Sikh homeland to be called Khalistan. Claimant's father was a member of the Akali Dal party which was highly critical of BTF terrorism in the Punjab and had given a speech which articulated the Alkali Dal party view. Subsequently, four armed men invaded the family home; they beat up applicant's father; demanded that the father cease his political activities; and they demanded that claimant and his brother fight for Khalistan, expressly so that they could not support the father financially in connection with the latter's political activities. The claim was based on persecution on account of the applicant's neutrality or, in the alternative, imputed political opinion.

The court set forth the law of "neutrality" as political opinion in the post-*Elias-Zacarias* environment as involving a four-part test:

> (i) Applicant can establish his or her neutrality either through pronouncements or through actions.
>
> (ii) The political neutrality must be the product of conscious, deliberate choice;
>
> (iii) The neutrality must be expressed sufficiently for it to serve as the basis for past or anticipated persecution; and
>
> (iv) Claimant can establish neutrality as political opinion persecution by refusing under threat of violence to serve in insurgent or illegal government forces.[130]

Using this test, the Ninth Circuit found that applicant had never adopted a conscious choice to remain neutral. Moreover, even if he had, there was no

---

[129] 103 F.3d 1482 (9th Cir. 1997). A caveat is in order here. A prior decision by the Ninth Circuit, *Ramos-Vasquez* v. *INS,* 57 F.3d 857 (9th Cir. 1995) established that "neutrality" as a political opinion could be used to ground a claim where the applicant has refused to be inducted into an army substantially engaged in "military action condemned by the international community". Refusal to become involved in atrocities had historically been accepted as a political opinion in any event, and there is nothing in the *Ramos-Vasquez* case which indicates that that decision adds anything to prior doctrine.

[130] Sangha v. INS, 103 F.3d 1482, 1488 (9th Cir. 1996).

evidence that the BTF intended to punish him for this choice. As concerns the imputed political opinion argument, moreover, the court ruled that there was no evidence in the case showing that the BTF would attribute the father's political opinion to the sons; on the contrary, the evidence indicated that the BTF members wanted to recruit claimant and his brother only so that they could cripple the father's ability to act against them through the latter's advocacy. The test applied by the court, however, is fairly stringent and would appear to be meaningful only in situations where some other principled outlook (e.g., opposition to becoming involved in atrocities) was also maintained by the claimant.

The Ninth Circuit's early decisions also confronted the fundamental problem of how to establish nexus between serious harm and a protected ground in the context of civil and political upheaval where the causes of persecution are not readily apparent. In a seminal decision, *Hernandez-Ortiz* v. *INS*,[131] the appeals court was confronted with the situation of a family which had been inexplicably made the subject of concerted action by the Salvadoran government. Resolving the ambiguous nature of this fact pattern in favor of the claimant, the Ninth Circuit ruled that, where a government's military strength is exerted against a definable group (in this case, a particular family), and there is no basis for believing that a criminal prosecution is intended, a presumption results that the government is being driven by political animus. As expressly found by the court:

> When a government exerts its military strength against an individual or a group and there is no reason to believe that the individual or group has engaged in any criminal activity or other conduct that would provide a legitimate basis for governmental action, the most reasonable presumption is that the government's actions are politically motivated.[132]

The Ninth Circuit clearly introduced, in the *Hernandez-Ortiz* decision, a proportionality test which would become more explicit in later cases. In *Blanco-Lopez* v. *INS*,[133] the appeals court had before it the claim of a Salvadoran asylum seeker who had been held incommunicado by security forces while being threatened with death. The Ninth Circuit found that such "excessive" treatment was not compatible with the requirements of a

---

[131] 777 F.2d 509 (9th Cir. 1985).

[132] *Id.* at 517. *But see* Sangha v. INS, 103 F.3d 1487, 1487 (9th Cir. 1996):

> [P]ersecution on account of political opinion can no longer be inferred merely from acts of random violence by members of a village or political subdivision against their neighbors who may or may not have divergent religious or political views.

[133] Blanco-Lopez v. INS, 858 F.2d 531 (9th Cir. 1988).

legitimate criminal investigation and so supported a grant of asylum based on the theory of imputed political opinion.[134]

In *Ramirez-Rivas* v. *INS*,[135] the appeals court formulated a succinct restatement of the proportionality doctrine. Members of the applicant's family (who were apparently both partisans and neutrals in the ongoing civil war) had been killed or injured extrajudicially by the Salvadoran government. The claimant herself, who had had no political attachments, was suspected because of the involvement of her family members. The appeals court upheld the asylum claim, ruling that the indiscriminate nature of the government's investigation, which swept in the innocent as well as the guilty, gives rise to an inference that the applicant has been targeted on account of a protected ground (attributed political opinion):

> It is at least as arbitrary and unjust for a government to persecute persons falsely accused of being ideological enemies as it is for a government to persecute real ideological enemies. *Whenever a government persecutes with a political motive, it engages in political persecution.*[136]

At the same time that these developments were transpiring, the Board continued to follow, and in fact to enlarge, its earlier rulings to the effect that harm or suffering arising out of civil strife would not support an asylum claim. In *Matter of T-*,[137] an ethnic Tamil from Sri Lanka had been compelled to give supplies to a militant Tamil-based rebel group (the LTTE). As a result of his "complicity", claimant had been severely mistreated by the EPRFL, another Tamil-based group but one allied to the Indian peacekeeping force.

The Board found that applicant had been punished because of his having provided aid to the LTTE, and not because of a "reason" contained in the refugee definition.[138] The Board treated the extreme beating to which claimant had been subject as merely reflective of the type of violence noncombatants could expect in a civil war environment, even if they have been misidentified with one of the belligerents. Harm or suffering arising from the conflict does not constitute persecution within the meaning of the Convention refugee definition. The Board was unmistakable with respect to how far it was prepared to apply the foregoing doctrine:

---

134 *Id.* at 534.

135 Ramirez-Rivas v. INS, 899 F.2d 864 (9th Cir. 1990), *vacated on other grounds,* 502 U.S. 1025 (1992).

136 *Id.* at 867. [Citations omitted; emphasis supplied].

137 Matter of T-, 20 I&N Dec. 571 (BIA 1992).

138 *Id.* at 577.

> It may be that the organizations seeking to curb the LTTE *were driven to acts of revenge* as the result of the militants' terrorism, *but this is in the nature of civil war.* Harm arising from general civil strife does not amount to persecution within the meaning of the Act.[139]

In *Matter of R-*,[140] a Sikh from the Punjab region of India had been mistreated by Sikh militants when he refused to be coopted by them. The police became suspicious of the claimant's contacts with the militants, however, and engaged in a brutal beating of him in an effort to discover the scope of his involvement.

The Board affirmed denial of the claim. It determined that the beating administered by the militants was not directed at a political opinion of the claimant, but was motivated by the rebels' need for manpower. The excessive harm imposed by the police was similarly not directed at a characteristic or belief, but resulted from the conduct of a lawful investigation into the claimant's association with the rebels.[141]

Consistent with its earlier line of cases, the Ninth Circuit rejected this approach in *Singh* v. *Ilchert.*[142] In *Singh*, a Sikh from India had been tortured in a putatively lawful investigation aimed at uncovering the applicant's suspected terrorist activities. In determining that the authorities' treatment of applicant had been politically motivated, the appeals court looked at:

> (i) the authorities' excessive use of anti-terrorist legislation to quell political dissent and efface secessionist sentiment; and
>
> (ii) reliable background materials which demonstrated that "terrorism" had been so broadly defined and those suspected of terrorism so harshly treated by the Indian authorities, that putatively lawful police investigations were in reality being used as a vehicle for political suppression.[143]

The Ninth Circuit's decision clearly drew upon the proportionality doctrine in reaching its result. Both the scope of legislation proscribing certain activity and the degree of force used against those suspected of offending the law were found to be disproportionate to legitimate governmental ends. Accordingly,

> The BIA's opinion in this case held that the security forces' activities were part of a legitimate inquiry into terrorist activities and thus, by the BIA's

---

139 *Id.* at 578. [Emphasis supplied].

140 Matter of R-, 20 I&N Dec. 621 (BIA 1992), *rev'd sub nom.* Rana v. Moschorak, No. 93-0274 SVW (SH), slip op. (C.D.Ca. May 24, 1993), *appeal dismissed,* 37 F.3d 1506 (9th Cir. 1994).

141 *Id* at 623-24.

142 Singh v. Ilchert, 63 F.3d 1501 (9th Cir. 1995).

143 *Id.* at 1508.

> reasoning, not politically motivated within the meaning of the immigration laws. The record in this case, however, chronicles without contradiction the Indian authorities' extensive use of vague anti-terrorism laws to suppress political dissent and stamp out secessionist ideologies in India. Documents introduced by the applicant included the State Department's 1990 *Country Reports on Human Rights Practices* and Reports from *Amnesty International*, which the IJ found "entitled to substantial weight." A review of these documents reveals that India defines "terrorism" so broadly, and treats those accused or suspected of terrorism so harshly, that police "investigations" of many suspected terrorists are not legitimate government functions but rather part of a pattern of political suppression.[144]

The modern Canadian approach, as set forth in the *Guidelines* promulgated by the Immigration and Refugee Board,[145] resembles in large measure that adopted by the Ninth Circuit. The *Guidelines* seek to address the types of concerns which have haunted the BIA's treatment of civil war cases. They describe the kind of methodology used in such cases as the "comparative" approach. Such a methodology is explicitly rejected by the *Guidelines* as being dominated by a sole inquiry, whether the claimant (or a group to which claimant belongs) would be "differentially treated" in comparison with other individuals and groups in the country of claimed persecution.[146] As an alternative, the *Guidelines* recommend a "non-comparative" approach which asks only whether the case is one of serious harm which can be linked to a refugee or a Convention ground.[147] The fact that the party imposing serious harm has not discriminated against the claimant individually is irrelevant in determining whether a protected ground can be made out.[148]

"Linkage" (or what the U.S. case law refers to as "nexus") is determined under the *Guidelines* by looking at a number of factors. The factor given the most weight is unquestionably the motivation of the parties in fighting the

---

144 *Id.*

145 *Canadian Civil War Guidelines, supra* § III.3, note 39.

146 *Canadian Civil War Guidelines, supra* § III.3, note 39, at 7. The premises of the "new" jurisprudence are in entire agreement with positions taken by the UNHCR. *See, e.g.*, *Refugees in Civil War Situations*, UNHCR Branch Office, Ottawa, November, 1990, *quoted in Civil War Guidelines, supra* § III.3, note 39, at 17:

> It should be noted at the outset that individuals are considered refugees when they flee or remain outside a country for reasons pertinent to refugee status. Whenever these reasons arise in a civil war situation, in international armed conflict or in peace time, is irrelevant. *There is nothing in the definition itself which excludes its application to persons caught up in a civil war.* [Emphasis supplied].

147 *Id.*

148 *Canadian Civil War Guidelines, supra* § III.3, note 39, at 7, *citing* Salibian v. M.E.I. (1990), 113 N.R. 123 (F.C.A.); Rizkallah v. M.E.I. (1992), 156 N.R. 1 (F.C.A.).

war. The *Guidelines* discuss the methodology announced in *Isa* v. *S.S.C.* (i.e., that all civil wars are fought for religious, political, ethnic or racial reasons, and therefore a grant based on religious, political, ethnic or racial attacks has the potential to qualify everyone affected).

However, far from negating the nexus between serious harm and a protected ground, the general animus underlying the conflict actually goes far toward establishing the vital element of linkage. *Internal wars are largely fought for "reasons" which are related to the grounds of refugee protection; an adjudicator should therefore exercise great caution before determining that serious harm is not "linked" to a predicate for refugee status.*[149]

Under the *Guidelines*, therefore, persecutory intent can be inferred from unlawful detentions, rape, murder and other inhuman treatment inflicted on "enemy civilians".[150] "Linkage" can also be established where human rights violations are committed against individuals whose views or status makes them particularly vulnerable in the armed conflict. The following classes are clearly exposed to persecution in the Convention sense:

> (i) persons facing persecution for refusing to join either side in the armed struggle out of a desire to remain neutral, a conscientious political choice or other valid reason of conscience;
>
> (ii) human rights activists, journalists or other citizens threatened with measures of persecution for investigating and/or criticizing military, para-military or guerilla activities and atrocities;
>
> (iii) persons fearing persecution for certain views attributed to them, such as "sabotaging the war efforts" or "collaborating with the enemy".

Also at risk for a Convention reason are the following groups:

> (i) members of an ethnic group against which a genocidal campaign is being waged.
>
> (ii) members of a religious faith expelled from their homes and suffering other forms of persecutory treatment as part of an "ethnic cleansing" agenda.[151]

---

[149] *Civil War Guidelines, supra* § III.3, note 39, at 7, noting:

> [A]s civil wars are often waged for reasons related to a Convention ground, caution should be exercised before determining that there is no linkage to a Convention ground.

[150] *Id.* at 8, *quoting* comments made by Dr. Joachim Henkel, German Federal Administrative Court, made at the International Judicial Conference on Asylum Law and Procedures, London, England, November 1995, *Who is a refugee? (Refugees from civil war and other internal armed conflicts), in* section entitled *Persecution versus 'general consequences' of civil war* at 3-4.

[151] *Id.* at 10.

Such claimants should be distinguished from those who are fortuitously swept up in the violence, i.e., non-combatants caught in a cross-fire, victims of indiscriminate shelling, or those subject to random (i.e., non-targeted) looting.

Deliberate targeting of a group will always lead to a finding of serious harm based on a Convention ground. Where targeting is unclear, however, the effect which the persecutor's actions produce on the claimant (or on her group) can be looked to as the basis for an inference that "linkage" to a refugee ground has been established.[152]

Materially in this respect, the Canadian Court of Appeal has specifically rejected the notion (previously embraced by the U.S. Board of Immigration Appeals) that excessive mistreatment of a refugee claimant can be consistent with a neutral and lawful investigation. In *Thirunavukkarasu* v. *M.E.I.*,[153] the appeals court applied the doctrine of proportionality to find that an ethnic Tamil who had been brutally beaten because of his suspected involvement with a rebel group had not been mistreated in an otherwise lawful investigation, but had been persecuted on account of a protected ground, his Tamil ethnicity. The "state of emergency in Sri Lanka," the court held:

> cannot justify the arbitrary arrest and detention as well as beating and torture of an innocent civilian at the hands of the very government from whom the claimant is supposed to be seeking safety.[154]

The *Thirunvukkarasu* case has its direct parallel in U.S. asylum law in *Matter of S-P-*.[155] Obviously, the Board, viewing practically identical facts regarding an overbroad investigation which resulted in persecutory mistreatment of an ethnic Tamil, granted asylum on the basis of imputed political opinion. Again, the grounds of refugee protection substantially overlap; thematic presentation tends to trump analysis rigidly linked to the refugee grounds; and the question of what constitutes "persecution" (mistreatment linked to a policy of discrimination) remains the dominant concern in refugee analysis.

Canadian case law (drawn upon by the Immigration and Refugee Board in drafting the *Guidelines*) is illuminating with respect to the manner in which the "non-comparative" approach may be applied, bearing in mind that

---

[152] *Id.* at 8.

[153] Thirunvukkarasu v. M.E.I. (1993), 163 N.R. 232 (F.C.A.).

[154] *Id.* at 238.

[155] 21 I&N Dec. 486 (BIA 1996), discussed *infra,* this section.

linkage to a refugee ground can be inferred in appropriate circumstances.[156] The case law makes clear in this respect that there must be *some evidence* linking serious harm to a recognized basis for persecution. Random shelling (which does not appear to target particular groups) will not satisfy the refugee definition, even where the claimant is consequently placed at risk.[157]

Similarly, where land mines remain unremoved at the end of a conflict, thus presenting a risk of injury affecting all persons indiscriminately, refugee status will not be recognized.[158] Moreover, in a short opinion, the Federal Court of Appeal has shown itself somewhat reluctant to infer serious harm based on imputed characteristics and beliefs. Accordingly, it has held that it will not ascribe a political opinion to all those victimized by government forces because they live in an area dominated by insurgents.[159] The *Guidelines* note that the case illustrates the need to "provide supporting evidence of targeting". Still, the *Shereen* decision appears to set an unduly restrictive standard with respect to inferring linkage to a protected ground in light of the fact that the government forces were clearly engaged in an impermissibly broad military action which swept in armed insurgents and innocent civilians alike.[160]

---

[156] The case law is summarized in the notes to the *Canadian Civil War Guidelines. See, Civil War Guidelines, supra* § III.3, note 39, at 16 -29, but especially note 14 at 19-20.

[157] *See, e.g.*, Hersi v. M.E.I., (F.C.T.D., no. 92-A-6574), May 5, 1993:

> The evidence of the applicants themselves speaks of general and indiscriminate shelling of cities and villages. Members of various clans become the victims, whether such clans could otherwise be regarded as friends or foes of the assailants.

*See also* Siad v. M.E.I. (1993), 21 Imm. L.R. (2d) 6 (F.C.T.D.):

> It is clear that the Refugee Division concluded that the fear felt was felt indiscriminately by all citizens [of Somalia] as a result of the civil war and random violence, and was not related to membership in a social group.

[158] Khalib v. M.E.I. (1994), 24 Imm. L. R. (2d) 149 (F.C.T.D.). The Refugee Division declined to accept that:

> [T]he mines were intended to harm only or even mainly the Issaqs living in the area of Hargeisa and that the mines placed by a former government and not yet removed constitute grounds for fear, recognized by the Convention, of persecution by a government that is no longer in authority.

[159] Shereen v. M.E.I. (F.C.A., no. A-913-90), March 21, 1994. *But see* Ahmed v. M.E.I. (F.C.T.D., no. A-1017-92), November 2, 1993, finding the CRDD to be in error on the question of targeting based on the claimant's documentary submissions.

[160] *See also* Khalib v. M.E.I. (1994), 24 Imm. L.R. (2d) 149 (F.C.T.D.), *quoted supra*, this section, note 158. The claimants, members of the Isaaq clan, based their claims to refugee status on the fact that the former government had indiscriminately placed a large number of mines in the roads and fields of Hargelsa, where a substantial number of the Isaaq

The foregoing situations should be distinguished from determinations in which targeting has been made out. Utilizing the "differentially treated" analysis, for example, the Convention Refugee Determination Division has recognized refugee status where the evidence indicates that claimant's group (the Harza) had suffered more frequent and more severe human rights violations than other groups in the Afghan civil conflict.[161] Also, in a decision of some moment, the CRDD determined that a Bosnian Moslem, as a member of a group which had been the collective victims of ethnic cleansing, should be recognized as a refugee.[162] Specifically, the CRDD held:

> Muslims are not merely the victims caught in the crossfire of war, but are a targeted group selected for elimination because of their religion.[163]

Moreover, the Federal Court-Trial Division has begun more regularly to overturn results where the "comparative" approach has been used by the CRDD to deny the claim. Accordingly, in *Hasan* v. *M.E.I.*, the court ruled that the CRDD had erred, reminding it that the *Rizkallah* decision:

> is not authority for concluding that the civil war situation in Somalia faces all Somalis indiscriminately.[164]

The court determined that the CRDD had not examined the claimant's individual situation, nor assessed his fear arising out of his clan membership. As noted in the *Guidelines*,[165] the Federal Court-Trial Division in *Hasan* had clearly held that the claim must be examined by the CRDD based on the claimant's fear as it relates to a refugee ground rather than following a differential risk analysis.

The *Canadian Guidelines* summarize the foregoing precedents by providing firm examples in which generalized violence crosses the line and

---

reside. The Federal Court-Trial Division upheld findings of the Refugee Determination Division of the Immigration and Refugee Board that targeting had not been made out. Claimants were clearly urging an "effects" type of analysis in their claims of persecution, rather than one showing that they would be, or had been targeted, based upon an inferential analysis.

161 CRDD T93-0900 and T93-09143, January 14, 1994.

162 CRDD T92-03148, September 9, 1992.

163 *Id.* at 5. *But see* Barisic v. M.C.I. (F.C.T.D., no. IMM-7275-93), January 26, 1995, where the court declined to set aside a determination by the CRDD to the effect that a Croatian who had been forced out of his village because of the latter's policy of "ethnic cleansing" was not a Convention refugee. The court ruled, in a rationale strikingly similar to that of *Matter of T-*, 20 I&N Dec. 571 (BIA 1992), that the claimant had not been "differentially treated". The decision in *Barisic* is clearly inconsistent with the "new" jurisprudence.

164 (F.C.T.D., no. IMM-39-93), June 9, 1994.

165 *See, e.g., Civil War Guidelines, supra* § III.3, note 39, at 23, n. 18.

becomes specifically directed against a particular group. Indiscriminate bombing of civilians should be distinguished from the "situation where one participant in a civil war bombs and shells the area of a town primarily inhabited by non-combatants who are members of another participant in the civil war".[166] Even where one of the participants shows "wanton disregard" for the safety of civilians (rather than deliberate targeting), such disregard may lead the Refugee Division to find that resulting serious harm is linked to a refugee ground.[167]

The reasoning in the *Guidelines* at this juncture quite clearly reflects prevailing standards in international humanitarian law which require belligerents to take certain precautions prior to launching an attack to assure that the collateral damage to civilians and their property will not be disproportionate to the military advantage to be gained from the attack. The *Commentary to Protocol I* sets forth criteria which should be considered by the commander in determining whether to launch an attack. Primarily, the commander should weigh the incidental damage to civilians and to civilian property which will flow as the result of the attack. Included in such a prospective analysis are the locations of the civilian population and property *vis-à-vis* the theater of operations; the terrain (including the potential for natural disasters resulting from an attack); the accuracy of the weapons used; the weather; the nature of the target of the attack (e.g., whether it contains explosives or other combustibles capable of inflicting ancillary damage); and the technical skill of the combatants. All of these must be weighed against the military importance of the object of attack. Where the case is a complex one, moreover, the result reached should be not to attack; the golden rule in such situations rests upon the "duty to spare civilians and civilian objects in the conduct of military operations".[168]

The Court of Appeal has recently placed its imprimatur on the model of adjudication put forward in the *Canadian Guidelines*. In *Ali* v. *M.C.I.*,[169] the court held that the proper test for establishing whether serious harm could be related to a protected ground was the "non-comparative approach". This approach, the court noted, does not emphasize comparing levels of risk

---

166 *See, e.g.*, *id.* at 26, n. 30.

167 *Id.* at 26, n. 29.

168 *See, e.g.*, Claude Pilloud, Jean de Preux, Yves Sandoz, Bruno Zimmermann, Philippe Eberlin, Hans Peter Gasser, Claude F. Wengel, *Commentary on the Protocol Additional to the Geneva Conventions of 12 August 1949, and relating to the Protection of the Victims of International Armed Conflicts (Protocol I) in* Commentary on the Additional Protocols of 8 June 1977 to the Geneva Conventions of 12 August 1949, 684 (Y. Sandoz *et al.* eds. 1987) [hereinafter *Commentary on Protocol I*].

169 (F.C.A., no. A-772-96), January 12, 1999.

(either between the applicant and other individuals or between applicant's and other groups). Echoing the jurisprudence of the *Guidelines*, the Court of Appeal ruled that the governing test in Canadian law examines simply whether the claimant has made out a risk of sufficiently serious harm, and whether that harm can be linked to a "reason" for persecution recognized in the Convention refugee definition.[170]

As concerns the role of excessive governmental action in identifying a protected ground, subsequent Canadian cases have largely followed the *Thirunavukkarasu* rationale,[171] although here some contradictions must be noted. It is clear that the Federal Court Trial-Division does not view all restrictions in time of national emergency as constituting persecution, nor as *per se* disproportionate to legitimate State ends.[172] For instance, the Trial Division has ruled that short-term detentions with a view to controlling disruptions[173] or terrorism[174] do not rise to the level of persecution. These cases must be understood as conceptually related to two basic methodologies in determining the scope of persecution. On the one hand, limited restrictions on derogable rights in a national emergency (which is publicly declared) will generally be regarded as non-persecutory. On the other hand, abridgements of non-derogable rights will always be viewed as disproportionate *per se*, and thus as meeting the standard required for serious harm.

Hence, *Interpretation of the Convention Refugee Definition in the Case Law* has approached the question presented in the following way:

---

170 On the other hand, the Court of Appeal has occasionally upheld decisions of the Immigration and Refugee Board which appeared to be following the "comparative" approach. In *Abdi* v. *M.C.I.* (F.C.A., no. A-602-94), June 10, 1997, the claimant had been a Somali who was a member of the Darod clan. Members of the Hawiye clan who also belonged to the United Somali Congress (USC) were involved in killing Darods in Mogadishu. Claimant's son-in-law had been arrested by members of the USC after which he effectively disappeared; his grandchild had been murdered by USC members; and another grandchild had been threatened with murder. Despite this evidence of targeting, the Immigration and Refugee Board denied the claim. A majority of the Court of Appeal found no errors of fact or law in this determination, ruling that a refugee claimant must show that he or she does not simply experience the fear of all citizens caught up in internal armed conflict. The fear must be that experienced by claimant himself or herself (or of a group in which the claimant is a member) of serious harm linked to a Convention ground. The case may be distinguished on the ground that it is really discussing the proximity of the serious harm (the objective reasonableness of the fear) rather than the problem of nexus.

171 The cases discussed herein are analyzed in Interpretation of the Convention Refugee Definition in the Case Law, *supra* § II.3, note 63, § 9.3.3.

172 *Cf.* Brar v. M.E.I. (F.C.T.D., no. IMM 292-93), September 8, 1993, at 3.

173 *Id.*

174 Mahalingham v. S.G.C., (F.C.T.D., no. A-79-93), November 2, 1993, at 6.

> [B]efore finding mistreatment to be non-persecutory because there is an emergency, the Refugee Division must consider several matters. Is there indeed an emergency? Is the particular right being violated a derogable right, or is it non-derogable? If the right is derogable, what is the nature of the particular emergency, what is the extent of this particular derogation, and is there a logical nexus between the emergency and the derogation?[175]

The required inquiry into the non-derogability of the right asserted has generally been taken seriously by the Trial Division. Thus in *Alfred* v. *M.E.I.*, the Trial Division held:

> The tribunal did not assess the physical mistreatment of the applicant by Colombo police in terms of persecution. Under the *International Covenant on Civil and Political Rights* Articles 7 and 4 make clear that no one shall be subjected to torture or to cruel, inhuman or degrading treatment or punishment, even in times of public emergency.[176]

Similarly, the last aspect of the test set forth in *Interpretation of the Convention Refugee Definition in the Case Law* relates, in essence, to whether the derogation is proportional to the ends envisioned, or, in other words, whether it constitutes the least restrictive alternative. The substance of the proposed test is, alternatively phrased, a striking parallel to that put forward by the UNHCR in its brief in *Canas-Segovia.*[177]

Where the claimant has highly distinct characteristics or beliefs which have resulted in individual targeting, the "comparative" versus "non-comparative" analysis does not play a role. In *Hotaki* v. *M.E.I.*,[178] the claimant had been a native and citizen of Afghanistan whose father had been a highly-placed communist official under the (previous) Najibullah regime. The father had arranged for claimant to be a schoolteacher, a position in which he instructed the children of other prominent communist officials. The claimant's brothers had disappeared; his father was killed in his office; and mujahidin guerillas visited claimant regularly. The Federal Court-Trial Division overturned the finding of the Immigration and Refugee Board that

---

[175] Interpretation of the Convention Refugee Definition in the Case Law, *supra* § II.3, note 63, § 9.3.3.

[176] Alfred v. M.E.I. (F.C.T.D., no. IMM-1466-93), April 7, 1994, at 5, *cited in* Interpretation of the Convention Refugee Definition in the Case Law, *supra* § II.3, note 63, § 9.3.3. The court might have added the non-derogable character of common Article 3 to the Geneva Conventions of August 12, 1949 (applicable to internal armed conflict) which includes a bar against torture. *See, e.g,* Commentary to Geneva Convention I, *supra* § I.2, note 40, at 39.

[177] *See, e.g., Brief Amicus Curiae of UNHCR, supra* § II.3, note 93, *in* 2 Int'l J. Refugee L. 390 (1990).

[178] (F.C.T.D., no. IMM-6659-93), November 22, 1994.

the claimant had not been differentially targeted, indicating that the prominence of the father and the regular contact with highly placed communist officials assured that claimant would not receive the same treatment meted out to others in the conflict.

Similarly, in *Osman* v. *M.C.I.*,[179] the claimant was a member of the Hawiye clan who had married a member of the Darod clan and of the Marehan subclan. Applicant's husband had been killed in the general shelling of Hargeissa. Applicant's fear was based on the fact that the Hawiye (her own tribe) now occupied Hargeissa, but that her safety was imperiled because of her marriage to a member of a rival clan. In overturning the Immigration and Refugee Board's original adverse determination, the Trial Division ruled that it was not proper to "hide behind" a civil war scenario in adjudicating claims with highly individualized facts. In this case, the fact that claimant had married a member of a rival clan distinguished her own case from that of other Somalis.

Like U.S. law on the subject, the Federal Court-Trial Division has ruled on occasion that beatings are not necessarily persecution, unless they are carried out for a prolonged period of time and are repetitive. This is highly questionable in light of *Thirunavukkarasu.* Beatings which meet the formal elements of the offence of battery under prevailing standards of criminal law should normally be viewed as violations of non-derogable rights, namely, as torture, inhuman or degrading treatment within the meaning of International Covenant on Civil and Political Rights[180] and under common Article 3 of the Geneva Conventions of August 12, 1949.[181]

U.S. law, as represented by the current jurisprudence of the Board of Immigration Appeals, has now largely followed the general direction taken by Canadian jurisprudence with respect to determining refugee status during periods of upheaval. The regulatory scheme, updated in 1990, provides clear guidance for adjudicating asylum claims where the individual is targeted as the member of a group: in such situations the refugee definition can be satisfied provided that a nexus between the serious harm and one of the enumerated grounds can be made out or otherwise inferred.[182] And, in a precedent case decided in 1996, the Board virtually placed its imprimatur on the non-comparative method.[183]

---

[179] (F.C.T.D., no. IMM-1295-94), January 26, 1995.

[180] ICCPR, *supra* § I.1, note 14, Art. 7.

[181] Geneva Conventions, *supra* § I.1, note 17, common Article 3.

[182] 8 CFR § 208.13(b)(2)(i).

[183] Matter of H-, 21 I&N Dec. 337 (BIA 1996).

*Matter of H-* involved a Somali asylum seeker who was a member of the Darod clan and of the Marehan sub-clan.[184] Applicant had been brutally beaten for 5 days by representatives of the United Somali Congress, a rival faction in the civil war, after being rounded up with other Darods.[185] Applicant's family had also been persecuted, a finding which lent support to the "pattern or practice" of the United Somali Congress in targeting members of the Marehan and their families. Applicant's father, a prominent businessman, had been killed by the United Somali Congress (consisting mostly of members of the Hawiye clan) at his place of business. The family home was attacked and applicant's brother, injured in the assault, was later killed by members of the United Somali Congress while receiving medical treatment in a hospital.[186]

The Board rejected the immigration judge's premise that asylum eligibility does not vest as the result of harm or suffering sustained in clan warfare or civil strife (since such an approach would arguably have the effect of qualifying all those on either side of the conflict).[187] Rather, the Board posed as the sole relevant question whether past persecution had been imposed as the result of a "reason" contained in the refugee definition. The Board answered that question affirmatively, finding that the Somali clans and sub-clans fit the definition of a "particular social group".[188]

---

184 *Id.* at 340. The clans, according to the Board's findings, were entities linked by kinship ties and vocal inflection. The Marehan had been closely associated with the "often brutal regime" of Siad Barre until the latter's overthrow orchestrated by the remaining clans. The revolting clans sought retaliation against those who had benefited from the regime

185 *Id.* at 341.

186 *Id.* at 340.

187 *Id.* at 338, 341. The opinion of the immigration judge in the case, at least on its surface, was a reflection of the Board's decisional law which has been discussed above. In conjunction with its main holding, the immigration court also determined that applicant was not entitled to relief simply because he had been detained by parties to the conflict or beaten by them.

188 *Id.* at 342, *citing Matter of Acosta,* 19 I&N Dec. 211 (BIA 1985), the Board defined a particular social group as being based either on an immutable characteristic (something the applicant cannot change) or one which is so fundamental to the applicant's identity or conscience that he or she ought not to be required to change it: "Clan membership is a highly recognizable characteristic that is acquired at birth and is inextricably linked to family ties." The Board was indebted for its analysis on the "particular social group" question to a Legal Opinion of the Immigration and Naturalization Service's General Counsel. *See* U.S. Immigration and Naturalization Service (Office of the General Counsel), Memorandum: *Whether Somali Clan Membership May Meet the Definition of Membership in a Particular Social Group under the INA* (December 9, 1993) *cited in* U.S. Immigration and Naturalization Service, Basic Law Manual, *supra* § I.1, note 26, at 48.

Three important doctrinal changes are apparent from the Board's fresh view of civil war cases. First, the axiom that "harm or suffering" arising from the conflict will not support an asylum claim is no longer being given preclusive effect as under prior law. Second, the individual seeking asylum clearly is not obligated to show individualized persecution (i.e., that the asylum seeker would be differentially treated or "singled out"), only that past or prospective harm is linked to a refugee ground.

Third and of equal importance, however, the concept originally advanced in *Matter of Vigil*[189] and followed in other cases, namely, that the generalized motives of the combatants in fighting the war could not serve to establish persecutory motive, stands squarely rejected. The Board took great pains to analyze the motives of various Somali clans in "retaliating" against the Marehan in light of the earlier political favoritism of Siad Barre. The Board viewed this historical background as providing important evidence that the harm suffered by the applicant was "on account of" a Convention ground.[190] The "non-comparative" approach virtually followed by the Board restores U.S. analysis to the interpretive standard deemed to govern refugee determinations by respected commentators: the number of persons affected is immaterial to the question of whether persecution in the refugee sense has been established.[191]

Some comment on the background of the case and the historical conditions which gave rise to it is appropriate here. As is evident, *Matter of H-* is technically a "particular social group" case, and not one dealing expressly with political opinion. Nonetheless, it is included in this section of the discussion because it is clear that the Board rested its decision largely on the attributed political profile of the Darod and of the Marehan. Historically, warfare among rival clans in Somalia was not aimed at political ends. Somalia had been dominated by nomadic groups which roved the countryside and fought. The organizing social principle of these group conflicts was that of family lineage, a genealogical network called *jiffo*. The conflicts themselves were subject to rules (called *xeer*). The *xeer* provided for peace

---

189 19 I&N Dec. 572 (BIA 1988).

190 Matter of H-, 21 I&N Dec. 337, 342-343 (BIA 1996).

191 As Atle Grahl-Madsen has written:

> Once a person is subjected to a measure of such gravity that we consider it 'persecution,' that person is 'persecuted' in the sense of the Convention, irrespective of how many others may be subject to the same or similar measures.

1 Grahl-Madsen, *supra* § I.1, note 7, at 213.

negotiations (*shir)* at which compensation by the loosing side may be agreed upon (*mag*).[192]

At the time of the applicant's claim, the clans had become substantially politicized. The various clans had organized into virtually rival political parties. In the wake of the overthrow of Siad Barre (January 1991), the warring factions organized themselves into hybrid entities which although they drew upon clan membership, were by no means based exclusively on the clan principle. Included in these self-styled organizations was the United Somali Congress (the organization which persecuted applicant) and the Somali National Front (principally supported by the Marehan, applicant's clan). The foregoing observations clarify that attributed political beliefs explain much of the background of the Somalian civil war (and thus much of applicant's claim). They also illustrate ongoing themes of this study: (i) that the grounds are, in fact, fluid and not fixed; and (ii) that they track the broader concept of "persecution" which is intended to create a framework of protection for situations in which there is a difference between the persecutor's views or status and that of the victim which the persecutor will not tolerate.

*Matter of S-P-*[193] pursues the broad direction introduced by *Matter of H-*, while clarifying the emerging framework of human rights and humanitarian law standards which is coming to dominate interpretation of the Convention refugee definition. According to the majority opinion in *Matter of S-P*, the asylum seeker had been kidnapped in November 1993 from a refugee camp by members of the LTTE, forcing him to work as a welder at one of their camps. In March of 1994, the camp was raided by the Sri Lankan army. Applicant was taken to Colombo prison where he was kept from March 25 until September 18, 1994. There he was suffocated, made the subject of water torture, and threatened with imminent death while being accused of being a member of the LTTE. He was released from prison after his father bribed one of the guards, eventually making his way to the United States. The immigration judge hearing the asylum claim denied the application, finding that the abuse inflicted on applicant arose by virtue of the "ongoing civil strife in Sri Lanka," and that, therefore, the relief sought was not contemplated by the Refugee Act.[194]

The critical question in the case was transparently whether the claimant had suffered on account of a protected ground for purposes of establishing

---

192 *See generally* G. Prunier, *Somalia: Civil War, Intervention and Withdrawal*, 15 (1) Refugee Survey Quarterly 35, 37 (1996).

193 21 I&N Dec. 486 (BIA 1996).

194 *Id.* at 487-488.

past persecution, or whether he had been molested in the course of an otherwise lawful investigation. In a long-overdue advance in refugee doctrine, the Board accepted that a claim could be based on characteristics or beliefs attributed to the claimant by the persecutor. Methodologically, the Board held that an asylum seeker is not under a burden to show that he or she would punished solely on account of one of the enumerated grounds. All that is required is that the claimant adduce some evidence showing that persecution on a protected ground is reasonable.[195] To hold the applicant to a higher burden, the Board opined, would contravene the Supreme Court's decision in *INS* v. *Cardoza-Fonseca*,[196]in which the Court clearly offered a "liberal" view of the claimant's burden with respect to the statutory standard for asylum, holding that the refugee definition would be satisfied if there were as little as a 10% chance of persecution resulting from the alien's return.

The Board clearly accepted that a political motive could be inferred from the factual setting (i.e., that the incentives of the persecutor in threatening or imposing serious harm need not be explicitly made out but could be established looking at the objective factors in the case). And the Board set out the criteria it would look to in determining whether this objective test was satisfied:

> (i) Indications in the particular case that the abuse was directed toward modifying or punishing opinion rather than conduct, e.g., statements or actions by the perpetrators of abuse out of proportion to non-political ends;
>
> (ii) Treatment of others in the population who might be confronted by government agents in similar circumstances;
>
> (iii) Conformity to procedures for criminal prosecution or military law including developing international norms regarding the law of war;
>
> (iv) The extent to which anti-terrorism laws are defined and applied to suppress political opinion as well as illegal conduct (e.g., an act may broadly prohibit "disruptive" activities to permit application to peaceful as well as violent expression of views);
>
> (v) The extent to which suspected opponents are subjected to arbitrary arrest, detention and abuse.[197]

---

195 *Id.* at 489-490, *citing* Matter of Fuentes, 19 I&N Dec. 658 (BIA 1988).

196 480 U.S. 421 (1987).

197 Matter of S-P-, 21 I&N Dec. 486, 494 (BIA 1996). The Board has not always been faithful to the inferential analysis to which it clearly gave its approval in Matter of *S-P-*. *See, e.g.*, Matter of T-M-B-, 21 I&N Dec. 775 (BIA 1997), discussed *infra*, this section.

The foregoing guidelines, the Board opined, were relevant to establish whether the abuse (i) "was directed toward punishing or modifying perceived political views" (rather than punishing criminal acts); (ii) arose out of a lawful act of war; or (iii) was connected to some reason unrelated to the refugee definition.[198] Taking as the cornerstone of its adjudicative analysis the doctrine of proportionality, the BIA concluded that the claimant had been mistreated because of an imputed political opinion (perceived identification with the LTTE cause). The Board supported its analysis in the present case with general findings regarding the treatment of Tamils by the Sri Lankan government, including their routine arrest in security-related incidents.[199]

The most important development of the case, however, is clearly the Board's reliance on human rights and humanitarian norms as providing the parameters of "legitimate" State action. Law enforcement or military action which exceeds the limits set by the normative standards of human rights and humanitarian law, at least where such excesses appear on their face to relate to specific classes, will give rise to an inference that harm or suffering is being inflicted because of a protected ground. As one noted human rights commentator has written:

> In determining whether State measures in a civil war situation have a legitimate military character, or whether they constitute political persecution, the German Federal Constitutional Court has followed exactly the same approach as is used by international courts and similar organs in international human rights and economic law. *Limitations of rights of individuals are only legitimate if they serve a legitimate goal and if, in their actual extent, they do not go further than necessary in order to achieve that goal.* If either they do not in fact serve the invoked interest or are disproportionate, they constitute political, racial or religious persecution if they take place in the context of a political, ethnic or religious conflict.[200]

*Matter of S-P-* has specifically adapted the foregoing proportionality doctrine to civil war situations. Naturally, human rights analysis will not

---

[198] Matter of S-P-, 21 I&N Dec. 486, 495-496 (BIA 1996). *See also Handbook, supra* § I.1, note 30, ¶ 57.

[199] Matter of S-P-, 21 I&N Dec. 486, 496-497 (BIA 1996). The Board followed *Singh* v. *Ilchert,* 63 F.3d 1501 (9th Cir. 1995), which governed the present case since it arose in the Ninth Circuit. The Board also proceeded to "harmonize" the *Singh* case with its own precedent so as to arrive at an essentially new methodology for deciding civil war cases, applicable nationwide. One limitation on this holding must be noted: *Matter of T-,* 20 I&N Dec. 571 (BIA 1992) remains valid precedent insofar as it holds that an asylum seeker must do more than establish serious mistreatment at the hands of the government or by a particular group to establish eligibility.

[200] Walter Kalin, *Refugees and Civil Wars: Only a Matter of Interpretation*, 3 Int'l J. Refugee L. 435, 450 (1991). [Emphasis in original].

have so much a bearing on claims arising out of internal armed conflict as will general principles of international humanitarian law. Indeed, *Matter of S-P-* reveals concretely the degree to which the Board was prepared to turn to the law of war in assessing whether those facing serious harm in a civil war context could claim refugee status.

> Although the Board has ruled that violations of the Geneva Conventions do not create an independent basis for asylum, Matter of Medina, 19 I&N Dec. 734 (1988), there may be situations in which the severity of the violations of the Geneva Convention [sic] may support an inference that the abuse is grounded in one of the protected grounds under the asylum law.[201]

Notwithstanding *Matter of S-P-,* the case law of the BIA dealing with the situation of recruitment by insurgents arising since *Elias-Zacarias* has placed strong reliance upon the decision's "conservative" aspects, and accordingly emphasized the applicant's burden to show affirmatively that serious harm is tied to the political opinion ground. Accordingly, in *Matter of T-M-B-,*[202] the asylum seeker, a native and citizen of the Philippines, had been approached by the New People's Army (NPA), a revolutionary group, with a view to recruiting claimant and obtaining financial support from her. The applicant was opposed to supporting the NPA "because they kill people, women and children". Representatives of the NPA became incensed at applicant's expression of opposition and demanded a "revolutionary tax" from her. When this was later doubled, applicant protested that she was unable to pay it. This led to applicant's being slapped and cut with a knife by NPA representatives.

Despite the conscientious opposition of the claimant to the insurgents' demands, the latter's' clear involvement in a political cause, and the act of serious harm which had been imposed on claimant as a result, the Board concluded that the NPA were motivated solely by the need for money and that the refugee definition did not protect against acts of extortion.[203] The

---

[201] Matter of S-P-, 21 I&N 486, 494, n. 3 (BIA 1996).

[202] 21 I&N Dec. 775 (BIA 1997). The case has now been reversed by the Ninth Circuit. *See* Borja v. INS, 175 F.3d 732 (9th Cir. 1999), discussed *infra* this section. The *T-M-B-* case is still damaging, however, because of the proclivity of the Board to apply its holding outside the circuit of decision.

[203] Introduced into the record was a "country profile" for the Philippines prepared by the [U.S.] Department of State. The profile revealed the following:

> [A] large proportion of Philippine asylum applicants allege that the NPA threatens them with death or other harm for refusing to support that organization financially. In most instances, the NPA is not interested in the political opinion of the intended victim but in the victim's wealth.

Board set forth the now established principle that an asylum applicant need not show "conclusively" her basis for fearing persecution. However, there must be some evidence that the harm feared or experienced relates to a protected ground. The Board indicated that the evidence pointed essentially to "criminal extortion" as the basis for the NPA's actions, not the political opinion of the applicant.

Similarly in *Matter of C-A-L-*,[204] the applicant had been a member of the Guatemalan armed forces who had been sent into the mountains to combat guerilla forces. His file, along with those of five other soldiers, had been retrieved by the guerillas at the time of his discharge in 1989. Subsequent to discharge, the applicant discovered that the guerillas were looking for him. The Board concluded that the predicate for the applicant's potential recruitment was his artillery expertise, not an imputed political opinion of the applicant's.[205]

Finally, in Matter of *V-T-S-*,[206] the respondent, a Philippine national and a native of the island of Mindano, had been receiving threatening letters from the Moro National Liberation Front (MNLF), a rebel Muslim group, since 1983. Respondent's father (who maintained a highly profitable business in the Philippines) had received similar letters since the early 1970s. The asylum seeker's brother and sister were kidnapped in 1989 and 1991 respectively, the latter development triggering applicant's asylum filing. The BIA dismissed the respondent's appeal, holding that, according to the evidence, the kidnappers were motivated by the respondent's wealth, not by a perception of his political leanings or other characteristic recognized as a reason for persecution.

The case is representative of the proclivity of both Canadian and U.S. tribunals not to recognize refugee status where wealth is the feature of the claimant's persona which serves as the basis for serious harm. Such cases appear to rest on the twin doctrines that (i) there is no internationally

---

Matter of T-M-B-, 21 I&N Dec. 775, 779 (BIA 1996). Yet the extortion efforts took place within an environment in which it was clear that those seeking the claimant's money would view her failure to pay the "revolutionary tax" as a political act. The divergence of the Board's methodology from that put forward in *Desir* v. *Ilchert*, 840 F.2d 723 (9th Cir. 1985) is self-evident.

204 21 I&N Dec. 754 (BIA 1997).

205 *Id.* at 757. Again, the results of applicant's non-cooperation with the insurgents (manifested by his flight) remained substantially unexamined by the Board. *Compare* Montecino v. INS, 915 F.2d 518, 520, holding that former members of the Salvadoran armed forces who fear being killed by insurgents after their discharge qualify for asylum under the particular social group ground.

206 21 I&N Dec. 792 (BIA 1997).

respected right to acquire assets; and, accordingly (ii) the claimant can be required to relinquish his or her wealth without compromising a "characteristic or belief" which is fundamental to the asylum seeker's conscience.[207] The case may demonstrate as well the unfairness of such an approach. Physical restraint and a consequent loss of personal liberty are certainly serious harm. Where the evidence shows that this punishment is being imposed because a politically-minded group perceives a non-complying individual as a threat to its program, a "reason" for persecution should be deemed to have been made out. In all such cases, however, those who do not cooperate should be distinguished from individuals who supinely accede to the insurgents' demands.[208]

In the area of recruitment, the Ninth Circuit has felt itself restricted by the Supreme Court's holding in *Elias-Zacarias*. As noted earlier, in *Sangha* v. *INS*,[209] the Ninth Circuit affirmed denial of an Indian asylum claim brought by the son of a prominent critic of Sikh insurgents after several rebels had attempted to recruit the claimant and his brother. The Ninth Circuit rejected the theory of imputed political opinion, holding that the evidence made it clear that the rebels' motivations were to deprive the father of claimant's support and to gain the applicant as a recruit in the struggle in Khalistan. For the most part, the court did not adopt a context-dependent analysis and looked austerely at the nexus requirement.

Yet the court in *Sangha* gave clear indications that, given an appropriate factual record, attributed political opinion remains a viable theory of asylum relief. In *Vera-Valera* v. *INS*,[210] the applicant was the president of a co-operative dedicated to constructing a building which would enable street vendors to sell their wares in a stable structure and environment. The building was opposed by the *Sendero-Luminoso*, a guerilla movement dedicated to the overthrow of the Peruvian government, because the existence of street vendors enabled the rebels to circulate propaganda on the street undetected. Members of the *Sendero Luminoso* both telephoned and left written messages advising applicant that if he did not cease to advocate for the construction project, he would be killed.[211]

---

[207] Hathaway, *supra* § I.1, note 7, at 166.

[208] As stated by the Ninth Circuit in *Maldonado-Cruz* v. *INS* , 883 F.2d 788 (9th cir. 1990), objective non-support for a politically motivated group gives rise to political opinion persecution, since the claimant's overt act of resistance will be perceived as a position of political opposition.

[209] 103 F.3d 1482 (9th Cir. 1997).

[210] 147 F.3d 1036 (9th Cir. 1998).

[211] *Id.* at 1037-38.

The Board had dismissed applicant's appeal noting that there was nothing "political" about the proposed construction. The Ninth Circuit disagreed, maintaining that what is "political" must be viewed from the perspective of the persecutor. In this case, there had been unequivocal evidence in the form of statements of the members of the *Sendero Luminoso* as to the latter's outlook toward those who were in favor of the construction project. Vera-Valera was accused of being a capitalist, a spy for the government, a bureaucrat and a traitor.[212] The very statements of applicant's putative persecutors, in other words, made it clear that they regarded his activity as political, and that they were prepared to punish it on that basis.

Recent jurisprudence of the Ninth Circuit reveals that the appeals court may be turning to actual political opinion as a way of resolving cases which previously would have fallen arguably under the "neutrality" rubric or have been resolved utilizing attributed political opinion. In *Gonzales-Neyra* v. *INS*,[213] for instance, the court had before it a situation closely resembling recruitment, that of extortion. A Peruvian businessman had been approached by members of the *Sendero Luminoso* with a view to obtaining financial support for their cause.[214] The asylum seeker made an initial "contribution" of $300, but advised the Shining Path representatives who approached him that he would make no further "donations" nor would be collaborate with a group which was ruining the country. Immediately after this encounter, applicant fled his home and his business, later learning that the two men who had approached him had been taken into custody by the authorities.[215] Fearing retribution because he would be perceived as the informant, applicant fled Peru.

The immigration judge hearing the case denied asylum, ruling that the insurgents were not motivated by a characteristic or belief of the claimant when they approached him for money and there was nothing in applicant's subsequent refusal to pay which caused their perception to change. The Board's determination upholding this theory and adding the rationale of changed country conditions, dismissed the appeal. The Ninth Circuit, however, ruled that the applicant's refusal to pay was an actual political opinion of being opposed to the *Sendero Luminoso.* The initial approach which was motivated by economic incentives had been transformed by the applicant's express refusal to "collaborate" Evidence showing that applicant's family were harassed and threatened only after the incident in which claimant

---

212 *Id.* at 1039.

213 122 F.3d 1293 (9th Cir. 1997).

214 *Id.* at 1295.

215 *Id.*

expressed his opposition to the guerrilla cause made clear that it was claimant's opinion which was the focus of guerilla attention, not his finances.[216]

A number of recent decisions expand the rationale developed in *Gonzalez-Neyra*. In *Borja* v. *INS*,[217] the asylum seeker feared serious harm at the hands of the New People's Army (NPA), a revolutionary group dedicated to overthrowing the Philippine government. The claimant's fear stemmed, in part, from her refusal to comply with the NPA's extortion demands. As noted earlier in analyzing the Board's treatment of this case,[218] Ms. Borja was a Philippine national who, in September 1992, had been approached by members of the NPA with the dual objective of getting the applicant to join the organization and to support it financially.

> The asylum seeker's initial response was to refuse the NPA's demands—explaining that she was pro-government. NPA members then pointed a gun at applicant. Claimant insisted on her position of not joining, asserting that NPA kills women and children, but agreed to pay the revolutionary "taxes" as a way of not being killed. The extortion demands continued to be paid until February 1993 when a demand for 6,000 pesos could not be met. At this juncture, NPA members became incensed, beat applicant, slashed her with a knife, and threatened her with death if she did not produce the money. This forced applicant to go into hiding and, ultimately, to flee the Philippines.

The Board had denied the claim, reasoning that, while the persecutor's motives could be mixed in imposing serious harm, there had to be some evidence that the applicant was being targeted because of a protected ground. And the Board ruled, based on the record, that the NPA's incentives had been exclusively economic. This determination was reversed by the Board as being hopelessly at odds with the record. The Ninth Circuit agreed with the Board's majority to some extent, finding that the NPA was motivated, at least in part, by economic incentives. But, the panel reasoned, no reasonable fact-finder could conclude that claimant's outspoken statement in opposition to the NPA played no role in her subsequent encounters with the guerilla group, the latter's physical abuse of her, and the threat to take her life. The *Borja* case thus provides a clear example of the kind of evidence "direct or circumstantial" which will point toward persecution on a protected ground in the extortion/recruitment context: an

---

216 *Id.* at 1296.

217 175 F.3d 732 (9th Cir. 1999).

218 The Ninth Circuit's decision reverses the Board of Immigration Appeals' decision in *Matter of T-M-B-*, 21 I&N Dec. 775 (BIA 1997).

outspoken expression of political partisanship hostile to the insurgent cause will take the case out of the otherwise preclusive rationale of *Elias-Zacarias*.

The ground of imputed political opinion was adopted by the Ninth Circuit to overturn the Board in *Del Agila* v. *INS*.[219] In *Del Aguila*, the asylum seeker was a Peruvian national who owned several gold mines. He had been forced, under threat of death, to make monthly payments to the *Sendero Luminoso*. Effective extortion went on for about two years, at which time the payments stopped. At this juncture, the guerillas kidnapped applicant, his brother and two of applicant's employees. All four were made subject to a "popular" trial. The four victims were forced to sign a statement of affiliation with the Shining Path and were then accused of being traitors to the guerilla organization. They were sentenced to death. Del Agila and his brother escaped to seek asylum in the U.S. The two employees, however, were killed.

As it had in *Matter of T-M-B-*, the Board ruled that, although motivations could be mixed, there was no evidence in the present case that the *Sendero Luminoso* were interested in anything but the claimant's finances. The facts presented, according to the Board, a pure case of criminal extortion. The Ninth Circuit took issue with the Board's majority on this point holding that, while extortion was undoubtedly one motive, it could not be said to be the exclusive one. The appeals court panel found that the overwhelming evidence in the record revealed that the claimant *was viewed* by the guerillas as hostile to the latter's cause. This flowed from the "popular" trial which the claimant had been forced to undergo as well as from the claimant's being characterized as a "traitor". Accordingly, at least one motive leading the guerillas to impose serious harm was their view of the applicant's political orientation.

*Del Agila* deals with the question of attributed characteristics and beliefs in the extortion/recruitment context while *Borja* deals with the same problem from the perspective of the claimant's own sincerely held and clearly articulated political beliefs. *Del Agila* shows clearly, however, that where the persecutor's own statements and actions reveal a political animus in imposing serious harm (as opposed to mere economic incentives), the dispute between the claimant and his persecutors can no longer be fairly characterized as a merely "personal" matter, but rather as an opposition in values leading to persecution, i.e., as a difference in the beliefs or status of the persecutor and those of the victim which the persecutor will not tolerate.[220]

---

219 216 F.3d 1082 (9th Cir. 2000).

220 *Cf.* Hernandez-Ortiz v. INS, 777 F.2d 509, 516 (9th Cir. 1985).

## § IV.4(b). International Humanitarian Law as the Basis for Resolving Refugee Claims Arising From Conditions of Armed Conflict

As the above recital shows, there has been considerable unevenness with respect to evolution of the case law in both Canada and the United States concerning the appropriate methodology for determining refugee status and asylum during periods of upheaval. The best models to date remain *Matter of S-P-*,[221] *Matter of H-*,[222] *Singh* v. *Ilchert*[223] and the *Canadian Civil War Guidelines*.[224] These models continue to follow the broad, flexible and inferential analysis which is the distinguishing characteristic of the jurisprudence covering asylum claims arising from civil war situations. The case law and the *Guidelines* clearly establish that the most critical evidence of linking persecution to a protected ground is to be found in systematic violations of the laws of war being practiced against a discernable group.

Insofar as internal armed conflict is concerned, lawful restraints on belligerent action are set forth in common Article 3[225] of the Geneva Conventions, as well as in Protocol II[226] to those Conventions. Common Article 3 proscribes violence to life and person, murder, mutilation, extrajudicial punishments, the taking of hostages and all forms of inhuman or degrading treatment with respect to those not actually involved in the combat. Common Article 3 has been supplemented by Protocol II which, as an aspect of the developing principles of humanity codified in common Article 3, contains specific principles which restrict the military actions of a belligerent in periods of civil war.

The extent to which customary international law controls the manner in which war is waged in civil conflicts had, prior to the efforts of the Yugoslavian War Crimes Tribunal, remained in doubt. As Theodor Meron had presciently written regarding the possible growth of customary law for internal wars:

> It is inevitable that, in developing international law for internal armed conflicts, the central source for the rules will be the principles of humanity. No self-respecting state would challenge the applicability of such principles in internal armed conflict. More specific rules, such as proportionality, the prohibition of direct attack on civilians, the prohibition of indiscriminate and

---

221 21 I&N Dec. 486 (BIA 1996).

222 21 I&N Dec. 337 (BIA 1996).

223 63 F.3d 1501 (9th Cir. 1995).

224 *Canadian Civil War Guidelines, supra* § III.3, note 39.

225 Geneva Conventions, *supra* § I.1, note 17, common Article 3.

226 Protocol II, *supra* § I.1, note 17.

> disproportionate attacks, the prohibition of means and methods of warfare that cause unnecessary suffering, can and should be regarded as necessary and proper derivations from the principles of humanity. The incorporation of such rules for internal wars in the national manuals of military law would be a necessary first step.[227]

The requirement that civilians be protected from the dangers of military operations in international wars was in fact a rule of long standing under customary law.[228] The *Commentary to Protocol II* adopts the view that this principle is equally applicable, as a matter of customary law, in internal conflicts.[229]

Jean Pictet has outlined the essential policies of the law of war in his seminal work, *Development and Principles of International Humanitarian Law*.[230] A core principle is that the civilian population must be protected from the dangers of military operations.[231] To that end, it is incumbent upon the parties to the conflict to differentiate between the civilian populace and the combatants.[232] The latter must never be the object of attack or reprisals. As set forth in the *Commentary to Protocol II*:

> The principle of immunity of those who do not participate directly in hostilities has in fact been recognized for a long time, in situations of both national and international armed conflict. Thus, in 1863, the Lieber Code [prepared for the Union Army in the American civil war] already provided that "an unarmed citizen is to be spared in person, property and honor, as much as the exigencies of war will permit."[233]
>
> * * *
>
> Further, it is not admissible that one of the parties could destroy or render useless objects indispensable to the civilian population living in the part of the territory under its control because it suspected that the latter supported or sympathized with the adversary. It should be recalled that collective punishments and pillage are prohibited by the Protocol.[234]

---

227 *See, e.g.*, T. Meron, Human Rights and Humanitarian Norms as Customary Law 74 (1989).

228 *See, e.g., Commentary to Protocol I, supra* § IV.4(a), note 168, at 593.

229 *Commentary to Protocol II, supra* § I.2, note 36, at 1450. *See also* S/RES/955, Nov. 8, 1994, the statute of the criminal tribunal established for violations of international humanitarian law deemed to have taken place in Rwanda. The latter resolution reposes jurisdiction in the tribunal for violations of common Article 3 and Protocol II. *Id.*, art 4.

230 Pictet, *supra* § I.1, note 18, at 71-78.

231 *See, e.g.,* Protocol II, *supra* § I.1, note 17*a*, Art. 13(1).

232 *Id.*, Art. 13(2).

233 *Commentary to Protocol II, supra* § I.2, note 36, at 1443.

234 *Id.* at 1459.

Accordingly, the starvation of civilians is prohibited,[235] and property essential to the survival of the population cannot be destroyed.[236] Acts which are intended to spread terror through the civilian population are unlawful.[237] Affirmative precautions are required to spare the civilian population or, at least, to minimize its injuries:

> The implementation of such practices requires that precautions are taken both by the party launching the attack during the planning, decision and action stages of the attack, and by the party that is attacked. For example, military installations should not be intentionally placed in the midst of a concentration of civilians with a view to using the latter as a shield for the purposes of making the adverse party abandon an attack, without forgetting any other safety measures which are explicitly laid down in Protocol II.[238]

A central doctrine in humanitarian law, as in human rights law, is that of proportionality: only the minimum force necessary to disable the enemy should be deployed, and no military force should be used where the collateral effects to civilians and their property would be disproportionate when measured against the utility of the attack. Under this broad prohibition, indiscriminate attacks are barred, as are attacks which are likely to cause excessive loss and injury to civilians and their property in light of the concrete and direct military advantages to be gained by the military action contemplated.[239] The idea that the proportionality rule applies in internal armed conflict by virtue of common Article 3 (as supplemented by Protocol II) is fully developed in the *Commentary to Protocol II*:

> It is appropriate to recall here the most important of these principles, i.e., the principle to use the minimum force required to harm the enemy, the principle of distinction and the principle of proportionality which only intervene when it is not possible to ensure the total immunity of the population:
>
> > - parties engaged in a conflict do not have the unlimited right as regards the means of injuring the enemy;
> >
> > - a distinction should be made at all times between persons participating in hostilities and the civilian population, so that the latter may be spared as far as possible;
> >
> > - the relation between the direct military advantage anticipated from an attack and the harmful effects which could result on the persons and objects protected should be considered in advance.

---

235 Protocol I, *supra* § I.1, note 17, Art. 54.

236 Protocol II, *supra* § I.1, note 17, Art. 14.

237 Protocol II, *supra* § I.1, note 17, Art. 13(2).

238 *Commentary to Protocol II, supra* § I.2, note 36, at 1449.

239 *Id.* at 1450.

These trends in humanitarian law and doctrine have been confirmed by developments in modern international penal law. Under recent jurisprudence of the Yugoslavian War Crimes Tribunal, a breach of the fundamental principles codified in common Article 3 or in Protocol II to the Geneva Conventions will give rise to criminal liability on the part of the perpetrator under the principle of universal jurisdiction.[240]

Violations of international humanitarian law carried out against those who are perceived to be identified with another party to the conflict may thus give rise to a finding that the victims of the violation have been persecuted within the meaning of the Refugee Convention and that the persecution relates to a Convention ground.[241] Such harm can result from implementation of a number of policies on the part of a belligerent, including the following:

1. **Compulsory depopulation programs.** An example of the suggested adoption of humanitarian law principles by refugee doctrine can be found in the forced migration policy which was pursued in El Salvador in the 1980s. That policy, one of scale, was aimed at emptying out pockets of guerilla resistance through the forcible transfer of civilians. The purpose of the program was to deprive the insurgents of needed shelter and provisions by a population thought to be sympathetic to the rebel cause.[242] Such displacement of the civilian population is clearly barred by Protocol II, Article 17 which provides:

> 1. The displacement of the civilian population shall not be ordered for reasons related to the conflict unless the security of the civilians involved, or imperative military reasons so demand. Should such displacements have to be

[240] Decision of the Defence Motion for Interlocutory Appeal on Jurisdiction in the Matter of Dusko Tadic, Case No. IT-94-AR72 (Int'l Trib. for the Prosecution of Persons Responsible for Serious Violations of International Humanitarian Law Committed in the Territory of the Former Yugoslavia since 1991) [hereinafter *Tadic Appeal*]. In the *Tadic Appeal,* the Yugoslavian War Crimes Tribunal virtually held that violations of the foregoing principles give rise to criminal liability despite the fact that neither common Article 3 nor Protocol II contains a criminal sanctions clause. The Tribunal's ruling implies, although it does not explicitly hold, that the fundamental principles codified in Article 3 and Protocol II constitute *jus cogens.*

[241] *Canadian Civil War Guidelines, supra* § III.3, note 39, at 26, n. 30.

[242] *See. e.g.*, Memorandum prepared by Dan Smulian to Patrick Young of CARECEN [Central American Refugee Center] and dated August 10, 1995 at 5, n. 9 *quoting Central America 1981: Report of the Committee of Foreign Affairs,* U.S. House of Representatives, March 1981, at 26. For a general discussion, *see* Mark R. von Sternberg, *Overview of Temporary Protected Status and the Deferred Enforced Departure Program With a Note on the Viability of Salvadoran Asylum Claims, in* 1 1995-96 Immigration and Nationality Law Handbook 462, 473-80 (American Immigration Lawyers' Association ed. 1995).

> carried out, all possible measures shall be taken in order that the civilian population may be received under satisfactory conditions of shelter, hygiene, health, safety and nutrition.
>
> 2. Civilians shall not be compelled to leave their own territory for reasons connected to the conflict.[243]

The *Commentary to Protocol II* confirms that the displacement of the civilian population can be effected only in two situations: (i) the security of the population involved; (ii) the imperative of military necessity. The *Commentary* also sets forth that such displacements should never be ordered for political incentives. In explaining what constitutes political motivation, moreover, the *Commentary* indicates:

> Clearly imperative military reasons cannot be justified by political motives. For example, it would be prohibited to move a population in order to exercise more effective control over a dissident group.[244]

A humanitarian law violation consisting of mass civilian displacements based on an incentive to control the affected group politically could thus also constitute an act of collective persecution for purposes of the refugee definition. Such forced internal movements should be viewed as instances in which humanitarian law principles are coming to converge with refugee analysis. In this case, serious harm has been imposed based on the government's views with regard to the political inclinations of the population (attributed political opinion or attributed membership in a particular social group). The government's conduct is thus both a humanitarian law violation and an act of serious harm which is linked to a protected ground.

2. **Official policies which are based on "ethnic cleansing".** The humanitarian law analysis suggested herein would have particular relevance with respect to wanton acts of "ethnic cleansing" (taking the form of forced displacements based on explicit ethnic lines) which have characterized the war in Yugoslavia as well as civil conflicts in the former Soviet Union (now the CIS). One writer has made clear the implications for the refugee definition of humanitarian law violations based upon the phenomenon of "ethnic cleansing":

> [F]or purposes of this study, the major political context which organizes impediments to the return of forcibly displaced populations to places of previous occupation is that of ethnic cleansing. This is a despicable term which has been coined as a euphemism for large scale deportations, expulsions, evictions and the removal of population groups from their places

---

243 Protocol II, *supra* § I.1, note 17, Arts. 17(1) and (2).

244 *Commentary to Protocol II, supra* § I.2, note 36, at 1473.

> of origin as a strategy for achieving specific political objectives. In its first *Interim Report*, the Commission of Experts established to investigate serious violations of humanitarian law committed in the former Yugoslavia viewed ethnic cleansing as a means of "rendering an area ethnically homogeneous by using force or intimidation to remove persons of given groups from the area." The Commission subsequently elaborated upon this view in its *Final Report* by defining ethnic cleansing as a "purposeful policy designed by one ethnic or religious group to remove by violent and terror-inspiring means the civilian population of another ethnic or religious group from certain geographic areas".[245]

Expulsions of this type have most recently materialized in the CIS after the dissolution of the former Soviet Union. Specifically, five conflicts have given rise to incidents of "ethnic cleansing": (i) Meskhetians in the Fergana Valley, Uzbekistan (June 1989); (ii) the Georgia-South Ossetian conflict (1990-1992); (iii) the Ingush-North Ossetian conflict (1992); (iv) the Georgia-Abkhaz conflict (1991-1994); and (v) the Armenian-Azerbaijani conflict (1991-1994).[246]

3. **The deliberate shelling of non-combatant sites with accompanying destruction of civilian homes and other property**. Perhaps the best example of this type of humanitarian law violation and its implications for refugee analysis can be gleaned from the relentless shelling of Sarajevo by the Bosnian Serbs during that phase of the Yugoslavian War which took place in Bosnia-Herzegovina. The deliberate targeting of civilian sites was unmistakable and included the destruction of hospitals, shopping and commercial districts, religious sites, and apartment complexes.[247]

Such attacks clearly offend the principle that the civilian population can never be made the object of attack.[248] As concerns the destruction of homes and other buildings which serve as civilian shelters, Rule 6 of the *Declaration of International Humanitarian Law Governing the Conduct of Hostilities in Non-International Conflicts* provides as follows:

---

[245] Chaloka Beyani, *A Political and Legal Analysis of the Problems of the Return of Forcibly Transferred Populations*, 16 (3) Refugee Survey Quarterly 1, 2 (1997).

[246] *See* Bohdan Nahajlo, *Forcible Population Transfers, Deportations and Ethnic Cleansing in the CIS: Problems in Search of Responses*, 16 (3) Refugee Survey Quarterly 26, 43-52 (1997).

[247] *Final Report of the Commission of Experts Established Pursuant to Security Council Resolution* 780, U.N. SCOR, 49th Sess., Annex at 3, U.N. Doc. S/1994/674, 45 (1994) [hereinafter *Final Report of the Commission of Experts for Yugoslavia*].

[248] Protocol II, *supra* § I.1, note 17, Art. 14.

> **Prohibition of attacks on dwellings and other installations used only by the civilian population**
>
> The general rule prohibiting attacks against the civilian population implies, as a corollary, the prohibition of attacks on dwellings and other installations which are used only by the civilian population.[249]

The serious harm entailed in these humanitarian law violations would clearly give rise to a finding that persecution had been imposed on a protected ground. The attack on Sarajevo was an aspect of the broader Serbian policy of "ethnic cleansing" which informed Serbian military policy throughout the war. The Bosnian Serbs, in formulating their attack, were seeking to weaken the resolve of those who were opposed to Serbian hegemony in the region.[250]

For purposes of refugee analysis, it is immaterial in the foregoing situations that those injured are not personally known to the belligerent inflicting the harm or that they have not been selected for differential treatment. In such cases, the asylum seeker has received injury as part of a larger aggregate of persons whom the persecutor is treating as a political or social threat. The "reasons" underlying the conflict round out the refugee analysis and show conclusively that the racial, ethnic, political or religious causes giving rise to the conflict inform the individualized act of persecution and show that it is related to a protected ground.

The essential precepts of humanitarian law go far to support the foregoing interpretation of the refugee definition as applied during periods of internal upheaval. As Jean Pictet has written, humanitarian law constitutes a balance between military necessity and the requirements of humanity.[251] Accordingly, a belligerent is not unrestricted with respect to the ways and means of warfare, but must weigh the respect due to humans against the rigors of military necessity and public order in executing military strategy.

Military action taken against an adversary which is disproportionate to the accepted goal of weakening or debilitating enemy strength offends the foregoing balance. Moreover, where military action is initiated against an undefended site consisting of non-combatants, the need for military necessity vanishes. It is at this juncture that the methodology set forth in

---

[249] International Institute for Humanitarian Law, *Declaration of International Humanitarian Law Governing the Conduct of Hostilities in Non-International Conflicts*, (Extract from *the International Review of the Red Cross, September* – October 1990), Rule 6 (San Remo, Italy 1990).

[250] *Final Report of the Commission of Experts Established Pursuant to Security Council Resolution* 780, *supra* this section, note 247, at 33.

[251] Pictet, *supra* § I.1, note 18, at 63.

*Hernandez-Ortiz* v. *INS*[252] (regarding the unexplained use of governmental force on innocent persons) becomes appropriately extended by analogy to the civil war context. Whenever a belligerent takes military action against civilians or their objects, and there is no basis to believe that a military advantage would be gained thereby, a presumption arises that the belligerents' actions are motivated by political, racial, ethnic or religious animus. Such an approach is consistent with *Matter of S-P-* which seeks to utilize humanitarian law standards in determining whether serious harm threatened or incurred in armed conflict can be said to derive from a Convention or a protected ground.

## § IV.5. Prosecution or Persecution: Refugee Status in the Context of the Purposes and Principles of the United Nations[253]

The law of refugee status is a creation of the 1951 Convention on Refugees which was adopted under the auspices of the United Nations and is deeply informed with the seminal objectives of the World Organization. Accordingly, it is essential to interpret the Convention refugee definition in light of the purposes and principles of the United Nations Charter[254] which include the full realization of individual human rights on a non-discriminatory basis.[255] The refugee definition's essential components must be interpreted

---

[252] 777 F.2d 517 (9th Cir. 1985). In *Hernandez-Ortiz,* the Ninth Circuit Court of Appeals ruled that where a government exercises its might against a family, and such use of force is not accompanied by a criminal prosecution, a presumption arises that the government is motivated by political considerations.

[253] This section draws upon a prior essay by the author. *See generally* Mark R. von Sternberg, *Political Asylum and the Law of Internal Armed Conflict: Refugee Status, Human Rights and Humanitarian Law Concerns,* 5 Int'l J. Refugee L. 153 (1993).

[254] *See* UN Charter, Preamble:

> WE THE PEOPLES OF THE UNITED NATIONS
> DETERMINED
>
> > to save succeeding generations from the scourge of war, which twice in our lifetime has brought untold sorrow to mankind, and
> >
> > to reaffirm faith in fundamental human rights, in the dignity and worth of the human person, in the equal rights of men and women and of nations large and small, and
> >
> > to establish conditions under which justice and respect for obligations arising from treaties and other sources of international law can be maintained, and
> >
> > to promote social progress and better standards of life in larger freedom.

[255] Convention on the Status of Refugees, *supra* § I.1, note 1, Preamble:

with a view to offering special protection to individuals and groups which advance fundamental human rights goals in the face of coercive governmental action as a matter of public policy.

Principally, the discussion which follows in the next two sections explores the asylum seeker's insistence upon basic human rights *vis-à-vis* putatively lawful State prosecution in two discrete areas: individuals resisting preemptively authoritarian regimes (the "democratic entitlement") and those asking for refugee protection based on their refusal to fight in armies engaged in widespread violations of the laws of war (the right not to be a persecutor). These individual refugee contexts raise important public policy issues because of their teleological relationship to the institutional aims of the United Nations, both as reflected in the World Organization's Charter and in historical practice.

Atle Grahl-Madsen has made explicit the view that punishment which is related to the asylum seeker's attachment to a fundamental human right constitutes political opinion persecution within the meaning of the refugee definition.[256] The discussion on draft resistance and rebellion as bases for refugee status is concerned with the human rights integument to the refugee definition mainly in connection with the prosecution versus persecution bar as applied in situations of internal armed conflict. The *Handbook* supports the view that analysis of the refugee definition is contextually dependent on prevailing human rights jurisprudence. Accordingly, where human rights norms are infringed by the State, those punished for conscientiously opposing State action will be deemed to have been persecuted based on the political opinion ground.[257] In assessing the "prosecution versus persecution" bar, moreover, it is essential to examine the status of the law being enforced, particularly in the light of normative standards established under the Universal Declaration on Human Rights,[258] as implemented by the Covenant

---

> Considering that the Charter of the United Nations and the Universal Declaration of Human Rights approved on 10 December 1948 by the General Assembly have affirmed the principle that human beings shall enjoy fundamental human rights and freedoms without discrimination.

256 1 Grahl-Madsen, *supra* § I.1, note 7, at 217.

257 Handbook, *supra* § I.1, note 30, ¶ 59: The prosecution versus persecution preclusion must be determined in the light of prevailing human rights standards. The law being applied may either violate these standards *per se*; or the law may be applied in a discriminatory way so as to frustrate the equal protection component of human rights doctrine. *See id.*, ¶ 60: Where this is the case, adjudicating States may have recourse either to their own human rights jurisprudence, or to general international law, including the human rights codified in the "International Covenants on Human Rights".

258 UDHR, *supra* § I.1, note 12.

on Civil and Political Rights[259] and the Covenant on Economic, Social and Cultural Rights.[260]

By way of introduction to the discussion which follows, it is important to remark here that international human rights and humanitarian law are relevant in two distinct ways where the "prosecution versus persecution" bar is concerned:

1. A violation of fundamental human rights may be considered persecution *per se* for purposes of the refugee standard. This will particularly be the case where a law is enforced in a "pretextual" manner (i.e., so as to reach, in fact, a protected ground) or where discriminatory enforcement is at issue.

2. Where a law of general application is supported by an arguably rational State interest and enforcement is not pretextual (e.g., where the law and its enforcement are supported by a rational, non-discriminatory State interest), application of the "prosecution versus persecution" bar becomes more nuanced. In such cases, the adjudicator must look to the relative primacy of the right being asserted by claimant *vis-à-vis* the State necessity in enforcing its law.[261]

3. The fact that an act involves excessive harm (or constitutes a violation of prevailing international law standards) does not resolve the question of whether the mistreatment is "on account of" a refugee ground. Violations of the Torture Convention, for instance, may not qualify the victim under the refugee definition where the punishment is inflicted in an exclusively criminal context.[262] Where, moreover, the State's criminal jurisdiction is predicated on concerns which are arguably legitimate (embracing, for instance, measures which are proportional to the sovereign's right to survival or to its general obligations regarding the public welfare), it must be shown that the

---

[259] ICCPR, *supra* § I.1, note 14,

[260] ICESCR, *supra* § I.1, note 15.

[261] Where, for instance, the asylum seeker fears punishment for activity which relates by its nature to a non-derogable norm of international law, such punishment may amount to persecution in all instances, irrespective of the severity of the punishment or the level of State interest involved.

[262] *Cf.* Bastanipour v. INS, 980 F.2d 1129 (7th Cir. 1992):

> Whatever its precise scope, the term "particular social group" surely was not intended for the protection of members of the criminal class in this country, merely upon a showing that a foreign country deals with them even more harshly than we do. A contrary result would collapse the fundamental distinction between persecution on the one hand and the prosecution of non-political crimes on the other.

harm or suffering of the claimant is connected to a value to which international public policy (or corresponding State constitutional practice) attributes overriding importance.[263]

U.S. law,[264] like that of Canada,[265] accepts that the conscientious assertion of a fundamental human right can constitute the basis for an asylum claim. The decisions to this effect clearly advance certain normative standards to the forefront of asylum analysis. Implicitly, those who vindicate human rights and humanitarian norms by challenging coercive State action will be held to have satisfied the criteria for refugee status when they face punishment putatively arising from the State's lawful exercise of criminal jurisdiction for their views or activities.

### § IV.5(a). The Refugee Definition in the Context of State Conscription: Avoiding Human Rights and Humanitarian Law Violations as a Basis for Refugee Status

In *Matter of Salim*,[266] the Board found that the Afghan army (in which the asylum seeker had avoided conscription) was engaged in certain inhuman acts, including the forced dragooning of men and boys as replacements for Afghan soldiers who had refused to fight under Soviet command against their fellow countrymen.[267] Based on these findings (which were strongly suggested by an Advisory Opinion by the U.S. Department of State), the Board concluded that the applicant's fear of punishment flowing from his refusal to be conscripted into the Afghan army constituted political opinion persecution.[268]

In *Matter of A-G-*,[269] the Board modified its original position on draft resistance as a basis for asylum considerably. It held that, under limited conditions, those who resist conscription or who desert out of a conscientious aversion to becoming involved in "inhuman conduct" are also eligible

---

[263] Handbook, *supra* § I.1, note 30, ¶ 59: States may use their own "national yardstick" on human rights standards in conjunction with norms protected under UDHR, ICCPR and ICESCR.

[264] *See generally* Matter of A.-G.-, 19 I&N Dec. 502 (BIA 1987), *rev'd sub nom.* M.A. v. INS (I), 858 F.2d 210 (4th Cir. 1988), *vacated,* M.A. A26 851 062 v. INS (II), 899 F.2d 304 (1990); Barraza-Rivera v. INS, 913 F.2d 1443 (9th Cir. 1990).

[265] *Zolfagharkhani* v. *M.E.I.* (1993), 155 N.R. 311 (F. C.A.).

[266] 18 I&N Dec. 211 (BIA 1982).

[267] *Id.* at 313.

[268] *Id.*

[269] 19 I&N Dec. 502 (BIA1987).

asylum seekers. The guidance urged by the applicant and relied upon by the Board[270] can be found in ¶¶ 169 through 171 of the *Handbook*, which constitutes persuasive authority regarding the manner in which such cases are to be adjudicated. Under the *Handbook*, a deserter or draft evader is not generally considered a refugee.[271] There are three broad exceptions, however, to this general rule. A claimant who would be made to suffer "disproportionately severe punishment" on account of a protected ground may be considered a refugee.[272] Apart from the situation of unusually harsh sanctions, a claimant who resists conscription may be a refugee where performance of the military obligation would involve the claimant in military action contrary to his genuine political, religious or moral convictions,[273] or where claimant conscientiously opposes becoming involved in military action condemned by the international community.[274]

In *Matter of A-G-*,[275] the Board clearly recognized the claimant's right to dissociate himself from "military action condemned by the military community" (the right not to participate in inhuman action) as a basis for asylum.

---

270 *Id.* at 506.

271 Handbook, *supra* § I.1, note 30, ¶ 168.

272 *Id.*, ¶ 169:

> A deserter or draft evader may also be considered a refugee if it can be shown that he would be suffer disproportionately severe punishment for the military offence on account of his race, religion, nationality, membership in a particular social group or political opinion. The same would apply if it can be shown that he has a well-founded fear of persecution on the grounds above and beyond the punishment for his desertion.

273 *Id.*, ¶ 170:

> There are, however, also cases where the necessity to perform military service may be the sole ground for a claim to refugee status, i.e., when a person can show that the performance of the military service would have required his participation in military action contrary to his genuine political, religious or moral convictions, or to valid reasons of conscience.

274 *Id.*, ¶ 171:

> Not every conviction, genuine though it may be, will constitute a sufficient reason for claiming refugee status after desertion or draft evasion. It is not enough for a person to be in disagreement with his government regarding the political justification for a particular military action. Where, however, the type of military action, with which an individual does not wish to be associated, is condemned by the international community as contrary to basic rules of human conduct, punishment for such desertion or draft evasion could, in light of all other requirements of the definition, in itself be regarded as persecution.

275 19 I&N Dec. 502 (BIA 1987). The case came to the Board by way of a motion to reopen initially made before an immigration judge, the issue being whether claimant had made out a prima facie case for asylum. *Id.* at 503.

Similarly, it accepted the claimant's contention that disproportionately severe punishment (provided that it were related to a refugee ground) would establish a basis for relief.[276] At the same time, however, the Board sharply distinguished its earlier decision in *Matter of Salim*, and it set up austere barriers to establishing when such internationally condemned military action might justify a refusal to be inducted or desertion.

The Board's distinguishing *Matter of Salim*[277] has always been viewed as controversial. The applicant had argued that the *Salim* decision supported the proposition that an alien who refuses induction into an army engaged in inhuman conduct is eligible for asylum. The Board held in this respect that the army in which the applicant did not wish to participate in *Salim* was not a "national" army, but one which was under the virtual control of a foreign sovereign, i.e., the Soviet Union. Notwithstanding this narrow interpretation, the *Salim* opinion is occasionally invoked to support the general proposition that an asylum seeker may qualify under the refugee definition by refusing to be inducted into an army that "persecutes."[278]

The applicant in *A-G-* had argued in support of asylum eligibility that he was opposed to serving in the Salvadoran army because the latter was engaged in widespread violations of international humanitarian law.[279] The Board essentially rejected claimant's contention that the background evidence (consisting of reports by Americas Watch) was sufficient to support a vital element of the claim, i.e., that the international humanitarian law violations reflected the *policy* of the Salvadoran government.[280] At the same time, the Board adopted the highly restrictive view that the "internationally condemned" criterion contained in § 171 of the *Handbook* (relating to the military action from which the claimant had sought to disassociate himself) could only be satisfied by an opinion issued by a recognized governmental body, such as a UN General Assembly resolution.

---

276 *Id.* at 506:

> We hold to the long-accepted position that it is not persecution for a country to require military service of its citizens. […]. Exceptions to this rule may be recognized in those rare cases where disproportionately severe punishment would result on account of one of the five reasons enumerated in section 101(a)(42)(A) of the Act, or where the alien would necessarily be required to engage in inhuman conduct as a result of military service required by the government.

277 18 I&N Dec. 311 (BIA 1982).

278 Basic Law Manual, *supra* § I.1, note 26, at 81, *citing* Matter of Salim, 18 I&N Dec. (BIA 1982).

279 Matter of A-G-, 19 I&N Dec. 502, 507 (1987).

280 *Id.* at 506.

The Fourth Circuit initially reversed, holding, in effect, that the requirements of the *Handbook* could be established by reliable evidence showing that common Article 3 of the Geneva Conventions of August 12, 1949 was being systematically violated by the military in El Salvador.[281] Common Article 3 specifically prescribes:

> (A) The obligation to treat humanely those taking no active part in the hostilities, including combatants who have been placed *hors de combat.*
>
> (B) The prohibition of certain acts with respect to the foregoing persons including violence to life and person; murder; mutilation; cruel treatment and torture; the taking of hostages; humiliating treatment; and the passing of sentences and carrying out of executions without previous judgment pronounced by a regularly constituted court.
>
> (C) The responsibility to care for the sick and wounded.[282]

Importantly, the Fourth Circuit determined that "private" human rights reports such as those issued by Americas Watch) and other credible sources were sufficient to meet the "condemned by the international community" standard of the *Handbook.*[283] With respect to the standard it would follow, the appeals court ruled:

> Paragraph 171 of the Handbook shelters those individuals who do not wish to be associated with military action "condemned by the international community as contrary to basic rules of conduct...". These basic rules are well-documented and readily available to guide the court in discerning what types of actions are considered unacceptable by the world community. The Geneva Conventions of August 12, 1949 represent the international consensus regarding minimum standards of conduct during wartime.[284]

The court had no difficulties finding that common Article 3 had been systematically violated. Among other things, the asylum seeker had submitted affidavits showing that government troops had engaged in the following practices both as a matter of course and in response to the commands of officers: the killing of women and children; the torturing of known guerillas; the raping of women considered guerilla sympathizers; the dragooning of minors who are forced to participate in search and destroy missions in which innocent civilians are killed. This testimonial evidence was supported by reports from Americas Watch and Amnesty International showing the Salvadoran military's violent policies toward civilians.

---

[281] M.A. v. INS(I), 858 F.2d 210 (4th Cir. 1990), *vacated,* M.A. A26 851 062 v. INS (II), 899 F.2d 304 (1990).

[282] *See, e.g.,* Geneva Conventions, *supra* § I.1, note 17, common Art. 3.

[283] M.A. v. INS(I), 858 F.2d 210, 218-19 (4th Cir. 1990).

[284] *Id.* at 218.

The Fourth Circuit also ruled that the violations need not reflect the policy of the Salvadoran government, only that the applicant would likely become entangled in them by virtue of their systematic and widespread nature.[285] Although it is presently of little precedential weight, the Fourth Circuit's initial decision in *M.A.(I)* remains of compelling interest. In this respect, the opinion of the panel unquestionably represents a comprehensive analysis of conscientious objector claims, setting forth a unique and probing restatement of the criteria to be applied under § 171 of the UN *Handbook*.

On motion for a rehearing, the Fourth Circuit, sitting *en banc,* vacated the panel's earlier determination, and issued a new decision which virtually reaffirmed the Board's earlier holding in *Matter of A-G-*.[286] The Circuit Court is now essentially in agreement with the Board on the critical elements which must be proved before a conscientious objector claim based on military misconduct can be established. The court ruled that the Board did not err in requiring that any violations of the laws of war reflect the policy of the Salvadoran government. Random misconduct by uncontrolled military units was a feature of civil war, the court ruled;[287] accordingly, it was reasonable to require that the asylum seeker establish a connection between the violations and governmental policy.[288] The court acknowledged that the reports of Amnesty International and of Americas Watch identified certain violations (including extrajudicial murder, acts of torture, "disappearances" and arbitrary detention) as flowing from Salvadoran governmental policy.[289] However, the appeals court upheld the most onerous of the restrictions announced by *Matter of A-G-,* namely, that the military misconduct be "condemned" by a recognized governmental source.[290]

The situation described in *Matter of A-G-* should be distinguished, at a minimum, from those in which there has been an effort to draw the claimant into the violations giving rise to conscientious objector status. In *Barraza-Rivera* v. *I.N.S.*,[291] the applicant had deserted from the Salvadoran military

---

[285] *Id.* On the critical question of whether the claimant was required to establish that the violations were being committed pursuant to a governmental policy, the court ruled that, since persecution under the refugee definition could flow either from the State or from a group which the State was unwilling or unable to control, in this case it was enough to show that the violations were emanating from the Salvadoran armed forces, a group which the government apparently could not control. *Id.*

[286] M.A. A26 851 062 v. INS (II), 899 F.2d 304 (4th Cir. 1990).

[287] *Id.* at 312.

[288] *Id.*

[289] *Id.*

[290] *Id.*

[291] 913 F.2d 1143 (9th Cir. 1990).

only after being pressured by his commanding officer to participate in paid assassination.[292] The Ninth Circuit held that the claimant had satisfied the refugee definition in that such paid assassination offended the common law of war as set forth in common Article 3 of the Geneva Conventions of August 12, 1949, and, therefore, stood "condemned" (virtually by operation of law) by the international community. Specifically, the appeals court ruled:

> In that case [*M.A. II*], a Salvadoran man who had never served in the military fled El Salvador because he wished 'to avoid serving in [the] violent military…'. The BIA denied the petitioner's motion to reopen on the ground that he failed to show that, as a matter of governmental policy, the Salvadoran military routinely engaged in unconscionable acts condemned by the international community…. In contrast to the Petitioner in *M.A.* v. *I.N.S.*, here Barraza does not claim general opposition to military service based on institutionalized practices of the Salvadoran military. He was actually threatened—a Salvadoran military officer ordered him to participate in two murders, internationally condemned acts. *See* Geneva Conventions, Aug. 12, 1949, Art. 3, T.I.A.S. Nos. 3362-3365, at 4-7, 75 U.N.T.S. 31.[293]

In *Ramos-Vasquez* v. *INS*,[294] the Ninth Circuit expanded upon the holding of *Barraza-Rivera* utilizing the doctrine of "neutrality" which was discussed, *supra*, in the civil war cases. Ramos-Vasquez was a native and citizen of Honduras who had been drafted into the Honduran army at an early age. He was placed in an elite intelligence unit which it was impossible to leave voluntarily. After serving for 13 years, the claimant deserted rather than execute a friend who had himself deserted. Ramos' evidence was to the effect that deserters were kept in water tanks for several days after which they were summarily executed, their bodies being later dumped in a river. Applicant had himself been kept in a water tank for 24 hours on several occasions for refusing to execute deserters.[295]

The immigration judge hearing the case treated Ramos' refusal to execute prisoners as reluctance to perform an unpleasant military duty; implicitly the applicant feared prosecution, not persecution. Again, the court cited as an authoritative guide in deciding such cases ¶¶ 170-71 of the UN *Handbook*, and concluded that, if the Honduran army regularly tortures and then summarily executes deserters, refusal to perform such acts would support a claim for asylum: conscientious opposition to performing "inhuman acts" (i.e., violations of the rules and customs applicable in armed conflict) was privileged and would not subject the claimant to lawful prosecution. The

---

[292] *Id.* at 1445-46.

[293] *Id.* at 1453, n. 14.

[294] 57 F.3d 857 (9th Cir. 1995).

[295] *Id* at 860.

court, however, declined to characterize the protected ground involved as "religious objection" (as it had in its first *Canas-Segovia* decision)[296] because it felt that, under *Elias-Zacarias*, the second Convention ground had been "discredited" as the basis for relief in such cases. Rather, the tribunal chose political opinion ("neutrality") as the relevant refugee ground which, it reasoned, constitutes a principled position which would adequately convey applicant's true status as a conscientious objector.[297]

Both *Barraza-Rivera* and *Ramos-Vasquez* were recently followed in *Martirosyan* v. *INS*.[298] In *Martirosyan,* the asylum seeker was a native and citizen of Armenia who had fled after refusing to serve in a prisoner-of-war camp. Applicant had had an extensive career in the Soviet military, serving as a trainer and counselor during the Afghan conflict. He was fired from the army in 1990, however, after expressing anti-communist views.

After his discharge, the applicant returned to Armenia and joined a group which designated itself "Officers Against the War". The group protested treatment of POWs, especially of Azeri prisoners at the camps located in Nagaro-Karabakh, an Armenian region of Azerbaijan. At the time the Russians and the Azeris were engaged in hostilities with respect to re-unification of Nagorno-Karabakh with the Republic of Armenia. Applicant testified that he had actually seen POWs who had been tortured and who had had body parts cut off. Subsequently, in 1991, applicant voluntarily joined a militia group which later became the Armenian National Army, but changed his mind when he discovered that he would be posted to a POW camp. Conscription became mandatory two years later, however, and applicant was conscripted. He refused to serve in light of his prior experiences with POWs. When the former Soviet republics signed an agreement to return all draft evaders to their home countries for prosecution and punishment, the applicant fled.

The Ninth Circuit adopted its prior decisions in *Barraza-Rivera* and *Ramos-Vasquez* to hold that "punishment based on objection to participation in inhuman acts as part of forced military service is 'persecution' within the meaning of [the refugee definition]". And the court concluded that the asylum seeker had adequately demonstrated, both through his testimony and through supporting background documentation, a reasonable possibility that his military service would require him to engage in inhuman treatment of POWs.

---

[296] 970 F.2d 599, 601 (9th Cir. 1992).

[297] 57 F.3d at 863-64.

[298] No. 98-70979, 2000 WL 1568686 (9th Cir. Oct. 23, 2000). The case is digested in 77 Interpreter Releases 1544 (October 30, 2000).

In support of his contention that he would be constrained to engage in inhuman acts, the asylum seeker introduced into evidence press releases from Amnesty International and Human Rights Watch showing gross violations of humanitarian law being committed by the armies fighting over Nagorno-Karabakh. The IJ had rejected the claim largely because the applicant had failed to adduce documentary evidence to the effect that *specific atrocities* were being committed against POWs (the severing of POWs' ears, for instance, and taking the mothers of POWs hostage while the prisoners were forced to commit atrocities in Azerbaijan). The reviewing court determined that imposing this requirement was improper, however, since persecutors were unlikely to supply their victims with affidavits attesting to their own misconduct. The decision helps to formulate a reasonable standard of proof where the "inhuman acts" which the asylum seeker is anxious to avoid are being clandestinely carried out by the persecutor.

U.S. asylum law relative to asylum seekers who conscientiously oppose becoming involved in internationally condemned military action remains unclear. The most austere requirement set forth in *Matter of A.-G.-*, upheld in *M.A. II*,[299] that there must be, as a predicate to conscientious objector status, a formal denunciation of the military action in question by a governmental source, constitutes a clear misreading of the law and has been criticized as such.[300] Neither the *Handbook*, nor the *Basic Law Manual*[301] set out as a requirement that military atrocities with which the asylum seeker wishes to avoid becoming entangled be formally condemned in an international political or legal process. The structure of the Refugee Convention (including the "exclusion" grounds relating to those who commit, for instance, "crimes against humanity" or violations of the Genocide Convention)[302] requires an interpretation permitting future refugees to avoid action which would render them "persecutors" and therefore ineligible for benefits under the Convention.

Deborah Anker[303] has cogently argued that two of the most restrictive elements of the *M.A.(II)*[304] decision have arguably been set aside in 1990 regulations promulgated by the Department of Justice governing asylum

---

299 *See generally* Matter of A.-G.-, 19 I&N Dec. 502 (BIA 1987), *rev'd sub nom.* M.A. v. INS (I), 858 F.2d 210 (4th Cir. 1988), *vacated,* M.A. A26 851 062 v. INS (II), 899 F.2d 304 (4th Cir. 1990).

300 *See, e.g.*, Anker 99, *supra* § I.2, note 32, at 362.

301 Basic Law Manual, *supra* § I.1, note 26, at 89.

302 Refugee Convention, *supra* § I.1, note 1, Arts. 1F(a) and (c).

303 Anker 91, *supra* § III.1, note 5, at 144.

304 M.A. A26 851 062 v. INS *(II)*, 899 F.2d 304 (4th Cir. 1990).

determinations.[305] In particular, the requirement that the alien be "singled out" has been replaced by a showing that the claimant belongs to a group which has been targeted for persecution.[306] Moreover, the quintessential holding of *M.A.(II)*, namely, that international condemnation of the military action in question must flow from a governmental source, has been displaced by a new rule which directs that the asylum adjudicator should consider background material from "private" human rights monitors in making findings on country conditions.[307]

Canada's initial response to the problems posed by refugee claimants who face putatively lawful prosecution for refusing to undergo induction was restrictive, great stress being laid on the fact that the draft law was one of general application. In *Musial* v. *ME.I.*,[308] the claimant, a Polish seaman, predicated his claim on the fact that he was subject to conscription as a result of which he might be sent to fight in Afghanistan, a war to which he was politically opposed. The Court of Appeal ruled that violation of a military conscription law would not support a claim to refugee status where all that was alleged was prosecution and punishment flowing from the offense of draft evasion or desertion.

> A person who is punished for having violated an ordinary law of general application is punished for the offence he has committed, not for the political opinions that may have induced him to commit it. ... [A] person who has violated the laws of his country of origin by evading ordinary military service, and who merely fears prosecution and punishment for offence in accordance with those laws, cannot be said to fear persecution for his political opinions even if he was prompted to commit that offence by his political beliefs.[309]

---

305 The Anker treatise has summarized the requirements of the *M.A. (II)* decision in the following way:

> (i) The military practices complained of must constitute the official policy of the government;
>
> (ii) the applicant must be singled out for punishment because of his political beliefs; and
>
> (iii) the acts which are said to be "condemned by the international community" must have been so adjudicated by international governmental bodies [such as the General Assembly of the United Nations]; in the alternative,
>
> (iv) applicant must be made subject to disproportionate punishment.

Anker 91, *supra* § III.1, note 5, at 144, *citing* M.A. v. INS, 899 F.2d 304 (4th Cir. 1990).

306 *Id., citing* 8 CFR § 208.13(b)(2)(i) (1990).

307 *Id.*

308 (1981), 38 N.R. 55 (F.C.A.).

309 *Id.* at 60.

The original position of the Court of Appeal has undergone significant modification in the case law. Modern Canadian law has adopted an approach similar to that of the Ninth Circuit in the area of conscientious objection. In *Zolfagharkhani* v. *M.E.I.*,[310] the Court of Appeal granted the applicant refugee status finding that his conscientious opposition to the use of chemical weapons in Iran's internal war against the Kurds was reasonable. The holding of *Zolfagharkhani* is considerably broader than any of the United States decisions discussed above and it adopts the correct standard for adjudicating such claims.

The claimant had served earlier in the Iranian army during the Iran-Iraq War for about 27 months commencing in 1986, both as a gunner and in a tank crew.[311] Subsequently, during the war against the Kurdish movement, he was requested by the Revolutionary Guard to serve as a paramedic. During a one-month training course, he discovered the intention of the government to use chemical warfare against the Kurds. The applicant objected repeatedly to this practice. And he based his claim to refugee status on flight and desertion predicated on his conscientious opposition to the unlawful use of chemical weapons.[312] It was not an aspect of the applicant's claim that he would be forced to fight against his fellow Kurds.[313]

The Immigration and Refugee Board originally denied the claim, largely on the basis that the claimant, as a paramedic, was not obligated to use any weapons during the conflict, but was solely responsible for tendering medical aid to the wounded.[314] The Court of Appeals rejected the Board's finding[315] that, since the claimant was involved solely as a paramedic, and not in the use of weapons, he was characterized as fulfilling a Florence Nightingale role of "helping his brothers on both sides of the conflict".

The Court of Appeal concluded, on the contrary, that there was a hidden military advantage in claimant's function which related directly to the use of chemical weaponry. Specifically, it was feared that Iranian forces might be caught by changing winds bearing the chemical clouds unleashed by their own army upon them. Applicant was expected to assist those Iranians thus

---

310 (1993), 155 N.R. 311 (F. C.A.).

311 *Id.* at 312.

312 *Id.* at 312, 313.

313 *Id.* at 311.

314 *Id.* at 312.

315 The Board made various factual findings in this regard which were not accepted by the Court of Appeal. Among these were that chemical agents were used by both sides during the conflict, whereas the reviewing court determined that only the Iranian forces utilized chemical warfare. *Id.* at 314.

affected. The claimant's participation as a paramedic could thus serve to advance the unlawful use of chemicals contemplated, i.e., by preserving the humanitarian law violators from the side-effects of their own breach.[316]

Reaching the merits of the claim, the *Zolfagharkhani* court rejected the contention that *Musial* v. *M.E.I.* was governing. The proposition that violating a neutral law of general application could never give rise to persecution in the Convention sense was overbroad, the court ruled, and did not take account of governmental laws in totalitarian states which operated as acts of oppression.[317]

The court noted that a refusal may well have been necessary to preserve the claimant from being a "persecutor," i.e. as one who had committed a crime against humanity.[318] The tribunal then set forth certain guiding principles which it regarded as binding where the prosecution versus persecution bar was present in an asylum adjudication based on the asylum seeker's non-compliance with a law of general application.[319]

These criteria are now governing generally in Canada with respect to claims in which individuals seek recognition as refugees based on conscientious opposition to laws of general application.[320] It is the intent (or effect) of the law which is the material consideration, rather than the motive of the claimant. The law must be objectively assessed by Canadian tribunals and enjoys a presumption of validity, the burden being on the claimant to show that the law (or its application) are persecutory. Finally, the fact that the law

---

316 *Id.*

317 (1982), 38 N.R. 55 (F. C.A.). The *Zolfagharkani* court ruled:

> This decision [*Musial*] has, I think, often been taken to establish the proposition that, where a government is merely enforcing "an ordinary law of general application", it cannot be guilty of persecution but is merely engaging in prosecution. With respect, I believe that to be only a half proposition, and in any event one not asserted by Pratte, J.A. Since any given ordinary law of general application in a dictatorial or totalitarian state may well be an act of political oppression, I believe it is self-evident that such an absolute proposition of prosecution, not persecution, could not be supported in relation to the majority of countries from which refugee cases arise.
>
> The essence of the reasoning of Pratte, J.A., in *Musial,* as it appears to me, is rather that the mental element which is decisive for the existence of persecution is that of the government, not that of the refugee.

Zolfagharkhani v. M.E.I. (1993), 155 N.R. 311, 315 (F.C.A.).

318 *Id.* at 314, *citing* Ramirez v. M.E.I. (1993), 135 N.R. 390 (F.C.A.).

319 Zolfagharkhani v. M.E.I. (1993), 155 N.R. 311, 317 (F.C.A.).

320 Interpretation of the Convention Refugee Definition in the Case Law, *supra* § II.3, note 63, § 9.3.6.

has been adopted by a generally oppressive regime is not sufficient to establish that the statute or regulation is persecutory; rather the law must be shown to entail persecution in relationship to a Convention ground. In the specific formulation of the court:

> (1) The statutory definition of Convention refugee makes the intent (or any principle effect) of an ordinary law of general application, rather than the motivation of the claimant, relevant to the existence of persecution.
>
> (2) But the neutrality of an ordinary law of general application, *vis-à-vis* the five grounds for refugee status, must be judged objectively by Canadian tribunals and courts when required.
>
> (3) In such consideration, an ordinary law of general application, even in non-democratic societies, should, I believe, be given a presumption of validity and neutrality, and the onus should be on the claimant, as generally is the case in refugee cases, to show that the laws are either inherently or for some other reason persecutory.
>
> (4) It will not be enough for the claimant to show that a particular regime is generally oppressive but rather that the law [in ] question is persecutory in relation to a Convention ground.[321]

The Canadian appeals court then pointed to ¶¶ 170 and 171 of the *U.N. Handbook* which (as shown above) develop specific circumstances under which the asylum seeker will be deemed to be persecuted on account of a political opinion if he seeks disengagement with internationally condemned military action as the basis for draft avoidance.[322] Critically, however, the appeals court did not insist upon a determination by an international governmental body that the military action in question stood condemned. Rather, the court looked to evidence that Iranian forces were engaged in some type of chemical warfare. The tribunal then cited the Convention on the Prohibition of the Development, Protection and Stockpiling of Bacteriological (Biological) and Toxic Weapons and on their Destruction as constituting conclusive proof that such means of warfare had received the "revulsion" of international law and society:

---

[321] Zolfagharkhani v. M.E.I. (1993), 155 N.R. 311, 317 (F.C.A.).

[322] The court cited with approval an earlier case, *Padilla* v. *M.E.I.* (1991),13 Imm. L.R. (2d) 1 (F.C.A.), in which the Court of Appeal reversed a denial of refugee status by the Immigration and Refugee Board with respect to a "conscientious objection" claim made by a Salvadoran. The decision rested apparently on the Board's mechanical application of the "prosecution versus persecution" bar. Also noted was the Court of Appeal's decision (discussed later in this essay) in *Cheung* v. *M.E.I.* (1993), 153 N.R. 145 (F.C.A.), which similarly rejected the Board's overbroad application of the doctrine that enforcement of a neutral law cannot constitute persecution in the Convention sense. 155 N.R. 311, 317 (F.C.A.).

> On the basis of the evidence in the record, it is impossible to say with scientific certainty that the gases in question in the case at bar would be included in these Convention definitions, though they would certainly appear to be. I believe that all that is necessary to dispose of the instant case, however, is evidence of the *total revulsion of the international community to all forms of chemical warfare, as revealed by the Convention on the Prohibition and the Development, Production and Stockpiling of Bacteriological (Biological) and Toxic Weapons and Their Destruction, for which both Canada and Iran voted on December 16, 1971.*[323]

The existence of the Convention on Biological Weapons, coupled with other international undertakings not mentioned in the opinion, led the court to conclude that the use of chemical weapons was "against international customary law." Accordingly, the asylum seeker would be punished not based on a neutral application of the sovereign's criminal statutes but rather based on the view of the Iranian authorities that a refusal to bear arms under these circumstances was predicated on an unacceptable political opinion.[324]

Other decisions of note have followed *Zolfagharkhani* in its analysis of the right not to participate in atrocities as the basis for a "conscientious objection" claim. In *Ciric* v. *M.E.I.*[325] the CRDD had concluded that a Serbian couple who had refused military service in the JNA (during the height of the 1991-1994 war in the former Yugoslavia) faced prosecution, and not persecution. The claimants had articulated their position with respect to the war by asserting that the government's "fighting their own people is wrong".

The Federal Court-Trial Division overturned the CRDD's conclusion that the couple would only be required to pay a fine, and remarked that the CRDD had ignored evidence that the international community had condemned the war (through, for instance, the establishment of a war crimes tribunal). Critically, however, the court did not rely on formal resolutions of the United Nations for its determination that avoidance of military service in the war was justified. Rather, the tribunal in substance adopted findings made by Amnesty International and other "private" human rights monitors in documenting the widespread atrocities which characterized the Yugoslavian war. This evidence established conclusively that violations of general humanitarian law such as woundings, killings, torture and imprisonment were being committed by the military against civilians; formal resolutions of

---

323 *Id* at 318. [Emphasis supplied].

324 *Id* at 319.

325 Ciric v. M.E.I. [1994] 2 F.C. 65 (T.D.). The case is noted with interest in Who is a Refugee? 193-194 (Jean-Yves Carlier, Dirk Vanheule, Klaus Hullmann and Carlos Pena Galiano, eds. 1997) [hereinafter cited as Who is a Refugee?].

the U.N. were not necessary to establish that such violations stood condemned by the international community. The court ruled:

> [R]espected organizations like Amnesty International, Helsinki Watch and I.C.R.C., are able to move quickly, study sufficiently and make pronouncements. And all did so here that surely the Board should have seen as condemnation by the world community. The atrocities committed were immediately abhorrent to the world community, eventually leading to a more public position by the United Nations. Basic human rights were violated through woundings, killings, torture, imprisonment and all clearly condemned by the international community.[326]

In *Diab* v. *M.E.I.*,[327] a Christian from South Lebanon had been forcibly recruited by the South Lebanese Army, a paramilitary force active during the Lebanese civil war. He performed initial service (to protect his life), but subsequently left South Lebanon and sought refugee status in Canada. The claimant contended that he was opposed to becoming involved in military activity which amounted to crimes against humanity and that, in all events, he would be perceived as a deserter and punished accordingly were he to return. The IRB rejected the application, ruling that the SLA was not an insurgent paramilitary force but the de facto government in South Lebanon. Accordingly, the claimant faced lawful prosecution for his desertion, not persecution. The Board also found the claimant's position untenable because the SLA had been established in South Lebanon to protect his own religious group (Christians).

The Court of Appeal overturned both bases for the denial. There was no indication in the record that the SLA was a "legitimate" government in South Lebanon, rather than a military faction maintained in power by virtue of foreign support. Moreover, the fact that the SLA had been established to protect Christians was not material: claimant's refusal to perform military service, his conscientious opposition to becoming entangled in criminal violations of human rights, constituted a recognized basis for refugee status. The *Diab* case remains one of overriding importance in that it demonstrates that conscientious opposition to committing atrocities can serve as the basis for refugee status not only where State conscription is concerned, but also where unlawful insurgent elements attempt to forcibly recruit the claimant.

The essence of "conscientious objection" basis for refugee status in Canada continues to center on cases in which the claimant is opposed to military service because the army into which he faces induction is particip-

---

326 *See* Who is a Refugee?, *supra* this section, note 325, at 193-94, *quoting* Ciric v. M.E.I. [1994] 2 F.C. 65 (T.D.).

327 (F.C.A., no. A-688-91), August 21, 1994.

ating in serious violations of the laws of war or is otherwise engaged in military action which contravenes in some important ways the purposes of the United Nations.[328] Critically, and in clear contradistinction to the Board's ruling in *Matter of A-G-*, such "military action condemned by the international community" may be proved by submissions from private human rights organizations such as Amnesty International or Helsinki Watch; actual condemnation by the United Nations is not necessary to the determination.[329]

Moreover, it is not only war crimes which can serve as the basis for a "conscientious objection" claim; violations of the law of peace (i.e., the waging of an "aggressive war") may also establish that military action has been undertaken which has been condemned by the international community. Accordingly, a non-defensive incursion into foreign territory (which was unprovoked) was held to violate fundamental standards of the United Nations, where the U.N. had formally condemned the incursion as contrary to basic rules of conduct.[330] Such action would have been an evident violation of Article 6(a) of the Nuremberg Charter (prohibiting aggressive wars) and Article 2(4) of the United Nations charter (relating to the prohibition of the use of force against another sovereign).[331]

*El Maisri* v. *M.E.I.*[332] brings to the forefront of refugee analysis modern proclivities in general international law. Among other things, the decision shows that international normative restraints on the exercise of sovereignty (including restrictions on the unlawful use of force) may be used to justify the refugee claimant's non-compliance with otherwise valid "national" measures. The claimant in *El Maisri* was a native and citizen of Yemen who had been called for active duty in the Yemenese army in 1990 to take part in the defense of Iraq subsequent to Iraq's unlawful invasion of Kuwait.[333] The claimant vehemently opposed the invasion of Kuwait and he acted on this belief to desert from Yemen's armed forces. The Court of Appeal overturned a denial of the claim ruling virtually that the refugee claimant's actions in refusing to fight were justified. In this respect, the United Nations had formally condemned Iraq's act of aggression against Kuwait as contrary to

---

[328] Interpretation of the Convention Refugee Definition in the Case Law, *supra* § II.3, note 63, § 9.3.6, and cases cited therein.

[329] Ciric v. M.E.I. [1994] 2 F.C. 65 (T.D.).

[330] Al-Maisri v. M.E.I. (1995), 183 N.R. 234 (F.C.A.).

[331] U.N. Charter, Art. 2(4).

[332] (1995), 183 N.R. 234 (F.C.A.).

[333] *See, e.g.*, S/RES/678, Nov. 29, 1990. The decision thus analyzes violations of the *jus ad bellum* (the right to go to war) as the basis for a refugee claim, as opposed to the *jus in bello* (the rights a belligerent has once hostilities are commenced).

"basic rules of conduct"; accordingly, any punishment faced by the claimant for declining to serve in a military action which supported Iraq's side in the conflict was persecution in the Convention sense.

Following *Zolfagharkhani*, the test in Canada with respect to claims based on induction by the government is confined to examining whether the facts disclose a nexus between serious harm and a refugee ground. As summarized in *Interpretation of the Convention Refugee Definition in the Case Law*,[334] the critical inquiry is whether the authorities view the claimant's refusal to serve as related to a protected ground which the authorities believe claimant to possess.[335]

Consistent with the general rule governing attribution principles, the claimant need not actually possess the political opinion (or other characteristic or belief) imputed to claimant by the authorities.[336] A claim can still be made out where refusal to serve will be regarded as motivated by a reason recognized as a basis for persecution under the refugee definition.[337] The case law appears to place emphasis not on the applicant's point of view (the values which motivated him to refuse to serve), but on the "intent or principal effect of the conscription law."[338]

An analysis of conscientious objector claims which focuses on attribution principles, however, would appear most appropriate where the sanction which the claimant faces is either excessive or will be extra-judicially administered. For example, in *Padilla* v. *M.E.I.*,[339] the claimant had deserted from El Salvador's armed forces engaged in combating guerilla insurgency urging as a basis "conscientious objection" and a fear of being killed in combat. The Immigration and Refugee Board disallowed the claim, finding that the claimant's fear was essentially one of prosecution for the offense of desertion, not a basis for refugee status. The Court of Appeals reversed: the evidence demonstrated that the claimant did not believe he would be charged with desertion in a formal context but that he would be made the subject of extrajudicial execution for his act. The Court of appeal thus ruled that the

---

334 Interpretation of the Convention Refugee Definition in the Case Law, *supra* § II.3, note 63, § 9.3.6.

335 Ahani v. M.C.I. (F.C.T.D., no. IMM-4985-93), January 4, 1995.

336 Interpretation of the Convention Refugee Definition in the Case Law, *supra* § II.3, note 63, § 9.3.6, and cases cited therein.

337 Zolfagharkhani v. M.E.I. (1993), 155 N.R. 311 (F.C.A.).

338 Interpretation of the Convention Refugee Definition in the Case Law, *supra* § II.3, note 63, § 9.3.6, *citing* Zolfagharkhani v. M.E.I. (1993), 155 N.R. 311 (F.C.A.).

339 (1991), 13 Imm. L.R. (2d) 1, 160 N.R. 156 (F.C.A.).

IRB had ignored the true basis for claimant's fear by concentrating on the legal consequences attending claimant's act of desertion.

The view that the intent of the law provides the critical consideration in "conscientious objector" cases seems incomplete. The claimant in *Zolfagharkhani* had adopted a position in which he had refused to violate fundamental international humanitarian norms relating to the protection of human rights in armed conflict as set forth in a critical treaty. His relationship to the law must be seen then as one of comparative privilege. His right not to violate such peremptory norms is not qualified; the claimant is not, in other words, obligated to demonstrate that application of the law would entail, as to him, a disproportionately severe punishment.[340] *Rather, the privilege obtaining with respect to a claimant's fundamental right not to violate the dignity of others is absolute. Any harm of a serious nature occasioned as the result of the claimant's having made this choice is persecution.*[341]

In any case, where refusal to be inducted arises, the Refugee Division must decide whether the reasons adduced by the claimant are sufficient to outweigh the State's right to require military service.[342] In general, however, the claim need not be based on some form of opposition to all militarism, or otherwise based on broad philosophical considerations In *Zolfagharkhani*, for instance, the claimant maintained that he was opposed to becoming an indirect party to violations of a specific treaty relating to the use of chemical

---

340 Subsequent cases have suggested that an element of "conscience" in opposing involvement with atrocities is required if there is no evidence that the punishment for draft evasion or desertion is not disproportionate. *See* Sladoljej v. M.E.I. (F.C.T.D. IMM-3160-94, July 4, 1995). In *Sladoljej,* the claimant had deserted from his Yugoslav army post in Croatia in 1993. The court acknowledged the general principle that "conscientious objection" provides the basis for a refugee claim where the army involved is engaged in military activity condemned by the international community, and it agreed that the Yugoslavian war satisfied the governing criteria. However, the court upheld denial of the claim in that claimant did not desert for reasons of conscience and there was no evidence that punishment would be excessive.

341 *See* Interpretation of the Convention Refugee Definition in the Case Law, *supra* § II.3, note 63, § 9.3.6, criticizing the view that the claimant's motivation is irrelevant and maintaining that some showing of an act of conscience is required:

> However, it would seem that the motivation of the claimant has not been completely discarded as a factor in claims concerning military service, although the cases do not make clear to which element or elements (nexus, serious harm) it may relate, and exactly how it should be worked into the consideration of a particular element. [...] [I]n subsequent decisions, the Trial Division has repeatedly considered the claimant's conscience, as well as the attitude of the international community to operations criticized by the claimant.

342 *Id.*

weapons.[343] Moreover, a claimant may base his opposition to serving in a particular conflict (rather than in war altogether) and still qualify under the Convention refugee definition.[344]

As the foregoing cases establish, the objection of the claimant may be regarded as sufficiently serious if the military actions in which the claimant fears participation are contrary to standards of the international community as manifested by the state of contemporary international law.[345] In making this determination, it is not permissible to rely on isolated or sporadic violations: the offending military conduct must be condoned in some way by the State.[346] Similarly, a claim cannot be grounded if the claimant would be offered some form of alternative service which would not involve him or her in the internationally condemned military action.[347] Finally, it is an independent basis to deny the claim if the penalties for refusing to serve are not harsh; however, the possibility of extra-legal measures being applied must be considered in this context.[348]

## § IV.5(b). The Modern International Law Setting of Conscription Claims: The *Jus Ad Bellum* and the *Jus In Bello*

As noted, conscription cases arise in a specific context which requires examination of contemporary international normative restraints on the exercise of sovereignty. The evolution of refugee status and asylum adjudications in the area of forced recruitment must be seen as enjoying significant parallels with developments affecting the United Nations itself and with the World Organization's endeavors to bring States into conformity with its purposes and principles as reflected in the U.N. Charter and related constituent documents. As outlined below, these developments have been directly related to (i) the prosecution of international humanitarian law violations; and (ii) the curbing of acts of "aggression" by States parties.[349] The parallels,

---

343 Zolfagharkhani v. M.E.I. (1993), 155 N.R. 311, 312-313 (F.C.A.).

344 Popov v. M.E.I. (1994), 24 Imm. L.R. (2d) 242 (F.C.T.D.).

345 Zolfagharkhani v. M.E.I. (1993), 155 N.R. 311, 318 (F.C.A.1993).

346 Popov v. M.E.I. (1994), 24 Imm. L.R. (2d) 242 (F.C.T.D.).

347 Talman v. S.G.C., (F.C.T.D., no. IMM-5874-93), January 11, 1994, at 7.

348 Frid v. M.C.I. (F.C.T.D., no. IMM-6694-93), December 15, 1994.

349 For a discussion of the *jus ad bellum* and the *jus in bello* in a modern context, and particularly with respect to the inclusion of *jus in bello* within the broad purposes and principles of the United Nations, *see Commentary on Protocol I, supra* § IV.4(a), note 168, at 26:

moreover, between U.N. enforcement action and refugee jurisprudence illustrate a persistent theme, namely, that the law of refugee status seeks to accommodate the seminal goals of the U.N., including the World Organization's objective of broadening and deepening human rights regimes.

Violations of the law of peace, specifically referenced and made the basis of decision in *El Maisri* v. *M.E.I.*,[350] wer invoked in 1990 and in 1991 by the Security Council when the Council concluded that there had been an "invasion" of Kuwait by Iraq and that this invasion constituted a threat to international peace and security.[351] The Council subsequently, acting under Chapter VII of the Charter, "authorized member States, cooperating with the government of Kuwait ... to use all necessary means" to expel Iraq from the territory thus unlawfully seized.[352] In undertaking this action, the Security Council was acting to enforce one of the most fundamental provisions of the U.N. Charter, namely Article 2(4) which bars the use of force by member States against the territorial integrity and political independence of other member States.[353]

Like common Article 3 of the Geneva Conventions of August 12, 1949 (discussed below), Article 2(4) of the Charter has been held by the International Court of Justice to constitute a rule of *jus cogens*, or a peremptory rule of customary international law.[354] Separate opinions filed in the *Nicaragua Judgment* by two justices illustrate the policy concerns which

---

> In short, as the prohibition on the use of force is not absolute, and is not immune to violation, it is necessary and justified to develop a body of law to govern international armed conflicts: the violation of the laws of peace, which includes certain exceptions (*jus ad bellum*) to the general prohibition of the use of force, neither prevents nor exempts any Party to a conflict from respecting the law applicable in such a situation (*jus in bello*). A moral and humanitarian argument can be added to this legal aspect: Just as the dissemination of humanitarian law contributes to the promotion of humanitarian ideals and a spirit of world peace among nations, the faithful application of such law can contribute to reestablishing peace, by limiting the effects of hostilities.
>
> Thus there is no contradiction between expressing a desire for peace on the one hand and developing a law of armed conflicts on the other, as both actions proceed from the same "faith in fundamental human rights, in the worth and dignity of the human person."

350 (1995), 183 N.R. 234 (F.C.A.).

351 *See, e.g.*, S/RES/661, Aug. 6, 1991.

352 S/RES/678, Nov. 29, 1990. For an overall discussion, *see* Thomas Franck, Fairness in International Law and Institutions 287 (1995).

353 U.N. Charter, Art. 2(4).

354 Military and Paramilitary Activities in and against Nicaragua (Nicaragua v. U.S.), 1986 ICJ Reports 14 [hereinafter *Nicaragua Judgment*], at 100-101.

underlie this determination. One opinion, submitted by Judge Sette-Camera referred broadly to the "non-use of force as well as non-intervention [...] as a corollary of equality of States and self-determination".[355]

Another separate opinion in the case, filed by Judge Nagendra Singh, articulated the significant connection between international preemption of the use of force and concern for the maintenance of international peace and security. Specifically, Judge Singh wrote that "the principle of non-use of force belongs to the realm of *jus cogens*, and is the very cornerstone of the human effort to promote peace in a world torn by strife".[356] This concept constitutes a logical extension of the Nuremberg Charter which included, in Article 6(a), charges relating to the "waging of a war of aggression".[357] As noted by Telford Taylor, this approach distinguished the war crimes effort at Nuremberg as an "idealistic prosecution" because it was clear that the bar against aggression was at the heart of international peace among sovereigns.[358] The "right to peace", furthermore, has gained considerable acceptance as being included within the "third generation of rights" which, although their realization lies in the future, constitute a part of the legitimate patrimony of mankind.[359]

The strength of the bar against aggression, therefore, while lacking the clear human rights implications of war crimes prosecutions, can be seen as a vital integument of the modern international order. Refugee claimants who advance as the basis for their claims a refusal to cooperate with violations of the law of peace (especially where the international community is acting to restrain sovereign acts of international "aggression") should receive international protection on the self-evident ground that they are advancing international public policy. A contrary result would create a glaring schism between refugee doctrine and the broader field of general international law to which refugee jurisprudence is inevitably related.

In a similar way, on February 22, 1993, the United Nations Security Council resolved, pursuant to Chapter VII of the Organization's Charter, to

---

[355] *Id.* at 199 (Sette-Camera, J., separate opinion).

[356] *Id.* at 153 (Singh, J., separate opinion).

[357] Charter of the International Military Tribunal, Aug. 8, 1945, 59 Stat. 1544, 82 U.N.T.S. 279 [hereinafter the Nuremberg Charter], Art. 6(a).

[358] *See, e.g.*, Telford Taylor, The Anatomy of the Nuremberg Trials 635 (1992).

[359] *See generally* Karel Vasak, *Pour un troisieme generation des droits de l'homme, in* Studies and Essays on International Humanitarian Law and Red Cross Principles in Honour of Jean Pictet 837, 840 (Christophe Swinarski ed. 1984). *See also* Henry Shue, Basic Rights: Subsistence, Affluence and U.S. Foreign Policy (2d ed. 1996), which stresses subsistence and security rights as being at the center of those basic rights which it is the primary responsibility of the international community to uphold.

establish an international war crimes tribunal responsible for prosecuting serious violations of international humanitarian law taking place in the former Yugoslavia since 1991.[360] By resolution dated November 8, 1994, a similar measure was adopted with respect to grave human rights violations arising out of the recent climactic violence affecting Rwanda.[361]

The United Nations Secretary-General in his first report on *Respect for Human Rights in Armed Conflict*, gave full recognition to the relationship between protecting international human rights and world peace and security:

> The Second World War gave conclusive proof of the close relationship between outrageous behavior of a Government towards its own citizens and aggression towards other nations, thus between respect for human rights and the maintenance of the peace.[362]

In the *Nicaragua Judgment*,[363] the ICJ found that common Article 3 of the Geneva Conventions was a peremptory norm of international law.[364] The ICJ held in effect that common Article 3, by virtue of its centrality to the Conventions as a whole, established a minimum standard of conduct which would apply in wars both of an international and of a non-international character.[365] The ICJ also characterized common Article 3 as setting forth "elementary considerations of humanity," which were governing with respect to both international and to non-international armed conflict.[366] For

---

360 S/RES 808, Feb. 22, 1993. *See also Report of the Secretary-General Pursuant to Paragraph 2 of Security Council Resolution 808* (1992), U.N. Doc. No. S/25704 (1993), discussing the law to be applied by the tribunal. In general, humanitarian law is modern usage for that body of principles which was previously referred to as the law of war, as established by treaty and by customary law. *See generally* Yoram Dinstein, *Human Rights in Armed Conflict: International Humanitarian Law, in* Theodor Meron (ed.), Human Rights in International Law 345 (1988).

361 S/RES 955, Nov. 8, 1994.

362 *Respect for Human Rights in Armed Conflict*, Report of the Secretary General, U.N. Doc. A/7120 (1969), ¶ 16.

363 *Nicaragua Judgment, supra* this section, note 354.

364 *Id.* at 114.

365 Article 55 of the Vienna Convention on the Law of Treaties explains the status of peremptory norms in the following way:

> A peremptory norm of general international law is a norm accepted and recognized by the international community of States as a whole as a norm from which no derogation is permitted and which can be modified only by a subsequent norm of general international law having the same character

Vienna Convention on the Law of Treaties, *in force* Jan. 22, 1980, 1155 U.N.T.S. 331, *reprinted in* 8 I.L.M. 679 (1969), Art. 55.

366 *Nicaragua Judgment, supra* this section, note 354, at 114 *citing* the *Corfu Channel* case (United Kingdom v. Albania), 1949 ICJ 4.

purposes of this analysis, the court viewed common Article 3 not so much as embodying treaty obligations but as a codification of customary law. A similar view was taken of common Article 1 which obligates signatory States to "respect" and to "ensure respect" for the Conventions. These responsibilities, the court found, flowed not from the Conventions themselves, but from "general principles of humanitarian law to which the Conventions merely give expression".[367]

The decision of the ICJ that common Article 3 sets forth peremptory norms of customary international law is supported by the *Commentary* to Geneva Convention I which clearly indicates that Article 3 is simply declarative of rules already extant at the time of its adoption.[368] Specifically, the Commentary provides that Article 3 demands respect for rules "already recognized as essential in all civilized countries, and enacted in the municipal law of the states in question, long before the Convention was signed".[369] Jean Pictet, the leading commentator on the Conventions, agrees with the foregoing judgment concerning the "pre-existing" character of Article 3 principles:

> [Humanitarian law] presents the rudiments of humanity; a minimum applicable at all times, in all places and circumstances ... [a]lthough based on written law, they are part of the customs of the people from which none may disengage himself.[370]

Treatise law thus provides a contextual underpinning for the development of common Article 3 in its relationship to internal wars. Central to this development is the principle of respect for the human personality (the philosophical mainstay of the Conventions, and in fact their core sustaining principle) which is "older" than the treaties, and is in fact independent of them.[371] The evolution of common Article 3 underscores the irreducible ethical character of the peremptory norms codified in the Conventions' provisions governing internal wars as well as their universal character. As set forth in the *Commentary* to Geneva Convention I:

> The principle of respect for human personality, which is at the root of all the Geneva Conventions, was not the product of the Conventions. It is older than they are and independent of them. Until 1949 it only found expression in the Conventions in its application to military personnel. But it was not applied to them because of their military status: *It is concerned with persons, not as*

---

367 *Id.*

368 Commentary to Geneva Convention I, *supra* § I.2, note 40, at 39. (Emphasis supplied).

369 *Id.* at 50.

370 J. Pictet, Principles of Humanitarian Law 26 (1966).

371 Commentary to Geneva Convention 1, *supra* § I.2, note 40, at 38, 41.

> *soldiers but as human beings without regard to their uniforms, their allegiance or their race, or their religious or other beliefs, without regard even to any obligations the Authority on which they depend may have assumed in their name or in their behalf. Wounded or sick, they are entitled as such to the care and aid which the respect for human personality enjoins.*[372]

As an illustration that central principles of international humanitarian law have universal reach, the Yugoslavian War Crimes Tribunal has recently ruled that certain prohibitions in both common Article 3 and Protocol II (relating to civil wars) were of such normative importance that a violation of them would give rise to criminal liability in the actor under the principle of universal jurisdiction. The Tribunal's ruling is in evident conformity with the broad policy goal of all international humanitarian law to protect, wherever possible, the individual human personality without regard as to which side the individual is identified with in the conflict:

> A State sovereignty approach has been gradually supplanted by a human-being oriented approach. Gradually the maxim of Roman law *hominum causa omne jus constitutum est* (all law is created for the benefit of human beings) has gained a foothold in the international community as well. It follows that in the area of armed conflict the distinction between interstate wars and civil wars is losing its value as far as human beings are concerned. Why protect civilians from belligerent violence, or ban rape, torture or the wanton destruction of hospitals, churches, museums or private property, as well as proscribe weapons causing unnecessary suffering when two sovereign States are engaged in war, and yet refrain from enacting the same bans or providing the same protection when armed violence has erupted "only" within the territory of a sovereign State? If international law, while of course safeguarding the legitimate interests of States, must gradually turn to the protection of human beings, it is only natural that the aforementioned dichotomy should gradually lose its weight.[373]

The foregoing ruling has significant implications with respect to the policy concerns which are shaping modern international law. In this instance, the Yugoslavian War Crimes Tribunal looked not merely at the "seriousness" of the rights violated (i.e., their putative character as *jus cogens*), but also at the potentially contradictory results produced by protecting some human rights in international conflict, while leaving these same rights unprotected in internal wars.

The result reached by the Yugoslavian War Crimes Tribunal is obviously in accord with the broad objectives of the law of Geneva and its aim of establishing an absolute standard of humanity applicable in all circumstances

---

[372] *Id.* at 39. [Emphasis supplied].

[373] *Tadic Appeal, supra* § IV.4(b), note 240, ¶ 54.

and from which none may disengage.[374] The *Tadic* decision now effectively extends the *jus cogens* status of humanitarian norms to fundamental principles of combat law (including the proportionality principle whereby attacks on legitimate military targets are not permissible if they produce disproportionate collateral consequences for civilians and their objects). The approach adopted in *Tadic*, however, only becomes possible by the comparative decline of State actors as subjects of international law, and the corresponding rise of the individual with respect to whom international humanitarian law now enjoys, in the area of internal armed conflict, primacy and direct effect.[375]

The fact that central principles of international humanitarian law are fundamental illustrates why a claimant's refusal to violate such norms should support an asylum claim, even in the absence of formal international condemnation. The universality of the principles involved shows clearly that serious military misconduct in armed conflict offends rules of long-standing which are viewed as matters of public policy by the international community. Claimants who refuse to contravene such norms present themselves as champions of the humane legal order codified in the law of Geneva. Their conscientious opposition to human rights violators, often undertaken at considerable risk, should receive appropriate treatment under the Refugee Convention. Such individuals have exposed themselves to political opinion persecution by refusing themselves to become persecutors.

---

[374] Pictet, *supra* § I.1, note 18, at 26.

[375] For arguments supporting the view that violations of Protocol II (as well as of common Article 3) should be included within the subject matter jurisdiction of the International Criminal Court Statute, *see* Lawyers' Committee for Human Rights, *Establishing an International Criminal Court: Major Unresolved Issues in the Draft Statute* 7 (August 1996):

> The Lawyers' Committee also endorses the view that crimes committed in non-international armed conflict currently covered by Common Article 3 of the Geneva Conventions and Additional Protocol II, should be included in the statute. The reality of armed conflict today proves that mass-scale violations of international humanitarian law are being committed in conflicts which are not international, or at least did not begin as such. Taking account of this reality, the Tribunal for the former Yugoslavia reiterated the customary law status of Common Article 3 in a recent ruling.

### § IV.5(c). The Refugee Definition and Insurgency Against the State: Opposition to Coercive Governments as a Basis for Refugee Status

Perhaps the most apparent application of the prosecution versus persecution bar arises when the individual asylum seeker has engaged or assisted in armed rebellion against the sovereign State. The State has an overriding right in such instances to defend itself, its capacity to uphold the human rights of its citizens depending on its ability to resist armed aggression.[376] The Board's initial treatment of the "right to rebel", accordingly, denied the underlying asylum claim despite a country background which showed that the sovereign in question (Ghana) had foreclosed all orderly democratic change and similarly engaged in widespread violations of fundamental human rights.[377]

In *Dwomoh*, the Board dismissed a claim brought by an asylum seeker who had been imprisoned and virtually sentenced to death by virtue of his having participated in a conspiracy to overthrow the (then) highly oppressive regime of Flight Lieutenant Jerry Rawlings. Dwomoh, a native and citizen of Ghana, had joined the Ghanaian army in 1974, eventually attaining the rank of sergeant.[378] In 1985, while he was a weapons instructor at the Military Academy, applicant discovered that a friend, Sergeant Tawiah, had been imprisoned for attempting to overthrow the Ghanaian government. In order to secure his friend's release, Dwomoh agreed with a warrant officer to join Sergeant Tawiah in a further effort to overturn the existing Ghanaian regime. The planned coup was discovered by agents of the government; Dwomoh was arrested and charged with mutiny. During the resulting interrogation, he was beaten several times. Applicant was then confined for approximately one year at Usser Fort Prison where prisoners, according to the evidence adduced, often "disappeared."[379] In 1986, during a visit to a prison hospital, Dwomoh managed an escape through the bathroom window.[380]

The Board looked to the *Handbook* for guidance in making its determination on the prosecution versus persecution bar. These factors were enumerated by the Board as: (i) the nature of the crime; (ii) the severity of

---

376 The sovereign's right to survival is described in J. Brierly, The Law of Nations 49 (6th ed. 1963).

377 Matter of Nana Asante Dwomoh, A26 805 882, Executive Office for Immigration Review (Board of Immigration Appeals), August 1, 1988 (unreported decision), *rev'd,* Dwomoh v. Sava, 696 F. Supp. 970 (S.D.N.Y. 1988).

378 *Id.* at 2.

379 *Id.*

380 *Id.* at 3.

the punishment; (iii) the political opinion motivating the asylum seeker to commit the crime; and (iv) the nature of the law upon which prosecution will be based.[381] Relying especially on the criterion of "proportionality" (i.e., between the level of punishment and the gravity of the offense), the Board concluded that, for the crime of treason, even the punishment of death would not be "excessive".[382] The BIA therefore ruled that any punishment meted out by the Rawlings regime would not be on account of the claimant's political opinion. An important and influential dissent in the case filed by Board member Michael Heilman clearly set down the framework for the future evolution of the case law. The dissent accepts the general right in the sovereign to defend itself against all forms of insurrection. Such a right, however, is conditioned on the State's continuing to uphold the "political freedoms" of its own citizens, as determined by existence of an implicit "social contract". Failure by the State to maintain such liberties will occasion a loss of legitimacy, so as to relieve the citizen of a corresponding duty to respect the State's authority.[383]

The District Court decision which reversed *Dwomoh* should now be viewed as an authoritative pronouncement regarding the law on insurrection as the basis for asylum. In *Dwomoh* v. *Sava*,[384] the U.S. District Court for the Southern District of New York ruled that Ghana's preemption of peaceful political discussion as a basis for orderly democratic change rendered the asylum claim viable: punishment for involvement in an attempted coup against such a preemptively authoritarian regime constituted persecution, not prosecution.[385] The District Court's decision relied extensively on the legislative history of the Refugee Act,[386] as well as the political offense exception to extradition in municipal law. Of significance, the *Dwomoh* court had no difficulty in arriving at a normative determination regarding Ghana's non-democratic status. Counsel for Dwomoh had secured a letter from the United Nations High Commissioner for Refugees regarding country conditions in Ghana. The letter reflected that "in Africa, a coup is often the only means

381 *Id.* at 3-4. *See generally Handbook* , *supra* § I.1, note 30, ¶¶ 56, 57, 85 and 86.

382 Matter of Dwomoh, *supra*, at 4. The Board drew an analogy in this respect to United States law criminalizing treason (18 U.S.C. §§ 2381-2385) to support its thesis that the punishment of treasonable acts by the sovereign was internationally accepted and, therefore, not disproportionate. *Id.*

383 Matter of Dwomoh, *supra*, at 6 (dissenting opinion).

384 Dwomoh v. Sava, 696 F. Supp. 970 (S.D.N.Y. 1988). Although normally District Court decisions are highly limited both jurisdictionally and in terms of precedential weight, they may become significant if they are later cited in a Circuit or a Board decision.

385 *Id.* at 979.

386 Pub. L. No. 96-212, 94 Stat. 102 (1980).

through which a change in the political regime can be effected...," and that, in such cases, a fear of punishment arising from an unsuccessful coup attempt may be regarded as "persecution" under the 1951 Convention on Refugees.[387]

*Dwomoh* was cited with approval in the leading administrative case on the subject, *Matter of Izatula*.[388] The immigration judge had denied asylum in *Izatula* largely on the basis that the Afghan State had engaged in lawful prosecution, not persecution, by seeking to punish the asylum seeker's provision of aid to the mujahidin, an organized coalition of Islamic forces attempting to overthrow the national Marxist government in Kabul.[389] In overturning this result, the Board held that Afghanistan essentially lacked legitimacy as a sovereign existing under international law.[390] In this respect, the Afghan State did not recognize peaceful democratic change, but was a totalitarian regime maintained in power by the Soviet Union.[391] The Board supported this result with general findings that Afghanistan did not tolerate any political opposition, but engaged in significant human rights violations with respect to opponents and perceived opponents of the regime. These violations included torture to punish such victims, extract information, or coerce confessions.[392]

Canadian law, like U.S. jurisprudence in this area, orients asylum analysis to the political offence exception in extradition law. It is important

---

387 Dwomoh v. Sava, 696 F. Supp. 970, 976 (S.D.N.Y. 1988). *See* Letter from the United Nations High Commissioner for Refugees to Bradford Smith, Esq., August 31, 1988, *quoted in* Dwomoh v. Sava, 696 F. Supp. 970, 979 (S.D.N.Y. 1988).

388 20 I&N Dec. 149 (BIA 1990).

389 *Id.*

390 *Id.* at 153-54.

391 *Id.*

392 Matter of Izatula, 20 I&N Dec. 149, 153 (BIA 1990). Torture techniques, which included physical and psychological abuses, consisted of electric shocks to sensitive parts of the anatomy, immersion in water, beatings, and prolonged deprivation of sleep. *Id.* For a recent decision in U.S. asylum law which accepts the principle of *Izatula*, but finds it inapplicable, *see* Chanco v. INS, 82 F.3d 298 (9th Cir. 1996). In *Chanco*, a Philippine military officer had participated in an attempted *coup d'état*. Essentially the court implicitly accepted that where a government does not respect the internationally recognized right of peaceful protest, punishment imposed on the asylum seeker for politically motivated violence may well constitute persecution, not prosecution. The *Chanco* court also agreed that "disproportionate" punishment for such a political act could support an asylum claim. However, under the facts of the case, the court found that neither of these conditions existed. The Philippine government had not restricted peaceful speech so that recourse to armed rebellion was not justified. Moreover, there was no evidence of disproportionate punishment.

to note, however, that Canadian law treats the question of whether armed insurrection is justified not in the context of qualifying under the refugee definition, but rather in the context of whether the exclusion ground (in Article 1F(b) pertaining to serious non-political crimes) precludes recognition of refugee status. By way of preface, in 1994, the Immigration and Refugee Board had prepared a Research Paper containing suggestive guidelines for determining when an offense may be deemed "political" under the Convention refugee definition so as to avoid application of the Article 1F(b) preclusion. The Research Paper set forth a four-part test under which a political crime:

> (a) is one committed out of genuine political motives, as opposed to personal reasons or gain;
>
> (b) is likely to be committed in a period of disturbance, in order to gain control of the country or in order to avoid or stop persecution; i.e., the crime is directed towards a modification of the political organization of the State;
>
> (c) is committed against a target which is closely connected to the political motive; in that respect the crime should not be out of proportion to the alleged political motive nor should it be of an atrocious or barbarous nature;
>
> (d) is ultimately committed when no other peaceful means of obtaining the desired political change is available.[393]

In *Gil* v. *M.E.I.*,[394] the Court of Appeal was required to rule on whether an Iranian asylum seeker whom the Immigration and Refugee Board had determined to have a well-founded fear of persecution should be excluded from refugee status in that he had putatively committed a serious non-political crime. The claimant had been an active supporter of the Shah's regime, his father having worked for the Shah's brother. After the Ayatollah came to power in 1979, the family began to experience harassment of a serious nature at the hands of the local revolutionary committee. Applicant joined an underground student group which eventually merged with a larger, more militant group of anti-Khomeni activists. In 1980 and 1981, applicant became involved in serious incidents of arson directed against wealthy supporters of the regime. These incidents involved the placing of bombs and Molotov cocktails in the businesses of these persons which were located in the bazaars; the bombs were apparently designed to explode at a time when

---

393 *Research Paper on Article 1F of the 1951 Convention Relating to the Status of Refugees in Canadian Law,* IRB Legal Services, December 14, 1994, at 47, *quoted in* Immigration and Refugee Board, *Interpretation of the Convention Refugee Definition in the Case Law* § 9.30 (June 30, 1995).

394 (1994), 174 N.R. 292 (F.C.A.).

the bazaars were frequented by innocent bystanders so that many innocent persons were injured and even killed in the resulting explosions.[395]

The Court of Appeals began its decision by noting that there was not an exact correspondence between the political offence exception on one hand and refugee status on the other, although there would necessarily, the court opined, be a substantial area of overlap. The differences noted by the tribunal were the following:

> (i) Extradition is carried out pursuant to a bilateral treaty under which the rights of States are invoked inter se.
>
> (ii) In extradition, the governing aim of the proceeding is for the requesting State to have the "fugitive" returned; in refugee status proceedings, there is generally no desire on the part of the country of nationality to have the putative refugee returned.
>
> (iii) In extradition, the "fugitive" generally contests his guilt; the refugee on the other hand admits the operative facts said to constitute his guilt but argues that they are "political " in nature.
>
> (iv) The refugee is putatively in danger of "persecution" if he is returned; with respect to an alien seeking to resist extradition, "it is generally assumed" that the requesting State will afford the defendant due process.[396]

The essential rationale of the decision adopts as its premise that for an offence to be of a political character (so as to be outside the exception) there must be proportionality between the activity of the asylum seeker (to whom the ground of exclusion is sought to be applied) and the political objective to be attained.[397] *Interpretation of the Convention Refugee Definition in the Case Law* also perceives the *Gil* case as requiring a balancing between the seriousness of the crime and the repressive nature of the regime in determining whether the claimant's crime is a political one, thus inviting an essentially open-ended analysis in which the total situation controls.[398]

The language ultimately adopted by the tribunal, however, strongly mirrors the general correlation between democratic norms on the one hand, and the right to engage in armed insurrection on the other, which has played so compelling a role in United States adjudications. In this respect, the *Gil* court emphasized that a crucial factor in determining the applicability of the political offence exception was the nature of the regime against which the crime was committed. A repressive regime which foreclosed freedom of

---

395 *Id.* at 295.

396 *Id.* at 296.

397 *Id.* at 309.

398 *Interpretation of the Convention Refugee Definition in the Case Law, supra* § II.3, note 63, § 10.3.2.

expression and orderly democratic process would provide the claimant with no option but rebellion to effect political change; constitutional governments guaranteeing freedom of speech and genuine democratic empowerment would tend to preempt violence as a legitimate means to effect reform:

> Where it is appropriate to use the proportionality test under paragraph 1(F)(b) is in the weighing of the gravity of the crime as part of the process of determining if we should brand it as "political." *A very serious crime, such as murder, may be accepted as political if the regime against which it is committed is repressive and offers no scope for freedom of expression and peaceful change of government or governmental policy. Under such a regime, the claimant might be found to have no other option to bring about political change.* On the other hand, if the regime is a liberal democracy with constitutional guarantees of free speech and expression (assuming that such a regime could ever produce a genuine refugee) it is very difficult to think of any crime, let alone a serious one, which we would consider to be an acceptable method of political action. To put the matter in concrete terms, the plotters against Hitler might have been able to claim refugee status; the assassins of John F. Kennedy could never do so.[399]

The court then ruled that, under the above formulation of the "serious non-political crime" ground of exclusion, the refugee claimant did not qualify: there was no nexus between his activities and a realistic political objective. The claimant's targeting of innocent non-combatants, moreover, was unacceptable irrespective of the "repressive, totalitarian or dictatorial" nature of the government to which opposition is asserted:

> Where the appellant's claim fails the incidence test, however, is in the second branch thereof. There is, in my view, simply no objective connection between injuring the commercial interests of certain wealthy supporters of the regime and any realistic goal of forcing the regime itself to fall or to change its ways or its policies. This, I think, is what the Board was attempting to convey when it talked of the appellant's crimes failing "to go beyond personal vindictiveness toward something which would alter political organizations that existed at that time". Even if we accept (which the Board appears to have done) that some of the businesses targeted were owned by highly placed members of the local revolutionary committees, the nexus between such businesses and the general structure of the government of Iran at the time appears far too tenuous to support or justify the indiscriminate violence which the applicant admitted to.[400]

*Gil* tends to oversimplify the questions which must be resolved in such cases. The eligibility of armed insurgents for asylum or refugee status really breaks down into two questions. The first of these is whether rebellion is privileged at all, and that question is determined by analyzing the nature of

---

399 *Id.* [Emphasis supplied].

400 *Id.* at 308.

the regime against which rebellion has been waged. The second step of the analysis, however, relates to the question of whether the claimant has conformed to prevailing standards of international humanitarian law in conducting hostilities, or whether the ground of exclusion in Article 1F(a) (precluding from refugee status those who have committed war crimes) applies. *Gil* deals with both sides of the required analysis without specifically identifying the second prong of it.

Another case of significance which deals with opposition to coercive governments in a context other than armed rebellion is *Mohamed* v. *M.E.I.*[401] In *Mohamed*, the claimant, a citizen of Sudan, had been Chief of Police in the City of Rashad when the previous democratic regime was overthrown by an illegal military coup. Claimant was ordered by the new regime to arrest the leaders of all opposition political parties and to seize their property. When he refused to execute these orders, he was removed from his post. The claimant later fled Sudan and sought refugee status in Canada. The Federal Court-Trial Division viewed claimant's fear not as one of prosecution, since the orders he received had no legal foundation. His refusal to execute them would give rise to persecution based on perceived political opinion. The court based its decision on the evident lack of legitimacy of the orders which claimant was required to carry out and on the regime's "abysmal" human rights record.[402]

The case is noteworthy because it provides a bridge between the conscription cases (discussed in the previous section) and the decisions dealing with insurrection. There is a growing inclination to view State "legitimacy" as being measured by human rights compliance (including conformity to prevailing principles of international humanitarian law). A regime which systematically declines to uphold human rights to an acceptable level loses its sovereign prerogative to enforce laws of general application. Opposition to such regimes, whether through armed rebellion or through peaceful non-

---

401 (1994), 176 N.R. 60 (F.C.A.).

402 As in conscription cases, an element of "conscience" is required where the claim is based on armed opposition to coercive regimes. In *Antonio* v. *M.E.I.*, (F.C.T.D., no. IMM-1072-93), September 27, 1994, the claimant had avoided military service in Angola by accepting employment as a telex agent with a governmental telecommunications office. Claimant used this position to obtain information regarding government troop movements for the FLEC and UNITA, rebel groups seeking to overturn the government. Claimant's incentive for cooperating had been the extrajudicial killing of his aunt (who had been a rebel activist) by government forces. Claimant's activity was discovered; he was arrested and accused of treason. He escaped and sought refugee status in Canada. The court found that the claimant's act of espionage was not inspired by a political opinion, and hence would not serve as a basis for refugee status. Moreover, the death penalty which claimant faced was not disproportionate in light of his crime of espionage.

compliance, can serve as the basis for refugee status or asylum. And the country of asylum will often decline to give the violated law extra-territorial application on the grounds that to do so would offend the public policy of forum.

## § IV.5(d). The International Framework of Rebellion Cases: The "Democratic Entitlement" in International Law

Principal among the guiding purposes and principles of the United Nations is the continuing development of normative standards regarding basic human rights, including now the collective right to democratic government. Significant recent scholarship has concluded that the "democratic entitlement" is an emerging norm under customary international law and that it occupies a position of centrality with respect to other basic human rights so as to form with these an ordered constellation. As noted by perhaps the most prominent advocate of this position:

> How coherent in this sense is normative canon of the democratic entitlement? It is apparent from the above examination of the global and regional texts and processes that the rules pertaining to self-determination, freedom of expression, and the right to participate in a free and open electoral choice are closely interwoven strands of the same fabric. These three generations of democratic entitlement, reinforced by regional systems, not only share many identical or similar norms, but also have common or comparable institutions, procedures and customs. Each thread reinforces, and is reinforced by, the weave of the cloth.[403]

The matrix for the contemporary right to "democratic entitlement" can be found in the Charter's principle of self-determination.[404] Supporting this "older", more pedigreed, principle, however, are basic guarantees outlined in succeeding constitutive documents of the United Nations. These include normative provisions under UDHR governing the right to participate in government; the right of equal access to the public service; and the principle that the will of the people is the sole basis of governmental authority.[405] The

---

403 *See, e.g.*, Franck, *supra* § IV.5(b), note 352, at 121.

404 *Id.* at 91:

> Self-determination is the historic root from which the democratic entitlement grew. Together with two newer forms—freedom of expression and electoral right—it constitutes the matrix of the democratic entitlement. As the oldest of the three generations of rights to political participation, self-determination endows the entitlement with an important gravitas of historically pedigreed legitimacy.

405 *See, e,g,* UDHR, *supra* § I.1, note 12, Art. 21:

guarantees laid down in the Universal Declaration have received concrete recognition in the International Covenant on Civil and Political Rights (ICCPR) which establishes the right to take part in public affairs and to vote at periodic and genuine elections.[406]

The electoral right must also be seen as closely connected with other fundamental freedoms, most particularly the rights to expression and peaceful assembly guaranteed both by UDHR (arts. 19 and 20) and by ICCPR (arts. 18 and 22). Importantly, Article 19(2) of ICCPR provides:

> Everyone shall have the right to freedom of expression; this right shall include freedom to seek, receive and impart information and ideas of all kinds, regardless of frontiers, either orally, in writing or in print, in the form of art, or through any other media of his [or her] choice.[407]

Importantly, the emerging customary norm of "democratic entitlement" has now received explicit recognition in the form of United Nations enforcement action under Chapter VII of the Charter. Accordingly, when a military coup overturned the elected government of Haiti in the fall of 1991, the General Assembly passed a resolution which "strongly condemned both the attempted illegal replacement of the constitutional President of Haiti and the use of violence, military coercion and the violation of human rights in the country". The resolution also demanded the "immediate restoration of the legitimate government".[408] In June of 1993, moreover, sanctions were imposed by the Security Council acting under Chapter VII of the United Nations Charter against the military junta. These measures were without precedent, and constituted a case of first impression in which the UN's

---

> 1. Everyone has the right to take part in the Government of his country, directly or through freely chosen representatives.
>
> 2. Everyone has the right of equal access to public service in his country.
>
> 3. The will of the people shall be the basis of the authority of the government; this will shall be expressed in periodic and genuine elections which shall be by universal and equal suffrage and shall be held by secret vote or by equivalent free voting procedures.

406 ICCPR, *supra* § I.1, note 14, Art. 25. Article 25 guarantees the right of everyone:

> (a) To take part in the conduct of public affairs, directly or through freely chosen representatives;
>
> (b) To vote at genuine periodic elections which shall be by universal and equal suffrage and shall be held by secret ballot, guaranteeing the free expression of the will of the electors.

407 ICCPR, *supra* § I.1, note 14, Art. 19(2).

408 G.A. Res. A/46/L.8/Rev. 1, ¶¶ 1, 2, 3 (1991). The resolution is discussed in Franck, *supra* § IV.5(b), note 352, at 112.

Chapter VII enforcement powers had been utilized to restore democratic government wrongly overthrown by an illegal coup.[409]

In summary, both democratic norms and self-determination have their common underpinnings in the concept of popular sovereignty[410] and the ideal that peoples should be free to shape their own political and social futures. This close connection between democratic theory and self-determination remains an important element of modern policy. There is an implicit linkage, for instance, between the core freedoms of the ICCPR (e.g., freedom of thought, conscience, expression, movement and association), and the broader collective freedom (the "democratic entitlement") within which these individual freedoms can be exercised in a meaningful way. As one commentator has framed it:

> The close link between self-determination and individual human rights is one of the main features of Western doctrine. As was stated in 1972 by the U.S. delegate to the Third Committee of the General Assembly, 'freedom of choice is indispensable to the exercise of the right of self-determination.' For this freedom of choice to be meaningful, there must be corresponding freedom of thought, conscience, expression, movement and association. Self-determination entails legitimate, lively dissent and testing at the ballot box with frequent regularity.[411]

The relationship between human rights in general (including the "democratic entitlement") and the law of refugee status is not novel, but has historically been recognized as critical to the evolution of the refugee definition. It is largely because the 1951 Convention was drafted in an environment of international concern for the protection of basic human rights that individual assertion of such rights will give rise to persecution if serious harm is threatened or imposed as a result. Atle Grahl-Madsen has saliently provided examples of those freedoms set forth in UDHR which will support the "political opinion" ground of refugee protection if conscientiously adhered to by the asylum seeker:

> (1) Article 19, which sets forth that 'everyone has the right to freedom of opinion and expression; this right includes freedom to hold opinions without

---

409 *See, e.g.*, Franck, *supra* § IV.5(b), note 352, at 112, *citing* S/RES 841 (1993):

> For the first time, collective measures had been employed to compel a violator government to give effect to the democratic entitlement.

410 *See generally* Ian Brownlie, *The Rights of Peoples in Modern International Law, in* The Rights of Peoples 1 (James Crawford ed. 1988).

411 A. Cassese, *Political Self-Determination—Old and New Developments, in* U.N. Law/Fundamental Rights: Two Topics in International Law 154-55 (A. Cassese ed. 1979), *quoted in* Eugene Kamenka, *Human Rights, Peoples' Rights, in* The Rights of Peoples 136 (James Crawford ed. 1988).

> interference and to seek, receive and impart information and ideas through any media and regardless of frontiers';
>
> (2) Article 20(2) which lays down that 'no one may be compelled to belong to an association'. The term 'association' here comprises political parties.
>
> (3) Article 21(3) which provides for periodic and genuine elections which shall be held by secret vote or by equivalent free voting procedures.
>
> (4) Article 26(2), which proclaims strengthening of respect for human rights and fundamental freedoms as well as promotion of understanding, tolerance and friendship among all nations, racial or religious groups as important goals of education.[412]

Consistently with the above, Grahl-Madsen maintains that it is "persecution" and not "prosecution" if the asylum seeker has engaged in armed resistance against a totalitarian or preemptively authoritarian regime.[413] Grahl-Madsen limits this basis for refugee status to those who resist sovereign authority in countries which persecute persons because of their beliefs and to countries where opposition is not tolerated.[414] In a parallel fashion, the exclusion ground otherwise governing "serious non-political crimes" clearly does not disqualify such a claimant where governmental enforcement action is based on his or her rebellion.[415]

Including within the refugee definition those who have opposed, even through armed insurrection, preemptively authoritarian (totalitarian) regimes has strong historical support. The International Refugee Organization refused in practice to apply the prosecution versus persecution bar to those who had transgressed the laws of totalitarian governments.[416] Recognizing refugee status in these instances was entirely appropriate in light of the

---

412 1 Grahl-Madsen, *supra* § I.1, note 7, at 227.

413 *Id.* at 253.

> For this contention we may find support in the wording of Article 1A(2). The words persecution 'for reasons of political opinion' may be read so as to imply that the Convention is designed to meet the needs of persons fleeing from a country where people are persecuted because of their beliefs, where opposition is not tolerated. The fact that anyone has taken up resistance or committed other acts for political motives against an oppressive government and thereby become liable to sanctions, shall not disqualify him from gaining refugee status. It is our assertion that this is, in a nutshell, the meaning of the provision just discussed.

414 *Id.*

415 Handbook, *supra* § I.1, note 30, ¶ 155.

416 *See generally* Dwomoh v. Sava, 969 F. Supp. 96, 97, *citing* International Refugee Organization, Manual for Eligibility Officers (May 1950).

standard exclusion existing for those who had cooperated with quisling regimes or those seeking to defeat the "United Nations".[417]

Recognizing such claimants as eligible refugees also draws considerable support from the origins of the political offense exception in extradition law. Nineteenth-century democracies developed a concern for protecting against extradition only those who had rebelled against "tyrannical" governments.[418] The development of the political offense exception to extradition treaties by nineteenth-century republics obviously drew its force from a liberal theory of constitutional formation pursuant to which the authority of the state was said to rest on the consent of the governed alone. Evolution of the exception has occasionally invoked its original rationale.[419]

In one remarkable British adjudication,[420] the Queen's Bench Trial Division upheld the exception with respect to several Polish seamen who had overpowered other members of the crew on board a trawler in the North Sea in order to flee to England and seek asylum there. The court stressed in its analysis that Poland was subject to a totalitarian regime in which any form of opposition (including flight) would be viewed as a political offense. Comparing contemporary conditions with those prevailing when the political offense exception was first being formulated by the courts, the tribunal noted:

> It was not then treason for a citizen to leave his country and start a fresh life in another. Countries were not regarded as enemy countries when no war was in progress. Now a state of totalitarianism prevails in some parts of the world and it is a crime for citizens in such places to take steps to leave. In this case the members of a crew of a small trawler engaged in fishing were under political supervision and they revolted by the only means open to them. They

---

417 Constitution of the International Refugee Organization, G.A. Res. 62, U.N. Doc. A/64/ Add.1 at 97 (1947), Part 1, section A(2) and Part II.

418 Such views are pronounced in both United States and French constituent documents. The [U.S.] Declaration of Independence, for instance, sets forth:

> [W]henever any Form of Government becomes destructive of these ends, it is the Right of the People to alter or abolish it.

The Declaration of Independence, ¶ 2 (U.S. 1776). On the other hand, the French Constitution of 1793 provided:

> *Le peuple français donne asile aux étrangers bannis de leurs patrie pour la cause de la liberté - Il le refuse aux tyrans.*

Fr. Const. of 1793, Art. 120. ["The French people grant asylum to those banished from their countries for the cause of liberty - They refuse it to tyrants"].

419 *See generally* C. Van den Wijngaert, The Political Offense Exception to Extradition 100 (1980)

420 Regina v. Governor of Brixton Prison (*ex parte* Kolczynski), [1954] 1 Q.B. 540.

> committed an offence of a political character, and if they were surrendered there could be no doubt that, while they would be tried for the particular offence mentioned, they would be punished as for a political crime.[421]

Similar reasoning has appeared from time to time in U.S. decisions. In *In re Gonzalez*,[422] for instance, a U.S. District Court allowed the extradition of a Dominican who had been charged with having killed two prisoners while acting as a military guard there. The court noted the evolution of British case law and concluded that there was nothing in the record to suggest that the defendant had acted in the cause of freedom against a totalitarian regime.[423]

In any case, the historical exception to extradition law relating to those who rebel against preemptively authoritarian regimes coupled with the seminal character of the "democratic entitlement" *vis-à-vis* other human rights explains the proclivity of both U.S. and Canadian tribunals to exempt armed insurrection against "totalitarian" governments from the prosecution versus persecution bar. The exemption makes sense when it is recalled that the utility of political expression depends upon the constitutional framework within which such speech is exercised. The collective right to internal self-determination, moreover, (the ancestor of the "democratic entitlement") is a *jus cogens* right which serves as the cornerstone for modern international organization. Democratic norms are thus often perceived as a necessary culture for the exercise of human rights in general. Their suppression clearly evidences a social condition in which the individual's political expression will at best constitute an act of futility and at worst invite political repression. These considerations confirm that upholding the "democratic entitlement" is a matter of public policy as concerns the community of States. Those individuals who place themselves at risk on behalf of that policy should be admitted as refugees in accordance with the corollary function of refugee law to advance the seminal goals of the United Nations.

## § IV.6. Violation of Exit Control Laws as a Basis for Political Opinion Persecution

An important area in which the prosecution versus persecution preclusion has been repeatedly tested is that of exit control violations. The *Handbook* treats this class of asylum case as governed by two separate issues (i) whether the alien's illegal departure was occasioned by political considera-

421 *Id.* at 543-44.

422 217 F. Supp. 717 (S.D.N.Y. 1963).

423 *Id.* at 721, n. 9.

tions; and (ii) whether he/she would suffer "severe penalties" as a result.[424] Both Canadian and United States law have undergone a considerable evolution with respect to these questions.

Historically, Canada's treatment of such cases has not been receptive. In *Valentin* v. *M.E.I.*[425] the Federal Court-Trial Division announced general considerations with respect to adjudication of "exit control" claims. In *Valentin*, counsel had contended that a claimant's violations of section 109 of the Czech Criminal Code (dealing with exit controls) would be viewed in all instances by the authorities as a political crime. The Court of Appeal responded:

> Neither the international Convention nor our Act [...] had in mind the protection of people who, having been subjected to no persecution to date, themselves created a cause to fear persecution by freely, of their own accord and with no reason, making themselves liable to punishment for violating a criminal law of general application. I would add [...] that the idea does not even appear to me to be supported by the fact that the transgression was motivated by some dissatisfaction of a political nature [...], because it seems to me, first, that an isolated sentence can only in very exceptional cases satisfy the elements of repetition and relentlessness found at the heart of persecution ..., but particularly because the direct relationship that is required between the sentence incurred and imposed and the offender's political opinions does not exist.

The *Valentin* decision reflects traditional adjudicative reluctance to approve claims where the applicant has the ability to "bootstrap" himself or herself into refugee status without incurring substantial risk within the country of claimed persecution. The opinion clearly goes beyond this historical caution, however, when it asserts that the essential elements of persecution and of nexus are completely lacking in such cases. As reflected below, the case law of both Canada and the United States is becoming progressively more receptive to "exit control" cases.

U.S. law similarly has viewed departure control violations as a basis for asylum with skepticism. A long line of decisions shaped the jurisprudence making clear that only in the most exceptional circumstances would violation of departure control laws, standing alone, be sufficient to satisfy a claim to asylum.[426] The *Basic Law Manual* refers to these decisions,

---

[424] Handbook, *supra* § I.1, note 30, ¶ 61.

[425] [1991] 3 F.C. 390 (C.A.).

[426] *See, e.g.*, Matter of Exilius, 18 I&N Dec. 276 (BIA 1982); Matter of Sibrun, 18 I&N Dec. 354 (BIA 1983); Matter of Matelot, 18 I&N Dec. 334 (BIA 1982); Matter of Williams, 16 I&N Dec. 697 (BIA 1979); Matter of Nagy, 11 I&N Dec. 888 (BIA 1966). *But see* Janus & Janek, 12 I&N Dec. 866 (BIA 1968), holding that the treatment which awaited the asylum seeker for violating Czechoslovakia's exit control laws did not constitute

commenting that exit restraints are often a legitimate exercise of sovereignty and remarking that the United States exercises such controls.[427]

The *Basic Law Manual* also comments, however, that enhanced consideration is required if the foreign sovereign persecutes persons who violate departure control laws, or who seek asylum abroad. And it sets down the following critical guideline for adjudicating such claims:

> Asylum officers should also consider that an applicant's illegal departure from his country may have been an escape, and so may indicate a fear of persecution.[428]

The new trend in the U.S. and Canada has begun to explore the implications of an excessive sanction in measuring the objective reasonableness of the claimant's fear that she would be made to suffer upon return on account of a protected ground. Canadian tribunals will consider, for example, excessive repercussions (beyond the scope of the criminal statute) as evidence of persecution. In *Castaneda* v. *M.E.I.*[429] the Federal Court-Trial Division was confronted with the case of a Cuban national who had been sent to the Soviet Union for a period of study. While in the USSR, claimant had spoken out against the Cuban regime and had consequently been expelled as a student with questionable political views. He was provided with a ticket back to Cuba, but instead boarded a plane for Canada where he applied for refugee status. As a consequence of applicant's "defection", his family had received discriminatory treatment in the home State. Claimant's father had been threatened with loss of his thirty-year job and reassignment to labor in the fields. His mother had similarly been demoted since she was no longer perceived as trustworthy.

The court found that the IRB had failed to consider this evidence in denying the claim. Moreover, the *Castaneda* tribunal also determined that abuse of the parents constituted extra-judicial punishment which went beyond the sanction applicable for violating exit control laws. Such methods of punishing departure control violations would satisfy the "repetition and relentlessness" criteria for persecution which the *Valentin* court had held were often lacking. Moreover, the mistreatment of applicant's family provided a direct link between the claimant's act of defiance and his well-founded fear of persecution: what had transpired to applicant's parents was probative evidence of the treatment which claimant could expect.

---

punishment for offending a law of general application but "persecution for a political offense which he [applicant] has committed against the State". *Id.* at 875.

427 Basic Law Manual, *supra* § I.1, note 26, at 77.

428 *Id.*

429 (F.C.T.D., no. A-805-92), October 19, 1993.

In the U.S. a comparable view was advanced in *Rodriguez-Ramon* v. *INS*.[430] In *Rodriguez-Ramon*, the claimant was a college-educated native and citizen of Cuba who had escaped to the U.S. in 1983 by jumping ship. Applicant maintained in the asylum claim which he filed shortly thereafter that Cuba would view his "defection" as an act of treason; he had received various benefits from the Cuban government (including his college education and his merchant marine job). Claimant contended that abandoning these benefits would be viewed as politically hostile acts.[431] In addition, as had the claimant in *Castaneda*, the asylum seeker in *Rodriguez-Ramon* showed that relatives had received extra-judicial mistreatment as the result of his own act of violating exit controls. Among other things, one of applicant's brothers had been arrested by the authorities because he was believed to have assisted Rodriguez-Ramon. Two other brothers had lost their jobs as well. Applicant's father had been interrogated and told that his son was a traitor.[432]

In determining whether Rodriguez Ramon would return to persecution in Cuba, the court looked for its customary guidance to the *Handbook*. Applying the *Handbook*'s criteria (outlined above), the court ruled that an asylum seeker would qualify under the refugee definition if he showed: (a) that he would be subject to disproportionate punishment flowing from his illegal departure or stay abroad; and (b) that his motivation in leaving or remaining outside the country was related to a protected ground. While the court found that the claimant in *Rodriguez-Ramon* had met both prongs of the governing test, its emphasis is clearly on attributed political opinion as the basis for finding the refugee definition satisfied:

> [A] state which severely punishes unlawful departure views persons who illegally leave as disloyal and subversive and seeks to punish them accordingly. Thus, the motive that a petitioner must show on the part of the state is initially established on the face of a statute that criminalizes illegal departure. To put it in different terms, the statute imputes to those who are prosecuted pursuant to it, a political opinion that the state believes warrants an extreme form of punishment.[433]

The exit control cases bear some resemblance to those decisions pertaining to draft resistance and to rebellion against preemptively authoritarian regimes in the limited sense that they grapple with the suppression of human rights as compromising the sovereign's right to apply its criminal statutes to

---

430 98 F.3d 416 (9th Cir. 1996).

431 *Id.* at 419.

432 *Id.*

433 *Id.* at 430.

the asylum seeker. Unlike the latter cases, however, it is clear that in departure control decisions there is significant adjudicative reliance on the State's characterization of the claimant's act which lies at the heart of the analysis. In the conscription and insurrection cases, refugee analysis tends to focus on the relationship between claimant's conscientious opposition to the State's human rights abuses and the punishment expected, irrespective of the sovereign's view of the applicant's conduct or the punishment faced upon return. It is the intrinsic features of the applicant's persona which are essentially at issue and the vindication of the underlying human right asserted.[434] In the departure control cases, however, the principal inquiry centers on the State's view of the claimant's violation and it is this perception which is largely dispositive of the claim. Departure control cases, in other words, depend explicitly on the doctrine of attributed characteristics and beliefs, and a claim does not appear possible in the absence of the State's treatment of the claimant's exit control violation as an act of political disloyalty.[435]

## § IV.7. "Political Opinion" Persecution and Coercive Family Planning

The present state of U.S. law with respect to the long-litigated and controversial issue of whether opposition to coercive family planning can serve as the basis for asylum has now been legislatively resolved. In 1996, Congress modified the definition of the term "refugee" contained in section 101(a)(42) of the Immigration and Nationality Act so as to include:

> [A] person who has been forced to abort a pregnancy or to undergo involuntary sterilization, or who has been persecuted for failure or refusal to undergo such a procedure or for other resistance to a coercive population control program, shall be deemed to have been persecuted on account of a political opinion, and a person who has a well-founded fear that he or she will be forced to undergo such a procedure or subject to persecution for such failure,

---

[434] Far less attention is paid, in the departure control cases, to the right to leave one's country and to return. *See, e.g., id.* at 428, n. 18, *citing* UDHR, *supra* § I.1, note 12, Art. 13(2).

[435] For instance, in *Li* v. *INS,* 92 F.3d 985 (9th Cir. 1996), the Ninth Circuit denied asylum to a Chinese claimant who asserted violation of the Chinese departure control laws as the foundation of his claim of persecution. The court found that there was no corroborative evidence that such violations would be met with anything but routine and mild punishments. *See also* Abedini v. INS, 971 F.2d 188, 191 (9th Cir. 1992), holding that violation of Iranian exit control laws through the use of a false passport would not support a claim of persecution: there was no evidence, the court held, that the claimant was motivated by a political opinion in violating Iran's exit control laws, or that Iran would attribute such an opinion to claimant.

> refusal or resistance shall be deemed to have a well-founded fear of persecution on account of political opinion.[436]

The modified definition now constitutes the source of U.S. law on the subject of coercive family planning as the basis for political asylum in the United States. Case law developing under the reconstituted definition is discussed below. Nonetheless, the history of family-planning cases in the United States is deeply revealing with respect to U.S. adjudicators' treatment of the refugee definition in an evolving context. Therefore, that history is outlined in the following paragraphs.[437]

In *Matter of Chang*,[438] the Board of Immigration Appeals first announced that implementation of China's one-family/one-child policy constituted a law of general application and that Chinese nationals fearing punishment because they violated that policy would not, by virtue of that fact alone, make out a claim "on account of" any of the grounds recognized by the law of refugee status. Of significance, so far as the rationale of the case is concerned, was the contention of the asylum seeker to the effect that he and his wife were in imminent peril of sterilization at the direction of their commune.[439]

Notwithstanding the exceptional punishment to which the asylum seeker (and his spouse) stood exposed,[440] the Board ruled that the one-family/one-child policy was directed at a disinterested policy need: limiting China's burgeoning population growth. Accordingly, application of the family-planning restrictions did not give rise to a claim of statutory persecution unless it could be shown that the policy was being applied selectively against certain individuals based on their religious or political beliefs.[441] As determined by the Board:

---

436 INA, *supra* § I.1, note 5, § 101(a)(42), 8 USC § 1101(a)(42).

437 Importantly, Canadian tribunals have arrived at opposite results to those of initial U.S. determinations with respect to their treatment of coercive family planning claims. However, Canadian jurisprudence evolved in connection with the particular social group category of refugee protection. *See* § V.5(a), *infra*.

438 Matter of Chang, 20 I&N Dec. 38 (BIA 1989).

439 *Id.* at 39.

440 This assertion was refuted by the Board only indirectly, i.e., through its rather oblique finding that there was no evidence that the People's Republic of China condones coercive measures, although the Board seemed to concede that such measures had been deployed in the past. *Id.* at 41.

441 Earlier, in August 1988, and in response to the Board's decision in *Chang*, the Department of Justice announced that refusals by nationals of the People's Republic of China to conform to the government's one family/one child policy could be considered persecution if it could be shown to have been undertaken "with full awareness of the urgent priority

> We do not find that the "one couple/one child" policy of the Chinese Government is on its face persecutive. China has adopted a policy whose stated objective is to discourage births through economic incentives, economic sanctions, peer pressure, education, availability of sterilization and other birth control measures, and the use of propaganda. Chinese policy makers are faced with the difficulty of providing for China's vast population in good years and bad. The Government is concerned not only with the ability of its citizens to survive, but also with their housing, education, medical services, and other benefits of life that persons in other societies take for granted. For China to fail to take steps to prevent births might well mean that many millions of people would be condemned to, at best, the most marginal existence. The record reflects that China was in fact encouraged by world opinion to take measures to control its population.
>
> * * *
>
> There is no evidence that the goal of China's policy is other than as stated, or that it is a subterfuge for persecuting any portion of the Chinese citizenry on account of one of the grounds enumerated in section 101(a)(42) of the Act.[442]

Earlier, in August 1988, and in response to the Board's decision in *Chang*, the Department of Justice announced that refusals by nationals of the People's Republic of China to conform to the government's one family/one child policy could be considered persecution if it could be shown to have been undertaken "with full awareness of the urgent priority assigned to that policy by … PRC officials … as well as the severe consequences which may be imposed". According to the Justice Department position, a grant of asylum could still be premised on a conscientious refusal to comply with one family/one child. The substance of this directive was later made a part of Executive Order No. 12711, § 4 (published on April 13, 1990).[443]

The Board[444] and the courts[445] generally continued to apply the *Chang* criteria despite non-rescission of the Attorney General's statement of policy and its express adoption in Executive Order No. 12711. A highly important memorandum by the General Counsel of the Immigration and Naturalization

---

assigned to that policy by … PRC officials … as well as the severe consequences which may be imposed." According to the Justice Department position, a grant of asylum could still be premised on a conscientious refusal to comply with one family/one child. The substance of this directive was later made a part of Executive Order No. 12711, § 4 (published on April 13, 1990). *See, e.g.*, 3 Charles Gordon, Stanley Mailman and Stephen Yale-Loehr, Immigration Law and Procedure § 33.04(1)(b) (August 200) for a discussion.

442 Matter of Chang, 20 I&N Dec. 38, 41 (BIA 1989).

443 *See, e.g.*, 3 Gordon, Mailman and Yale-Loehr, *supra* this section, note 441, § 33.04(1)(b).

444 Matter of G-, 20 I&N Dec. 764 (BIA 1993).

445 *See, e.g.*, Huan v. Carroll, 852 F. Supp. 460 (E.D. Va. 1994), *aff'd without opinion sub nom.* Yang v. Carroll, 70 F.3d 114 (4th Cir. 1995); Chen Zhou Chai v. Carroll, 858 F. Supp. 569 (E.D. Va.), *aff'd,* 48 F. 3d 1331 (4th Cir. 1995).

Service made salient criticism of the *Chang* rationale and pointed to a number of theories under existing law whereby asylum claims based on coercive family planning policies could be granted. The ground upon which these theories rested was that of attributed political opinion.[446] In this respect, the memorandum concluded:

> PRC family planning policy is one of those rare cases in which the persecutors have declared that they regard their victims not just as lawbreakers but as political enemies.[447]

The second premise upon which relief could have been afforded is that the punishment (fines several times the asylum seeker's salary; involuntary abortions in the case of women; and involuntary sterilizations in the case of both sexes) was disproportionately severe.[448] Disproportionate punishment was said to consist of: (i) fines amounting to three times yearly income; (ii) abductions of pregnant women to clinics where they were forced to undergo involuntary abortions; (iii) compelling men and women to undergo involuntary sterilization; (iv) revocation of business licenses, crop permits and other permits necessary to maintain a livelihood; and (v) appropriation of family property (including, on occasion, the family home).[449]

Thirdly, execution of the policy entailed a gross violation of fundamental human rights, including the right to procreate and the individual's right to bodily integrity.[450] Finally, enforcement (often involving the brutal slaying of infants at the point of birth through crushing of the skull or formaldehyde injection) brought individuals into conflict with conscientiously held beliefs and thus forced them to engage in "inhuman action".[451]

---

[446] Memorandum from Grover J. Reese, III, to Jan Ting dated January 19, 1993 re: *Continued Viability of the Doctrine of Imputed Political Opinion*, at 8. The memorandum is reprinted in 70 Interpreter Releases 498 (April 12, 1993).

[447] *Id.*

[448] *Id.* at 8-9.

[449] *Id.* at 9.

[450] *Id.* at 9:

> [I]n order to be effective, a regime of coercive family planning must be carried out by means of a comprehensive and unrelenting control over the most intimate aspects of family life. In the PRC, for example, local family planning authorities record individual women's menstrual cycles and couple's methods of birth control, and unauthorized pregnancies are dealt with by "work units" which also exercise almost unlimited control over the economic and personal lives of unit members. Both the right to bodily integrity and the right to procreate are universally recognized human rights. *See, e.g.*, Universal Declaration of Human Rights Arts. 12, 16(3); *Skinner* v. *Oklahoma*, 316 U.S. 535 (1942).

[451] *Id.*:

Prior to the statutory reversal, *Chang* had suffered a material setback at the hands of an immigration judge in New York City. Although a social group case rather than one based on political opinion, *Matter of C-X- and C-S-*[452] is discussed here in that it relies, in large measure, on the General Counsel memorandum of April 12, 1993 and because discussion of U.S. law on coercive family planning would be incomplete without it. Study of the decision reveals convincingly that, in the absence of legislative intervention, the evolving case law might well have "cured" the aberrant view announced in *Chang* that forced late term abortion and involuntary sterilization were not persecution within the meaning of the Convention refugee definition.

In *Matter of C-X- and C-S-*, a couple sought asylum, alleging persecution under the Chinese one family/one child program. The claim was based upon a showing that the female spouse was four months pregnant with a third child having previously suffered an involuntary abortion in China with respect to a second pregnancy.[453]

The immigration judge found that "sex" (gender) was an immutable characteristic for purposes of the particular social group category, but determined that gender, standing alone, was too broad for purposes of finding a necessary causative element linking the anticipated harm to a recognized ground of persecution. Rather, the tribunal ruled, the applicant in this case could show that she had been persecuted because of her membership in a sub-group, namely:

> those Chinese women who find the one child policy so abhorrent that they refuse to conform, even though the routine punishment for violation can be forced sterilization or even as severe as late term abortion.[454]

---

> [I]n many cases, the PRC program may require its victim to engage in "inhuman conduct". See Matter of A-G-, supra, at 506-07; United Nations High Commissioner on [sic] Refugees, Handbook on Procedures and Criteria for Determining Refugee Status Under the 1951 Convention and the 1967 Protocol Relating to the Status of Refugees 39-41 [pages relating to conscientious objection to military service]. A pregnant woman who wishes to carry her child to term but who is compelled (either by physical force or by threats of severe punishment) to terminate her pregnancy becomes not only a victim but also an unwilling participant in an almost uniquely violent and intrusive violation of bodily integrity and family privacy. Indeed, coerced pregnancy termination under the PRC program has been reported to occur even during the process of giving birth.

452 (IJ, New York, Dec. 14, 1995) (Jeffrey Chase, IJ), *abstracted in* 73 Interpreter Releases 296 (March 11, 1996).

453 *Id.* at 296-97.

454 *Id.* at 296-97.

The tribunal distinguished the Board's decision in *Chang* and an otherwise controlling opinion by the Second Circuit Court of Appeals in *Zhang* v. *Slattery*.[455] The immigration judge held that, in this case, the asylum seeker had an immutable characteristic (gender) which had caused her to be discriminatorily treated by the Chinese authorities administering the family planning program.[456] In addition, applicant's was no mere "political statement" (mere opposition to the policy, in other words) but a moral conviction which would cause her compliance with the family planning program to bring her into conflict with deeply held religious beliefs:

> The respondent in this case is not merely disagreeing with her government regarding the political justification for the one child policy. Her violation of the one child policy is not a political statement. The respondent opposes the policy because of genuine moral convictions and for reasons of conscience. In this respect, the respondent's beliefs are analogous to a person who is required to violate deeply held religious beliefs.[457]

The respondent's "moral convictions" served to support the second prong of the analysis, namely, her belief in reproductive liberty. The court determined that this belief was "so fundamental to her human dignity that she is willing to violate the policy and suffer the severe consequences of the violation." The asylum seeker's genuinely held religious beliefs thus served a dual purpose: they helped include her in a particular social group and they made her undergoing involuntary abortion persecution (by causing her to involve herself in what she clearly perceived as an inhuman act).[458]

The immigration court thus relied, in reaching its result, on a combination of the considerations raised in the General Counsel's memorandum of April 12, 1993 (serious harm based upon the exercise of fundamental rights; conscientious opposition to inhuman action; and excessive punishment for violation of the norm). However, rather than looking at the three grounds separately, the court examines them in conjunction with one another. Could any of these grounds have satisfied a grant of asylum? In light of the fact that the *Chang* decision was then law, probably not. The court, however, produces an irresistible momentum in cumulating these arguably distinct bases for refugee status, thus confronting the BIA with the clear contradictions between *Chang* and its own prior doctrine.[459]

---

455 13 F.3d 732 (2d Cir. 1995).

456 73 Interpreter Releases 296 (March 11, 1996), at 297.

457 *Id.*

458 *Id.*

459 The tribunal's elevation of right being defended by the applicant (i.e., from a political to a religious status) raises interesting implications with respect to the "conscientious

It is clear, however, that conscientious attachment to a human right is coupled here with discriminatory administration of a State policy and excessive methods of execution to make application of the one-family/one-child program persecutory under the facts of this case.[460] At the heart of the analysis is a theme which will play a progressively greater role when gender-based claims are examined: One of the most fundamental policies underlying modern human rights jurisprudence is that human rights must be enjoyed on an equal basis and without discrimination. Where the equal protection component of human rights doctrine is violated, affected individuals and groups may conscientiously protest their discriminatory treatment. An asylum claim can be grounded in these circumstances irrespective of the asserted "neutrality" of the program or measure (or social practice) which is at issue:

> While a forced abortion does not rise to the level of infanticide or matricide, it is nevertheless much more severe than a forced sterilization. Requiring a woman to undergo a forced long-term abortion is very distinct from sterilization. Forced abortions distinguish between the sexes both physically and socially. On the most basic level the harm is that the forced abortion is gender-specific. Physiologically, only women have the capacity to bear children. Because only women become pregnant, they are the only persons targeted for forced abortions. They suffer disproportionately the profound physical, emotional, and psychological consequences of a forced late term abortion. *Unlike the case of a forced sterilization that can be applied to both sexes, the utilization of a forced (late) term abortion can never be a law of general application because it can only be applied to women. This is a practice that affects a limited and defined group of people and does not have general consequences.*[461]

---

objector" basis for asylum. Quite clearly, the mere fact that an asylum seeker views the imposition of a law of general application as "inhuman" will not, *per se*, render the applicant a refugee; the law may well be mild and the restraint reasonable in light of its social aim. For purposes of analysis, however, it may be important to make careful note of the precise "right" which claimant is "conscientiously" exercising: Is she insisting upon the right to absolute procreative autonomy, or the right not to have that autonomy curtailed by dramatic invasions of one's bodily integrity?

Relevant in this respect is the fact that certain rights set forth in the International Covenant on Civil and Political Rights may not be derogated from, even during a state of national crisis. Among these is the right to be free from inhuman treatment or torture (including unwanted medical experiments). The right to form a family, however, is subject to derogation during time of national emergency which is publicly proclaimed. *See, e.g.*, ICCPR, *supra* § I.1, note 14, Art. 4-1, making the provisions of Article 6 (the right against torture) non-derogable, but not making similar provision with respect to Article 23 (family rights). *Id.*, Arts. 4-1 and 6.

460 UDHR, *supra* § I.1, note 14, Art. 2.

461 *See Matter of C-X and C-S-*, (IJ New York Dec, 14, 1995) (Jeffrey Chase, IJ), 73 Interpreter Releases 296 (March 11, 1996), at 298. [Emphasis supplied].

An implicit requirement under the *Chang* decision is that the persecutors have an intent to "punish" or persecute the asylum seeker as a threshold requirement of refugee status. The rationale of the Board in *Chang* was that the one-family/one-child program was uniform and directed toward a legitimate public policy need, restriction of population growth within China. The law was not, in other words, "being used to punish individuals for their political opinions or for other reasons enumerated under section 101(a)(42)(A) of the Act." The Board's analysis left completely unanswered how such a result could live comfortably with now established refugee jurisprudence, particularly with respect to:

> (i) The protection of non-derogable human rights asserted against a putatively valid law of general application;[462]
>
> (ii) The problems posed when the equal protection component of human rights doctrine is violated;[463] and
>
> (iii) The accepted rule that excessive punishment for offending a law of general application will provide the basis for refugee status where objective circumstances identify the applicant's views or behavior with a protected ground.[464]

The provisions of IIRIRA which create an asylum right for victims of coercive family-planning policies fail to indicate why these victims conform to the refugee definition. These provisions also do not examine the human rights implications of coercive family planning and how these play a role in the refugee analysis. Are these empowering provisions which overrule *Matter of Chang* and allow the Board to find that victims of family-planning programs are refugees under appropriate conditions? Or is the new definition of "refugee" under § 101(a)(42) of the Immigration and Nationality Act a directive that all such victims (or potential victims) qualify for refugee status provided they are credible? The former is a more reasonable interpretation of the new law. Current interpretation by the Board of Immigration Appeals has not resolved the issue.

In *Matter of X-P-T-*,[465] the applicant had already been sterilized as the result of her violating the one-family/one-child policy. The Board overturned the immigration judge's denial of the case (issued prior to the IIRIRA amendments and based on *Chang*) finding that IIRIRA "superseded" the

---

462 *Cf.* Matter of Izatula, 20 I&N Dec. 147 (BIA 1990).

463 *See, e.g., U.S. Gender Guidelines, supra* § I.5, note 61.

464 *See generally* Matter of A.-G.-, 19 I&N Dec. 502 (BIA 1987), *rev'd sub nom.* M.A. v. INS (I), 858 F.2d 210 (4th Cir. 1988), *vacated,* M.A. A26 851 062 v. INS (II), 899 F.2d 304 (1990); Barraza-Rivera v. INS, 913 F.2d 1443 (9th Cir. 1990).

465 21 I&N Dec. 634 (BIA 1997).

earlier decision, so that the sterilization incurred by claimant constituted past political opinion persecution within the meaning of the governing standard.[466]

In *Matter of C-Y-Z-*,[467] a second, more complex and interesting case, the Board found that a male asylum seeker whose wife had been sterilized had also suffered, on that account, past political opinion persecution under the amended refugee definition in § 101(a)(42). The Board in *C-Y-Z-* relied on a memorandum prepared by the Immigration and Naturalization Service in reaching its decision.[468] A compelling concurrence by Board member Lory Rosenberg, however, treated the case in connection with the growing human rights framework of analysis governing refugee and asylum adjudications. Essentially, the Rosenberg concurrence would focus on the rights being violated (procreative autonomy and the right against unwanted medical experiments and inhuman treatment) to conclude that those who conscientiously opposed such restrictions are asylum eligible under the political opinion ground:

> The right to privacy, the right to have a family, the right to bodily integrity, and the right to unfettered reproductive choice are fundamental individual rights, recognized domestically and internationally. The view that these are fundamental rights, and that the election to exercise them should be respected, constitutes a political opinion.
>
> * * *
>
> Neither sterilization nor abortion, in and of itself, is a violation of fundamental human rights, nor does either constitute persecution, *per se*. [...] [A]s a consequence of *opposition* to these practices, however, either procedure, imposed involuntarily, may constitute persecution. Being forced to comply with the very violation of fundamental human rights which one opposes on political, religious or other grounds, constitutes a type of punishment for a characteristic which the persecutor, in this case, the Chinese government, wishes to overcome.[469]

---

466 *Id.* at 4-5.

467 21 I&N Dec. 915 (BIA 1997).

468 As noted in the opinion and order:

> The Service also conceded [its position] in its brief on appeal in this case, stating, "The Service is aware that its legal perspective as directed by the General Counsel is that the husband of a sterilized wife can essentially stand in her shoes and make a bona fide and non-frivolous application for asylum based on problems impacting more intimately on her than on him".

*Id.* at 918.

469 Matter of C-Y-Z-, 21 I&N Dec. 915, 921-922, 923 (concurring opinion of Board member Lory Rosenberg).

## § IV.8. Gender-Based Claims and the Fifth Convention Ground

The limits of the refugee definition exclude those situations in which the claimant merely flees some form of "personal" violence or other harm.[470] As will be developed below, during discussion of the fourth Convention ground, such injury is based on purely "personal" considerations and essentially lacks the "public" dimension which is ordinarily required to satisfy the refugee definition. To establish linkage to a protected ground, serious harm must be generalized; the claimant's suffering cannot flow from a dispute which is "private" in nature or one which is highly individualized. No class of case has explored more successfully the limits of this restriction on refugee status than have gender-based asylum claims.

Hard line-drawing here is extremely difficult. Although personal problems obviously cannot form the basis for a claim, they can "cause a person to be imputed with a quality that would result in persecution."[471] Cases which most completely illustrate the problems involved in this area are treated under the "particular social group" category. "Particular social group" covers potentially two areas of refugee protection which are significant for gender-based asylum claims, namely, (a) immutable characteristics and (b) voluntary associations or beliefs which the claimant should not be required to relinquish because they are fundamental to her identity or conscience. Because the particular social group category embraces beliefs which would ordinarily constitute political opinion, but weds those beliefs to gender (an immutable characteristic), the fourth refugee ground will often provide a more compelling explanation of the persecution which the claimant fears. However, "political opinion" as the basis for such claims has certainly not been absent from the jurisprudence.

In Canada, *Interpretation of the Convention Refugee Definition in the Case Law*[472] indicates that some acts may fairly be characterized as vendettas or misuse of official position. Resulting harm is not generally "persecution" within the meaning of the refugee definition.[473] On the other hand, some acts

---

[470] Basic Law Manual, *supra* § I.1, note 26, at 85; Interpretation of the Refugee Definition in the Case Law, *supra* § II.3, note 63, § 3.1.1.4.

[471] Basic Law Manual, *supra* § I.1, note 26, at 85.

[472] Interpretation of the Convention Refugee Definition in the Case Law, *supra* § II.3, note 63, § 3.1.1.4.

[473] *Id.* In one conspicuous example, a claimant maintained that he suffered from a lack of State protection in that the police had refused to act unless bribed with respect to a crime affecting the claimant. The Federal Court-Trial Division ruled that the claimant had failed to establish either persecution or (assuming serious harm had been made out) linkage to a protected ground. Rawji v. M.E.I. (F.C.T.D., no. IMM-5929-93), November 25, 1994.

which might be characterized as "personal problems" involve domestic abuse.[474] The Court of Appeal has ruled that the Refugee Division might find "persecution" in such instances, although it was not required to do so.[475] The Federal Court-Trial Division has held unequivocally, however, that domestic abuse constitutes persecution.[476] As a material consideration in such cases, *Interpretation of the Convention Refugee Definition in the Case Law*[477] sets forth that:

> In assessing these sorts of claims, it is suggested that members inquire whether the harm is serious, whether it is inflicted for a Convention reason, and whether state protection is available.

Two cases in the United States tend to show the demarcation point between attributed political opinion (a basis for asylum) and a claim which (according to the tribunal) was based only on personal considerations. In *Campos-Guardado* v. *INS*,[478] the applicant had been a native and citizen of El Salvador. She had witnessed the murder of her uncle and a male cousin by guerilla members, as well as the rape of three female cousins in the same incident in which she herself was raped. She suffered a nervous breakdown, was hospitalized, and went to work in a factory upon her recovery. When she returned home, she was introduced by her mother to two young men who had allegedly deserted recently from the guerilla forces. Claimant recognized one of these young men as a participant in the atrocity. Applicant had been recognized in turn by the youth and threatened with death if she revealed his identity.[479]

The Fifth Circuit found that the claimant's real fear (that her assailant would kill her if she identified him) was personal in nature, and so did not constitute a cognizable claim.[480] The case has been substantially criticized,

---

474 Interpretation of the Convention Refugee Definition in the Case Law, *supra* § II.3, note 63, § 3.1.1.4.

475 M.E.I. v. Mayers (1993), 150 N.R. 60 (F.C.A.).

476 Diluna v. M.E.I. (F.C.T.D., no. IMM-3201-94), March 14, 1995, at 4. *See also* Narvaez v. M.C.I. [1995] 2 F.C. 55 (T.D.).

477 Interpretation of the Convention Refugee Definition in the Case Law, *supra* § II.3, note 63, § 3.1.1.4.

478 809 F.2d 285 (5th Cir. 1987).

479 *Id.* at 287.

480 The holding of the Fifth Circuit is predicated on its factual determination that the sole basis for the threatened persecution is applicant's potential to reveal the identity of the insurgent. *Id.* at 288. The case has been substantially criticized for failing to take account of the evidence and as having "rejected the theory of imputed political opinion in the context of rape and other violence against women by military personnel". Anker 91, *supra* § III.1, note 5, at 119, n. 625.

particularly on the ground that the court went to excessive lengths to deny protection to a victim of violent abuse because it was not sufficiently demonstrated that the "reasons" for persecution conformed to the "five-factor catalog".[481] The Fifth Circuit, moreover, merely placed its imprimatur on the Board's findings. And, as noted by Deborah Anker, *Campos-Guardado* arose before the Board's acceptance of the notion of attributed political opinion.[482]

A claim which resembled *Campos-Guardado,* however, resulted in a grant of asylum by the Ninth Circuit. In *Lazo-Mejano* v. *INS*,[483] the applicant, a national of El Salvador, had been raped and abused by a member of the Salvadoran military, a sergeant who threatened to expose applicant as a subversive if she resisted his demands. While the case appears at first blush to resemble *Desir* v. *Ilchert,* analysis of its holding shows that much more is involved.

For the Ninth Circuit took a dualistic view of the case. On the one hand, the court was prepared to view the applicant as suffering serious harm on account of a protected ground in that Zuniga (the sergeant) had advised the claimant that resistance would occasion his reporting her as a subversive, a clear instance of imputed political opinion on purely conventional grounds.[484] On the other hand, the court clearly went beyond this analysis to find that the persecutor was attempting to force upon Olympia (the applicant) the view that a man has the right to dominate women through physical abuse; Olympia's implicit rejection of this claim creates the basis for asylum eligibility by elucidating an opposition in principle between persecutor and victim, an opposition which the persecutor will not tolerate:

> Was Olympia, however, persecuted by an agent of the government because she had a political opinion or was the relation of Olympia and Zuniga purely personal? When "political opinion" in the sense used by the two statutes is

---

481 David A. Martin, *The Refugee Concept: On Definitions, Politics and the Careful Use of a Scarce Resource*, *in* Refugee Policy: Canada and the United States 30, 43 (Howard Edelman ed. 1990).

482 Anker 99, *supra* § I.2, note 32, at 334, n. 380.

483 813 F.2d 1432 (9th Cir. 1987).

484 *Id.* at 1435:

> Olympia has suffered persecution because of one specific opinion Zuniga attributed to her. She is, she has been told by Zuniga, a subversive. If she complained of Zuniga, she was informed she would be killed as a subversive.
>
> Olympia does have a political opinion, camouflage it though she does. She believes that the Armed Force is responsible for lawlessness, rape, torture and murder. Such views constitute political opinion and she has been persecuted for possessing it.

> analyzed, it must mean "the political opinion of the victim as seen by the persecutor". At times in the history of persecution the victims have been persons who did not share the prejudices and enthusiasms of their persecutors. Their opinions have been politically unacceptable only because of the opposition and hostility the persecutors have read into their silence or non-commitment. So in this case, if the situation is seen in its social context, *Zuniga is asserting the political opinion that a man has a right to dominate and he has persecuted Olympia to get her to accept this opinion without rebellion.*[485]

The Ninth Circuit thus sets up traditional and accepted notions of "imputed political opinion" as a bedrock basis upon which to grant the claim. The true rationale of *Lazo-Mejano,* however, as can be seen from the court's language, goes well beyond this and is suggestive of later methodologies underlying gender-based asylum determinations in which resistance to a social world dominated by men (feminism) will be considered a basis for refugee status. *Lazo-Mejano*, however, constitutes a prototype of this analysis and illustrates the evolving nature of the Convention refugee definition.

*Lazo-Mejano* emphasizes that refugee claims must be adjudicated in their social context and that it is the perception of the persecutor which is the governing consideration in determining who is a refugee. Although the doctrine of attributed "characteristics and beliefs" is long-established, application of the principle necessarily gives rise to novel interpretations of the refugee definition. As emphasized throughout this study, the categories can now no longer be viewed as being fixed in time; rather, the rise of imputed grounds will occasion situations in which it is the outlook and behavior of the persecutor which determines the scope of refugee protection. The doctrine that refugee claims must be interpreted in their social context assures that the "reasons" for persecution operate not so much to protect against "known forms of harm", but to establish a flexible standard which will accommodate the machinery of international protection to forms of persecution which could not have been anticipated at the time the refugee definition was initially adopted.[486]

There can be no doubt in this respect that the *Canadian Guidelines on Gender-Based Persecution* have had an immeasurable influence on the

---

[485] *Id.* [Emphasis supplied].

[486] *Cf.* Helton, *Persecution on Account of Membership in a Social Group as a Basis for Refugee Status*, *supra* § I.1, note 23, 15 Columbia Human Rts. L. Rev. 39 (1983). The concept of attribution as applied to the "particular social group" category of persecution is developed in Part V, *infra*.

growth of U.S. law in this area.[487] Gender-based persecution, then, presents a useful context in which to examine the ways in which refugee doctrine can develop using the comparative method.[488] The *United States Guidelines for Women's Asylum Claims,*[489] following the *Canadian Guidelines*[490] set forth a framework in which women's asylum claims can be related to the protected grounds.[491] However, the *U.S. Guidelines'* treatment of "political opinion" persecution (like its treatment of the particular social group)[492] clearly elucidates and possibly serves to enhance the current definition of refugee

---

[487] *Compare* Guidelines Issued by the Chairperson Pursuant to Section 65(3) of the Immigration Act, *Women Refugee Claimants Fearing Gender-Related Persecution* (Immigration and Refugee Board, Ottawa, Canada, March 9, 1993) (*Canadian Gender Guidelines*) *and* *U.S. Gender Guidelines, supra* § I.5, note 61. The *Canadian Gender Guidelines* were recently updated. Guidelines Issued by the Chairperson Pursuant to Section 65(3) of the Immigration Act, Guideline 4, *Women Refugee Claimants Fearing Gender-Related Persecution*: Update (Immigration and Refugee Board, Ottawa, Canada, November 25, 1996). The source of both *Canadian Gender Guidelines* and *U.S. Gender Guidelines* can be found in seminal doctrinal promulgations by the United Nations High Commissioner for Refugees. *See, e.g.*, Ex. Comm. Conclusion No. 39 (XXXVI) on Refugee Women and International Protection (36th Session 1985); UNHCR *Guidelines on the Protection of Refugee Women* (Geneva, Office of UNHCR, EC/SCP/67, 22 July 1991); Conclusion No. 73 (XLIV) on Refugee Protection and Sexual Violence (44th Session 1993).

[488] For early proposals concerning the *U.S. Gender Guidelines* which adopt a comparative perspective reflecting the influence of Canadian jurisprudence on the substantive field of U.S. refugee law, *see generally* Kelley, Anker and Beasley, *supra* § III.3, note 26, at 814. The same study recognizes the use of general international and comparative law materials as a means of establishing a governing standard for refugee status.

> The United Nations High Commissioner for Refugees (UNHCR), the European Parliament, the Immigration and Refugee Board of Canada, and other bodies have interpreted the refugee definition to incorporate the specific gender related claims of women applicants.

*Id.* The *U.S. Gender Guidelines* draw upon all of the foregoing sources as persuasive authority in shaping criteria for refugee status with respect to women asylum seekers.

[489] *See U.S. Gender Guidelines, supra* § I.5, note 61.

[490] *See Canadian Gender Guidelines, supra* this section, note 487.

[491] Several of the categories pertinent to the refugee definition (race and nationality) raise no discrete issues as concerns gender-based persecution; accordingly, these categories are not independently discussed in the *U.S. Guidelines*. *See U.S. Gender Guidelines, supra* § I.5, note 61, at 10-16.

[492] *Id.* at 18. *See also* Kelley, Anker and Beasley, *supra* § III.3, note 26, at 818. The imposition of gender-specific cultural norms is often treated as a case arising under the "religion" category of persecution. Kelley, Anker and Beasley make provision for this approach to analysis (*see id.*) but tend on the whole to treat such claims as arising under the imputed political opinion or the social group categories.

status developed by the case law.[493] Relevant provisions of the *U.S. Guidelines* (with cross-references to the *Canadian Guidelines* and comparative law commentary[494] upon which the *U.S. Guidelines* are largely based) are summarized below.

1. **Political Opinion**. Consistent with the "social" theory of human rights enforcement advanced by CEDAW, the *U.S. Guidelines* identify a woman claimant's "political opinion" as going beyond the conventional definition of politics, and as including any opinion which pertains to gender.[495] Accordingly, the term political opinion must be understood as including:

> an opinion regarding the treatment or status of women within her country, culture or social, religious or ethnic group.[496]

This essentially "new" definition of "political opinion" is critical. The modified definition reflects received doctrine that political opinion persecution flows not merely from governmental sources, but also from significant groups within society (e.g., cultural or religious aggregates). More importantly, however, is what the definition has to say regarding the nature of the recognized reasons for persecution. The new interpretation of "political opinion" establishes that the protected grounds are not limited to characteristics or beliefs which define the claimant *vis-à-vis* the formal structure of the State, but can be based on claimant's views concerning her "status" *vis-à-vis* social aggregates (including cultural, religious and ethnic groups).[497] The inspiration for this development can clearly be gleaned from the *Canadian Gender Guidelines* which provide in material part:

> **Political Opinion:**
>
> A woman who opposes institutionalized discrimination of women, or expresses views of independence from male social/cultural dominance in her society, may be found to fear persecution for reasons of imputed political opinion (i.e., she is perceived by the established political/social structure as expressing politically antagonistic views). Two considerations are of importance when interpreting the notion of "political opinion":

---

493 *U.S. Gender Guidelines, supra* § I.5, note 61, at 10-16.

494 Kelley, Anker and Beasley, *supra* § III.3, note 26, at 813.

495 *U.S. Gender Guidelines, supra* § I.5, note 61, at 11:

> However, the case [Fatin v. INS, 12 F.3d 1233 (3d Cir. 1993)] does make clear that an applicant who could demonstrate a well-founded fear of persecution on account of her (or his) beliefs about the role and status of women in society could be eligible for refugee status on account of that opinion.

496 Kelley, Anker and Beasley, *supra* § III.3, note 26, at 817.

497 *But cf.* Hathaway, *supra* § I.1, note 7, at 135-188.

> (1) In a society where women are "assigned" a subordinate status and the authority exercised by men over women results in a general oppression of women, their political protest and activism do not always manifest themselves in the same way as those of men.
>
> (2) The political nature of oppression of women in the context of religious laws and ritualization should be recognized. Where tenets of the governing religion in a given country require certain kinds of behavior exclusively from women, contrary behavior may be perceived by the authorities as evidence of an unacceptable political opinion that threatens the basic structure from which their political power flows.[498]

2. **Imputed Political Opinion**. It is difficult here to distinguish entirely between actual political opinion and attributed political opinion as these two concepts are developed in the *U.S. Guidelines*. The *Guidelines* stress that serious harm may flow from a woman's position of independence from the "social or cultural dominance of men" in a given society.[499] Such a posture may, under the comparative law commentary to the *U.S. Guidelines*, involve the claimant as being perceived by the "established political/social structure" as holding antagonistic views to the accepted order. Inability to conform to religious or cultural norms may give rise to attributed beliefs.[500]

Canadian case law has relied practically exclusively on "membership in a particular social group" as a basis for gender-based refugee claims and a highly significant case decided by the (U.K.) House of Lords[501] has similarly stressed the fourth Convention ground as constituting the most appropriate basis for protection. For that reason, gender-based claims are for the most part dealt with in the discussion of "social group" persecution.[502]

---

[498] *Canadian Gender Guidelines*, *supra* this section, note 487, at 3.

[499] *See U.S. Gender Guidelines, supra* § I.5, note 61, at 11. *See also* Kelley, Anker and Beasley, *supra* § III.3, note 26, at 817-818:

> *Imputed political opinion.* A woman who opposes institutionalized discrimination against women or expresses views of independence from the social or cultural dominance of men in her society may be found to have been persecuted or to fear persecution because of her actual political opinion or a political opinion that has or will be imputed to her (i.e., she is perceived by the established political/social structure as expressing politically antagonistic views through her actions or her failure to act). These views may be imputed to her for any reason, including her refusal to conform to religious or cultural norms or the roles assigned to women within her country or culture.

[500] *Id.*

[501] Islam (A.P.) v. Secretary of State for Home Department, Regina v. Immigration Appeal Tribunal and Another Ex Parte Shah (A.P.), [1999] 2 All ER 545 (House of Lords).

[502] *See* § V.5(b), *infra*.

Case law in the United States has seldom reached the level of analysis which characterized the Ninth Circuit's decision in *Lazo-Mejano* v. *INS*, and many decisions fall far short of it. Nonetheless, as noted earlier, the Third Circuit in *Fatin* v. *INS*[503] did accept that an opinion regarding the status of woman in society would constitute a political opinion for purposes of the fifth Convention ground. Several decisions, moreover, decided by immigration judges have drawn upon political opinion persecution to find that the applicant qualified under the refugee definition. In *Matter of A- and Z-*, decided December 20, 1994, a Jordanian woman was awarded asylum based on abuse she had suffered at the hands of her husband, her political opinion being identified as "belief in Western values," i.e., a belief in the autonomy of women which was in contradistinction to the views of her husband regarding the status of women in Jordanian society.[504] In a highly similar case, *Matter of M- and K-*, the same immigration judge granted relief to a woman from Sierra Leone who had been beaten by her husband and forced to undergo FGM under extremely unsanitary conditions. The immigration judge concluded that the claimant's political opinion consisted of a belief in the "values and integrity of the individual", the right to "seek her own identity" through education, and the corresponding right not to be a "slave".[505]

Finally, in *Matter of Sonia Sharmin*, another immigration judge granted asylum to a young woman from Bangladesh who had been badly beaten by members of her family because of her efforts to define herself as an individual and, consistently with the foregoing, to enter political life in Bangladesh as an advocate for women's rights.[506] As to the political opinion ground upon which relief was predicated, a memorandum of counsel had identified the protected ground involved as flowing from applicant's political activity on behalf of the women's wing of the Jatyo Party. The tribunal did not quarrel with this characterization but found the respondent's political opinion was in fact more encompassing, consisting of applicant's efforts to lead a life which was independent and socially unfettered by the oppressive norms of her society.[507] In sum, the court drew heavily upon the equal

---

503 12 F.3d 1233 (3d Cir. 1993).

504 A72 793 219 (IJ Arlington, Va. Dec. 20, 1994) (Nejelski, IJ), *abstracted in* 72 Interpreter Releases 521 (April 17, 1995).

505 A72 374 558 (IJ Arlington, Va. Aug. 9, 1995) (Nejelski, I.J.), *abstracted in* 72 Interpreter Releases 1188 (September 1, 1995).

506 A73 556 033 (IJ New York, NY Sept. 30, 1996) (Joanna Bukszpan, IJ).

507 *Id.*, at 12-13:

protection component of universal human rights norms in formulating the opinion which applicant had in fact advanced through her activities and behavior in Bangladesh:

> The court notes the obvious: while the respondent might be characterized as having a "feminist" political opinion, her political opinion is essentially the Jeffersonian concept that one has an unalienable right to life, liberty and the pursuit of happiness. That the Jeffersonian concept is a profound and fundamental political concept of this country to this very day can be seen in the recent holding of the United States Supreme Court in which the court noted that "(sex) classifications may not be used, as they once were, to create or perpetuate the legal, social and economic inferiority of women." *United States* v. *Virginia et al.*, __ S.Ct. __ 1996, Nos. 94-1941 and 94-2107, 1996 WL 345786 (U.S.).[508]

This advanced and eloquently expressed view of political opinion persecution, however, has not been given meaningful application in either federal court or Board decisions interpreting the refugee definition in connection with gender-based claims. The more limited jurisprudence of the Board and of the federal courts is set out below.

In *Fisher* v. *INS*,[509] the asylum seeker sought to qualify under the political opinion ground by virtue of her experiences in Iran. Applicant had left Iran with her eleven-year-old son in 1984. She had been divorced from the child's father in Iran because of specific "incidents" occurring before her departure. Applicant had been handcuffed and taken to a local "Comite" as the result of seeing her host at a social gathering in bathing attire. She was kept for several hours suffering, as she demonstrated, psychological anguish which required the attentions of a psychiatrist.[510] Subsequent to this,

---

> In a memorandum submitted by counsel, the respondent claims that, as a person who was abused by her husband and family, specifically because she was exercising her political rights by participating in the activities of a political party, she was persecuted on account of political opinion. In fact, counsel refers to this as "political opinion par excellence." While the court does not dispute this characterization of the claim, it is also the court's view that this claim encompasses a much broader view of "political opinion" in that the respondent claims that, as a person who was abused by her husband and family, specifically *because she was attempting to lead an independent life, which included participation in a political organization*, she was also asserting a political opinion and that she was persecuted because of her attempt to voice that opinion in both words and actions. [Emphasis supplied].

508 *Id.* at 13.

509 *See, e.g.*, 61 F.3d 1366 (9th Cir. 1994), *amending* 37 F.3d 1371 (1994), *redecided en banc*, Fisher v. INS, 79 F.3d 976 (9th Cir. 1996).

510 *Id.* at 1369.

applicant was stopped on the street by government agents and ordered into a car at gunpoint. The detention had occurred because applicant had several strands of her hair outside her *chador*. She was warned not to appear in public again. A final confrontation with the authorities took place when several agents searched her home. Applicant believed that this incident was prompted by activities of her sister's husband who was against the Khomeni regime. The immigration judge and the Board rejected the claim ruling that such oppressive cultural norms, although harsh, did not reach the level of persecution.[511]

In its initial ruling, the Ninth Circuit determined that the Board had erred in denying asylum and ordered a remand to the Board.[512] In arriving at this result, the appeals court issued an interpretation of "persecution" in the context of asylum seekers with conscientiously held beliefs which has remained significant: when a person of religious views must comply with a religious regime fundamentally opposed to those views, or is punished for failing to comply with laws which he or she holds as abhorrent, the resulting "anguish" should be considered in assessing whether that person has experienced persecution.[513]

The appeals court later amended its earlier ruling, while, at the same time, ordering that the case be reheard *en banc*.[514] The amended decision, while of limited precedential weight, sets forth, like its predecessor, substantially correct principles of application with respect to gender-based claims.

In its second determination of the case, the Ninth Circuit found that the Board had erred by considering only the treatment actually received for violating the regime's ultraconservative rules, and had not analyzed the prospective serious harm which might befall the claimant. The court cited convincing scholarly opinion to the effect that severe sanctions would follow violations of Iran's ultraconservative laws.[515] The U.S. State Department,

---

[511] *Id.*

[512] Fisher v. INS, 37 F.3d 1371 (1994).

[513] *Id.* at 1381, *citing* Fatin v. INS, 12 F.3d 1233 (3rd Cir. 1993). The initial *Fisher* holding was cited with approval both in the *Basic Law Manual* (*supra* § I.1, note 26, at 38) in the *U.S. Gender Guideline* (*supra* § I.5, note 61, at 10). As discussed earlier, the fact that *Fisher* was later virtually overturned does not prevent this broad operating language from remaining a part of U.S. asylum doctrine in light of its earlier formulation in *Fatin*.

[514] *See, e.g.*, 61 F.3d 1366 (9th Cir. 1994), *amending* 37 F.3d 1371 (1994).

[515] *Id.* at 1372, n. 5 *citing* Freda Hussain & Kamela Radwan, *The Islamic Revolution and Women: Quest for the Quaranic Model, in* Muslim Women 44, 47 (Freda Hussain ed. 1984).

*Country Condition Reports on Human Rights Practices*, cited by the court,[516] reflected that women were often attacked in the street for violating the gender-based dress code.

Although not specifically developed by the tribunal, it would appear that this aspect of the analysis relates to the attributed political opinion category of refugee protection. In an important observation, the Ninth Circuit took issue with the Third and Eighth Circuits to the effect that an asylum seeker would be required to take a conscientious and deliberate step to violate the dress code and suffer the consequences or relinquish all hope of applying for asylum. In a correct rejection of the requirement that the asylum seeker must deliberately place herself at risk, the Ninth Circuit ruled that the codes could be inadvertently violated: the excessive punishment to which the claimant would then be subject gives rise to an inference that the sanction was not a lawful one but had been imposed on account of a protected ground.[517]

Subsequently, however, the Ninth Circuit vacated its earlier ruling, and issued an *en banc* opinion which virtually set down a preclusive framework of decision for women seeking asylum based on their opposition to discriminatory gender-specific codes.[518] Looking at the same facts, the court ruled that the claimant had established no more than that she would face the possibility of prosecution for having committed an act which was deemed criminal in her homeland and which applied to "all women". The court noted (with apparent indifference to the implicit contradictions in its ruling) that the law had not been shown to be "pretextual", nor had it been demonstrated that "disproportionate" punishment was involved. In effect, the court held that a body of regulations which, on their face, applied only to women

---

[516] *Id.* at 1373 *citing* U.S. Department of State, *Country Condition Reports on Human Rights Practices for 1986,* 100th Cong., 1st Sess., 1165 *et seq.* (Comm. Print 1987).

[517] 61 F.3d at 1376. The Ninth Circuit also disagreed with the Board's analysis regarding the question of whether compliance with an oppressive norm could itself ever constitute persecution. The *Fisher* court indicated at the outset of its opinion that "persecution" within the meaning of the refugee standard embraces more than simply a "threat to life and freedom." The court then quoted with approval central language used in *Fatin* v. *INS* describing emotional anguish flowing from forced compliance with an ethical or religious regime which the applicant finds to be repugnant:

> *The concept of persecution is broad enough to include governmental measures that compel an individual to engage in conduct that is not physically painful or harmful but is abhorrent to that individual's deepest beliefs.* An example of such conduct might be requiring a person to renounce his or her religious beliefs or to desecrate an object of religious importance. [Emphasis supplied; footnote omitted].

[518] Fisher v. INS, 79 F.3d 976 (9th Cir. 1996).

constituted a law of general application which was entitled to judicial deference in the absence of selective prosecution or excessive sanctions.[519]

It is of moment to note at this juncture that Canadian refugee law takes the opposite view of this situation. In *Namitabar* v. *M.E.I.*,[520] the Federal Court Trial Division determined that violation of Iran's gender-based dress codes would give rise to disproportionate punishment without procedural safeguards and therefore could be considered as overt opposition to a theocratic regime.[521] This ruling was refined in *Fathi-Rad* v. *S.S.C.* where the requirements relating to a woman's donning of the *chador* could not be considered as a law of general application applicable to all citizens alike, but was on its face gender-specific. The *Fathi-Rad*[522]court also concluded that enforcement of the law could be exceptionally draconian in light of the law's objective. Such a showing was made out where claimant had been repeatedly arrested, detained and interrogated, not for her deliberate defiance of the law but for her imperfect compliance with it.[523]

The rights raised by women who seek protection in these circumstances are largely those explicitly set forth in or emerging under CEDAW and by the equal protection component of international human rights law. Women's claims in a "conscientious objector" environment should not be viewed as arising in a novel context since conscientious advocates of human rights standards are not a new species of asylum seeker. It has long been received doctrine that those who advance an internationally recognized human right, including the enjoyment of fundamental rights on an equal basis and without discrimination, will be deemed to fear persecution by reason of a protected ground if they confront serious harm as the result of their insistence.[524]

Finally, the Board of Immigration Appeals decision in *Matter of R-A-*[525] purported to deal a substantial blow to the political opinion ground as it relates to gender-based claims which are predicated on domestic violence.[526]

---

519 *Id.* at 962.

520 [1994] 2 F.C. 42 (T.D.), *rev'd on other grounds sub nom.* Canada (Secretary of State) v. Namitabar (F.C.A., no. A-709-93), October 29, 1996.

521 *Id.* at 49.

522 (F.C.T.D., no. IMM-2438-93), April 13, 1994.

523 *Id.* at 4-5.

524 1 Grahl-Madsen, *supra* § I.1, note 7, at 227.

525 Interim Decision 3403 (BIA 1999).

526 As noted in § V.5(b)(4) of this study, *Matter of R-A-* has been vacated by the Attorney-General with a directive to re-adjudicate in the light of pending proposed regulations. The prefatory section of the proposed rules, however, clearly indicates that nothing contained in them shall be deemed to affect that aspect of the *R-A-* decision which rests on the political opinion ground. *See generally* 65 Fed. Reg. 76588, 76592 (December 7, 2000).

In *R-A-*, a case arising in the Ninth Circuit, the Board overturned a decision by an immigration judge granting asylum to a Guatemalan woman who had been the victim of prolonged mistreatment by her husband including kicks to the spine; dislocating applicant's jaw-bone; repeated rapes; blows to the genitalia; and using applicant's head to break windows. Persistent efforts to secure State protection had been of no avail. The Board rejected both political opinion and attributed political opinion as constituting grounds upon which the claim could be grounded, despite the Ninth Circuit's earlier ruling in *Lazo-Mejano* v. *INS.*[527]

The Board rejected as an evidentiary basis for determining that serious harm was related to a protected ground the background material showing a pattern or practice of violence committed against a discernable group. This method of analysis, applicable in civil war cases,[528] is found inapplicable by the Board because internal armed conflicts are informed with an inherent "political" dimension, a context which relates the harm or suffering more easily to a protected ground. This manner of analysis quite clearly ignores the expanded view of political opinion which maintains that political opinion can embrace a woman's beliefs (or perceived beliefs) concerning the role or status of women *vis-à-vis* social or cultural norms and practices, including by implication cultural norms which postulate the domination of men over women. The opinion of the Board thus adopts a restrictive interpretation of "political" opinion as being limited to matters relating to the conquest of public power which characterize civil wars.

In any case, as will be developed at greater length in the "social group" discussion, Canadian law clearly accepts that household domestic violence constitutes persecution within the meaning of the refugee definition. Therefore, women who are subject to such abuse in an environment indicative of a

---

527 813 F.2d 1432 (9th Cir. 1987). As noted earlier, in *Lazo-Mejano*, the Ninth Circuit had awarded asylum to a Salvadoran woman in claimant's position on the theory that, by offering opposition to her male companion's conduct, applicant had shown herself as an opponent of male domination in a society which largely embraced such domination as the governing standard. The Board found that *Lazo-Mejano* had been restricted by the Supreme Court's decision in *Elias-Zacarias* v. *INS*, 502 U.S. 478 (1992), holding that the insurgents' broad political incentives in seeking to overturn the government could not be used to establish an attributed political opinion in those who resist recruitment on an individualized basis. The facts of *R-A-*, however, clearly involve something more than the forced recruitment of non-combatants by insurgent elements: indeed they resemble generalized practices of discrimination against specific classes culminating in serious harm which the Board had approved as the basis for asylum in the civil war context.

528 *See* Matter of S-P-, 21 I&N Dec. 486 (BIA 1996).

lack of State protection will be recognized as refugees under the fourth Convention ground.[529]

[529] *See, e.g.*, Diluna v. M.E.I. (F.C.T.D., no. IMM-3201-94), March 14, 1995.

# V. SOCIAL GROUP PERSECUTION AND THE PARAMETERS OF REFUGEE PROTECTION: THE ROLE OF INTERNATIONAL LAW AND POLICY IN DETERMINING REFUGEE CLAIMS

## § V.1. Membership in a Particular Social Group: The Essential Framework

Of all the protected grounds, the particular social group category has undergone the most substantial evolution. Canadian law has historically been receptive to this particular basis for refugee status,[1] while the United States has only of late begun to look to the "particular social group" as a meaningful predicate upon which asylum can be granted.[2] A relationship clearly exists between this ground and the other four bases for asylum.

The *Handbook* indicates in this respect that since the social group category describes persons of similar backgrounds, habits or social status, the fourth ground may conveniently overlap with other bases for persecution, e.g., race, religion or nationality.[3] Similarly, a group may be unified not only through its internal features (i.e., immutable characteristics or the exercise of fundamental human rights), but also in effect because it is viewed as a collective threat by the government, either on account of its economic activities or by its very existence.[4]

---

1 *Cf.* Hathaway, *supra* § I.1, note 7, at 157-169.

2 For an interesting study on the early limitations on the social group category in United States asylum law, *see* Daniel Compton, *Asylum for Persecuted Social Groups: A Closed Door Left Slightly Ajar*, 62 Wash. L. Rev. 913 (1987).

3 Handbook, *supra* § I.1, note 30, ¶ 77:

> A "particular social group" normally comprises persons of similar background, habits or social status. A claim to fear persecution under this heading may frequently overlap with a claim to fear persecution on other grounds, i.e., race, religion or nationality.

4 *Id.*, ¶ 78:

> Membership in such a particular social group may be at the root of persecution because there is no confidence in the group's loyalty to the Government or because the political outlook, antecedents or economic activity of its members, or the very existence of the group as such, *is held to be an obstacle to the Government's policies.* [Emphasis supplied].

The *Handbook* also makes it clear that mere membership in a particular social group will not, in the absence of special circumstances, be sufficient to establish a claim to refugee status. As with the other categories which relate to group identification, additional evidence must be adduced showing that the claimant is at risk.[5]

## § V.2. The Social Group Ground in a Modern Context: The *Acosta, Ward* and *Shah* and *Islam* Decisions

The relationship between the "particular social group" concept and the remaining grounds of persecution was initially developed in a seminal decision of the Board of Immigration Appeals, *Matter of Acosta*.[6] There, the Board reasoned, the "particular social group" category enjoys certain features of the other four grounds and must be interpreted as embracing qualities which are of like kind [*ejusdem generis*] with the remaining classes.[7] Under *Acosta*, therefore, the "particular social group" rubric is broadly divided into three principal categories:

> (i) individuals possessing fixed characteristics which they lack the capacity to alter;
>
> (ii) individuals who voluntarily associate in pursuits which are so fundamental to their identity or conscience that they should not be required to abandon these associations; and
>
> (iii) individuals linked by past associations for which they will be persecuted irrespective of their current status.

The rationale of the *Acosta* case has now been adopted by the Canadian Supreme Court in a decision of considerable scope interpreting the refugee

---

5 *Id.*, § 79.

6 19 I&N Dec. 211 (BIA 1985).

7 *Id.* at 233. Specifically, the Board held:

> We find that the well-established doctrine of *ejusdem generis*, meaning literally "of the same kind," to be the most helpful in construing the "particular social group". That doctrine holds that general words used in an enumeration with specific words should be construed in a manner consistent with the specific words.... The other grounds of persecution ... listed in association with "membership in a particular social group" are persecution on account of "race", "religion", "nationality", and "political opinion." Each of these grounds describes persecution aimed at an immutable characteristic: a characteristic that is either beyond the power of an individual to change or is so fundamental to individual identity that it ought not to be required to be changed.

standard in general and the particular social group in particular.[8] In *Ward,* the refugee claimant was an Irish national who had joined the Irish National Liberation Army (INLA), a "ruthless para-military organization". He had previously been convicted of assorted "terrorist" activities, including possessing firearms. One of his chief responsibilities was to guard hostages on behalf of INLA. Upon discovering that the hostages were to be executed, Ward arranged for their escape.

Claimant was later tortured by INLA members for his part in the hostages' release, and sentenced to death. He managed to escape from INLA, however, and sought police protection. This resulted in the claimant's being tried for the hostages incident and sentenced to three years' imprisonment. Exposed to the possibility of extra-judicial killing at the hands of INLA, Ward made his way to Canada (with the help of the prison chaplain), and there advanced a claim for refugee status.[9] His application rested on membership in a particular social group (INLA) and on imputed political opinion (a basis added during oral argument).

The Supreme Court concluded that Ward had not made out a claim in the particular social group category, specifically ruling that requiring Ward to relinquish violent means to secure political ends (unification between Northern Ireland and the Republic of Ireland) did not entail an abdication of the claimant's human dignity.[10] The Court also determined, however, that Ward might have a claim by virtue of certain views which would be attributed or imputed to him by INLA arising from his freeing of the hostages.[11]

In assessing the scope of the "particular social group" category, the Supreme Court took up two competing models which could, arguably, satisfy the definition. The first of these (which was rejected) was the broad "safety net" definition which had been advanced by leading commentators on the refugee definition.[12] A variant of this theory would have included as eligible those who had suffered a form of "common victimization" as objects of persecution.[13] The Court rejected these approaches to the "particular social group" definition in favor of a narrower view which it believed was appropriate in light of the historical evolution of the refugee definition which

---

8 Canada (Attorney General) v. Ward, [1993] 2 S.C.R. 689.

9 *Id.* at 669-700.

10 *Id.* at 745.

11 *Id.* at 747-49. This aspect of the case is discussed in § IV.2, *supra.*

12 Helton, *supra* § I.1, note 23, at 45.

13 Isi Foighel, *The Legal Status of the Boat People*, 48 Nordisk Tidsskrift for International Relations 222-23 (1979).

draws upon both human rights and discrimination concepts as these have been shaped by general international law:

> Underlying the Convention is the international community's commitment to the assurance of basic human rights without discrimination. This is indicated in the preamble to the treaty as follows:
>
>> CONSIDERING that the Charter of the United Nations and the Universal Declaration of Human Rights approved on 10 December 1948 by the General Assembly have affirmed the principle that human beings shall enjoy fundamental rights and freedoms without discrimination.
>
> This theme outlines the borders of the objectives sought to be achieved and consented to by the delegates. It sets out, in a general fashion, the intention of the drafters and thereby provides an inherent limit to the cases embraced by the Convention.[14]

The Court found that the Convention's references to "race, religion, nationality, membership in a particular social group, or political opinion" were illustrative of categories considered worthy of special protection under the non-discrimination component of UDHR. These same factors, the Court opined, following Guy Goodwin-Gill, have "figured in the development of the fundamental principle of non-discrimination in general international law, and have contributed to the formation of other fundamental human rights".[15]

Essentially, the *Ward* decision looks to the same three criteria emphasized by the Board of Immigration Appeals in *Acosta*. Because the formulation of social group membership arrived at in *Ward* has come to command a considerable international consensus, it will be set out in full:

> The meaning assigned to "particular social group" in the Act should thus take into account the general underlying themes of the defence of human rights and anti-discrimination that form the basis for the international refugee protection initiative. The tests proposed in *Mayers, Cheung* and *Matter of Acosta, supra,* provide a good working rule to achieve this result. They identify three possible categories:
>
>> (1) groups defined by an innate or unchangeable characteristic;
>>
>> (2) groups whose members voluntarily associate for reasons so fundamental to their human dignity that they should not be forced to forsake the association; and
>>
>> (3) groups associated by a former voluntary status, unalterable due to historical permanence.[16]

---

[14] Canada (Attorney General) v. Ward, [1993] 2 S.C.R. 689, 733.

[15] *Id.* at 734, *citing* Guy Goodwin-Gill, The Refugee in International Law 39 (1st ed. 1983).

[16] *Id.* at 739. While thus following the *Acosta* criteria, the *Ward* Court continued to explain the significance of the third prong of the particular social group definition in greater detail:

"Race," "nationality," and, to some extent, "religion," are clearly examples of characteristics which the individual has no capacity to change. Related to such truly immutable features of the individual persona are sexual orientation, family and class or clan affiliation. On the other hand, "political opinion" and "religion" (when it is actively practiced or advocated) set forth the voluntary bases for refugee status.[17] These categories refer to beliefs or outlooks which it would be unconscionable to force the individual to relinquish.[18] Accordingly, claims to refugee status predicated on membership in voluntary associations often involve groups which are held together by the exercise of fundamental human rights which have gained recognition in international law.[19] Analysis often borrows from both associational and fixed characteristic elements.[20]

In *Islam (A.P.)* v. *Secretary of State for Home Dept., Regina* v. *Immigration Appeal Tribunal and Another Ex Parte Shah,*[21] the British House of Lords ruled that "women" constitute a particular social group for purposes of the Convention refugee definition. The opinion found eligible for asylum two Pakistani women largely on the basis of a systematic lack of State protection against spousal abuse in their homeland. The Lords' decision, which is likely to influence substantially the future evolution of the

---

> The first category would embrace individuals fearing persecution on such bases as gender, linguistic background and sexual orientation, while the second would encompass, for example, human rights activists. The third is included more because of historical intentions, although it is also relevant to the anti-discrimination influences, in that one's past is an immutable part of the person

17 *See generally* 1 Grahl-Madsen, *supra* § I.1, note 7, at 217.

18 Hathaway, *supra* § I.1, note 7, at 168:

> Thus membership in a voluntary association defined by a non-fundamental purpose, such as recreation or personal convenience, would normally be seen to be outside the scope of a particular social group. Conversely, where the purpose of the voluntary association is essential to individual identity or conscience, it is reasonable that individuals should have access to international protection where there is a risk of persecution for failure to renounce such basic interests.

19 *Cf.* Hathaway, *supra* § I.1, note 7, at 168:

> Students are thus logically included within the social group category, since the pursuit of education is a basic international human right.

20 *See, e.g.*, Annan v. M.C.I., [1995] 3 F.C. 25 (T.D.) (implicitly finding Catholic women fleeing the Muslim practice of clitoral excision in Ghana to be members of a social group). *See also* the definition of the "social group" offered in *Fatin* v. *INS*, 12 F.3d 1233, 1241 (3d Cir. 1993):

> "Iranian women who refuse to conform to the government's gender-specific laws and norms".

21 [1999] 2 All ER 545 (House of Lords).

fourth Convention ground, is analyzed in greater detail in § V.5(b)(4) in connection with gender-based claims predicated on domestic violence. Importantly, for purposes of the "social group" category, both Lord Steyn (who wrote the Lords' opinion) and Lord Hoffman (who supplied the most substantive rationale for the decision) looked to *Acosta* and to *Ward* as providing critical guidance with respect to the relevant criteria for social group formation.[22] Importantly, both opinions also accept the non-discrimination component of modern human rights doctrine in determining which "social groups" are entitled to international protection.

The most far-reaching of the Lords' opinions is clearly that of Lord Hoffman. Drawing a creative analogy between refugee law and human rights doctrine, Lord Hoffman concludes that it is not simply violations of human rights which satisfy the Convention refugee definition, but violations which are based on acts of discrimination. The Universal Declaration of Human Rights sets out in Article 2 certain forms of status which may be deemed to qualify for refugee protection under UDHR's mandate of equal treatment and concern for purposes of human rights analysis. Included in this category are not only those groups held together by innate characteristics (race, social origin, gender), but also those united by economic conditions which they are powerless to alter (specifically groups identified by "property" but including implicitly those economically marginalized by their societies and therefore placed in peril). Having concluded that gender is included within the embrace of Article 2, Lord Steyn goes on to develop the theme of "gender" as a social group in conformity with the *Ward* and *Acosta* criteria relating to "immutable" characteristics.

This largely revolutionary ruling must be understood, however, in the context of an even more dramatic pronouncement to be found explicitly in the opinion of Lord Hoffman, namely, that any class which can be located in UDHR Article 2 will potentially meet the social group definition. The open-ended nature of this approach can be understood by the fact that UDHR is itself non-exclusive, and the categories warranting protection against discrimination are still being developed both by the Human Rights Committee[23] and by the Committee on Economic, Social and Cultural Rights.[24]

---

22 The decision is reprinted and analyzed in 11 Int'l J. Refugee L. 496 *et seq.*

23 McGoldrick, *supra* § I.3, note 45, at 269-300.

24 Craven, *supra* § II.2, note 50, at 153-193.

## § V.3. Evolution of the "Social Group" Ground

*Interpretation of the Convention Refugee Definition in the Case Law*[25] notes that the Federal Court of Appeal and the Federal Court Trial Division have found the following collectivities to constitute "particular social groups" for purposes of refugee analysis

> (i) The family (immutable characteristic).[26]
>
> (ii) Homosexuals (sexual orientation—an immutable characteristic).[27]
>
> (iii) Trade unions[28] (exercise of fundamental human rights).
>
> (iv) The poor[29] (based on a finding that the poor were mistreated in Haiti as developed in background materials: attributed characteristics and beliefs).
>
> (v) Women subject to domestic abuse;[30] forced into marriage without their consent;[31] or made subject to involuntary circumcision[32] (combination of immutable characteristic and exercise of fundamental human rights without discrimination).
>
> (vi). "Women who have been subjected to exploitation resulting in the violation of the person and who, in consequence of the exploitation have been tried, convicted and sentenced to imprisonment"[33] (combination of immutable characteristic and exercise of fundamental human rights without discrimination).
>
> (vii). Persons exposed to compulsory sterilization (exercise of fundamental human rights).[34]
>
> (viii) Children of police officers who are terrorized by Muslim groups because they are perceived as being anti-terrorists (combination of "external" perceptions and immutable characteristics).[35]
>
> (ix) Women who have recently immigrated to Israel from the former Soviet Union and who, despite generous support by the host government, fail to

---

25 *See* Interpretation on the Convention Refugee Definition in the Case Law, *supra* § II.3, note 63, § 4.5.

26 Chan v. M.E.I., [1993] 3 F.C. 675 (C.A.).

27 Pizarro v. M.E.I., (F.C.T.D., no. IMM-2051-93), March 11, 1994 at 3-4.

28 Rodriguez v. M.E.I. (F.C.T.D., no. IMM-4109-93), October 25, 1994, at 2.

29 Sinora v. M.E.I. (F.C.T.D., no. 93-A-334), July 3, 1993. The claim was nonetheless denied in that applicant could not demonstrate targeting

30 Narvaez v. M.C.I., [1995] 2 F.C. 55 (T.D.).

31 Vidhani v. M.C.I., [1995] 3 F.C. 60 (T.D.).

32 Annan v. M.C.I., [1995] 3 F.C. 25 (T.D.).

33 Cen v. M.C.I. (F.C.T.D., no. IMM-1023-95), November 2, 1995, at 7.

34 Chan v. M.E.I., [1995] 3 S.C.R. 593 and Cheung v. M.E.I. (1993), 153 N.R. 145 (F.C.A.).

35 Badran v. M.C.I. (F.C.T.D., no. IMM-2472-95), March 29, 1996.

integrate, are subsequently lured into prostitution, and are confronted with indifference by the front-line supervisors responsible for their safety (combination of immutable characteristics and exercise of fundamental human rights based on analogy to domestic violence cases).[36]

(x) Educated women from Afghanistan (immutable characteristics).[37]

(xi) Former employees of a Mexican mayor who will be terrorized because of what they know regarding the mayor's corrupt political practices (combination of "external" perceptions and immutable characteristics).[38]

Apart from the foregoing adjudications by federal tribunals, the Convention Refugee Determination Division has also rendered some administrative decisions of scope concerning social group membership.[39] According the the CRDD,[40] the following classes have been held to qualify under the fourth Convention ground:

(i) Divorced women in Somalia whose rights to personal security and as parents received no protection under Sharia law[41] (combination of immutable characteristics and exercise of fundamental human rights without discrimination—including violation of equality rights under Articles 15 and 16 of the Convention on the Elimination of All Forms of Discrimination against Women).[42]

---

36 Litvinov v. S.C.C. (F.C.T.D., no. IMM-7488-93), June 30, 1994, at 4.

37 Ali v. M.C.I. (F.C.T.D., no. IMM-3404-95), October 30, 1996.

38 Reynoso v. M.C.I. (F.C.T.D., no. IMM-2110-94), January 29, 1996.

39 Several of the CRDD decisions which are discussed in this section are cited and analyzed in Who is a Refugee, *supra* § IV.5(a), note 325, at 190-191 and 208-212.

40 The predecessor to the CRDD, namely, the Immigration Appeal Board had issued some highly relevant opinions on social group membership. *See, e.g.,* Incirciyan v. Canada (10 Aug. 1987), No. M87-1541X (Imm. App. Bd.) holding that "single women living in a Moslem country without the protection of a male relative" constitute a particular social group. The Immigration Appeals Board gave a particularly elastic interpretation of the social group category, ruling both that young Tamil males and young Salvadoran males constitute social groups within the meaning of the fourth Convention ground. *See generally* Nalliah v. Canada (20 Oct. 1987), No. M84-1642 (Imm. App. Bd.); Cruz v. Canada (26 June 1986), No. V83-6807 (Imm. App. Bd.).

41 CRDD T93-12198, T93-12199, **T93-12197**, May 10, 1994. A similar rationale was adopted in CRDD V97-01419 *et al.*, August 9, 1999. There, the CRDD found that a widowed mother who would lose custody of her children under Iranian law as well as the ability to influence guardianship decisions faced persecution by virtue of her membership in a social group.

42 CEDAW, *supra* § I.1, note 22, Arts. 15 and 16. Article 15 guarantees a woman's right to equality with men before the law. Article 16 requires States parties to adopt all appropriate measures to eliminate discrimination against women in social matters, including marriage and family relations. CEDAW is discussed in greater detail in § V.5(b), *infra*.

(ii) Minor female children in Somalia who stand exposed to female genital circumcision[43] (combination of immutable characteristics and exercise of fundamental human rights without discrimination—specifically the claimant's right to liberty and security of the person within the meaning of Article 3 of UDHR, as well as her rights under Articles 37, 19 and 24 of the Convention on the Rights of the Child).[44]

(iii) Minor male children in Somalia who are deprived of expressing any view in the determination of which parent is to have custody of them and who are separated from a parent against their will[45] (combination of immutable characteristics and exercise of fundamental human rights without discrimination—specifically the requirement under Article 3 of the Convention on the Rights of the Child governing the best interests of the child—as well as the claimant's rights under Article 9 of the Convention on the Rights of the Child not to be separated from a parent against his will, and under Article 12 conferring upon the child a right to express a view concerning a matter affecting him).[46]

(iv) Individuals persecuted on account of sexual orientation—including claimants from Argentina,[47] Russia[48] and Venezuela[49] (immutable characteristics).

---

43 CRDD T93-12198, T93-12199, **T93-12197**, May 10, 1994.

44 Convention on the Rights of the Child, *supra* § I.1, note 21, arts 37, 19 and 24. Under Article 37, children are to be protected against acts of cruelty and torture. Article 19 requires States parties to adopt all appropriate measures (including social programs) to assure that children are protected from physical or mental violence, neglect or exploitation (including sexual abuse), while in the care of parents, guardians or others having custody of the child. Article 24 mandates that the child enjoy the highest attainable standards of health.

45 CRDD T93-12198, T93-12199, **T93-12197**, May 10, 1994. *See also* CRDD V97-01419, *et al.*, finding that children of widowed Iranian mothers had a well-founded fear of being persecuted by virtue of their membership in a social group; their automatic separation from their mother under Iranian law was deemed to violate the Convention on the Rights of the Child and, therefore, to constitute serious harm based on a protected ground.

46 Convention on the Rights of the Child, *supra* § I.1, note 21, arts 3, 9 and 12. Article 3 requires that in all matters affecting children the best interests of the child shall be the primary consideration. Article 9 mandates that a child shall not be separated from a parent against his/her will except when the best interests of the child requires it. Article 12 sets forth that children who are capable of expressing a view shall be provided with the right to express such view in all matters affecting their interests, and especially in proceedings wherein their interests are at stake.

47 CRDD T95-06913, March 25, 1998. The Argentinean claimant had suffered egregiously in his country: he had been expelled from school, detained several times by the authorities, and, on one occasion, had been beaten and raped by the police.

48 CRDD A98-00268, July 29, 1998.

49 CRDD T94-07129, August 14, 1995.

> (v) Ticketing agents in Sri Lanka having access to classified information of value to terrorist groups[50] (attributed characteristics and beliefs).
>
> (vi) Civil servants in Sri Lanka responsible for implementing governmental policy who for that reason are targets of terrorist groups[51] (attributed characteristics and beliefs).

The Trial Division has consistently ruled that wealthy individuals and landlords do not satisfy the "particular social group" definition.[52] Here again, the developing jurisprudence for refugee status has relied heavily on the human rights analysis which forms the centerpiece of *Ward* coupled with the broad conclusion that there is no international human right to accrue or retain wealth. The prevailing principle has been summarized by James Hathaway:

> A fourth form of particular social group encompasses immutable forms of class and caste. While it is often suggested that notions of class and social group are essentially coterminous, the general definition posited above excludes social class defined by a changeable characteristic of a non-essential nature. For example, the members of a privileged social class who resist renunciation of economic privilege are not protected, since it is within their ability voluntarily to renounce their property, an interest which is not protected under core human rights norms.[53]

According to the case law, therefore, economic criteria may be relevant to the determination of whether a particular social group exists. Wealthy industrialists do not necessarily fall under the rubric since possessing assets is not an international human right and the asylum seeker can disencumber himself/herself of the characteristic attracting persecution.[54] The poor,

---

[50] CRDD T90-02283, August 13, 1991.

[51] CRDD T90-02709, July 11, 1991.

[52] *See generally, Interpretation of the Convention Refugee Definition in the Case Law, supra* § II.3, note 63, § 4.5, citing e.g., Mortera v. M.E.I. (F.C.T.D., no. A-1084-92), December 8, 1993.

[53] Hathaway, *supra* § I.1, note 7, at 166.

[54] In one leading case, the Trial Division ruled:

> [I]t does not necessarily follow that, merely because the historical underpinning of including the term 'particular social group' as found in the Convention was based on the desire to protect capitalists and independent businessmen fleeing eastern block persecution during the cold war, should it lead to the conclusion that the [asylum seeker] in this case was persecuted for the same reason.

Karpounin v. M.E.I. (F.C.T.D., no. IMM-7368-93), March 10, 1995. In commenting on the above case, furthermore, Immigration and Refugee Board concludes that the

> claimant, an independent businessman, was targeted because of the size of his bank account and not because of his choice of occupation or the state of his conscience.

however, are in a different position; unlike their wealthy counterparts, they cannot alter their economic station.[55] Since the right to subsist is an internationally respected human right, and since the asylum seeker is powerless to alter his/her position, refugee status on the basis of a disadvantaged economic situation can often be appropriate. The results here are consistent with those espoused by Hathaway:

> In contrast to wealth or even middle class status, both of which can ordinarily be the subject of voluntary alienation, poverty as an economic class may constitute a particular social group, since membership cannot always be given up.... Similarly, an economic class is within the scope of the particular social group where membership, though nominally voluntary, is the only means of ensuring basic subsistence, an interest protected under core norms of human rights law.[56]

On the other hand, Canadian case law (as determined by the federal courts) also makes it clear that the human rights protections recognized by international law and incorporated into the refugee standard are not limited to State actors but may be asserted against exclusively non-State agents. Accordingly, in the leading case of *Meyer* v. *M.E.I.*,[57] the Court of Appeal affirmed a decision of the Immigration and Refugee Board which concluded that Trinidadian women subject to wife abuse constituted a particular social group for purposes of the refugee definition. And in the more recent case of *Vidhani* v. *M.E.I.*[58] the court determined that women forced into marriage without their consent formed a particular social group in that they were bound together by an immutable characteristic (gender) and had been denied a fundamental human right (the right to enter freely into marriage) on that basis.

Review of the decisions entered by the Convention Refugee Determination Division prior to *Ward* clearly reveals that the CRDD has been historically inclined toward a "liberal" interpretation of the social group category. Of significance in these adjudications is the willingness of the CRDD to apply attribution principles flexibly in determining the parameters of social group membership. Individuals who are targeted by guerillas because they are ticket agents with access to classified information[59] or

---

*Interpretation of the Convention Refugee Definition in the Case Law, supra* § II.3, note 63, § 4.5.

55 *Cf.* Sinora v. M.E.I. (F.C.T.D., no. 93-A-334), July 3, 1993.

56 Hathaway, *supra* § I.1, note 7, at 167.

57 (1992), 150 N.R. 60 (F.C.A.).

58 [1995] 3 F.C. 60 (T.D.).

59 CRDD T90-02283, August 13, 1991.

government officials executing national policy[60] are obvious examples of groups held together not by intrinsic characteristics but by their constituting a collective threat in the perception of their persecutors. The CRDD's willingness to treat these as social groups for refugee determination purposes reveals a proclivity to adopt a context-dependent method of analysis when interpreting the scope of social group membership.

Finally, it is important to note that the demarcation line between personal problems and the refugee definition is not limited to gender claims. A central question which arises under refugee law is whether individuals subjected to lawlessness (e.g., by drug traffickers) may make out a claim for refugee status. Canadian case law has generally resolved this question in the negative, even in the presence of exceptional circumstances such as the targeting of specific family members by drug lords.[61] Such results are becoming extremely difficult to justify in those countries wherein narcotics trafficking has developed into a significant social force, especially where those targeted are viewed as being opposed to the drug lords' overall goal of commercial dominance through widespread social dependency on narcotics.

In the wake of early BIA decisions, United States adjudications regarding the fourth Convention ground were initially highly conservative. In *Matter of Martinez-Romero*,[62] the Board rejected the approach that students could, as a general matter, constitute a particular social group, at least in the absence of evidence regarding collective persecution. Subsequently, in *Matter of Acosta*,[63] the still leading case in the U.S., the Board rejected the idea that membership in a Salvadoran taxi cooperative could form the basis of a "particular social group" claim. The Board ruled that the cooperative was formed for merely commercial purposes, and that there was nothing in the voluntary association thus created which related to the asylum seeker's dignity or conscience:

> In the respondent's case, the facts demonstrate that the guerillas sought to harm the members of COTAXI, along with members of other taxi co-operatives in the city of San Salvador, because they refused to participate in work stoppages in that city. The characteristics defining the group of which respondent was a member and subjecting that group to punishment were being a taxi driver in San Salvador and refusing to participate in guerrilla-sponsored work stoppages. Neither of these characteristics is immutable because the members of the group could avoid the threats of the guerillas either by changing jobs or by cooperating in the work stoppages. *It may be unfortunate*

---

60 CRDD T90-02709, July 11, 1991.

61 Calero v. M.E.I. (F. T.C.T., no. IMM-336-93), August 8, 1994.

62 18 I&N Dec. 75 (BIA 1981).

63 19 I&N Dec. 211 (BIA 1985).

> *that respondent would have had to change his means of earning a living or cooperate with the guerillas to avoid the threats. However, the internationally accepted concept of refugee simply does not guarantee an individual the right to work in the job of his choice.*[64]

As emphasized throughout this study, *Acosta* has come to be recognized internationally as constituting an appropriate restatement of the criteria for social group persecution, at least so far as intrinsic characteristics are concerned.[65] Nonetheless, the way in which those criteria were *interpreted* by the Board presents grave problems with respect to application of the refugee standard, problems which, to some degree, have now come to inform Canadian jurisprudence through the reliance upon *Acosta* by the (Canadian) Supreme Court's decision in *Ward*.[66]

It is imperative to note, in this respect, the fundamentally insensitive dismissal of the right being asserted by those in the taxi cooperative itself, a dismissal essential to the Board's finding that the COTAXI members could withdraw from their economic activity (and their cooperative), thus escaping further persecution. The Board commented that the right to one's choice of employment was not guaranteed by international law. One noted commentator has characterized the Board's treatment of COTAXI's members as "elitist":

> The BIA mischaracterized Acosta's claim. The seriousness of Acosta's potential plight and the complexity of this aspect of refugee law deserve more reflective analysis. Contrary to the BIA's implication, Acosta did not claim that either United States or international law guarantees individuals the unqualified right to work in the job of their choice. Acosta simply testified that by carrying out the job he had managed to find in an economy suffering from high unemployment, he had received serious death threats from a group that apparently had no difficulty in making such threats come true. The BIA's

---

64 *Id.* at 234. [Emphasis supplied].

65 *See generally* Islam (A.P.) v. Secretary of State for Home Dept., Regina v. Immigration Appeal Tribunal and Another Ex Parte Shah, [1999] 2 All ER 545 (House of Lords).

66 The *Ward* formulation seems especially troublesome in this regard:

> Surely there are some groups, the affiliation in which is not so important to the individual that it would be more appropriate to have the person disassociate him-herself from it before Canada's responsibility should become engaged. Perhaps the most simplified way to draw the distinction is by opposing what one is against what one does at a particular time. For example, one could consider that facts in *Matter of Acosta* in which the claimant was targeted because he was a member of a taxi driver cooperative. Assuming no issues of political opinion or the right to earn some basic living are involved, the claimant was targeted for *what he was doing and not for what he was in an immutable or fundamental way.* [Emphasis supplied].

Canada (Attorney General) v. Ward , [1993] 2 S.C.R. 689, 738-39.

> evaluation of Acosta's particular social group claim was narrow and elitist and the BIA vividly demonstrated how cramped an interpretation is possible under its proposed definition.[67]

As noted earlier, Grahl-Madsen maintains that a refugee claimant's insistence on any of the rights set forth in UDHR will give rise to political opinion persecution if serious harm is threatened or imposed as a consequence. Rights recognized under UDHR include those "social" rights[68] which now form part of customary international law and which are contained in the International Covenant on Economic, Social and Cultural Rights.[69] ICESCR assures as one of its core norms the right to work.[70] The centrality of the right to work can be gleaned, at least in part, from its relationship to other rights. Essential "survival rights" are often dependent on the individual's access to employment in that the income generated thereby constitutes the means to secure food, medical care, clothing and housing. Apart from these "basic rights", however, employment may also be critical with respect to the enjoyment of less fundamental rights such as education and culture. As concerns the status of the right to work under general international law, a leading commentator makes the following observation:

> Article 6 [of ICESCR], however, is not so much concerned with what is provided by work (in terms of remuneration), or the conditions of work, *but rather with the value of employment itself. It thus gives recognition to the idea that work is an element integral to the maintenance of the dignity and self-respect of the individual.*[71]

The right to work, moreover, must be considered in conjunction with the following correlative rights:

1. **The right to choice of work.**[72] The Board in opining that international law does not confer the right to work in the employment of one's choosing conflates two important aspects of this right which, for convenience sake, may be termed its "positive" and "negative" dimensions. International law has not advanced (nor is it likely to) to the point at which the individual may place a legitimate demand on the State that he/she be employed in a specific

---

67 *See generally* Fullerton, *supra* § I.5, note 60, at 547.

68 *See, e.g.*, UDHR, *supra* § I.1, note 12, Arts. 23-1 (free choice of employment); 23-4 (right to form and join trade unions); art 23-3 (right to just and favorable remuneration); Art. 25-1 (right to a standard of living adequate for the wage earner's health and well-being and that of his family); and Art. 2 (right to enjoy the foregoing rights without discrimination).

69 ICESCR, *supra* § I.1, note 15, Arts. 7 and 8.

70 *Id.*, Art. 6-1.

71 Craven, *supra* § II.2, note 50, at 194. [Emphasis supplied].

72 *Id.*

vocation (the "positive" right). On the other hand, it is evident that the individual has the right, under international law, to be protected against arbitrary deprivation of productive labor by the State as well as by third parties (the "negative" right).

**2. The right not to be arbitrarily deprived of work.**[73] The right to have one's labor protected against arbitrary interference by third parties ("horizontal" enforcement of human rights in the private sphere) has its usual application in the employer-employee context, rather than in the situation of insurgents attempting to coerce civilian non-combatants to do their bidding. However, in its more customary social setting, the right against arbitrary termination of employment has compelling public policy underpinnings in general international law. As noted by Mathew Craven:

> Indeed, the question of horizontal effectiveness is of particular importance in the field of economic, social and cultural rights. In the context of Article 7, for example, [relating to just and favorable conditions of employment], if State obligations were limited to ensuring that public employees enjoyed fair conditions of work, the right would be largely deprived of effect (especially in the case of 'mixed' or 'market' economies). Similar considerations apply to the right to work (Article 6), the right to housing (Article 11) and in certain circumstances, the right to health (Article 12) and education (Article 31). *It must be assumed that where the State is not in a position to ensure the rights itself, it must regulate private interactions to ensure that individuals are not arbitrarily deprived of the enjoyment of these rights by other individuals.*[74]

**3. The right of workers to form and join a workers' organization.**[75] The taxi cooperative (COTAXI) which resisted guerilla demands in *Acosta* was clearly a workers' organization formed for the purpose of engaging in trade but also with a view to enhancing the members' economic interests. For instance, the members of COTAXI were to "pool" their resources to purchase new taxi-cabs.[76] The *travaux preparatoires* to ICESCR Article 8(1)(a) reveal that the term "trade union" was to be broadly interpreted (so as to include, for instance, employers' associations) and would embrace voluntary associations of workers formed for mutual economic advancement (such as would be covered by the French term *syndicats*).[77]

---

[73] *Cf.* ICESCR, *supra* § I.1, note 15, art 6(a).

[74] *See, e.g.*, Craven, *supra* § II.2, note 50, at 112. [Emphasis supplied].

[75] ICESCR, *supra* § I.1, note 15, Art. 8(1)(a) (relating to the right to form and join trade unions).

[76] Matter of Acosta, 19 I&N Dec. 211, 216 (BIA 1985).

[77] *See. e.g.*, UN Doc. A/3525, 11 UN GAOR, Annexes (Ag. item 31), 8-12, ¶¶ 54-75 (1955). For an overview of the social rights described above, *see* David B. Trubick, *Economic,*

The Board's ruling does not take these important rights into account in rendering its judgment. If *Matter of Acosta* is viewed, moreover, as involving a group of workers in voluntary association with one another seeking to maintain a livelihood in the only way open to them, it is hard to see how the situation presented cannot be characterized as one of serious harm flowing from the exercise of important social rights which the international community has determined to be worthy of protection. It is apparent in this respect that the *Acosta* decision raises (although it does not adequately address) the problem of horizontal enforcement of individual rights in the private sphere which has been developed through the substantive jurisprudence of both human rights and humanitarian law.[78] The fact that the Board did not even consider how seriously these social rights were taken by claimants constitutes, in the view of Maryellen Fullerton, a glaring omission in the Board's approach:

> More significantly, the BIA did not apply to Acosta's testimony the "matter of conscience" aspect of its social group definition. The BIA did not even examine whether members of a work cooperative might find that their membership is fundamental to their identities and to their views of themselves as members of society. This failure of examination by the BIA reflected a significant class bias in the BIA's view of social group. For example, the BIA decided in *Acosta* that taxi drivers resisting work stoppages can be required to change their views and actions when faced with threats of persecution, but it is difficult to imagine that the BIA would come to the same conclusion if the facts indicated that doctors throughout the city of San Salvador were routinely persecuted for practicing medicine. Similarly if lawyers in San Salvador risked death by practicing law or university professors were threatened with death for holding classes, it is hard to imagine the BIA blithely saying that it was unfortunate that these groups of individuals have to change their jobs, but they have no right under international law to do the work of their choice. Undoubtedly, doctors, lawyers and professors all are in occupations that require more training than that necessary for taxi drivers. More education and training does not, however, guarantee more commitment to work. Nor is more highly skilled and more highly paid work necessarily more fundamental to one's identity.[79]

---

*Social and Cultural Rights in the Third World: Human Rights Law and Human Needs Programs, in* Human Rights in International Law 205, 232 (Theodor Meron ed.1984).

78 The death threats said to constitute serious harm were issued by a group of insurgents in clear violation of an injunction imposed on them by international humanitarian law to respect non-combatant civilians taking no part in the hostilities. *See, e.g., Commentary to Protocol II, supra* § I.2, note 36, at 1448. The Board's lack of interest or concern in this aspect of the case opens it up to legitimate skepticism with respect to its commitment to the human rights underpinnings of the law of refugee status.

79 Fullerton, *supra* § I.5, note 60, at 547.

The ruling of the Board that the claimants' exercise of important social rights was not linked to their identity or conscience indicates that the Board may be drawing too high an eligibility test in determining the scope of social group protection. A similar observation may be made of the *Ward* decision,[80] which quotes the Board's ruling with approval and relies on *Acosta*'s interpretation of the Board's social group criteria, at least in part.[81] In holding that the claimant can be obliged to withdraw from such social rights, the Board rules (implicitly) that violation of these rights does not constitute "persecution". In this connection, although the Hathaway definition of "persecution" may not be entirely free of ambiguity, its linkage of serious harm to a denial of core human rights which offends human dignity in a key way may be appropriately invoked in this instance. Hathaway writes:

> The dominant view, however, is that refugee law ought to concern itself with actions which deny human dignity in a key way, and that the sustained or systemic denial of core human rights is the appropriate standard.[82]

The Hathaway formula accepts that infringement of some of the rights set forth in ICESCR may give rise to persecution on a Convention ground. Included within this category of ICESCR violations are those which result from the State's discriminatory allocation of resources (or its failure to deploy available resources at all). Indeed Hathaway acknowledges that violations of many of these rights set forth in ICESCR will give rise to refugee status, but confines his analysis to the State's role in protecting these rights. Such a doctrinal approach, it is submitted, fails to acknowledge the principle that persecution can consist of a violation of human rights by third parties, and that the rights thus violated do not depend for their validity on the existence of a State apparatus to enforce them. Hathaway writes:

> Third are those rights contained in the UDHR and carried forward in the International Covenant on Economic, Social and Cultural Rights. In contrast to the ICCPR, the ICESCR does not impose absolute and immediately binding standards of attainment, but rather requires States to take steps to the maximum of their available resources to progressively realize rights in a non-discriminatory way. The basic values protected are the right to work, including just and favorable conditions of employment, remuneration and rest, entitlement to food, clothing, housing, medical care, social security and basic education; protection of the family, particularly children and mothers; and freedom to engage and benefit from cultural, scientific, literary and artistic

---

80 [1993] 2 S.C.R. 689.

81 *Id.* at 738-739. Reliance seemed especially critical with respect to the Court's distinction between what one *is* (*a* predicate for social group persecution) and what one *does* (not a predicate).

82 Hathaway, *supra* § I.1, note 7, at 108.

> expression. While the standard of protection is less absolute than that which applies to the first two categories of rights [non-derogable and derogable rights under the UDHR and the ICCPR] a state is in breach of its obligations where it either ignores these interests notwithstanding the fiscal ability to respond, or where it excludes a minority of the population from their enjoyment.[83]

The Hathaway analysis thus confines itself to infringements which are the product of some failure on the part of the State to meet its affirmative responsibilities under the Convention. The submission of this study, on the other hand, is that the rights enshrined in the UDHR and developed in the ICCPR and the ICESCR are not limited to violations by States but may, in appropriate instances, be invoked *vis-à-vis* non-State actors (*Drittwirkung*).[84]

As concerns the ICESCR, moreover, the Convention's aspirational aspects (the "right" to full employment, the "right" to demand a remunerative position in a particular occupation from the State, etc.) must be kept separate and apart from deliberate violations which negatively impact the instrument's normative provisions. As the analysis offered by Matthew Craven demonstrates, the right to engage in work which one has freely chosen is deeply related to the maintenance of individual self-respect. Deliberately displacing those who are pursuing this right (especially in light of a conscientious choice which they have made) affects their human dignity in a more than incidental way.[85] Consistent with its role of protecting human rights which relate to the inherent worth or dignity of the individual, the law of refugee status should intervene where such fundamental social interests have been irreparably affected and offer surrogate protection to those in need of it.

*Acosta* was followed by a highly disappointing decision from the Ninth Circuit, *Sanchez-Trujillo* v. *INS*.[86] By way of preface, it is important to note that the generally preclusive criteria for social group formation announced in *Sanchez-Trujillo* continue to be given a narrow interpretation. Freshly

---

[83] Hathaway, *supra* § I.1, note 7, at 110-111.

[84] *See, e.g.*, Clapham, *supra* § I.2, note 41, at 178-244, discussing *Drittwirkung* and alternative theories for the application of human rights in disputes between private parties.

[85] The case would also appear to contradict the now received doctrine that the imposition of severe economic disadvantage constitutes persecution within the meaning of the refugee definition. Accordingly, it was considered persecution for a trained chef in Yugoslavia to be forced to work as an untrained cook because of his refusal to join the Communist Party. *See* Kovac v. INS, 407 F.2d 102 (9th Cir. 1987). How could it have been persecution of Kovac to bar him from being a chef, if he had no right to be one? *See also* Gonzalez v. INS, 82 F.3d 903 (9th Cir. 1996).

[86] 801 F.2d 1571 (9th Cir. 1986).

proposed regulations, for instance, indicate that such considerations are permissive, not mandatory.[87] The decision is still viewed as valid precedent with respect to the conditions under which members of a social group can be viewed as having a fear of persecution in the statutory sense. The four-part test set forth by the appeals court is as follows:

> (i) The class of persons identified by the applicant must be cognizable as a particular social group.
>
> (ii) The applicant must have established that he/she qualifies as a member of the group;
>
> (iii) The particular social group must in fact have been targeted on account of the characteristic of its members; and
>
> (iv) It must be determined whether "special circumstances" are present which warrant the decision-maker to regard mere membership in the "social group" as constituting eligibility for refugee status.[88]

In *Sanchez-Trujillo*, the Ninth Circuit ruled that young working class Salvadoran males who were of military age did not qualify for social group treatment. Beyond this, however, the Ninth Circuit developed a highly restrictive view of the social group ground. Specifically, the appeals court looked solely to "internal" characteristics in defining the group whose members should be linked together in an active relationship and in pursuit of a goal which is fundamental to their identities.[89] As explained by the court:

> [T]he phrase 'particular social group' implies a collection of people closely affiliated with one another, who are actuated by some common impulse or interest. Of central concern is the existence of a voluntary associational relationship among the purported members, which imparts some common characteristic that is fundamental to their identity.[90]

The decision is obviously completely inconsistent with *Ward* and *Acosta*, and the emphasis of those cases on immutable characteristics as the basis for

---

87 *See* 65 Fed. Reg. 76588, 76597 (December 7, 2000) (to be codified at 8 CFR § 208.15).

88 801 F.2d 1571, 1574-75. These criteria reflect the general point which was made earlier, namely that qualifying under one of the Convention grounds is seldom enough, standing alone, to merit relief under the Refugee Convention. The "well-founded fear" aspect of the refugee definition also must be met. Accordingly, it is usually essential to make some showing that the focus of the persecutor has become narrowed, either upon the claimant herself or to a restricted body of persons who share the applicant's "characteristic or belief". The claimant stands in the most advantageous posture if she can show that serious harm has actually befallen her either individually or as the member of a group. *See, e.g.*, 8 CFR § 208.13(b)(2)(i).

89 *Id.* at 1576

90 *Id.*

"social group" formation. *Sanchez-Trujillo* has, moreover, been internationally discredited, particularly by the recent *Shah* and *Islam* decision of the House of Lords. As Deborah Anker has noted,[91] the social group category was, according to the *travaux preparatoires,* intended to cover groups which did not fall within the remaining grounds of persecution, namely, race, religion, nationality and political opinion. In order to accomplish this objective, it is essential that the term "social group" have flexible boundaries. Moreover, there was ample precedent for defining the social group in terms of the perceptions of the persecutor, i.e., by "external" characteristics:

> Following WWII, cases in European courts of nations party to the 1951 UN Convention recognized the importance of defining the group "externally" in terms of the persecutor's (i.e., the communists) perceptions and placed less emphasis upon the "internal" characteristics of the group such as the existence of a "voluntary associational relationship". The *Sanchez-Trujillo* court can be criticized for failing to recognize the importance of the persecutor's perception in defining a social group and for performing its group cognizability in a vacuum; the underlying purpose of recognizing "particular social groups" is to protect such groups from persecution (i.e., from external agents interfering with the rights and safety of the members).[92]

One early decision of growing importance, *Ananeh-Firempong* v. *INS*,[93] was far more promising with respect to liberal development of the "social group" category. In *Ananeh-Firempong,* an appeals court recognized that a Ghanaian asylum seeker could establish[94] her membership in a particular social group by demonstrating inclusion in any of the following categories:

> (i) those associated with the former government;
>
> (ii) members of the Ashanti tribe; or
>
> (iii) professional business persons who were highly educated.[95]

This ruling determines social group membership as flowing from past associations of the asylum seeker which she is powerless to alter. Although this basis for social group membership is accepted by U.S. case law, jurisprudence interpreting the fourth Convention ground has tended to ignore the

---

[91] Anker 91, *supra* § III.1, note 5, at 147-48.

[92] *Id.*

[93] 766 F.2d 621 (1st Cir. 1985).

[94] The case came before the Ninth Circuit on petition for review of a denial of a motion to reopen. Accordingly, all that the appeals court held was that there were sufficient specific facts alleged which, if proved, would make out eligibility for withholding of deportation under § 243(h) of the Immigration and Nationality Act. *Id.* at 626.

[95] *Id.* at 623.

possibilities raised by past associations (together with the group's "external" features),[96] and instead has focused largely on immutable characteristics or pursuits which the asylum seeker should not be constrained to alter as a matter of conscience (exercise of fundamental human rights). Quite clearly, past associations which have ceased, but which are viewed by the persecutor as being permanent, bear some relationship to attributed characteristics and beliefs. Guy Goodwin-Gill cogently develops this element of the fourth Convention ground:

> The *Ward* judgement is of major importance on a variety of issues, but the analysis of the social group question raises a number of concerns. What is meant by 'groups associated by a former voluntary status', is far from clear. The Court said that this sub-category was included 'because of historical intentions'. However, there is no evidence to suggest that those apparently intended to benefit from the social group provision, the former capitalists of eastern Europe, were ever formally associated one with another. They may have been, but equally they may not. What counted at the time was the fact that they were not only *internally* linked by having engaged in a particular type of (past) economic activity, but also *externally* defined, partly if not exclusively, by the perceptions of the new ruling class.
>
> As the Supreme Court in fact recognized, capitalists were persecuted historically, 'not because of their contemporaneous activities, but because of their past status *as ascribed to them by the Communist leaders*.' In this sense, they were persecuted not because they were *former* capitalists, but because they *were* former capitalists; not because of what they had done, but because of what they were considered to be today; not because of any actual or imagined voluntary association, but because of the perceived threat of the class (defined *incidentally* by what they had once done) to the new society. The approach of the new ruling class to the capitalist class reveals a clear overlap between past activity and/or status and the perception of the *present* threat to the new society.[97]

Interpretations of the fourth ground of refugee protection giving the social group concept meaningful scope did not begin to become prevalent until the 1990s. For instance, in *Carranza-Hernandez* v. *INS*,[98] persecution on account of membership in a particular social group was held to be made out by the

---

[96] One notable exception to this trend was the decision of the Second Circuit Court of Appeals in *Gomez* v. *INS*, 947 F.2d 660, 664 (2d Cir. 1991), where the court defined the 'social group' category as including:

> A particular social group is comprised of individuals who possess some fundamental characteristic in common which serves to distinguish them in the eyes of a persecutor—or in the eyes of the outside world in general.

[97] *Cf.* Goodwin-Gill, *supra* § I.1, note 11, at 360-61. [Emphasis in original].

[98] 12 F.3d 4 (2d Cir. 1993).

asylum seeker's belonging to a Honduran union.[99] Even *Acosta* 's restrictive reading of social rights should not be extended to situations in which the asylum seeker was being punished explicitly for his association with a union and the concomitant political and social values which are advanced through such membership.

Family or clan membership clearly constitutes a ground for particular social group persecution for asylum seekers who can show serious harm on this basis. In *Gebremichael* v. *INS*,[100] the claimant was an Ethiopian national of Amhara descent. His father and brother had been imprisoned for participating in a Seventh Day Adventist service. Applicant had himself been imprisoned and tortured for more than three months for assisting his brother to escape from prison and later from the country. As noted in the decision:

> [T]he link between family membership and persecution is manifest; as the record makes clear and the INS conceded, the Ethiopian security forces applied to petitioner the time honored theory *cherchez la famille* ("look for the family"), the terrorization of one family member to exact information about the location of another family member or to force the missing family member to come forward. As a result, we are compelled to conclude that no reasonable fact-finder could fail to find that petitioner was singled out for mistreatment because of his relationship to his brother. Thus, this is a clear case of "past persecution on account of ... membership in a particular social group".[101]

Thus, while seemingly resting on the immutable ties of family, *Gebremichael* contains an analysis which focuses largely on the perception of the persecutor in defining the relevant group.

It is possible for government employees to constitute a particular social group.[102] However, former members of the police were held not to constitute a social group in *Matter of Fuentes.*[103] And, although members and former

---

99 *Id.* at 8:

> It is of course correct that Carrenza had the burden of showing that the persecution he fears is based on the union activities and organization of the Braceros march rather than on criminal activity such as arson.... We are persuaded that he did so.

100 10 F.3d 28 (1st Cir. 1993).

101 *Id.* at 36.

102 Aguiler-Cota v. INS, 914 F.2d 1375, 1380 n. 3 (9th Cir. 1990).

103 19 I&N Dec. 658, 661 (BIA 1988). Again, the comment of the *Basic Law Manual* is salient:

> Former members of the Salvadoran National Police, as a social group, was not developed in *Matter of Fuentes,* 19 I&N Dec. 658, 661-62 (BIA 1988), but it could be a social group since the former officers cannot undo their past.

Basic Law Manual, *supra* § I.1, note 26, at 45.

members of the military have been held not to constitute a particular social group,[104] this result has been called into question by the *Basic Law Manual*. Specifically, the *Manual* explains:

> As stated above, the Ninth Circuit has concluded that the " social group" classification does not extend to every social group, but particular social groups. This may explain the court's holding concerning former military membership. Clearly, former military membership is a grouping that the member cannot change; it is immutable. Other courts may find it to be a particular social group.[105]

In fact, the Ninth Circuit had earlier determined that former Salvadoran soldiers who could demonstrate that they would be killed if they returned could qualify as members of a particular social group.[106] The decision is based upon the third prong of *Acosta*, i.e., past associations which have become immutable through the passage of time:

> In a civil war persons engaged in military service will be shot at by the other side. But when a person has abandoned his military service and is resuming life as a civilian, it is not civil war to kill him. It is an act of barbarism, of terrorism, of persecution. It is the persecution of a distinct group—ex-soldiers—who become the object of harm because their persecutors identify them politically with the government they served. We are, of course, not laying down the rule that every former soldier of the Salvadoran army may seek asylum in the United States because he has a well-founded fear of persecution. We are holding only that fear of reprisal from guerillas on the part of an ex-soldier is a type of political persecution and that if such a soldier, on the basis of objective circumstances personally known to him, believes that he has at least a one in ten chance of being killed by the guerillas, he meets the statutory test of eligibility.[107]

Similarly, in a recent decision of some moment, the Board determined that a member of the Darod clan and of the Marehan sub-clan in Somalia who had been detained, beaten and tortured by members of the United Somali Congress had been persecuted on account of membership in a particular social group.[108] The "social group" classification of the warring clans may be cited as some authority that struggles between human aggregates not related explicitly to political objectives may constitute a basis for refugee status.

---

[104] Arriaga-Barrientos v. INS, 925 F.2d 1177, 1180 (9th Cir. 1991), *superseded* 937 F.2d 411.

[105] Basic Law Manual, *supra* § I.1, note 26, at 45.

[106] Montecino v. INS, 915 F.2d 518, 520 (9th Cir. 1990).

[107] *Id.*

[108] Matter of H-, 21 I&N Dec. 337 (BIA 1996). As noted previously, warfare among rival clans in Somalia was not originally aimed at political ends. Rather, nomadic groups roved the countryside and engaged in ritualistic warfare. *See* Prunier, *supra* § IV.4(a), note 192, at 37.

The Board has also been disinclined to view those opposed to a national policy which has lawful objectives and is not directed to particular groups as constituting a particular social group.[109] This has tended to be true even where enforcement of the law violated fundamental human rights, such as compulsory sterilization and abortion under China's one family/one child policy.[110]

With some exceptions,[111] this was also the view of federal courts called upon to adjudicate asylum claims arising under China's coercive family-planning policy.[112] The recently passed Illegal Immigration Reform and Control Act of 1996 overturns these decisions by making opposition to family-planning restraints a basis for asylum under the political opinion category.[113] Nonetheless, the Board's prior decisions interpreting the "social group" category restrictively with respect to violators of China's family-planning policy suggests that similar considerations may govern those seeking asylum on the fourth refugee ground urging opposition to similar national programs as a basis.

As with Canadian adjudications, moreover, U.S. law does not generally view as asylum-eligible those fleeing from criminal elements, even when these have been targeted because of their opposition or perceived opposition to unlawful enterprise. In *Bartesaghi-Lay* v. *INS*,[114] asylum was denied where the applicant showed that the Peruvian revolutionary political party (MRTA) would inflict harm or suffering on him because of his refusal to smuggle drugs.[115] However, such cases clearly show the existence of dis-

---

[109] Matter of G-, 20 I&N Dec. 764 (BIA 1993).

[110] Basic Law Manual, *supra* § I.1, note 26, at 42-43, *citing* Matter of Chang 20 I&N Dec. 38 (BIA 1989).

[111] *Cf.* Guo Chun Di v. Carroll, 842 F. Supp. 858 (E.D. Va. 1994) (finding eligibility for relief on the political opinion ground), *rev'd and remanded without opinion sub nom.* Guo Chun Di v. Moscatto, 66 F.3d 315 (4th Cir. 1995).

[112] *See, e.g.*, Yang v. Carroll, 852 F. Supp. 460 (E.D. Va. 1994), *aff'd without opinion sub nom.* Yang v. Carroll, 70 F.3d 114 (4th Cir. 1995); Chen Zhou Chai v. Carroll, 858 F. Supp. 569 (E.D. Va. 1994), *aff'd*, 48 F. 3d 1331 (4th Cir. 1995).

[113] *See, e.g.*, Matter of X-P-T-, 21 I&N Dec. 634 (BIA 1996).

[114] 9 F.3d 819 (10th Cir. 1993).

[115] *Id.* at 822. The rationale of the case reveals that it may well be ripe for overruling in light of the now clearly accepted doctrine of attributed characteristics and beliefs which has gained acceptance in treatise law, in the law of the Ninth Circuit, and presently by the Board of Immigration Appeals. As stated by the 10th Circuit, when quoting the Board with approval:

> Taking the respondent's testimony as true for purposes of analysis, the record is clear that the respondent was solicited for MRTA's drug smuggling operations by virtue of his employment as a sailor, not for any political reasons. When the

crimination directly aimed at the applicant's conscientious desire not to become involved with a widespread and pernicious practice over which there is no effective social control. The scope of the criminal enterprise involved and the applicant's standing as one dedicated to the upholding of public law illustrate clearly that public policy considerations are raised by the applicant's refusal and subsequent flight: attachment to the integrity of public law over private interests (a conscientiously maintained belief which it would be unconscionable to force applicant to relinquish) could easily form the basis for a particular social group; those seeking reprisals against the claimant for his activity are clear agents of persecution for purposes of the refugee definition, provided they are acting in an environment of impunity. There is no requirement in the social group category that serious harm be imposed on account of "political" reasons.

By way of contrast, it seems evident that those who have sustained criminal convictions for serious common law offences and who face excessive punishment for their crimes do not constitute a particular social group for purposes of the refugee definition. The decisions seem to rest on the conclusion that the framers of the 1951 Convention specifically sought to exclude such common law criminals from consideration as refugees. As noted by the Seventh Circuit in *Bastanipour* v. *INS*,[116]

> Whatever its precise scope, the term 'particular social group' was not intended for the protection of the criminal classes in this country, merely upon a showing that a foreign country deals with them more harshly than we do. A contrary result would collapse the fundamental distinction between persecution on the one hand and the prosecution of non-political crimes on the other. [...] We suppose there might be an exception for some class of minor or technical offenders in the U.S. who were singled out for savage punishment in their native land, but a drug felon sentenced to thirty years in this country (though Bastanipour's sentence was later reduced to fifteen years) cannot be viewed in this light.[117]

Gender-based claims have received the most administrative and judicial attention. In the early cases, youth and gender had a tendency to be treated as

---

> respondent refused, he placed himself at risk of harm since the MRTA members wished to insure secrecy of their plans, not due to any concern about the respondent's political opinion. *The fact that the MRTA has an ultimately political rather than a purely criminal purpose does not alter their motive to silence the respondent in that regard.*

*Id.* [Emphasis supplied].

[116] 980 F.2d 1129 (7th Cir. 1992).

[117] *Id.* at 1132. *See also* Saleh v. U.S. Dept. of Justice, 962 F.2d 234, 240 (2d Cir. 1992).

an insufficiently distinct category. Accordingly, in *Matter of Vigil*,[118] the Board held that young male Salvadorans do not constitute a particular social group, a result which (as noted earlier) was reaffirmed by the Ninth Circuit in *Sanchez-Truillo* v. *INS*.[119] Moreover, in *Gomez* v. *INS*,[120] an appeals court affirmed the Board's denial of a claim postulating particular social group membership as:

> women who had been previously battered or raped by the Salvadoran government.[121]

Like *Vigil* and *Sanchez-Trujillo, Gomez* rejects the principle that, standing alone, gender may constitute a ground of refugee protection, even where there is evidence in the record to show that serious harm or suffering has been directly incurred "on account of" an immutable characteristic. The court's language is especially troubling in this respect.

> As the BIA noted, Gomez failed to produce evidence that women who have previously been abused by the guerillas possess common characteristics—other than gender and youth—that such would-be persecutors could identify them as members of the purported group.[122]

A growing body of jurisprudence, however, has found women to be a "particular social group" under a variety of circumstances.[123] Basically, these cases view female gender as constituting an immutable characteristic.[124] Standing alone, such a "characteristic or belief" has generally been held not sufficient to establish a claim since women are not usually found to fear persecution *qua* women.[125] Narrower classes of gender-based claimants clearly qualify, however, and women seeking to throw off unconscionable restrictions imposed on them by their societies, religious communities, or cultural environment who are punished for their non-conformity can, in principle, establish that they satisfy the Convention refugee definition.[126] The common rationale of these decisions rests on the fundamental principle of

---

[118] 19 I&N Dec. 572 (BIA 1988).

[119] 801 F.2d 1571 (9th Cir, 1986).

[120] 947 F.2d 660 (2d Cir. 1991).

[121] *Id.* at 663-664.

[122] *Id.* at 664.

[123] *See generally* Kelley, Anker and Beasley, *supra* § III.3, note 201, at 814.

[124] Fatin v. INS, 12 F.3d 1233 (3rd Cir. 1993).

[125] *Id.* at 1242. Importantly, this trend may well be altered by *Shah* and *Islam,* 2 All ER 545 (House of Lords), finding two Pakistani women eligible for asylum in light of the systematic lack of State protection against spousal abuse provided them in Pakistan.

[126] *Cf.* Safaie v. INS, 25 F.3d 636 (8th Cir. 1994).

the Universal Declaration of Human Rights that human rights (including the right to the free exercise of expression) are to be enjoyed without discrimination.[127]

In *Fatin* v. *INS*,[128] the court classified as a possible social group women within applicant's country (Iran) who had refused to comply to restrictive gender-specific legislation and customs:[129] Women conscientiously opposed to such oppressive practices could base their claims to asylum on infringement of beliefs which were so fundamental to their identities and consciences that they ought not to be required to relinquish them.[130]

Similarly, in *Safaie* v. *INS*,[131] the Eighth Circuit rejected the proposition that women in Iran, without more, constituted a particular social group simply because of the restrictions which had been placed on them. The court agreed, however, that those who protested such religious restraints could make out a claim. Under *Fatin,* moreover, women who "unhappily complied" with such restrictions might also be included in the group, but generally a showing of conscientious objection would be necessary to establish the required element of individualized persecution.[132] Such "overt manifestation" of opinion makes clear both that the applicant is within a group which merits protection (e.g., she is not among those women who have accepted the regime) and that the resulting punishment (extreme according to most accounts) is the equivalent of serious harm. The gender-based cases in other words demonstrate that there is a substantial link between the protected grounds and the concept of persecution.

Finally, in a precedent decision of exceptional breadth, the Board of Immigration Appeals found that a young women from Togo who demonstrated that she would be subject to Female Genital Mutilation (FGM) if she were returned to her country made out a claim based on the membership in a particular social group category, namely members of applicant's particular

---

[127] UDHR, *supra* § I.1, note 12, Art. 2.

[128] 12 F.3d 1233 (3rd Cir. 1993).

[129] *Id.* at 1241.

[130] *Id. quoting* Matter of Acosta, 19 I&N Dec. 211, 234 (BIA 1985).

[131] 25 F.3d 636 (8th Cir. 1994).

[132] As will be noted *infra*, both the *Fatin* and the *Sefaie* courts crafted unrealistically high standards for women attempting to show that they would suffer persecution through their forced conformity with gender-specific codes. In contradistinction to prevailing doctrine, both the Third and Eighth Circuits virtually required the asylum seeker to show that she was prepared to be a martyr in order to qualify as oneconscientiously opposed to inherently discriminatory religious laws and customs.

tribe (the Tchamba-Kunsuntu) who had not been subjected to FGM and who were conscientiously opposed to the practice.[133]

The case of household domestic violence for which there is no recourse in the home country, but which has not been brought about by the applicant's opposition to cultural, political or social norms, constitutes an emerging type of claim in both jurisdictions. Canadian case law has expressly found this class of claim to provide a basis for refugee status. On the other hand, U.S. law is coming into line with the overwhelming international consensus in this area both through adoption of the *U.S. Gender Guidelines*[134] and in recently proposed regulations which are tailored to the issues generated by domestic violence.[135] Eligibility here must be premised on parallel developments taking place in international human rights law which essentially characterizes violence in a "private" marital dispute as having significant public policy implications.[136] Major public policy implications flow from the relevant society's overall tolerance toward violent abuse of a particular group and the want of State protection which accompanies that tolerance. As Theodor Meron has written:

> [Article 1] of the Convention on the Elimination of All Forms of Discrimination Against Women clearly extends the prohibition of discrimination to private life.[137]

The 1993 Declaration on the Elimination of Violence Against Women clearly constitutes an effort to enlarge the protection of women against discrimination and abuse by recognizing that violence against women is a *per se* violation of fundamental human rights which operates as an obstruction to the realization by women of other basic rights.[138] On the other hand, a growing body of literature maintains that the concerns generated by domestic violence raise acute issues of distress for women who are seen as

---

[133] Matter of Kasinga, 21 I&N Dec. 357, 367 (BIA 1996). The case was followed in *Abankwa* v. *INS*, 185 F.3d 18 (2d Cir. 1999). While *Abankwa* goes into great depth with respect to the evidentiary standards governing a gender-based claim predicated on the threat of FGM, it adds little, if anything, to the eligibility requirements as initially set forth in *Matter of Kasinga*, 21 I&N Dec. 357 (BIA 1996).

[134] *United States Gender Guidelines, supra* § I.5, note 61, at 17. For a more specific discussion of the issue *see* Kelley, Anker and Beasley, *Guidelines on Women's Asylum Claims, supra* note 201, 71 Interpreter Releases 813, 821 (July 27, 1994), *citing* Mayers v. M.E.I. (1992), 97 D.L.R. (4th) 729.

[135] *See* 65 Fed. Reg. 76588, 76597 (December 7, 2000) (to be codified at 8 CFR § 208.15).

[136] *See, e.g., U.S. Gender Guidelines, supra* § I.5, note 61, at 2.

[137] Theodor Meron, Human Rights Law-Making in the United Nations 60 (1986).

[138] Declaration on the Elimination of Violence Against Women, *adopted* 20 December 1993, G.A. Res. 48/104, UN Doc. A/48/29, *reprinted in* 33 ILM 1049 (1994).

being left out of conventional human rights analysis which is reserved for "public" (i.e., political) situations. The role of women is portrayed as occupying mainly a "private" sphere which is often not within the human rights field of vision. As argued by Catherine MacKinnon:

> Why isn't this [torture of women by men] political? The abuse is neither random nor individual. The fact that you may know your assailant does not mean your membership in a group selected for violation is irrelevant to your abuse. *This abuse is systematic and group-based.* It defies the quality of community life and the distribution of power in society. It would seem that something is not considered political if it is done to women by men, especially if it is considered to be sex. Then, it is not considered political or even violent because what is political is when men control and hurt and use other men, persons who are deserving of dignity, on some basis men have decided is deserving of dignity, like political ideology. *So their suffering has the dignity of politics and is called torture.*[139]

Related to the growing body of gender-based persecution claims are cases based on sexual orientation. In the now leading case, *Matter of Toboso-Alfonso*,[140] the Board noted that the Immigration and Naturalization Service did not challenge the contention that the asylum seeker's homosexuality for which he had been persecuted in Cuba placed him within the particular social group category. The Board cautioned that membership in a particular social group was not sufficient to establish a claim if such showing is not accompanied by a parallel demonstration of proximate or past persecution on account of the statutory ground. Representative of this growing class of case is the Ninth Circuit's decision in *Pitcherskaia* v. *INS*[141] in which the appeals court determined that a Russian lesbian had established a well-founded fear of future persecution by showing a reasonable expectation that she would be subjected to electric shock treatment and drug therapy.[142]

A recent case which develops sexual orientation as a basis for asylum is *Hernandez-Montiel* v. *INS*.[143] *Hernandez-Montiel* involved a Mexican youth who had been expelled from school and thrown out of the parental home because of his being gay. Applicant was subsequently harassed by Mexican

---

139 Catherine MacKinnon, *On Torture: A Feminist Perspective on Human Rights*, *in* Human Rights in the Twenty-First Century 21 (Kathleen Mahoney and P. Mahoney eds.1993), *reprinted in* Steiner and Alston, *supra* § I.1, note 13, 953. [Emphasis supplied].

140 20 I&N Dec. 819 (BIA 1990).

141 118 F.3d 641 (9th Cir. 1997).

142 *Id.* at 646-648. Following the *Kasinga* decision, the Ninth Circuit ruled that treatment which the asylum seeker reasonably regards as offensive will qualify as persecution, and it is irrelevant that the persecutor seeks to "cure" the victim, rather than to "punish her. *Id.*

143 No. 98-70582, 2000 WL 1199531 (9th Cir. Aug. 24, 2000). The case is digested in 77 Interpreter Releases 1283 (September 1, 2000).

police officers for dressing in women's clothing (although no charges were filed) and attacked by a street gang which resulted in knife wounds and hospitalization. The asylum seeker returned to Mexico in 1993 after an aborted effort to flee to the U.S. When a counseling program failed to "cure" the applicant, he fled a second time to the United States and applied for asylum.

The Ninth Circuit recognized that the "voluntary associational relationships" which had been the basis for its earlier decision in *Sanchez-Trujillo* v. *INS*[144] were not appropriate for every type of "social group" case and it specifically adopted the "immutable characteristics" basis first announced in *Acosta* and now followed in the First, Third and Seventh Circuits. The appeals court rejected the Board's characterization of the relevant group ("homosexual males who dress like females"). Rather the tribunal determined the "social group" of which applicant was a member to consist of "gay men with female sexual identities in Mexico". This characterization of the protected ground was essential in light of expert testimony before the immigration judge which showed that it was claimant's female identity which was viewed with hostility in Mexico. Social group membership (like political opinion) is largely a reflection of how the persecutor perceives the asylum seeker.[145]

The "poor" (as that generic description applies contextually in specific country settings) may be a "particular social group" under appropriate factual determinations. Relevant where disadvantaged groups are concerned is Article 11 of the International Covenant on Economic, Social, and Cultural Rights pursuant to which States parties recognize the "right of everyone" to an adequate standard of living, including adequate food, clothing and housing.[146] The Committee on Economic, Social and Cultural Rights has been comparatively clear, requiring that: "States parties must give due priority to those social groups living in unfavorable conditions by giving them particular consideration." As noted by the Committee:

> Policies and legislation should correspondingly not be designed to benefit already advantaged social groups at the expense of others. The Committee is aware that external factors can affect the right to continuous improvement of living conditions, and that in many States overall living conditions declined

---

[144] 801 F.2d 1571 (9th Cir. 1986).

[145] Also relevant here is a memorandum from the General Counsel of the Immigration and Naturalization Service to the effect that HIV (human immunodeficiency virus)-positive individuals can constitute a particular social group for purposes of satisfying the refugee definition. *See* Memorandum from David Martin, INS Office of General Counsel, Feb. 16, 1996, *reprinted in* 73 Interpreter Releases 909 (July 8, 1996).

[146] ICESCR, *supra* § I.1, note 15, Art. 11.

> during the 1980's. However, as noted by the Committee in its General Comment Number 2 (1990) (E/192/23, annex III), despite externally caused problems, the obligations of the Covenant continue to apply and are perhaps even more pertinent in times of economic contraction. It would appear to the Committee that a general decline in living and housing conditions, directly attributable to policy and legislative decisions by States parties, and in the absence of compensatory measures, would be inconsistent with obligations under the Covenant.[147]

International humanitarian law also recognizes affirmative responsibilities in parties to the conflict to provide sanitary conditions, sustenance and minimum health care to those under their control.[148]

No asylum case in the U.S. has held that the poor as such constitute a particular social group. Nonetheless, in *Haitian Refugee Center* v. *Civiletti*,[149] a group of Haitian asylum seekers sought to challenge the categorical determination of the Immigration and Naturalization Service that they were mere economic migrants and not refugees. The district court held that the procedures under which this determination had been made were constitutionally defective, finding that economics in Haiti was largely a function of the country's political system.[150] The court concluded that, in substantial measure, extensive Haitian poverty was due entirely to the corruption and oppression of the Duvalier regime. The Duvaliers' method of maintaining political power had such pervasive effects on the economy that it was appropriate to characterize the asylum seekers' "economic situation as a political condition".[151] An influential law review note contains this revealing comment on the *Civiletti* case:

> The court in *Haitian Refugee Center* concluded that Duvalier "had made his country weak so that he could be strong". This simple formulation invokes the fundamental democratic principle that political power should be exercised for the benefit of the governed—that political conditions are illegitimate when those holding power exercise it for their own aggrandizement at the expense of some or all of the citizenry. The asylum statutes are at bottom an expression of this principle. *By offering asylum to members of any "particular social group," these statutes hold foreign governments to the democratic ideal of exercising power in the interests of all. The issue that must guide the judicial inquiry is whether the political system being considered makes of one group*

---

[147] *See* General Comment Number 4 (1991), UN ESCOR, Supp. (No. 3), Annex III, at 117, ¶ 11, UN Doc. E/1992/23, (1992), *reprinted in* Craven, *supra* § II.2, note 50, at 377, *et seq*.

[148] *See, e.g.*, Geneva Convention IV, *supra* § I.1, note 17, Arts. 85, 89.

[149] 503 F. Supp. 442 (S.D. Fla. 1980), *aff'd as modified,* 676 F.2d 1023 (5th Cir. 1982).

[150] *Id.* at 508-10.

[151] *Id.*

> *of citizens merely the means for another group's prosperity, privilege and continued power.*
>
> When such exploitation amounts to a "threat to life or freedom," the refugee's showing is complete.[152]

The holding in *Haitian Refugee Center* v. *Civiletti* elucidates that the "poor", for purposes of the law of refugee status, can be as clearly defined a group as "race" or "nationality" where widespread economic oppression is concerned. Under these circumstances, the "poor" may be seen as possessing an immutable characteristic (poverty or extreme economic disadvantage which the members are powerless to alter or alleviate).[153] As noted above, where societies are stratified according to rigid ethnic or caste lines, an affected individual may qualify for asylum if the impending injury approaches destitution or other serious harm.[154]

The decision also reveals the close linkage which exists between the equal protection component of human rights doctrine and the refugee standard. Failure on the part of the State to uphold human rights to an acceptable level may well expose human beings who are affected by a distorted allocation of resources to substantial risks flowing from their economic position within society.[155] Marginalization which the State has a duty to redress under international law can thus give rise to a finding of persecution in affected classes, if the resulting harm is of a particularly serious dimension (e.g., destitution or a threat to life itself).[156] A broad reading of the *Civelleti* case, moreover, suggests that where the State fails to correct social arrangements which foreclose identifiable groups from realizing basic economic and social rights, the refugee definition may well be satisfied for individuals seriously affected by such practices. Such an approach is clearly consistent with modern trends as represented by the current position of the Committee on Economic, Social and Cultural Rights. Mathew Craven writes:

> In practice, the actual intention of the State concerned seems to be of little importance. It is clear that in the majority of States some form of discrimina-

---

152 Note: *Political Legitimacy in the Law of Political Asylum,* 99 Harv. L. Rev. 450, 465 (1985). [Emphasis supplied]

153 *See, e.g.*, Hathaway, *supra* § I.1, note 7, at 166-167.

154 Jaeger, *supra* § II.2, note 52, at 7.

155 This view has now been advanced by the Human Rights Committee. *See* McGoldrick, *supra* § I.2, note 45, at 274.

156 It is received doctrine, for instance, that the "deliberate imposition of substantial economic disadvantage" (directed toward a protected ground) constitutes persecution in the refugee sense. Kovac v. INS, 407 F.2d 102 (9th Cir. 1969).

tion is inherent in the civil, political, social, economic, and cultural traditions of the country. A particular government at any given juncture cannot be considered to have willed that situation, whether expressly or impliedly. *The necessity of eliminating discrimination requires that the government take action to remedy circumstances for which it is not itself responsible.* This is particularly clear insofar as States are obliged to eliminate discrimination between private individuals. Thus although discriminatory intention might be determined merely by the existence of discriminatory polices and legislation, the Committee has not refrained from criticizing governments on the basis of the *de facto* situation alone.

* * *

[E]ven though there is often distinct correlation between covert discriminatory situations and general stratification of power, wealth, prestige and education, it is more important to recognize that discrimination is not merely a consequence of that stratification but also a cause. As such the recognition and elimination of discrimination is central to the well-being of such groups.[157]

## § V.4. Commentary on the Protected Grounds in General with Special Reference to the Particular Social Group Category

Related to the evolving nature of modern refugee doctrine is the question whether the "particular social group" classification is a Convention ground which may be liberally expanded by signatory States in their discretionary development of the refugee definition. A subsidiary issue concerns the degree to which States are obligated, in implementing the 1951 Convention and the 1967 Protocol, to adopt an analysis of "social group" which remains anchored in the four remaining grounds of refugee protection.

The "liberal" viewpoint, i.e., that the fourth Convention ground is essentially "catch-all" has been expounded by Arthur Helton. Helton contends that the seminal goal of the Convention (to protect individuals and groups against "persecution") requires a construction which would allow States parties substantial flexibility in determining the scope of the "social group" category. Such an approach is essential, Helton maintains, to confer an effective remedy against future forms of harm which could not be adequately anticipated by the Convention's framers.[158]

---

[157] Craven, *supra* § II.2, note 50, at 166, 178. [Emphasis supplied].

[158] Helton, *supra* § I.1, note 23, at 44:

> The intent of the framers of the Refugee Convention was not to redress prior persecution of social groups, but rather to save individuals from future injustice. The "social group" category was meant to be a catch-all which could include all the bases for and types of persecution which an imaginative despot could conjure

The view advanced by Helton was clearly original but hardly radical, and seems in well-established agreement with what other commentators have had to say about the "particular social group" category. Atle Grahl-Madsen certainly views the adoption of the "particular social group" ground as included in the refugee definition "in order to stop a possible gap," noting that there would be some overlap with other protected grounds.[159] Significantly, the "liberal" view is also the one put forward by Guy Goodwin-Gill who argues that the "particular social group" classification is essentially "open-ended", especially in light of the attitude toward the group on the part of State authorities and other social groups:

> In determining whether a particular group of people constitutes a 'social group' within the meaning of the Convention, attention should therefore be given to the presence of linking and uniting factors such as ethnic, cultural, and linguistic origin; education; family background; economic activity; shared values, outlooks and aspirations. Also highly relevant are the attitude to the putative social group of other groups in the same society, and, in particular, the treatment accorded by the State authorities. *The importance, and therefore the identity, of a social group may well be in direct proportion to the notice taken of it by others—the view which others have of us—particularly at the official level. The notion of social group thus possesses an element of open-endedness potentially capable of expansion in favor of different classes susceptible to persecution.* How far decision-makers are prepared to go is another matter, but in arguing for expansion appropriate reference could be made to the linking factors of the group in question and to the elements of distinction which make it the object of persecution.[160]

Notwithstanding this apparent consensus, the "liberal" approach to the "particular social group" category has been criticized by some commentators, most particularly by James Hathaway.[161] Hathaway contends that

---

up. Thus the framers' general intent is illustrated by the subsequent recognition of the many types of invidious persecution prevalent in the world today.

[159] *See, e.g.*, 1 Grahl-Madsen, *supra* § I.1, note 7, at 219. Grahl-Madsen also observed that the "social group" class was necessarily broader than the specifically covered ethnic, national and religious groups already contained in the definition, and could embrace such aggregates as:

> Nobility, capitalists, landowners, civil servants, businessmen, professional people, farmers, workers, members of a linguistic or other minority, even members of certain associations, clubs or societies....

[160] Goodwin-Gill, *supra* § I.1, note 11, at 47-48. [Emphasis supplied].

[161] For the (comparatively) conservative view, *see* Hathaway, *supra* § I.1, note 7, at 159:

> [The purpose of the framers] was anything but the creation of a regime to address new, future injustices. [...] It is clear from the comments of the Swedish proponent of the social group category and others that the Convention was

expanding the "particular social group" classification in the manner recommended by Helton does disservice to the specific intent of the framers of the 1951 Convention which was to protect individuals only from certain known forms of harm. Critically, the "known forms of harm" must be linked to "civil or political status".[162] Hathaway writes:

> The notion of social group as an all-encompassing category is seductive from a humanitarian perspective, since it largely eliminates the need to consider the issue of linkage between fear of persecution and civil or political status.... The drafters of the Convention did not wish to avoid drawing distinctions among various types of refugees, but rather intended to establish a demarcation line between those whose fear was attributable to civil or political status (refugees) and those whose concern to flee was prompted by other concerns (not refugees).

Helton's interpretation seeks a teleological construction of the refugee definition, one which would interpret the grounds of refugee protection in the light of the framer's paramount desire to provide protection against "persecution".[163] The Helton analysis thus identifies "persecution" as the central term in the refugee definition, and makes the protected grounds of essentially derivative importance. Hathaway, on the other hand, sees the protected grounds as informing the core concept of persecution and defining the limits of refugee protection.

This study resists the conclusion that nexus to "civil or political status" constitutes the unifying criterion of the protected grounds while recognizing its suggestive appeal and, with respect to specific types of cases, its utility. Alternatively, the present study recommends a refugee analysis which incorporates more fully the liberal (or "open-ended") approach, with the necessary constraining element of discriminatory motive or effect. Initially, it should be noted that critiques of the "liberal" view of "social group" persecution seem unduly restrictive in a number of respects.[164] It does not appear unreasonable to maintain that the term "refugee" should be interpreted consistently with the overriding "social purpose" of the framers which was to afford protection against "persecution." Such an interpretive approach is

---

designed simply as a means of identifying and protecting refugees from known forms of harm.

162 *Id.* at 159.

163 *See also* Anker 91, *supra* § III.1, note 5, at 148-149, discussing the relevant test.

164 Examination of the views advanced by Goodwin-Gill, Helton and Hathaway are of moment for a number of reasons. Principal among these is that the broader interpretations offered by Goodwin-Gill and by Helton were rejected by the Supreme Court of Canada in the *Ward* decision, the Supreme Court listing toward the more restrictive view of Hathaway. *See* Canada (Attorney General) v. Ward, [1993] 2 S.C.R. 689 728-739.

especially appropriate in light of the fact that human rights and humanitarian concerns provide important public policy underpinnings to the refugee definition.[165]

Linking the protected grounds to "civil or political status" seems forward-looking in a number of respects. Most notably, such an approach stresses the implications for refugee analysis which arise when the State fails to relieve, through affirmative action, specific groups suffering from acute distress.[166] However, the term "civil or political status" implies that the substantive grounds upon which a showing of persecution may be based must be connected in some way to the alien's formal status within his/her country of nationality or last residence.

The limitations on the scope of the protected grounds identified by Hathaway are clearly related to his defining persecution by reference to a lack of State protection.[167] It seems highly unlikely that Hathaway intended to exclude "social" or "economic" status from the ambit of the refugee definition. On the other hand, it does seem likely that he did intend to restrict the protected grounds (as he had restricted the concept of "persecution") to some element in the claimant's persona which would have defined her relationship to a *national* community. The Hathaway approach is in stark contrast to the more elastic standard recommended here which is to analyze the protected grounds in connection with the applicant's relationship either to her national community or to some powerful aggregate within that community able to assert actual power and dominion over her.

A claim within the meaning of Article 1(A)(2) of the 1951 Convention may be based on persecution either by the government or by a group or groups which the government is unable or unwilling to control. A failure of State protection is, therefore, an essential showing where the refugee's claim of future serious harm is at the hands of third parties since such lack of protection goes to the reasonableness of the fear itself: it simply cannot be plausibly maintained that a well-founded fear remains ongoing where the government of the refugee's country of nationality (or former residence) is prepared to offer "adequate" protection. Similarly, an absence of State pro-

---

[165] On the need to interpret the refugee definition liberally, and particularly in light of its human rights dimension, *see generally* Goodwin-Gill, *supra* § I.1, note 11, at 35:

> Given "protection" of refugees as one of the Convention's objectives, a liberal interpretation of the criteria is called for.

[166] James Hathaway, *Reconceiving Refugee Law as Human Rights Protection*, 4 Journal of Refugee Studies 122, 123 (1991).

[167] *See, e.g.*, Hathaway, *supra* § I.1, note 7, at 125-133.

tection is also relevant to showing that an "agent" of persecution is present for Convention purposes.

But a failure of State protection does not explain *by itself* the causal relationship between serious harm and a protected ground. Where the actions of private groups form the basis of the claim, linkage must be established between a characteristic of the claimant (real or perceived) and the animus of the third party. Such animus is often unrelated to the conventionally "public" sphere of political life and is often associated with the social and cultural life of the community, sometimes regarded as the "private" sphere. As this study has maintained throughout, however, so long as the practice against the social group is systematized (i.e., relates to enforcement of generally maintained objective standards of the community) and is being exercised in an environment of impunity, persecution on a protected ground can be made out.

The UN *Handbook* is specific in this respect by showing how the *reasons for persecution* may be entirely divorced from the government and its authorities, resting instead on the claimant's failure to conform to religious, cultural or social codes:[168]

> Persecution is normally related to action by the authorities of a country. It may also emanate from sections of the population that do not respect the standards established by the laws of the country concerned. A case in point may be religious intolerance, amounting to persecution, in a country otherwise secular, but where sizable factions of the population do not respect the religious beliefs of their neighbours. Where serious discriminatory or other offensive acts are committed by the local population, they can be considered as persecution, if they are knowingly tolerated by the authorities, or if the authorities refuse, or prove unable, to offer effective protection.

Linking the grounds of persecution, therefore, to "civil or political status" draws the State into the refugee analysis in a way not contemplated by the 1951 Convention. A State which is unable to control elements of its own population (viz., a government defending itself against insurgents who have gained dominion over a substantial portion of the former's territory) cannot be held realistically responsible for the latter's *discriminatory incentive* in committing violations of fundamental human rights.[169] Hence, if there is a common thread or threads holding the grounds of protection together, it must be one other than "civil or political status" which appears too dependent on a

---

[168] Handbook, *supra* § I.1, note 30, ¶ 65.

[169] Under these circumstances, the persecution complained of simply does not emanate from State actors, just as the "characteristic or belief" causing persecution is entirely unrelated to the State's outlook toward the refugee. The motivation to persecute in this instance is attributable entirely to a non-State agency.

State action requirement as a causative element in the serious harm threatened or imposed.

On the other hand, the exclusion from Convention coverage of specific forms of harm (e.g., lawful acts of prosecution by the sovereign; general conditions of upheaval; and harm arising from putatively "private disputes") strongly suggests that relief under the Convention is circumscribed and that there are limits beyond which the refugee definition cannot be extended. Notwithstanding this general conclusion, it is evident that the refugee definition was intended to look to human rights violations as its quintessential organizing principle. And it is not only those who are prejudiced by a lack of State protection who suffer from human rights abuses; also affected are individuals whose dignity has been deliberately compromised by private groups.

Consistent with this basic notion, modern international humanitarian law governing internal conflicts confers broad protections on non-combatants both against State and against insurgent military action. The proscriptions of both common Article 3 of the Geneva Conventions of August 12, 1949, and of Protocol II to those Conventions confer protection against human rights violations committed by the government and the insurgents alike.[170] A counterpart to the advances made by humanitarian law can be found in the "horizontal" enforcement of human rights which has now gained acceptance in general international law [*Drittwirkung*].[171] Related to the latter development is the special protection conferred by modern customary law and treaty upon specific groups with a view to relieving the latter from the effects of social discrimination and to assure their enjoyment of human rights on an equal basis. Many modern human rights treaties aim at social transformation as their ultimate goal. Article 5 of CEDAW seeks, among other things, to "modify the social and cultural patterns of conduct of men and women," and Article 10(c) contemplates the elimination of "any stereotyped concept of the roles of men and women...".[172] The fact that modern human rights instruments seek to relieve human rights violations committed by non-State agents in the "private" sphere constitutes compelling evidence that the refugee grounds are not conditioned by a failure of State protection.

Another, perhaps more telling argument supports the view that "nexus to civil or political status" does not constitute an appropriate litmus test for the

---

170 *See, e.g.*, Commentary to Geneva Convention I, *supra* § I.2, note 40, at 51-52.

171 Clapham, *supra* § I.2, note 41, at 89-133.

172 CEDAW, *supra* § I.1, note 22, arts 5 and 10(c). Such Conventions virtually create affirmative obligations toward specific groups in order to eliminate previous conditions associated with broad patterns of social discrimination.

protected grounds and particularly for the "social group" concept. The view advanced by the Board of Immigration Appeals in *Acosta* (and supported by Hathaway as constituting a sound application of the "civil or political status" test) lays singular stress on internal characteristics and beliefs. The now internationally accepted test of social group persecution (i.e., immutable characteristics, fundamental beliefs and associations, and past activities which have become fixed through the passage of time) does not take sufficient account of beliefs and associations which may be imputed to the claimant by his or her persecutor.

### § V.4(a). "Policy of Discrimination" Approach

Lord Hoffman's separate opinion in *Islam* and *Shah*[173] points to the anti-discrimination mandate of UDHR Article 2 as establishing an appropriate test with respect to whether persecution can be related to a protected ground. International law has developed the parameters of the concept of "discrimination" in such a way that it can be used (as it was in *Shah* and *Islam*) to provide direct relevance to claims of persecution based upon an explicit form of status: groups falling within the penumbra of Article 2 can claim refugee protection based on a precise analogy to human rights doctrine.[174]

An act of discrimination can be discerned wherever protected human rights are systematically negated or restricted on the basis of "objective and reasonable criteria".[175] There is no requirement that the discrimination result from a specific intent on the part of the actor, only that some defined group is adversely affected on an objective basis.[176] Nor need the discrimination be linked to particular grounds or bases specifically mentioned in human rights instruments.[177] Under prevailing international law standards, so long as a

---

[173] [1999] 2 All ER 545 (House of Lords).

[174] *See generally* McGoldrick, *supra* § I.3, note 45, at 274 *et seq*. *See also* Matter of S-P-, 21 I&N Dec. 486 (BIA 1996); Interpretation of the Convention Refugee Definition in the Case Law, *supra* § II.3, note 63, § 9.2.1. The most essential criteria for establishing persecutory motive is thus a configuration of systematic human rights violations affecting persons who are objectively linked to the claimant.

[175] *See e.g.*, McGoldrick, *supra* § I.3, note 45, at 283.

[176] South West Africa Cases, 1966 ICJ Reports 6, 293 (dissenting opinion of Judge Tanaka ):

> The arbitrariness which is prohibited means the purely objective fact and not the subjective condition of those concerned. Accordingly, the arbitrariness can be asserted without regard to ... motive or purpose.

[177] The UDHR provides that human rights are to be enjoyed without distinction based on race, color, sex, language, religion, political or other opinion, national or social origin, property, birth *or other status*. UDHR, *supra* § I.1, note 12, Art. 2. [Emphasis supplied].

discernable collectivity has been the victim of generalized practices (governmental or social) which have the effect of curtailing internationally respected rights or freedoms, the requirements of discrimination will have been met.[178] *International equal protection standards thus make clear that the question of discrimination rests essentially on an examination of objective circumstances in which systematic violations of the human rights of a defined group will constitute the governing criterion.*[179]

In his seminal work, *Taking Rights Seriously*, Ronald Dworkin distinguishes between "personal preferences" and "external preferences" in the following manner:

> Preference utilitarianism asks officials to attempt to satisfy people's preferences so far as this is possible. But the preferences of an individual for the consequences of a particular policy may be seen to reflect, on further analysis, either a personal preference for his own enjoyment of some goods or opportunities, or an external preference for the assignment of goods and opportunities to others, or both. A white law school candidate might have a personal preference for the consequences of segregation, for example, because the policy improves his own chances of success, or an external preference for these consequences because he has contempt for blacks and disapproves of situations in which the races mix.[180]

The limits on refugee status must be seen as deeply related to the dichotomy which Dworkin invokes. A claim which is based purely on a personal dispute between gang-lords intent on controlling the dominant share of a relevant market does not give rise to a claim to refugee status on the part of the participant who looses. Feuding businesses do not normally rise to the level of international protection.[181] However, where the persecutor's motiva-

---

Both the ICCPR and the ICSECR contain similarly open-ended provisions. *Compare* ICCPR, *supra* § I.1, note 14, Art. 2-1 and ICESCR, *supra* § I.1, note 15, Art. 2-2.

178 *See, e.g.*, General Comment 18(37), UN Doc. A/45/40, at 174, ¶¶ 7,8, 45 UN GAOR, Supp. (No. 40) (1990), *quoted in* McGoldrick, *supra* note 45, at 276.

179 For parallelism with the refugee definition, in this respect, *see, e.g.*, 8 CFR 208.13(b)(2)(i) setting forth the governing test for group persecution as whether claimant can show:

> a pattern or practice [...] of persecution of groups of persons similarly situated to the applicant on account of race, religion, nationality, membership in a particular social group, or political opinion.

180 Dworkin, *supra* § I.1, note 29, at 234-45.

181 This would not necessarily be the case, however, in a country dominated by clan warfare (or other form of rivalry engaged in by groups with fixed characteristics). Under such conditions, an innocent party who is made the victim of serious harm could make out a claim based on his actual or perceived membership in one of the contending aggregates. *Cf.* Matter of H-, 21 I&N Dec. 337 (BIA 1996). Here, harm or suffering is not based on "personal" animosity, but rather on a principled aversion to a "characteristic or belief" in the applicant which reflects a general policy of discrimination.

tion relates to what Dworkin classifies as an "external preference" (i.e., one not based on personal needs or proclivities of the persecutor, an essentially private dispute), the threshold criterion of refugee status should be viewed as being met. In such instances, the analysis can begin to develop the relationship between persecutor and victim and to examine whether that relationship is based on a real or implied difference in principle having as its foundation a "public" or community-based scheme of values. As noted in the *Basic Law Manual*:[182]

> These grounds should not be considered in a narrow and technical fashion as clear-cut "categories." They are broad categories, and are not meant to exclude from consideration people who can demonstrate persecution or fear of persecution that is targeted and is not only the result of private or personal vengeance or of proximity to civil strife.

Where attributed characteristics or beliefs are concerned, there must be an intention to modify some feature of the claimant's persona, although this need not be the exclusive drive behind the persecutor's actions.[183] From an evidentiary point of view, the dividing line between a "personal" preference and an "external" one is not the subjective state of mind of the persecutor, but general configurations of mistreatment aimed at a particular class of which the claimant is a member. And it is here that the usefulness of the law of non-discrimination becomes apparent: a course of conduct consisting of systematic human rights violations indicative of an implicit policy of discrimination remains the appropriate test for determining whether serious harm is based on a refugee ground.[184]

---

[182] *See* Basic Law Manual, *supra* § I.1, note 26, at 36.

[183] It is important to note the limitations of applying the non-discrimination standards of human rights law to the refugee context. Protected classes under international human rights instruments do not include victims who have had characteristics or beliefs mistakenly attributed to them. Guy S. Goodwin-Gill, *Judicial Reasoning and Social Group After* Islam *and* Shah, 11 Int'l J. Refugee L. 537 (1999). The "categories" benefiting from non-discrimination standards in general international human rights law are those having objective (internal) characteristics which they enjoy in common. Such characteristics can be broadly conceived to include various forms of marginalization based on economic or social status. But the relevance of the non-discrimination mandate of UDHR Art. 2 to attributed characteristics and beliefs should not be underestimated. The open-ended nature of the grounds upon which discrimination may be imposed under UDHR Art. 2 indicates clearly the relevance by analogy of the Universal Declaration's equal protection component to situations where the refugee has been *identified* (rightly or wrongly) as having a particular status or a specific belief.

[184] These are, in fact, the essential criteria put forward in the Board's decision in *Matter of S-P-*, I&N Dec. 486 (BIA 1996).

The "policy of discrimination" approach seeks to draw upon attributed characteristics and beliefs to define the limits of the grounds of refugee protection.[185] As a descriptive term, "policy of discrimination" orients the "reasons" for persecution to the claimant's relationship (through group characteristics which she shares with others or is perceived to share with others) to some community held together by objective criteria (race, religion, caste, economic grouping, social origin, etc.). Unlike the term "civil or political status", however, the proposed analysis rejects as a litmus test the claimant's membership in a national community. Rather, a "characteristic or belief" for Convention refugee purposes would be any component of the claimant's persona which defines her relationship either to the State, or to some important social aggregate within that larger national community.[186] This *public* persona[187] may be manifested through the applicant's faith, political proclivities, ethnicity or some other feature of claimant's makeup which is deemed offensive either by the political authorities of the asylum seeker's homeland, to values maintained by prominent religious or social elements within the country, or to its cultural traditions.

---

[185] In this respect, one noted authority has defined "discrimination" as consisting of:

(i) a difference in treatment;

(ii) linked to certain prohibited grounds;

(iii) having a certain purpose or effect; and

(iv) in selective fields.

E. Schelb, *The International Convention on the Elimination of All Forms of Racial Discrimination*, 15 Int'l and Comp. L. Q. 996, 1001 (1966).

[186] Often analysis conflates this question (i.e., the "public" nature of the applicant's persona) with whether the government is unable or unwilling to control the agent of persecution. The two questions are related. However, as the case law shows, the issue of State protection is essentially one of fact. It matters little in the analysis whether State institutions of protection are available if they are, in fact, ineffective to provide the needed protection. *See, e.g.*, Bobrik v. M.C.I. (F.C.T.D., no. IMM-5519-93), September 16, 1994.

[187] On the use of the term "public" as employed in this study, *see, e.g.*, Black's Law Dictionary 1193 (4th ed.1968) offering the following definition:

Common to all or many; general; open to common use.

## § V.4(b). Attributed Characteristics and Beliefs and the Expanding Concept of Social Group Protection

The idea that attribution or imputation applies not merely to the "political opinion" category but with equal force to all the refugee grounds is in accord with seminal refugee doctrine.[188] The *Basic Law Manual*[189] has correctly adopted this approach to the notion of attributed characteristics and beliefs:

> The holding in *Elias* directly concerned only "political opinion" persecution. It is reasonable to infer, however, that the reasoning of *Elias-Zacarias* applies as well to persecution "on account of" the other statutory grounds. The Ninth Circuit has expressly held, for example, that the reasoning of *Elias-Zacarias* applies to claims on account of religion. Thus, the applicant must present direct or circumstantial evidence that the perpetrator may seek to inflict the harm because of the applicant's race, religion, nationality, membership in a particular social group, or political opinion, *or because the perpetrator may erroneously impute one of these five characteristics to the applicant.*

Canadian doctrine reaches the same result through the case law. As noted in the *Ward* decision:[190]

> The examination of the circumstances should be approached from the perspective of the persecutor since it is the perspective which is determinative of the persecution. The political opinion that lies at the root of the persecution, therefore, need not necessarily be correctly attributed to the claimant. *Similar considerations would seem to apply to the other bases of persecution.*

The principle of attribution, in fact, makes it clear why reasonable extensions of the refugee definition by analogy are both doctrinally possible and desirable. In this respect, the implications of attribution must be interpreted as conferring upon the grounds of international protection an exceptional degree of elasticity. Guy Goodwin-Gill has argued persuasively, for instance, that the *travaux preparatoires* to the Convention reveal a concern on the part of the framers to protect groups against serious harm flowing from the social perceptions of those holding political power. Specifically, former landlords and "capitalists" would be viewed in a hostile light by the

---

[188] This outlook constitutes received doctrine as developed in the writings of principal treatise writers. For instance, Atle Grahl-Madsen has written:

> As I see it, it is the behavior of the persecutor which determines which persons shall be considered refugees in the legal sense.

[189] Basic Law Manual, *supra* § I.1, note 26, at 35-36, n. 9. [Emphasis supplied; citations omitted].

[190] Canada (Attorney General) v. Ward, [1993] 2 S.C.R. 689, 747. [Emphasis supplied].

emerging communist regimes of eastern Europe. The *Ward* case emphasized the past associations aspect of the Convention's negotiating history in its social group formulation, yet failed to acknowledge that it was not previous affiliations which were of most concern to the Convention's drafters, but the perceived "present threat" which past activity or status posed to the new governments.[191]

Similarly, Maryellen Fullerton has described the dramatic reach of the imputation doctrine in commenting upon a previously issued Position Paper by the Canadian Refugee Board relating to the "particular social group" category.[192] Fullerton concludes that decision-makers should not "limit themselves to internal group characteristics," but should "examine external perceptions". In the latter case, persecution can be imposed either based on the erroneous belief that the group actually exists (i.e., that it possesses putatively immutable characteristics or is informed with a common belief going to the identity or conscience of its members) or to the mistaken view that the group poses a present threat or danger.[193]

In all events, the critical definition embraces situations where the group is believed to exist or where it is believed to pose a threat of any kind, not necessarily a political one. A group believed to exist (which does not) will satisfy the refugee definition if the individuals comprising it are persecuted on this basis. On the other hand, a validly constituted group may be persecuted for values with which it has become mistakenly associated. Again these values need not be political ones but may arise in any context that the persecutor perceives as threatening.[194] In this sense, it matters little if an asylum seeker is technically not a member of a particular ethnic group if the government of the day perceives the asylum seeker to be so included and is prepared to persecute him or her on that basis.

---

191 Goodwin-Gill, *supra* § I.1, note 11, at 360-61.

192 Fullerton, *supra* § I.5, note 60, at 541, *citing* Preferred Position Paper, *Membership in a Particular Social Group as a Basis for a Well-Founded Fear of Persecution*, Immigration and Refugee Board, Ottawa, Canada, Mar. 1992.

193 *Id.*

194 *Id.* The passages analyzed by Professor Fullerton from the Preferred Position Paper do not take into account the (subsequent) decision of the Canadian Supreme Court in *Attorney General* v. *Ward,* [1993] 2 S.C.R. 689. As noted earlier, the *Ward* decision deals exclusively with the "internal" characteristics of "social group" persecution, and does not purport to define what the parameters of social group persecution based on "external" perceptions might be. That *Ward* did not rule out attributed social group persecution is strongly supported by the Court's *obiter dictum* that attribution applies to all five "reasons" for persecution listed in the refugee definition. *Id.* at 747.

The significance of the attribution approach to the particular social group ground is self-evident. The question where group membership has been attributed to the asylum seeker by the persecutor is not whether the applicant possesses an immutable characteristic or is exercising a human right which attaches him or her to the group (the "internal characteristics" analysis).[195] Rather, the inquiry should be whether the persecutor has violated (or threatens to violate) a fundamental human right of the applicant based on the perception that he or she is the member of a hostile human aggregate.

Under attribution principles, the protected grounds are reflections of a perceived difference in principle between the persecutor's views or status and those of the victim which the persecutor will not tolerate.[196] Where acts of non-State agents are involved, such differences in principle should satisfy the refugee definition, provided that the perception of the persecutor is linked in a not incidental way with the "public" life of the community, its political sphere, social norms, its culture, or way of life.

Modern jurisprudence has been remarkably reluctant to accept the broader implications of the foregoing doctrine.[197] Contemporary comment-

---

[195] The approach of using attributed characteristics and beliefs to interpret the "social group" ground has been substantially criticized as looking to "common victimization" as a unifying factor of group identity. Anker 99, *supra* § I.2, note 32, at 378. The argument that "common victimization" could unite a group for refugee purposes was rejected in *Ward*. Canada (Attorney General) v. Ward, [1993] 2 S.C.R. 689, 729. Yet while "common victimization" cannot constitute a *reason motivating persecution*, it can serve as *significant evidence* that the serious harm the claimant fears flows from an implicit policy of discrimination which affects the claimant and others in like circumstances. *Cf.* Goodwin-Gill, *supra* § I.1, note 11, at 362.

[196] Hernandez-Ortiz v. INS, 777 F.2d 509, 516 (1985).

[197] The most noted opinion, internationally, regarding "external" perceptions as the basis for social group persecution remains a decision of the *Verwaltungsgericht Weisbaden* (Administrative Court in Weisbaden) in its judgement of April 26, 1983, No. IV/1 E 06244/81, which adopted the "objective observer" approach. The decision is summarized in Maryellen Fullerton, *Persecution Due to Membership in a Particular Social Group: Jurisprudence in the Federal Republic of Germany*, 4 Geo. Imm. L.J. 381, 408 (1990). On the other hand, the concept of attributed membership in a particular social group has been generally rejected in New Zealand jurisprudence. *See, e.g.*, Roger P. G. Haines, *Gender-Based Persecution: New Zealand Jurisprudence*, Int'l J. Refugee L. 128, 153 (Special Issue: Autumn 1997), *discussing* Refugee Appeal No. 1312/93 Re GJ (30 Aug. 1995):

> It was our conclusion that the difficulty with the 'objective observer approach' is that it enlarges the social group category to an almost meaningless degree. That is, by making societal attitudes determinative of the existence of the social group, virtually any group of persons in a society perceived as a group could be said to be a particular social group. We were of the view that the Refugee Convention was not intended to afford protection to every such persecuted group and we once again relied on the *Ward* decision.

ators on U.S. asylum law, for instance, note the proclivity of the case law to allow "external" perceptions to form the basis for social group persecution, but only in conjunction with "immutable" characteristics.[198] The relevance for gender-based claims of such an approach is self-evident and cannot be underestimated.[199] But the courts have been extraordinarily reluctant to extend the concept of attribution to broader social aggregates ("internally diverse demographic groups"). It is important to add that the application of attribution principles to refugee claims is highly dependent on evidentiary criteria (showing that the claimant is indeed within a broader human aggregate which has been targeted) and the failure of decided cases may well be explicable on evidentiary grounds.[200] Still Deborah Anker maintains that such denials are consistent with the *Acosta* criteria as these set forth the parameters of the fourth Convention ground.[201]

It is of moment to note that Canadian jurisprudence has been less reticent in finding that diverse demographic groups fall within the social group ground. For instance, the "poor" have been found to constitute a social group largely on the basis that Haiti's economically destitute were perceived collectively in a hostile light and were so mistreated by their social oppressors.[202] In an analogous vein, former municipal employees who were terrorized because of what they knew about a former corrupt mayor[203] and the children of Egyptian police officers who were perceived as being anti-terrorist by virtue of their fathers' positions[204] have similarly been recognized

---

The reliance on *Ward* seems extravagant in light of the fact that, while *Ward* stresses internal characteristics or beliefs, it leaves the door open to attributed membership in such groups. Moreover, as noted throughout this study, the needed discipline in identifying social group membership is supplied by evidentiary criteria showing systematic human rights violations of individuals who are linked to the claimant on an objective basis.

198 Anker 99, *supra* § I.2, note 32, at 380.

199 Gomez v. INS, 947 F.2d 660, 664 (2d Cir. 1991):

> A particular social group is comprised of some individuals who possess some fundamental characteristic in common which serves to distinguish them in the eyes of a persecutor—or in the eyes of the outside world generally.

200 Anker 99, *supra* § I.2, note 32, at 383-84, *citing* Sanchez-Trujillo v. INS, 801 F.2d 1571 (9th Cir. 1986); Del Valle v. INS, 901 F.2d 787 (9th Cir. 1990); Uktor v. INS, 930 F. Supp. 881 (2d Cir. 1996).

201 *Id.* at 384.

202 Sinora v. M.E.I. (1993), 66 F.T.R. 66 (F.C.T.R.). The degree to which the rationale of this case is preempted by *Ward*'s language regarding "collective victimization" remains unclear.

203 Reynoso v. M.C.I. (F.C.T.D., no. IMM-2110-94), January 29, 1996.

204 Badran v. M.C.I. (F.C.T.D., no. IMM-2472-95), March 29, 1996.

under the fourth Convention ground. The latter two decisions rest on attribution principles merging into "immutability"; in the first case the knowledge of former employees regarding corrupt practices was something they could not change and, in the second, perceptions flowing from a relationship were similarly unalterable. The opinions reflect a decidedly liberal direction in determining the scope of "immutable" characteristics.

And indeed, the potential scope of fixed or immutable characteristics is broad. Social origins, after all, are aspects of one's existence which one cannot change. Economic status is often beyond one's power to alter.[205] Hathaway recognizes this aspect of social life while recommending that the "poor" be classed as a social group, while the "rich" (landlords, capitalists, etc.) should not be because they had the power to change their social condition (by disencumbering themselves of the cause of persecution) and international human rights law does not recognize a right to acquire assets.[206] Guy Goodwin-Gill has suggested that the state of being unprotected may itself be enough to qualify under the third prong of *Ward*.[207] But these insights may overlook the fact that unless there is a connection between the protected ground established and future serious harm, the claim will fail. That "nexus" or "linkage" can only be supplied by examination of how the persecutor views the claimant and her status. Again, we are back to the foundation of all refugee law: it is the viewpoint of the persecutor that matters.

Yet the reluctance of the case law and of the commentators to take a more assertive stance on social group persecution can only be explained by anxieties concerning an overbroad (and therefore meaningless) interpretation of the fourth Convention ground. Such misgivings surely are not well-founded. As noted earlier, similar anxieties attended development of imputed political opinion ground in the U.S. when that notion first gained acceptance in U.S. asylum law. The civil war cases have developed the doctrine of attributed political opinion to track patterns of human rights violations against discernable groups, the backdrop of political incentives informing

---

205 *Cf.* Goodwin-Gill, *supra* § I.1, note 11, at 361:

> In fact this approach is not as restrictive as might appear; this list is illustrative and in principle other innate or unchangeable factors relevant to non-discrimination in the enjoyment of fundamental rights may also be included, such as ethnic or cultural factors, education, family background, property, birth or other status, national or social origin; in short the very sort of *social* factors that are or ought to be irrelevant to the enjoyment of fundamental human rights. [Emphasis in original].

206 Hathaway, *supra* § I.1, note 7, at 166-67.

207 Goodwin-Gill, *supra* § I.1, note 11, at 365.

the motivations of the belligerents in threatening serious harm. Attribution principles applied to the social group ground clarify that configurations of abuse aimed at particular classes need not have such a conventional "political" backdrop to link serious harm to a protected ground.

The "public" dimension of the Convention refugee definition need not flow from a contest over public political power between the State and insurgent elements; patterns of persecution taking place in a *social context* can similarly satisfy the needed public dimension. This result is broadly consistent with the growing importance of social rights as contained in both UDHR and ICESCR; by the "horizontal" enforcement of human rights as a matter of public policy; and by the need to offer protection where essentially private groups are acting in an environment of impunity. As noted earlier, attributed characteristics or beliefs are created by an implicit difference in principle between persecutor and victim which the persecutor will not tolerate. Where that difference is tied to an objective political or social standard (or what this study has defined as the "public" life of the community) the threshold criteria for refugee status will have been met. Systematic violations of human rights at the political or social level are compelling evidence that the public life of the community is involved.

### § V.4(c). Intrinsic Characteristics or Beliefs and the Protections of International Human Rights Law

The Convention must be interpreted in light of its historical and ideological underpinnings, namely, the principle of UDHR that human beings should enjoy, on a universal basis, human rights without discrimination. There is every reason to adopt a construction allowing the equal protection component of international law to define the generic kinds of discrimination which would be considered social group persecution. The Human Rights Committee has made clear its own understanding that ICCPR Article 2-1 is entirely open-ended. Accordingly, any "distinction, exclusion, restriction or preference" which is based on any ground such as "race, colour, sex, language, religion, political or other opinion, national or social origin, property, birth or other status" should be considered as discrimination if it has the "purpose or effect" of nullifying or impairing the recognition or exercise of rights and freedoms by all persons on an equal footing.[208]

---

[208] *See, e.g.*, General Comment 18(37), UN Doc. A/45/40, at 174, ¶¶ 7, 8, 45 UN GAOR, Supp. (No. 40)(1990), *quoted in* McGoldrick, *supra* § I.3, note 45, at 276.

The growth of international human rights jurisprudence is influencing the scope of "social group" coverage for purposes of the refugee definition. In *Matter of Kasinga*,[209] for instance, the Board supported a finding of social group persecution based on the Tchamba-Kunsuntu's practice of FGM, even though there was no indication that imposition of FGM was based on any difference in principle between persecutor and victim. Asylum was granted, on the contrary, on the theory that the persecutor had intended to "overcome" a characteristic or belief in the claimant, namely her right to "unmutilated" womanhood.

This analysis, however desirable the result it yields, does not appropriately take account of the conceptual elements actually at play. It is clear that the nexus requirement in U.S. asylum law is really assuming a flexible dimension and that "persecutory intent" will not be required where the human rights of a vulnerable group are protected under international law or policy and the harm or suffering threatened in an individual case relates to specifically protected rights. In such instances, it is enough that the serious harm which the claimant fears *has the effect* of negatively impacting a protected characteristic or belief.

This analysis is hardly novel, and has obvious antecedents in the case law interpreting the political opinion ground. Individuals who are prosecuted for seeking to overturn totalitarian regimes are asylum eligible even though there is no intention on the part of their States to target them specifically for their views. Draft resisters conscientiously opposed to becoming involved in grave humanitarian law violations are also recognized as refugees even though the State is simply interested in enforcing in regard to them a law of general application. These individuals are asserting human rights to which international law and policy have assigned relative primacy; their activity, in terms of the refugee definition, is privileged. The persecutor's intent in each case remains simply to prosecute criminal law violations and not, in the immediate term, to treat the claimant adversely because of one of the enumerated grounds.

Notwithstanding the absence of specific intent in such instances, the model of discrimination does not lose its relevance. In such cases, by prosecuting the claimant, the persecutor is taking action which has discriminatory effect with respect to the exercise of a human right which is privileged under international or municipal law. *As indicated previously, the agent of persecution must act with discriminatory motive with respect to a defined group or must act in disregard of the rights of a specifically protected class so that the underlying action is discriminatory in effect.*

---

[209] 21 I&N Dec. 357 (BIA 1996).

Expanding upon earlier rationales, the decision of the CRDD in *B.(P.V.) (Re)*[210] is certainly suggestive of an emerging method of examining refugee claims having a far-reaching potential. In *B.(P.V.) (Re)*, a Somali mother argued that her divorce would result in (i) her being separated from her children in Somalia; (ii) her daughter's being subjected to Female Genital Mutilation (FGM); and (iii) her son's being permanently separated from her without his consent or participation in the decision. The CRDD's adjudication recognized refugee status in the mother and her two children based on the fourth Convention ground. In each case, the claimant was found to be the member of a "social group" by virtue of a protective human rights treaty governing his or her rights (CEDAW in the case of the mother and daughter; the Convention on the Rights of the Child in the case of her son). Persecution was then identified based on potential violations of the relevant treaty as well as possible violations under general international human rights law. The rights determined to play a role in this analysis were the following:

> (i) the mother's rights under Articles 7 and 16 of UDHR as well as under 15 and 16 of CEDAW (equal protection and family rights);
>
> (ii) the minor daughter's rights against FGM under Article 3 of UDHR (security of the person) and under Articles 19, 24 and 37 of the Convention on the Rights of the Child (relating, among other things, to the child's health).
>
> (iii) the minor son's rights under Articles 3, 9 and 12 of the Convention on the Rights of the Child (relating to the best interests of the child being respected).

The methodology used by the CRDD is of interest in that, like *Matter of Kasinga*,[211] the decision completely relinquishes any effort to conceive of "persecution" as arising out of an intention on the part of the persecutor to inflict serious harm, with that serious harm being linked to a characteristic or belief in the claimant. Rather, the injury constituting persecution in *B.(P.V.) (Re)* flows from the claimants' identification with groups whose rights are defined under international law. The CRDD's conclusion that the rights of specifically protected classes were being made the subject of "nullification" or "impairment" in the circumstances led it to hold that the individual claimants faced persecution by virtue of a protected ground.[212]

---

[210] CRDD T-93-12198, T93-12199, **T93-12197**, May 10, 1994.

[211] 21 I&N Dec. 357 (BIA 1996).

[212] For a highly original piece of scholarship having a direct bearing on the creation of "sub-groups", particularly as these affect gender-based claims, *see* David Neal, *Women as a Social Group: Sex-Based Persecution as Grounds for Asylum*, 20 Columbia Hum. Rts. L. Rev. 203 (1988).

*B.(P.V.) (Re)* illustrates the expanding relevance of a human rights model in adjudicating refugee claims. For the case clearly supports the growing recognition that, where international law stipulates a duty toward a defined group (that duty running both to State and to non-State actors),[213] failure to observe the duty will constitute persecution for purposes of the refugee definition. Such a methodology effectively brings the law of refugee status into broad conformity with the international law of discrimination and equal protection.

It may be of moment to note that the principle of refugee recognition outlined above may have significant implications with respect to granting relief to socially disadvantaged classes whose plight has become hopeless by virtue of the home State's economic order.[214] For affirmative action is not limited to gender and age, but may be extended to classes which have been socially oppressed. As noted by McGoldrick:

> In the Third Committee there had been no objection to the interpretation of draft Article 2 under which special measures for the advancement of any socially and educationally backwards sections of society should not be construed as 'distinction' within the meaning of Article 2. In the General Comment on 'non-discrimination' the HRC stated that 'Reports of States parties ... very often lack information which would reveal discrimination in fact.... The Committee wishes to know if there remain any problems of discrimination in fact which may be practiced either by the public authorities, by the community, or by private persons or bodies. The Committee wishes to be informed about legal provisions and administrative measures directed at diminishing or eliminating such discrimination. The Committee also wishes to point out that the principle of equality sometimes requires States parties to take affirmative action in order to diminish or eliminate conditions which cause or help to perpetuate discrimination prohibited by the Covenant. For example, in a State where the general conditions of a part of the population prevent or impair their enjoyment of human rights, the State should take specific action to correct those conditions...'.[215]

Modern human rights law applied by analogy supports the view that socially or economically marginalized classes may constitute "social groups" within the meaning of the Convention refugee definition. Failure to redress the condition of these human aggregates on the part of the State rises to the level of "persecution" where individual health, safety, or environmental interests are adversely affected in a dramatic way.

---

[213] The duty would clearly run to non-State actors in the present situation since Somalia (during the time in question) was virtually without a government. *See generally* Prunier, *supra* § IV.4(a), note 192, at 37.

[214] *See generally* McGoldrick, *supra* § I.3, note 45, at 275.

[215] *Id.*

## § V.5. Specific Situations Involving the Fourth Convention Ground

The following sections concern application of the fourth refugee ground in specific situations. Throughout, it must be remembered that the Convention refugee definition lends itself to thematic presentation (i.e., to an analysis which seeks to apply the definition to specific fact situations rather than looking at the definition in an abstract context). Such an approach emphasizes (i) the overlapping nature of the refugee grounds in specific areas of application; and (ii) the mutually dependent relationship existing between the concept of persecution on the one hand, and the scope of the protected grounds on the other.

### § V.5(a). Particular Social Group Persecution and Coercive Family-Planning Policies

United States law in the area of coercive family-planning has stressed political opinion as the appropriate refugee ground. Canadian refugee jurisprudence on the other hand has resorted to the social group basis. Yet, as will be seen, the principal underpinning of the social group analysis in the Canadian cases has been the human rights dimension of parenting, i.e., the second prong of *Ward* (associations the claimant should not be forced to relinquish because they are fundamental to claimant's identity or conscience). This aspect of the comparison of U.S. and Canadian approaches demonstrates forcefully the essential fluidity of the categories and the relative dominance of "persecution" within the refugee definition *vis-à-vis* the protected grounds. It also reveals that the most fruitful approach to refugee analysis is thematic, i.e., a discussion organized around particular problems rather than piecemeal discussion of the grounds.

Canadian tribunals have adopted, for the most part, an alternative approach to that of U.S. jurisprudence in the area of coercive family-planning. In this regard, Canadian adjudications have accentuated the effect of the law's application rather than the intent of those administering it.[216] Under this rationale, Canada's Court of Appeal has found that women in China who have had more than one child and are faced with sterilization constitute a particular social group so as to be eligible for refugee status.[217] Interestingly, the asylum seeker in *Cheung* (like the asylum applicant before

---

[216] *See, e.g.*, Interpretation of the Convention Refugee Definition in the Case Law, *supra* § II.3, note 63, § 9.3.7 and cases cited therein.

[217] Cheung v. MEI. (1993), 153 N.R. 145 (F. C.A.).

the Board of Immigration Appeals in *Chang*) alleged that forced sterilization would be the result if repatriation were effected.[218]

On the question of whether such claimants could constitute a particular social group, the appeals court found that women thus affected hold "a similar interest in common" which is:

> so fundamental to their human dignity that they should not be required to alter it on the basis that interference with a woman's reproductive liberty is a basic right "ranking high in our scale of values".[219]

On the engaging question of whether forced sterilization would constitute "persecution" in the circumstances, the court found that, even if the law were one of general application, such a characterization would not be conclusive on whether applicant would suffer serious harm under it.[220] The tribunal found that the forced sterilization of women who had had more than one child in China was not uniform, and was in fact contrary to the expressed policy of the Chinese government.[221] The court looked in this respect to Articles 3[222] and 5[223] of the Universal Declaration of Human Rights

---

218 *Id.* at 147. Claimant also alleged that her second child would:

> not be given food subsidies, would receive low grade education, and might not even be allowed to register for school. This evidence was confirmed in the documentary material.

*Id.*

219 *Id.* at 150, *citing* In re Eve, [1986] 2 S.C.R. 388.

220 *Id.*:

> Even if forced sterilization were accepted as a law of general application, that fact would not necessarily prevent a claim to Convention refugee status. Under certain circumstances, the operation of a law of general application can constitute persecution. In *Padilla* v. *M.E.I.*, [1991] 13 Imm. L.R.(2d) 1 (F.C.A.), the court held that even where there is a law of general application, that law may be applied in such a way as to be persecutory. In *Padilla*, the court ruled that the Board must consider extra-judicial penalties which might be imposed. Similarly, in our case, the applicant's fear is not simply that she may be exposed to the economic penalties authorized by China's one child policy. That may well be acceptable. Rather the applicant in this case, genuinely fears forced sterilization; her fear extends beyond the consequences of the law of general application to include extraordinary treatment in her case that does not normally flow from that law.

221 *Id.* at 150.

222 UDHR, *supra* § I.1, note 12, Art. 3:

> Everyone has the right to life, liberty and the security of the person.

223 *Id., Art.* 5:

> No one shall be subjected to torture or to cruel, inhuman or degrading treatment or punishment.

(guaranteeing the right to life, liberty and the security of the person, and the right not to be subjected to torture or other cruel, inhuman or degrading treatment, respectively) and concluded that the treatment which the asylum seeker feared (compulsory, non-therapeutic sterilization) was dramatically inconsistent with these fundamental human rights. Then, in a passage which since has become celebrated, the court observed:

> Furthermore, if the punishment under a law of general application is so Draconian as to be completely disproportionate to the objective of the law, it may be viewed as persecutory. This is so regardless of whether the intent of the punishment or treatment is persecution. Cloaking persecution with a veneer of legality does not render it any less persecutory. Brutality in the furtherance of a legitimate end is still brutality.[224]

The scope of this ruling has been called into question by a subsequent decision[225] in which the Federal Court of Appeal found that a man who had alleged prospective forced sterilization as the result of his violation of the one-family/one-child program did not establish a claim. The case raises important potential limitations both on the political opinion category and on the "particular social group" concept.[226]

With respect to the social group ground, the court initially set forth the definition codified in *Ward* and found (based on application of the first and second criteria of the case) that couples in China having more than one child did not have an immutable characteristic (having more than one child was a choice), nor could the couple be said to have associated for reasons fundamental to their identities or consciences (there was no active association in this case and, in all events, applicant was being punished for what he did, not what he was). The court's discussion of the limits which it believed had been imposed on the scope of "social group" by *Ward* is of moment:

> In reaching its decision to restrict the meaning of "particular social group" to these categories, the Supreme Court initially discussed and then rejected a broad definition of the phrase "comprising basically any alliance of indi-

---

[224] Cheung v. M.E.I. (1993), 153 N.R. 145 (F. C.A.).

[225] Chan v. M.E.I. (1993), 156 N.R. 279 (F. C.A.). The decision was later affirmed by the Supreme Court, but largely on the evidentiary ground that the claimant did not demonstrate that sterilization was a reasonable possibility. Chan v. M.E.I., [1995] 3 S.C.R. 593.

[226] A differentiating factor underlying the appeal tribunal's treatment of the refugee grounds in the *Chan* decision (not present in the *Cheung* case) was the intervening decision of the [Canadian] Supreme Court in *Canada (Attorney-General)* v. *Ward,* [1993] 2 S.C.R. 689. Under the *Ward* decision, as discussed in the majority opinion in *Chan* (written by Justice Heald), the appeals court was constrained to adopt a more restrictive view of both the political opinion category and the particular social group rubric than it had done previously. Chan v. M.E.I. (1993), 156 N.R. 279, 285-89 (F. C.A.).

> viduals with a common objective" or an interpretation which characterized a group "merely by virtue of their common victimization as the objects of persecution". The enumerated grounds were not "superfluous" and were "intended to function as another built-in limitation to the obligations of signatory states".[227]

For similar reasons, the criterion relating to past historical association which had become permanent was held inapplicable. The court then noted the Supreme Court's rejection of "common victimization" as constituting a unifying factor of the fourth refugee ground. Based largely on this consideration, a definition of the class was rejected which would have included "parents with more than one child who are faced with and oppose forced sterilization". The court was careful to note that having a fear of persecution, while a valid component of the statutory definition of refugee, could not be included in formulating (or otherwise qualifying) the refugee grounds.[228]

With respect to the political opinion category, the court noted the broad definition offered by Guy Goodwin-Gill ("any opinion on any matter in which the machinery of the state, government, and policy may be engaged").[229] Here, however, the court invoked a strict causative nexus test: The applicant was not being punished because he had voiced opposition to the family planning control policy (a political opinion within the meaning of the Convention grounds), but because he had breached that policy. This was not a case, in the court's view, of persecution on account of a protected ground, but rather of legitimate punishment because the applicant had violated a disinterested law of general application.

This aspect of the analysis borders on the limited view of the protected grounds which was announced by the [U.S.] Board of Immigration Appeals in *Matter of Chang*.[230] Wholly ignored were the (non-derogable) status of the right asserted by claimant and the issue of whether the punishment imposed was extreme. As stated by the court:

> There is no indication that the breach of the one child policy and the reluctance to undergo sterilization will be perceived by the central government or the local authorities as anything more than what it is—breach of a law and reluctance to undergo the ensuing penalty. An analogy to the Criminal Code is apt. Breach of Criminal Code provisions is not, in general, viewed as a political statement.[231]

---

227 *Id.* at 286.

228 *Id.* at 287.

229 *Id.* at 288, *citing* Guy S. Goodwin-Gill, The Refugee in International Law 31 (1st ed. 1983).

230 20 I&N Dec. 38, 44 (BIA 1989).

231 Chan v. M.E.I. (1993), 156 N.R. 279, 288 (F.C.A.).

At the heart of the case stands the central question of what is to be made of forced sterilization. Here, the court found that the evidence of coerced sterilization was equivocal,[232] and it implied that the fines applicant faced upon return were not sufficiently serious as to amount to persecution within the meaning of the Convention. The court concluded that, even if the refugee claimant had established a case of prospective sterilization, he would have failed to meet the Convention's standards: sterilization merely followed the breach of a disinterested policy.[233]

The concurring opinion of Justice Desjardins draws the "persecution" definition into sharper focus: The concurrence sets forth unequivocally that the Convention refugee definition does not embrace human rights violations by State authorities who proceed under a "legitimate" State objective, population control.[234] The concurrence similarly dismisses the "excessive punishment" principle by offering that, were disproportionate punishment the issue, those facing capital punishment (still employed by democratic governments) for a criminal offense would "automatically" qualify as refugees:

> The legitimacy of the Chinese Government's population control policy is not in question. Therefore, as a general proposition, it cannot be said that when a foreign government employs means that violate basic human rights, as known in Canada, so as to ensure respect for a valid social objective, such means amount to persecution under the Convention. If so, those who face capital punishment as a consequence of breach of a valid and legitimate piece of legislation would automatically become refugees under the Convention. This would be a startling proposition since capital punishment is still currently used by a number of democratic states.[235]

The arguments urged in the concurrence raise troubling concerns. The appeals court in *Chan* had before it two essential issues for decision: (i) whether forced sterilization as a punishment for exercising a fundamental human right is persecution *per se*; and (ii) whether sterilization is excessive in light of China's social goal of population control. Justice Desjardins' analysis (postulating that there are situations within democracies where capital punishment is a "legitimate" and acceptable punishment, e.g., for a

---

232 *Id.* Importantly, the court concluded that the claimant had failed to demonstrate, on the facts, that he would be subject to coerced sterilization.

233 *Id.* at 285.

234 *Id.* at 299:

> I conclude that, unless amended, the Convention Relating to the Status of Refugees would not cover violations of human rights imposed by local authorities in the pursuit of what the record shows is a legitimate state objective, namely, population control.

235 *Id.* at 297.

capital offense) essentially begs both these questions. Excessiveness must always be viewed in the context of international, comparative and domestic standards. And the issue of whether one's bodily integrity should be violated by a State as lawful punishment for exercising the fundamental human right to procreate is not addressed by a finding that there may be circumstances in which an individual's life may be taken as lawful punishment for a particularly serious common law offense.

The Canadian Supreme Court has declined to rule on the substantive legal questions involved, finding that sterilization was not a reasonable possibility.[236] A strong dissent issued by Justice La Forest,[237] however, (not questioned by the majority) has reasoned that the applicant's exercise of a recognized human right (procreative autonomy) places him within the particular social group category: such rights are fundamental to human dignity and so should not be required to be abandoned.[238] The dissenting opinion is now viewed as containing the germ of the law's future growth in this area.[239]

Justice La Forest begins his analysis by asserting that forced sterilization certainly constitutes "persecution" within the meaning of the case law. The putative "persecution" need not emanate from the State itself. In the present case, for instance, there was evidence in the record that forced sterilization was not an aspect of official Chinese policy, but was engaged in at the local level by those administering the program (without official sanction). Serious harm under the Convention can originate with those whom the government is unable or unwilling to control.[240]

As concerns the overriding question of whether the claimant's fear was of prosecution rather than of persecution, moreover, the dissent notes that an otherwise legitimate governmental goal (population control, for instance)

---

[236] Chan v. M.E.I., [1995] 3 S.C.R. 593.

[237] The fact that Justice La Forest dissented in especially significant. The critical basis for the Court of Appeal's decision in *Chan,* (1993), 156 N.R. 279 (F. C.A.), was its conclusion that the newly announced *Ward* criteria constrained it to offer a highly conservative interpretation of the protected grounds. Justice La Forest, however, was the author of the majority opinion in *Ward;* accordingly, his interpretation of the refugee definition as contained in the *Ward* opinion is of some weight. For an analysis of the La Forest dissent in context, *see* Interpretation of the Convention Refugee Definition in the Case Law, *supra* § II.3, note 63, § 9.3.7.

[238] Chan v. M.E.I., [1995] 3 S.C.R. 593, 600-659 (dissenting opinion of Justice La Forest).

[239] Interpretation of the Convention Refugee Definition in the Case Law, *supra* § II.3, note 63, § 9.3.7.

[240] Chan v. M.E.I., [1995] 3 S.C.R. 593, 630-631 (dissenting opinion of Justice La Forest).

may be enforced in a way which is illegitimate (e.g., by violating non-derogable rights relating to the security of the person):

> Whether the Chinese government decides to curb its population is an internal matter for that government to decide. Indeed, there are undoubtedly appropriate and acceptable means of achieving the objectives of its policy that are not in violation of basic human rights. However, when the means employed place broadly protected and well-understood rights under international law such as the security of the person in jeopardy, the boundary between acceptable means of achieving a legitimate policy and persecution will have been crossed.[241]

The dissent similarly takes issue with the assertion contained in the Desjardins concurrence in *Chan* (analyzed above) that violations of fundamental human rights (assessed under Canadian standards) cannot be said to be necessarily persecution. Rather, international law could be looked to (as could municipal law) in determining whether sterilization was "serious harm" within the meaning of the refugee standard:

> These basic rights are not to be considered from the subjective perspective of one country, as Desjardins, J.A., suggests. By very definition, such rights transcend subjective and parochial perspectives and extend beyond national boundaries. This does not mean, however, that recourse to municipal law may not well animate a consideration of whether the alleged feared conduct fundamentally violates basic human rights. Accordingly, this court's decision in *Eve, supra,* which concerned an application for non-therapeutic sterilization of a mentally incompetent adult by a parent, may be looked to for guidance.[242]

As concerns the Convention ground upon which the claim could be based, moreover, the La Forest dissent concludes that the conditions of the "particular social group" category had been met, using the second prong of the *Ward* test. Noting the Court of Appeals' reliance on the *Ward* definition of "particular social group" and that decision's putative differentiation between what the claimant *is* and what he or she *does,* the dissent remarks that the applicant herein was advancing a basic human right, the right to reproductive autonomy. Concluding that there is no requirement for the members of the group to be involved in active association with each other,[243] the dissent maintains that individuals implicitly united in their defense of a fundamental freedom (the right to determine the size of their own families) were held together by a common belief so fundamental to their dignity that they should not be obligated to forsake it. The author of *Ward* quite clearly spells out the

---

241 *Id.* at 631-632.

242 *Id.* at 635-636.

243 *Id.* at 644-645.

criteria which continue to characterize treatment of the "particular social group" category:

> The distinction between what one fundamentally *is* as opposed to what one merely *does* offers ... the most simplified way of discerning when Canada's obligations to refugees should be able to be invoked. Such an inquiry only comes after consideration of whether an issue exists concerning basic human rights has been undertaken. This simplified distinction was never intended to replace the *Ward* categories. It is still necessary under the second category to consider whether an association exists which is so fundamental to its members' human dignity that they should not be required to forsake it. To apply this simplified distinction without proper consideration of the context in which it arose can lead to ludicrous results. Accepting that appellant's own particular social group has yet to be yielded by my analysis up until this point of my reasons, I find it difficult to conceive that the associative qualities of having children may be considered so sufficiently analogous to the associative qualities of being a member of a taxi-driver cooperative as to warrant any meaningful comparison. Moreover, if the distinction was treated as a hurdle claimants are obliged to pass, behaviour fundamental to one's basic humanity, such as having children, could always be classified out of context as something one merely *does* rather than something one actually *is*. To pursue this example, however, surely it is nonsensical to find other than that one fundamentally is a parent. Parenting cannot be considered activity that one merely does, as interchangeable as a particular occupation, without distorting the primary focus of refugee law: the assurance that basic human rights are not fundamentally violated without international recourse.[244]

The dissent thus adopts international human rights in its analysis in two ways. The right to procreative autonomy provides the underlying value which unites the social group for purposes of determining whether a protected ground is present. In this respect, the Universal Declaration of Human Rights provides in Articles 16-1 and 16-3 that men and women have the unqualified right to marry and to found a family. The UDHR also stipulates that the family is the "fundamental group unit" of society and is, accordingly, entitled to State protection.[245] The Universal Declaration's provisions have received expression in the International Covenant on Civil and Political Rights which provides in Articles 23-1 and 23-2 that:

---

[244] *Id.* at 643-644.

[245] UDHR, *supra* § I.1, note 12, Arts. 16-1 and 16-3:

> 16-1. Men and women of full age, without any limitation due to race, nationality or religion, have the right to marry and to found a family. They are entitled to equal rights as to marriage, during marriage and at its dissolution.
>
> 16-3. The family is the natural and fundamental group unit of society and is entitled to protection by society and the State.

> 23-1. The family is the natural and fundamental group unit of society and is entitled to protection by society and the State.
>
> 23-2. The right of men and women of marriageable age to marry and to found a family shall be recognized.[246]

Similarly, the Universal Declaration provides for a general bar on inhuman treatment and torture.[247] Implementing this provision, the Covenant establishes in Article 7 that:

> 7. No one shall be subjected to torture and to cruel, inhuman or degrading treatment or punishment. In particular, no one shall be subjected without his free consent to medical or scientific experimentation.[248]

A question arises as to whether the right to marry and to found a family (absolute procreative autonomy) can be reasonably limited under international law. What, in other words, is the scope of a couple's legal right to have children? The Desjardins concurrence in *Chan* concludes that international law sets forth no conclusive guidance on this question, and that broad insistence on unlimited procreative rights comes at the expense of other (third generation) rights, e.g., the right to development. Some commentators have insisted that the latter right be given consideration in connection with the citizen's rights to found a family:

> Clearly, certain extralegal steps taken by the citizenry in reaction to the policy—such as female infanticide and coerced abortion and sterilization are abhorrent from the standpoint of human rights as expressed in the international instruments, and warrant stronger approbation than the PRC government has provided. The more difficult question lies in assessing the one-child policy as the PRC government intends it to work. An argument can be made that even when functioning as intended, the policy violates Article 16 of the Universal Declaration of Human Rights. After all, if mature adults are not free to have a family when they choose, is that not a violation of that portion of Article 16 providing that 'men and women of full age … have the right to … found a family'? But one may argue in response that a basic and broadly shared precept underlying human rights is that of the fundamental human 'dignity' spoken of in Article 1 of the Declaration and reflected throughout the whole body of international human rights documents. Given the best demographic and agricultural projections, there is currently little doubt that mass malnutrition and even starvation—and a concomitant loss of human dignity—would ensue early in the next century if all Chinese were free to bear children whenever they chose.

---

[246] ICCPR, *supra* § I.1, note 14, Arts. 23-1 and 23-2.

[247] *Id.*, Art. 5:

> No one shall be subjected to torture or to cruel, inhuman or degrading treatment or punishment.

[248] *Id.*, art 7.

> Confronted with what is arguably the PRC's most compelling challenge to human rights, the Universal Declaration and other major international human rights documents—which, after all, were drafted predominantly by western men having little direct interest or experience with the type of population pressures confronting nations such as China—provide faint, if any, guidance.[249]

The analysis proposed here does not attempt to resolve the question of the scope of family-based rights either under UDHR[250] or ICCPR.[251] It does, however, suggest that there is a relationship between procreative rights and the bar against invasions of bodily integrity (found in both UDHR[252] and ICCPR[253]) and that this relationship effectively sets limits to the power of the State to restrict family-based rights.

It is relevant, in this respect, that the Covenant indicates some rights to be derogable by national authorities in time of national emergency "which threatens the life of the nation".[254] Such derogation must be "strictly required by the exigencies of the situation" and not inconsistent with "other obligations under international law".[255] The rights pertaining to family formation are among those which may be derogated from; the rights pertaining to freedom from torture (including freedom from unwanted medical experimentation) are non-derogable.

The derogability of family-formation rights suggests (as indicated earlier) that moderate legislation may "affect" the exercise of procreative autonomy, at least where a case of compelling national necessity is made out. The

249 Chan v. M.E.I. (1993), 156 N.R. 279 (F.C.A.), at 295 and 309-310 (concurring opinion of Justice Dejardins, *quoting* W. P. Alford, *Making a Goddess of Democracy from Loose Sand: Thoughts on Human Rights in the People's Republic of China, in* Human Rights in Cross-Cultural Perspectives 65, 73-74 (Abdullahi Ahmed An-Naim ed. 1992).

250 UDHR, *supra* § I.1, note 12, Art. 16.

251 ICCPR, *supra* § I.1, note 14, Art. 23.

252 UDHR, *supra* § I.1, note 12, Art. 5.

253 ICCPR, *supra* § I.1, note 14, Art. 7.

254 The derogation principles set forth here are, it is submitted, applicable by analogy. Whether a qualifying emergency exists in the People's Republic of China, which *might* satisfy the requirements of Article 4 of the ICCPR is beyond the scope of this discussion. The essential point is that, given an appropriate national emergency which has been publicly proclaimed, the family formation rights contained in Article 23 of ICCPR are subject to derogation by States parties.

255 ICCPR, *supra* § I.1, note 14, Art. 4-1. It is of moment to note that derogations are becoming the focus of a growing regime of supervision. Accordingly, while there at present exists no established criteria for determining how emergencies are proclaimed, or the conditions upon which they may be determined to exist, derogations based on public emergencies must be reported to the Human Rights Committee. *See generally* McGoldrick, *supra* § I.3, note 45, at 302-05 (1994).

discretion to determine the number of one's offspring, in other words, does not appear to be absolutely protected so that *any* infringement or limitation would qualify an individual for refugee status if restraints of a proportionate nature were to follow a violation. Accordingly, those who protest proportional and necessary restrictions would not automatically conform to the requirements of the refugee definition.[256]

The sanctions imposed by the State to control those resisting family planning measures are thus arguably informed with a valid State interest to contain dangerous population levels and to "limit" family formation rights to that end; hence, implementing restrictions which are moderate in nature may not constitute persecution in all instances. In a similar way, conscientious objectors who are confronted with overbroad draft laws making no exception for opposition to military service on religious grounds may (pursuant to UNHCR interpretation) qualify under the refugee definition, *even assuming arguendo that conscientious objection is not a human right*. In such instances, measures to implement an otherwise legitimate policy must be reasonably directed to achieve the social end envisioned and must not be disproportionate. Circumscribing regulation must constitute, in other words, the least restrictive alternative.[257]

Such an analysis applies by analogy to the situation of PRC nationals who have undergone (or who face) either involuntary sterilization or involuntary abortion. For in these instances, it would be impossible to make out a

---

[256] Thus family-planning cases must be distinguished from the situation in which the asylum seeker declines military service in order not to become involved in genocide or other violation of the laws of war. Fundamental norms protected by the Geneva Conventions of August 12, 1949 (including Protocols I and II thereto), by the Genocide Convention, and by Articles 6(b) and 6(c) of the Nuremberg Charter are *jus cogens*. *See generally* Parker & Neylon, *supra* § I.1, note 16, at 430-431 and 432-435. Such rights are, by definition, non-derogable. An individual who shows conscientious attachment to these principles (for instance, by refusing to become involved in atrocities) and suffers or reasonably fears punishment as a result can claim absolute protection under the refugee definition; it is immaterial in such instances whether the punishment inflicted is "proportional" to the State ends envisioned. *See generally* Matter of A.-G.-, 19 I&N Dec. 502 (BIA 1987), *rev'd sub nom.* M.A. v. INS (I), 858 F.2d 210 (4th Cir. 1988), *vacated,* M.A. A26 851 062 v. INS (II), 899 F.2d 304 (1990); Barraza-Rivera v. INS, 913 F.2d 1443 (9th Cir. 1990).

A similar case can be made out for those who take up arms against totalitarian regimes which pursue policies of systematic and widespread violations of basic human rights. In the latter case, the absolute protection of the asylum seeker's position flows from the sovereign's complete abrogation of all basic human rights as well as the non-derogable right to self-determination which claimant is advancing. *Cf.* Matter of Izatula, 20 I&N Dec.149 (BIA 1990). On the peremptory norm character of self-determination, *see* Parker and Neylon, *supra* § I.1, note 16, at 440-441.

[257] *Brief Amicus Curiae of UNHCR in Canas-Segovia, supra* § II.3, note 93, at 407.

showing that a more restrained approach is not possible to limiting China's population growth. At a minimum, the right to establish a family, the fundamental right described above, must be brought into balance with the sovereign's right to achieve control of its social environment.

State and society have a recognized and legitimate interest in population growth. Enforcement efforts, however, which are inconsistent with measures "reasonably necessary in a democratic society,"[258] should be viewed as repugnant to the international human rights norm being asserted and therefore as persecution within the meaning of the refugee definition. In support of this analysis, it is clear under Article 4 of the International Covenant on Civil and Political Rights that legitimate derogations from any of the rights contained in the Covenant cannot at the same time constitute a violation of the State's obligations under international law. This condition flows from the language of Article 4 which delimits the power of the State to make derogations from certain rights (i.e., other than those contained in Articles 6,7,8 (paragraphs 1 and 2), 11, 16 and 18) with the following proviso:

> [S]uch measures [shall not be] inconsistent with their other obligations under international law and do not involve discrimination solely on the ground of race, color, sex, language, religion or social origin.[259]

It follows from the above that it cannot be a lawful derogation from the right to procreate for the State to enforce its policy by violating the non-derogable right contained in ICCPR Article 7 against degrading treatment and involuntary medical experimentation.

The means chosen by some officials in China to implement one-family/ one-child (forced abortion and/or coerced sterilization) quite clearly offend the non-derogable rights protected in Article 7 (the right against torture and unwanted medical experimentation).[260] The State cannot address an emergency by violating non-derogable rights under the Covenant without being found to have engaged in disproportionate conduct. Such excessive enforcement measures constitute at once a violation of the asylum seeker's Article 7 rights (degrading treatment and involuntary medical experimentation) as well as his or her family formation rights under Article 23 (since the proportionality rule has been breached). Under this set of circumstances, the State's actions must be viewed as persecution.

A final word on the international human rights analysis needs to be made. The question of whether an international right has been violated (in this case,

---

[258] *Id.*, *citing* Akar v. Attorney-General of Sierra Leone [1970] AC 853.

[259] ICCPR, *supra* § I.1, note 14, Art. 4-1.

[260] *Id.*, Art. 7.

the right against inhuman treatment and unwanted medical interference) provides a cogent basis for analysis with respect to the question of whether persecution has been threatened or imposed. The imposition of serious harm, however, is not necessarily dispositive with respect to the broader question of whether a protected ground is involved, although the violation is certainly relevant to this question.

As noted previously, violation of a human right in an exclusively criminal context does not give rise to a finding of serious harm based on a refugee ground.[261] Atle Grahl-Madsen has made explicit, however, the view that punishment which is related to the asylum seeker's exercise (or insistence upon) a fundamental human right constitutes political opinion persecution within the meaning of the refugee definition.[262] The attachment of the claimants in these cases to family formation rights (which are substantially protected under UDHR and thus under general international law) completes the criteria for refugee status in family-planning cases. Such insistence on the exercise of a fundamental human right illustrates that the harm or suffering presented by forced sterilization and late term abortions is clearly for a "reason" which is recognized by the law of refugee status. It seems largely irrelevant, moreover, whether protection is conferred using the political opinion ground, or adopting the social group basis under the second prong of *Ward*.

The foregoing analysis may appear to the reader as unremarkable. One further point, however, must be made. The dissenting opinion by Mr. Justice La Forest in *Chan*[263] seems implicitly to agree with the majority that "collective victimization" is not sufficient as a unifying factor for the particular social group ground. In this respect, the dissent does not pause to analyze the question of whether excessive mistreatment of individuals who are united by a common characteristic or shared belief may give rise to a claim to refugee status based on attribution principles, i.e., either under the attributed political opinion rubric or under imputed membership in a particular social group.[264]

This is a surprising feature of the opinion in light of its otherwise clearly "liberal" and "remedial" interpretation of the social group ground. The dissent, nonetheless, quotes with apparent approval a law review article which gives implicit approval to attribution principles in applying the social group concept:

---

261 *Cf.* Bastanipour v. INS, 980 F.2d 1129 (7th Cir. 1992).

262 1 Grahl-Madsen, *supra* § I.1, note 7, at 217.

263 Chan v. M.E.I., [1995] 3 S.C.R. 593-659 (dissenting opinion of Justice La Forest).

264 *Id.* at 249.

> In principle, an anti-discrimination approach should look at the imposed social consequences of possessing certain attributes. After all, it hardly matters to a racist whether a person of color sees himself or herself as united with other people of color in a stable association to achieve common purposes. *As long as perpetrators of persecution treat people with a shared attribute as comprising a group by virtue of that common characteristic, whether individuals so identified would choose to see themselves as united in any meaningful sense has little impact.*
>
> The point can also be illustrated using students as a social group. Assume that a Chinese student is persecuted by police in the wake of the Tianamen Square pro-democracy, anti-government demonstrations. The student may be entirely apolitical, have taken no part in the protest, and indeed have little or nothing to do with fellow students outside the classroom. The police may not even care whether the student shares views of those who participated in the demonstrations. The student cannot be said to 'voluntarily associate' with other members of the designated social group, but may be understood as being voluntarily associated with the status of student for reasons fundamental to human dignity.[265]

Having quoted the above language, however, Justice La Forest then draws the conclusion that it is "internal" characteristics which matter, i.e., the quality of students organized for purposes of their human dignity. The dissent does not abstract from the language in the Macklin article (italicized above) which clearly emphasizes the perception of the persecutor as much as it does the internal features of the claimant's persona.

Notwithstanding this feature of the *Chan* decision, it must be observed that both United States refugee law and that of Canada are moving in quite the opposite direction. "Collective victimization" involving excessive punishment to individuals comprising a definable group may be considered as a factor (i.e., is probative from an evidentiary viewpoint, although clearly not dispositive) in determining whether those individuals have suffered under an implicit policy of collective discrimination. Under the imputation theory, moreover, it is the outlook of the persecutor (the persecutor's inclination to treat a given class as a group, an outlook evidenced by the persecutor's activity leading to collective victimization) which serves to unite the group for purposes of refugee analysis. Showing that the members of the group have been similarly treated (victims of collective victimization) is certainly probative with respect to the question of whether the persecutor *perceives*

---

[265] *See generally id., quoting with approval* Audrey Macklin, *Canada (Attorney-General)* v. *Ward: A Review Essay*, 6 Int'l J. Refugee L. 362, 375 (1994). [Emphasis supplied].

the group's members to be united by a common characteristic and is prepared to impose persecution on that basis.[266]

## § V.5(b). Gender-Based Claims: The Social Dimension of Refugee Status

Of all the classes of cases which have virtually forced evolution of the fourth Convention ground, none has surpassed gender-related persecution claims. Perhaps a logical reason for this can be found in the fact that "women" *per se* easily satisfy the first criterion set down in the *Acosta* case (immutable characteristics)[267] for determining that a social group exists. More important, however, is the growth of international law norms which mandate protection for women as a group. These international law developments clarify that, in some instances, it may not be necessary to "contextualize" a claim (i.e., to analyze its elements to determine whether a "persecutory animus" is present). Rather, certain forms of harm with respect to women may be viewed as absolutely protected against by international law and policy with the result that they constitute persecution irrespective of the agent's intent.

As will be outlined in greater detail below, the Convention on the Elimination of All Forms of Discrimination against Women mandates programmatic realization of equal protection standards over time with respect to the status and treatment of women in public and in private life. The existence of such standards triggers on the part of the State an affirmative duty of protection which is not dependent on its good or its evil intentions. The law of State responsibility must be seen as providing an important element in refugee analysis so that whether "linkage" can be made out may well be determined by reference to a right/duty relationship between a specific class and affirmative obligations owed to that class by the State and its agents.

As noted previously in this study, the Convention refugee definition does not contain the "on account of" formulation largely pursued by States parties implementing the well-founded fear standard. Article 1A(2) rather uses a "for reasons of" formulation in determining whether serious harm can be linked to a Convention ground.[268] The Convention, therefore, implicitly allows for an examination which rests not so much on the intent of the persecutor to "punish" individuals because they have a particular character-

---

[266] *Cf.* Basic Law Manual, *supra* § I.1, note 26, at 35-36, n. 9; 8 CFR § 208.13(b)(2)(i)(B) providing that asylum seekers do not need to show that they will be "singled out" if they can demonstrate their inclusion in a wider aggregate of similarly situated persons which has been the target of a pattern or practice of persecution.

[267] Matter of Acosta, 19 I&N Dec. 211 (BIA 1985).

[268] Goodwin-Gill, *supra* § I.1, note 11, at 51.

istic or viewpoint, as it does on identifying forms of harm which have the effect of seriously prejudicing specific groups held together by common status or shared beliefs. Accordingly, where State responsibility runs to a specific class, failure to protect the class may well give rise to persecution based on the fourth Convention ground in instances where State inaction is a contributing cause of the serious harm feared or experienced.

Basic policy guidance in determining the scope of the "social group" category as it applies to gender-based claims can be gleaned from the U.S. and Canadian *Guidelines*.[269] In general terms, the *Guidelines* provide that the particular social group and political opinion protected grounds enjoy broad areas of commonality and may, in given instances, be coextensive.[270] The *U.S. Guidelines* incorporate the view of the Third Circuit that "sex" (i.e., gender standing alone) might in some circumstances qualify the claimant as the member of a social group, particularly when the claimant faces especially harsh treatment for having transgressed the social mores of the society in which she lives.[271] The comparative law commentary to *U.S. Guidelines*[272] gives several instances of the particular social group refugee ground. These include:

> (i) Women who do not conform to restrictive religious or social codes because of deeply held beliefs or because they are simply unable to comply.[273]
>
> (ii) Women who, through circumstances such as the death of a spouse, are subject to abuse because they live alone and without male protection.[274]
>
> (iii) Women who are seriously stigmatized because they have been raped or sexually abused.[275]

---

269 *Compare U.S. Guidelines, supra* § I.5, note 61 *and Canadian Gender Guidelines, supra* § IV.8, note 487.

270 *Cf.* Kelley, Anker and Beasley, *supra* § III.3, note 26, 71 Interpreter Releases 813, (July 27, 1994).

271 *U.S. Gender Guidelines, supra* § I.5, note 61, at 15. The *U.S. Guidelines* quote with approval Conclusion No. 39(k) of UNHCR to the effect that States might in the exercise of their sovereign discretion in interpreting the refugee definition conclude that:

> [W]omen asylum seekers who face harsh or inhuman treatment due to their having transgressed the social mores of the society in which they live may be considered as a "particular social group" within the meaning of Article 1A(2) of the 1951 United Nations Refugee Convention.

*Id., citing Conclusion on the International Protection of Refugees*, adopted by the Executive Committee of the UNHCR Programme, No. 39(k) (36th Session 1985).

272 Kelley, Anker and Beasley, *supra* § III.3, note 26.

273 *Id.* at 819.

274 *Id.*

275 *Id.* at 820.

> (iv) Women who have been, or may be, subjected to serious household domestic violence.[276]

The foregoing examples bring to the fore a common principle which is fundamental to all refugee analysis: it is the perception of the persecutor which determines whether an act is persecutory and whether it relates to a protected ground. The examples fortify the conclusion that these ultimate findings relative to refugee status are largely "social", i.e., they are based on a study of country conditions and the treatment by society of the group of women seeking protection. The nuanced nature of the fact-specific situations found in the comparative law commentary to the *U.S. Gender Guidelines* owe a clear debt to the *Canadian Gender Guidelines* which provide in material part as follows:

> **Membership in a particular social group:**
>
> In applying the "membership in a particular social group" category as a ground for gender-related fear of persecution, two considerations are necessary:
>
> (1) Most of the gender-specific claims involving fear of persecution for transgressing religious or social norms may be determined on *grounds of religion or political opinion*. Such women may be seen by the governing authorities or private citizens as having made a religious or political statement in transgressing those norms of their society, even though UNHCR Conclusion No. 39 above, contemplates the use of particular social group as an appropriate ground.
>
> (2) For a women to establish a well-founded fear of persecution by reason of membership in a gender-defined particular social group:
>
> * * *
>
> what is relevant is evidence that the particular social group suffers or fears to suffer severe discrimination, or harsh or inhuman treatment *that is distinguished from the situation of the general population, or from other women.*
>
> A sub-group of women can be identified by reference to the fact of their exposure or vulnerability for physical, cultural or other reasons, to violence, including domestic violence, in an environment that denies them protection. These women face violence amounting to persecution, because of their particular vulnerability as women in their societies and *because they are so unprotected.*[277]

The following subsections look at the foregoing context-specific situations as they have been developed as a basis for relief in U.S. and Canadian

---

276 *Id.*, at 821.

277 *Compare Canadian Gender Guidelines, supra* § IV.8, note 487, at 5. [Emphasis supplied].

refugee law. Generally, the following types of claims will be examined: (i) women who defy gender-specific norms of their society and fear State-sponsored sanctions as a result; (ii) women who are concerned that they will be made the subject of severe bodily disfigurement if they are repatriated; and (iii) women whose essential fear is of serious harm imposed in a family setting. It must be conceded at the outset that demarcation lines between the three types of cases are not always clear and that the subject matter of the claims will often overlap. All three types of cases do enjoy a common background in international human rights law which provides a necessary context within which the claims must be discussed.

### § V.5(b)(1). The International Law Context

Implementation of the United Nations Convention on the Elimination of all Forms of Discrimination against Women (CEDAW),[278] has been accompanied by rapid and far-reaching advances in the field of interpretive law-making in order to achieve the Convention's underlying remedial purposes. The Committee on the Elimination of Discrimination against Women (having oversight responsibility under CEDAW) has pressed for the application of the Convention's human rights regime beyond the level of combating discrimination flowing from State action. As a result, the body of individual protections contemplated by CEDAW is now widely viewed as governing not merely the "public", but also the "private" sphere. In broad outline, CEDAW adopts the "social" or affirmative approach to human rights enforcement which seeks to relieve endemic patterns of private discrimination.[279] Inherent in such a methodology is the residual notion that a

---

[278] CEDAW, *supra* § I.1, note 22.

[279] *See* Steiner and Alston, *supra* § I.1, note 13, at 888, for a discussion of the social context in which gender-based discrimination often arises:

> Legal norms capture and reinforce deep cultural and community practices. They entrench ideas and help give them the sense of being natural, part of the order of things.
>
> Social forces and analysts insist that change is possible, so that what was seen as natural, if not inevitable, comes to be understood as socially constructed and thus contingent, open to change.
>
> Property rights and economic dependence interact with patterns of authority within family and workplace, and with vital issues like education and health.
>
> Major economic and political programs, like a development or privatization scheme or structural adjustment requirements, impose particular and severe costs on women that are not apparent on the face of the programs.

policy which appears facially to be neutral will be adjudged to have discriminatory effect if it produces adverse consequences for a group recognized as being worthy of special protection in international law.[280]

Establishing a comprehensive body of norms which could relieve conditions of social injustice was thus clearly at the core of the concerns leading to adoption of CEDAW. These considerations, furthermore, still provide the principal policy guidance with respect to implementation of the Convention's provisions. Consistently with the above, CEDAW places upon States affirmative obligations to correct social discrimination against women in the fields of:

> (i) political representation;[281]
>
> (ii) education;[282]
>
> (iii) employment (including terms of payment and access to health care);[283]
>
> (iv) health care;[284]
>
> (v) economic and social life;[285]
>
> (vi) problems arising in rural life (including access to health care and social security programs);[286]
>
> (vii) equality before the law;[287]
>
> (viii) the family (including the right to marry freely, guardianship and ownership of property).[288]

Article 5 of CEDAW summarizes the thrust of the equal protection component of the Convention and restates CEDAW's primary policy of eliminating unequal treatment in the private sphere through an affirmative program of human rights enforcement.[289] Important among CEDAW's goals is the

---

> The statistics created by bureaucracies or scholars structure and confine our imaginations. We often view them as objective data, without awareness of what contentious concepts and information determine their formulation.

[280] Craven, *supra* § II.2, note 50, at 166.

[281] CEDAW, *supra* § I.1, note 22, arts 7 and 8.

[282] *Id.*, Art. 10.

[283] *Id.*, art 11.

[284] *Id.*, art 12.

[285] *Id.*, art 13.

[286] *Id.*, art 14(2).

[287] *Id.*, art 15.

[288] *Id.*, art 16.

[289] *Id.*, Arts. 5(a), 5(b). States Parties shall undertake the following measures:

elimination of cultural and other practices which are based on the subordination of one sex to the other.

CEDAW thus represents the "horizontal" enforcement[290] of human rights utilizing the mechanism of affirmative State action.[291] The possibilities for analysis are twofold. Persecution can emanate from third parties, i.e., from the claimant's husband and other family members who proceed to impose serious harm in an environment of impunity, whether made possible by State incapacity or by the State's being subordinated to dominant social elements. On the other hand, the State is under an affirmative obligation to respond to human rights violations by third parties under CEDAW; where the injury can be traced, directly or indirectly, to the State's failure to afford protection, a case of State persecution may be made out as well.

Equal protection as an affirmative normative standard[292] thus becomes an important human right. Indeed, equal protection has established itself as a primary guiding principle with respect to interpretation and implementation of human rights doctrine on an historical basis.[293] This flows not merely from

---

> (a) To modify the social and cultural patterns of conduct of men and women, with a view to achieving the elimination of prejudices and customary and all other practices which are based on the idea of the inferiority or the superiority of either of the sexes or of stereotyped roles for men and women;
>
> (b) To ensure that family education includes a proper understanding of maternity as a social function and the recognition of the common responsibility of men and women in the upbringing and development of their children, it being understood that the interest of the children is the primordial concern in all cases.

290 On the horizontal enforcement of human rights generally [*Drittwirkung der Grundrechte*], *see* Craven, *supra* § II.2, note 50, at 111-112.

291 *See, e.g.*, Steiner and Alston, *supra* § I.1, note 13, at 894:

> The status of women within the international human rights regime and the task of ensuring human rights for women are incomprehensible without taking into account the social and economic conditions that characterize women's lives around the world.
>
> * * *
>
> According to virtually every indicator of social well-being and status—political participation, legal capacity, access to economic resources and employment, wage differentials, levels of education and health care—women fare significantly and sometimes dramatically worse than men.

292 CEDAW seeks to implement one of the most fundamental objectives of modern international law and policy, namely, that of equal protection and the right to enjoy human rights without discrimination. *See, e.g.*, UDHR, *supra* § I.1, note 12, Art. 2.

293 On the critical role of equal protection to international human rights doctrine under the Covenants, *see* Craven, *supra* § II.2, note 50, at 153-191. *See also* McGoldrick, *supra* § I.3, note 45, at 269-300.

the fact that anti-discrimination law has served as a principal matrix for the development of human rights in general, but also from the fact that (as noted above) equal protection is itself the most effective vehicle for realizing the normative content of human rights protections within society's sub-structures.[294]

### § V.5(b)(2). Claims Based on Opposition or Perceived Opposition to Gender-Based Cultural, Social or Governmental Norms

The rationale supporting refugee relief for women without the social protection flowing from an accompanying family member was developed in one of Canada's leading cases, *Incirciyan* v. *Minister of Employment and Discrimination*.[295] In *Incirciyan*, an Armenian woman and her daughter were living in Turkey without the protection of a male relative. They sought protection from the Turkish authorities on several occasions and were denied. The Immigration Appeal Board concluded that there was a lack of adequate State protection and granted the refugee claims. The refugee ground was determined to be membership in a particular social group made up of:

> single women living in a Moslem country without the protection of a male relative (father, brother, husband, etc.).[296]

This seminal decision illustrates more than the use of "tailoring" the particular social group concept to fit the circumstances of the particular claimant. An immutable characteristic (gender) has been fused with specific narrowing criteria which are equally "immutable" in the sense that they are beyond the claimant's power to control (absence of a male companion), and which, in all events, offend equal protection standards (why should women be exposed to physical risk in such situations when men are not?). *Incirciyan*, was followed in a decision by the Convention Refugee Determination Division [CRDD][297] which concluded that a Somali woman had established a claim based on her membership in a particular social group consisting of "young women without male protection".

On the other hand, the CRDD has recognized that "women and girls who do not conform to Islamic fundamentalist norms" constitute a particular

---

[294] *See especially* Steiner and Alston, *supra* § I.1, note 13, at 888.

[295] Immigration Appeal Board Decision M87-1541X, slip op. (Aug. 10, 1987).

[296] The case is discussed in *Canadian Gender Guidelines, supra* § IV.8, note 487, at 13, n. 7.

[297] CRDD T89-06969 (December 4, 1994).

social group so as to be eligible for refugee status.[298] It now seems evident from the case law that conscientious opposition to repressive social or cultural norms constitutes the most potent predicate for a gender-based claim to international protection. The initial views of the CRDD have found doctrinal acceptance in the decisions of the Federal Court-Trial Division.

In *Namitabar* v. *M.E.I.*,[299] a woman claimant demonstrated that she would be subject to disproportionate punishment imposed without procedural guarantees for refusing to wear the *chador*. Accordingly, the claimant's breach of the dress code could properly be characterized as overt opposition to the repressive practices of a theocratic regime.[300] The Federal Court-Trial Division has also ruled in *Fathi-Rad* v. *S.S.C.*[301] that the social prescription relating to the donning of the *chador* could not be considered as a "law of general application" which would govern the conduct of all citizens alike.[302] Like the *Namitabar* court, the tribunal in *Fathi-Rad* found that strictly minor infractions of the Islamic dress code could lead to severe treatment which was out of proportion to the objectives of the norm.[303]

However, where the record is not clear regarding demonstrated opposition or excessive penalty, a grant of refugee status may not be appropriate. In *Hazarat* v. *S.S.C.*,[304] the Trial Division found that restrictions on women flowing from mujahidin laws and practices in Afghanistan constituted discrimination only, even though those norms reached "dress, movement outside the home, travel, education and work".[305] Implicit in the *Hazarat* decision, however, is that both the Refugee Division and the Federal Court-Trial Division were prepared at least to consider the possibility that the regime itself (restricting the rights outlined above) might be tantamount to persecution *per se*.

In the area of forced marriage, however, the judicial proclivity has been to find persecution based on a protected ground. In this field, the Federal Court-Trial Division has made it clear that the regime itself permitting such social arrangements will constitute persecution without more. In *Vidhani* v.

---

298 CRDD U91-04008 (December 24, 1991). The case is discussed in the *Canadian Gender Guidelines, supra* § IV.8, note 487, at 13, n. 7.

299 [1994] 2 F.C. 42 (T.D.), *rev'd on other grounds sub nom.* Canada (Secretary of State) v. Namitabar (F.C.A., no. A-709-93), October 28, 1996.

300 *Id.* at 49.

301 (F.C.T.D., no. IMM-2438-93), April 13, 1994.

302 *Id.* at 4.

303 *Id.* at 4-5.

304 (F.C.T.D., no. IMM-5496-93), November 25, 1994.

305 *Id.* at 2-4.

*M.C.I.*,[306] a Moslem woman from Kenya sought refugee status on the basis that her father had arranged a marriage which she opposed. The claimant feared the abuse which would follow if she declined to follow her father's wishes, alleging that the police would sexually assault her if she complained to them. The Trial Division based its reasoning on the legal premise that the right to marry freely was a basic human right which had been violated in this instance. Resulting persecution might flow from any one of four sources:

> (i) the fact that the claimant would be forced into the marriage without more;[307]
>
> (ii) potential mistreatment by the claimant's husband;[308]
>
> (iii) abuse by her father;[309] or
>
> (iv) serious mistreatment by the police.[310]

Included in this broad category of claims are those of women who stand exposed to future persecution because they have already been subject to abuse. In *Cen* v. *M.C.I.*,[311] the Federal Court-Trial Division found that women who had "been subject to exploitation resulting in the violation of the person and who, in consequence of the exploitation have been tried, convicted and sentenced to imprisonment" constituted a particular social group.[312] As in the case of forced marriage, a regime which punishes on this basis must be viewed as persecutory *per se*.

Recent decisions of the Federal Court-Trial Division have not been so clear with respect to this particular class of gender-based claims. As concerns one woman claimant who asserted that the means by which the gender-based Islamic dress codes were maintained constituted persecution as to those obligated to conform, the Trial Division ruled:

> There was not evidence that her activities and commitments or beliefs would challenge the policies and laws of Iran, if she were to return, in a manner that

306 [1995] 3 F.C. 60 (T.D.). For a discussion of the decision, *see* Interpretation of the Convention Refugee Definition in the Case Law, *supra* § II.3, note 63, § 9.3.8.1.

307 *Id.* at 2-5.

308 *Id.* at 2.

309 *Id.* at 5 and 6.

310 *Id.* at 6.

311 (F.C.T.D., no. IMM-1023-95), November 2, 1995, at 7.

312 *Id.* at 7.

> might result in retributive action by the state that would constitute persecution. Her expressed fear was thus found not to be objectively based.[313]

Along similar lines, the Federal Court Trial Division also determined in *Pour* v. *M.C.I.*[314] that not all women who "disagree" with Islamic gender-based dress codes will be recognized as refugees on that basis, noting that previous decisions concerned women who had engaged in prior acts of defiance towards the discriminatory regime. *Interpretation of the Convention Refugee Definition in the Case Law*[315] observes that the case appears to hold that the claimant must demonstrate some past act indicating a readiness to dissent from the codes to satisfy the criteria for refugee status. The circumscribing limit to this emerging doctrine, however, is that claimants will not be obligated to forsake basic human rights (e.g., those of a nine-year-old child to pursue an education) in order to avoid placing themselves in harm's way.[316]

The CRDD has also advanced the law here considerably. As discussed previously, CRDD has recognized as a refugee a divorced Somali woman able to demonstrate that she would, under Sharia law and custom, be deprived of her two children.[317] Such deprivation is violative of Articles 15 and 16 of CEDAW (requiring respectively that women receive equal protection before the law and that they not be discriminated against in social matters).[318] Moreover, the serious harm in the case clearly arose by virtue of the mother's natural and instinctive grief (psychological harm) flowing from the loss of her children whom she had striven to keep with her for about 10 years.

U.S. cases have not been generally as favorable as their Canadian counterparts in determining application of the refugee definition to women who defy gender-based religious codes. There remain two important circuit court decisions dealing with the "social group" category as it applies to women's asylum claims based on conscientious opposition (real or perceived) to

---

313 Ameri v. M.C.I. (F.C.T.D., no. IMM-3745-94), January 30, 1996, at 9, *quoted in* Interpretation of the Convention Refugee Definition in the Case Law, *supra* § II.3, note 63, § 9.3.8.1.

314 (F.C.T.D., no. IMM-3650-95), June 6, 1996, at 5-6.

315 Interpretation of the Convention Refugee Definition in the Case Law, *supra* § II.3, note 63, § 9.3.8.1.

316 Ali v. M.C.I. (F.C.T.D., no. IMM 3404-95), October 30, 1996, at 2.

317 CRDD T93-12198, T93-12199, **T93-12197**, May 10, 1994.

318 CEDAW, *supra* § I.1, note 22, arts 15 and 16.

gender-specific codes.[319] These decisions constitute a starting point (rather than a dispositive methodology); nonetheless, the reasoning of the tribunal in each instance contains implications which may enhance development of the law of refugee status in the area of gender-based claims.

In *Fatin* v. *I.N.S.*,[320] the asylum seeker was a native and citizen of Iran. She sought relief predicated both on future forced compliance with unconscionable social and religious norms and on consequences attaching to certain actions which she had taken before leaving Iran.[321] Applicant had left her country and entered the U.S. an a non-immigrant at the age of eighteen. At this time (1978) the Shah was in power, although he left Iran a short two weeks after the applicant's own departure. Specifically, claimant alleged that she had belonged to a student group which favored the Shah; that she had deliberately refused to don the veil "which was a sign or badge that I favor Khomeni".[322] If she were returned, she alleged, she would be required "to do things that [she] never had to do".[323] Applicant also alleged that she was a feminist and that her complete subordination as a second class citizen would contravene her right to enjoy human rights on an equal basis with men, a predicate for asylum in applicant's submission.[324]

With respect to applicant's claim that she feared persecution because of her membership in a particular social group, the court made the following observation in an exceptionally important ruling:

> In the excerpt from *Acosta* just quoted above, the Board specifically mentioned "sex" as an innate characteristic that could link the members of the "particular social group". Thus, to the extent that the petitioner in this case suggests that she would be persecuted in Iran simply because she is a woman, she has satisfied the first of the three elements.[325]

Of equal importance, however, the court concluded that the petitioner could not establish "persecution" under this broad a category, noting that the

---

[319] Fatin v. INS, 12 F.3d 1233 (3d Cir. 1993); Sefaie v. INS, 25 F.3d 636 (8th Cir. 1994). *See also* Fisher v. INS, 37 F.3d 1371 (9th Cir. 1994), *amended* , 61 F.3d 1366 (1994), *redecided en banc*, Fisher v. INS, 79 F.3d 976 (9th Cir. 1996). As noted earlier in this study [§ IV.8], the *Fisher* decision essentially explores political opinion as the protected ground in such cases, and it arrives at a highly questionable result (the serious harm feared flows from a legitimate act of prosecution) using a methodology which, for the most part, stands rejected in the cases discussed in this section.

[320] 12 F.3d 1233 (3d Cir. 1993).

[321] *Id.* at 1235.

[322] *Id.*

[323] *Id.* at 1236.

[324] *Id.*

[325] *Id.* at 1240.

applicant herself was suggesting that a narrower definition of the protected ground applied to her. Materially, the court noted:

> Thus, we interpret *Acosta* as recognizing that the concept of persecution does not encompass all treatment which our society regards as unfair, unjust, or even unlawful or unconstitutional. If persecution were defined that expansively, a significant percentage of the world's population would qualify for asylum in this country—and it seems most unlikely that Congress intended such a result.[326]

As noted throughout this study, the above reasoning inverts the proper analysis. The critical inquiry is not to examine how many would be affected, but rather whether the claimant has shown an objectively reasonable fear of serious harm based on one of the reasons contained in the refugee definition. If she has done that, then the serious harm complained of will constitute persecution irrespective of how many are affected. The court's *obiter*, however, does illustrate the important relationship between "serious harm" on the one hand, and the scope of the social group put forward as the basis for the claim on the other. If being subjected to a discriminatory norm alone is persecution, then the protected class is all women within the country of claimed persecution; if more is needed (severe punishment arising from a challenge to the gender-specific norms), then a sub-group will normally have to be found.

In this respect, although several variations of a possible particular social group were put forward in applicant's brief, the formulation upon which the decision was actually rendered defined the group as:

> a very visible and specific subgroup: Iranian women who refuse to conform to the government's gender-specific laws and social norms.[327]

The court found, however, that applicant would, albeit reluctantly, don the veil if she returned to Iran.[328] Her opposition to the regime in question was, therefore, not "of the depth and importance required" to establish persecution. The excessive penalties which accompanied non-compliance ("74 lashes, a year's imprisonment, and in many cases brutal rape and death") were held to be of no moment, since the only showing that applicant had made was that she would seek to avoid conforming to the regulation, but could not say unequivocally that she would not do so.[329]

---

[326] *Id.*

[327] *Id.* at 1241.

[328] *Id.*

[329] *Id.* The court noted significantly:

It is significant that the court appeared to accept that if the regime were not sustainable for applicant emotionally, conformity alone might entail persecution. ("Nor did she testify that wearing the *chador* or complying with any of the other restrictions was so deeply abhorrent to her that it would be tantamount to persecution.").[330] The tribunal's *obiter* in this connection is a firm reminder that persecution contains a subjective aspect and that the outlook and emotional composition of the asylum seeker must be born in mind in determining whether the putative persecutor's action is tantamount to serious harm. At the same time, in light of the tribunal's findings, it would give the *Fatin* case an impermissibly restrictive reading to conclude that repatriation to a gender-specific regime can only constitute persecution if the applicant testifies that she will defy the oppressive standards applied to her.

The decision appears to have been wrongly decided, but for another, unrelated reason. The court's insistence on a deeply-held conscientious opposition, one which was of sufficient emotional depth that subjecting the asylum seeker to the Khomeni regime would entail persecution *per se*, seems unnecessary in light of the facts. It was clear from the applicant's evidence that she had already refused to put on the *chador*, having participated with students who supported the Shah in opposition to those who advanced the cause of Khomeni.[331] As recorded by the appeals court, the witness testified:

> I personally belonged to a student group that favored the Shah. We refused to demonstrate with students who favored Khomeni. *I refused to wear a veil which was a sign that I favor Khomeni.*[332]

This element of the applicant's claim is not discussed in the court's opinion, and examination of it might well have led to a different result. If in fact applicant had been identified as someone who had opposed or who would oppose the austere Islamic regime with its clearly negative human rights implications, the degree of her attachment would be irrelevant. In such a situation, the asylum seeker would be perceived as someone inimical to the regime in question, and would be subject to disproportionate punishment as a result. Excessive or disproportionate penalties in response to the assertion

> This definition ["Iranian women who refuse to conform to the government's gender-specific laws and social customs"] does not include all Iranian women who hold feminist views. Nor does it include women who find the Iranian government's "gender-specific laws and repressive social norms" objectionable and offensive.

330 *Id.*

331 *Id.* at 1235.

332 *Id.* [Emphasis supplied].

of a colorable human right quite clearly constitutes persecution within the meaning of the refugee definition.[333]

Such a claim could have been advanced under the attributed political opinion category or on the premise that applicant was the member of a particular social group. The group could have been characterized as Iranian women who have been identified as being opposed to fundamentalist Islamic gender-specific laws and customs. It must be recalled that the definition of "particular social group" given in *Acosa*[334] (and accepted by the instant tribunal) included a third prong which permitted the relevant class to consist of those who are targeted because of past voluntary associations which have become permanent through the passage of time (one's past is a part of one's present).

More troubling, however, is the tribunal's conclusion that a woman wishing to lead an independent life (to adopt feminism openly) and who will be exposed to severe punishment for doing so (74 lashes, imprisonment, rape, or death, according to the tribunal's findings) does not qualify for refugee status. All of the factors of the discriminatory regime in relation to the applicant's claim must be taken into account at this juncture. In the first place, the law is not one of general application (as noted in several of the Canadian cases annotated *supra*), but is one which is tailored to imposing severe restrictions on a specific class in contravention to the equal protection component of modern human rights law. Secondly, punishment in this instance (corporal laceration for violating a dress code) is extreme by any standard. Finally, and most critically, however, the claimant is not asserting an incidental or marginal activity as the basis for her claim: Feminism, brought into conflict with the gender-specific norms of the Iranian State, must be perceived as a framework of beliefs which is fundamental to the claimant's identity or conscience.[335]

At the heart of applicant's case lies the exercise of her freedom of thought, conscience and religion,[336] as well as of opinion and expression.[337] The nature of these rights, moreover, must be examined in the light of Article 16 of CEDAW, which imposes on States affirmative obligations to eliminate discrimination between the sexes with respect to social matters, including the administration of family life.[338] The asylum seeker's claim thus

---

[333] Handbook, *supra* § I.1, note 30, ¶ 57.

[334] 19 I&N Dec. 211, 229 (BIA 1985).

[335] Matter of Acosta, 19 I&N Dec. 211, 233 (BIA 1985).

[336] ICCPR, *supra* § I.1, note 14, Art. 18.

[337] *Id.*, Art. 19.

[338] CEDAW, *supra* § I.1, note 22, art, 16.

becomes one in which the claimant is asserting a right to "equal protection and concern," as contemplated by CEDAW.[339] Against this must be weighed a State interest which is nugatory by any standard and, even if such an interest could be identified, a completely disproportionate method of enforcement.[340]

Finally, there is no justification for questioning the sincerity of the claimant's beliefs (in the guise of insisting that she defy at all times the coercive authority with which she was confronted). Applicant had already shown opposition to the Khomeni movement while in its incipient stages. And, in all events, there is no requirement that the claimant announce her deeply held beliefs to her persecutors and thereby incur punishment deliberately in order to qualify under the refugee definition. As Hathaway has maintained in connection with the political opinion ground, the test is whether the strength of the applicant's views will, at some juncture, bring her into conflict with the authorities:

> Since political expression is a core human right, the claimant must enjoy a reasonable expectation of tolerance of peacefully articulated views. It is therefore, inappropriate simply to discount the risk of harm on the ground that the claimant could avoid detection by keeping silent.[341]

Another leading case at the circuit level interpreting the refugee definition as applied to women opposing cultural, social or governmental norms is *Safaie* v. *INS*.[342] Like the claimant in *Fatin*, the asylum seeker in *Sefaie* was a native and citizen of Iran who had left Iran at the outset of the Khomeni "revolution", although her adverse contacts with the new Islamic regime had been more substantial.

Specifically, the claimant had been discharged from her job as secretary to a governmental official as the result of her having overtly opposed the government's dress regime. She later enrolled in the University of Teheran

---

339 *Id.*

340 *See also Brief Amicus Curiae of UNHCR in Canas-Segovia, supra* § II.3, note 93, at 407.

341 *Cf.* Hathaway, *supra* § I.1, note 7, at 150. *Id. See also* Handbook, *supra* § I.1, note 30, ¶ 82:

> As indicated above, persecution "for reasons of political opinion" implies that an applicant holds an opinion that either has been expressed or has come to the attention of the authorities. There may, however, also be situations in which the applicant has not given any expression to his opinions. Due to the strength of his convictions, however, it may be reasonable to assume that the applicant will, as a result, come into conflict with the authorities. Where this can reasonably be assumed, the applicant can be considered to have fear of persecution for reasons of political opinion.

342 25 F.3d 636 (8th Cir. 1994).

from which she was expelled three years later, again for not wearing conservative Islamic dress and other infractions of the Islamic State's gender-based code.[343] Safaie had been detained and interrogated several times in connection with associations deemed suspect by the Islamic authorities and she had experienced extreme mental anguish flowing from these encounters. Of particular moment was an interrogation in 1982 when the University of Tehran was temporarily closed resulting from demonstrations in which the applicant had participated. The questioning lasted for eight hours during which Safaie's interrogator had threatened to kill her. Applicant adduced some evidence that she suffered from post-traumatic stress disorder as the result of this and other experiences.[344]

Safaie sought to establish her claim based on her membership in a particular social group which she defined in the alternative as "sex" (a characterization which the *Safaie* court found to be overbroad[345]—just as the *Fatin* court had before it)—or as:

> Iranian women who advocate women's rights or who oppose Iranian customs relating to dress and behavior.[346]

The court accepted this definition with the qualification that the opposition be sufficiently pronounced so that the asylum seeker would "choose to suffer the severe consequences of non-compliance" rather than keep silent.[347] The court noted that the applicant had taken "affirmative steps" to articulate her position of opposition to the Islamic regime.[348] However, in the tribunal's view, applicant did not demonstrate the "missionary fever" which would be required to establish inclusion in the putative particular social group (as defined by the court), noting that the applicant had begun to adopt the Islamic dress code in 1982. Furthermore, with respect to any severe consequences flowing to applicant as the result of her past non-conformity with the regime, these were undermined by the asylum seeker's apparently

---

343 *Id.* at 638.

344 *Id.*

345 *Id.* at 640:

> We believe this category is overbroad, because no fact finder could reasonably conclude that all Iranian women had a well-founded fear of persecution based solely on their gender.

346 *Id.*

347 *Id. citing* Fatin v. INS, 12 F.3d 1233, 1241 (3d Cir. 1993).

348 *Id.*

lenient treatment at the hands of the authorities after her non-compliance became known.[349]

The links between applicant's overt manifestation of dissent in Iran and the subsequent reaction by the authorities is clearer in *Safaie* than it is in *Fatin*. The court does not follow, however, with sufficient rigor the possible implications of this linkage. For instance, the asylum seeker in *Safaie* had quite clearly experienced a loss of normally available educational benefits which both the *Basic Law Manual*[350] and the comparative law commentary on the *U. S. Guidelines*[351] describe as "persecution".[352] There was also some evidence that she had been terminated from her employment on account of her opposition, a form of persecution consisting of the deliberate imposition of economic disadvantage recognized in *Kovac* v. *INS*.[353]

Most important, however, was the strong evidence of severe emotional destabilization, a showing that the applicant had in fact been made the subject of dramatic emotional abuse[354] flowing from serious death threats made against her during interrogation. The court does not discuss this form of punishment as resulting from applicant's status either as a member of a putative social group (consisting of Iranian women opposed to Islamic gender-based regulations) or based upon applicant's imputed political opinion (her non-conformity with Islamic dress code and her repeated suspect associations which caused her to be seen as a threat to the regime). In light of the facts brought forth in the case, this seems a material omission.

---

349 *Id.*

350 Basic Law Manual, *supra* § I.1, note 26, at 25 (1994).

351 *See* Kelley, Anker and Beasley, *Guidelines on Women's Asylum Claims*, *supra* § III.3, note 26, 71 Interpreter Releases 813, 820 (July 27, 1994):

> [D]iscriminatory practices applied specifically to women that deprive them of fundamental human rights, or substantially affect their right to earn a livelihood or to obtain normally available educational benefits, constitute persecution within the meaning of the refugee definition.

352 On the right to an education generally, *see* UDHR, *supra* § I.1, note 12, Art. 26.

353 407 F.2d 102 (9th Cir. 1969).

354 Safaie v. INS, 25 F.3d 636, 639 (8th Cir. 1994). The Torture Convention, which may be applied by analogy, includes:

> any act by which severe pain or suffering, whether physical or mental, is intentionally imposed on a person ... based on discrimination of any kind.

Convention Against Torture and Other Cruel, Inhuman or Degrading Treatment, *adopted* Dec. 10, 1984, *entered into force* June 26, 1987, G.A. Res. 39/46, 39 UN GAOR, Supp. (No. 51), UN Doc. A/39/51, at 197 (1984), *reprinted in* 23 ILM 1027, Art. 1 (1984), *minor changes reprinted* in 24 ILM 535 (1985), 5 HRLJ 350 (1984) [hereinafter Torture Convention].

At a minimum, where there is some evidence of the asylum seeker's having overtly challenged the regime, a strict adherence to the very heightened "conscientious opposition" requirement, initially crafted in *Fatin*, is misplaced. In the situation involving a prior overt manifestation of dissent, the question is not whether the asylum seeker will be repatriated to a regime which would be unsustainable for her emotionally (i.e., is persecution *per se*). Rather, the relevant question is whether applicant has been (or will be) subjected to serious harm as the result of her opposition, irrespective of whether that opposition is of a religious or emotionally intense nature.[355]

In connection with this analysis, it must be born in mind that the regime opposed does not constitute a body of administrative rules which are of general application, but a corpus of norms which are gender-specific, which deny the availability of human rights on an equal footing between the sexes and which are, on their face, discriminatory. The requirement of conscientious opposition developed in *Fatin* (and mirrored in *Safaie*), insisting that the applicant virtually place herself in harm's way in order to demonstrate the sincerity of her beliefs, is not a feature of generally accepted principles of asylum law.[356]

What seems clear from the *Safaie* and *Fatin* decisions, however, is that the claimant's individual response to the repressive regime in question will be analyzed both with a view to determining whether conformity to the regime constitutes serious harm and as a criterion defining the "particular social group" (women who conscientiously oppose gender-based fundamentalist norms). This treatment of the refugee definition illustrates, with respect to such cases, the growing difficulty in interpreting the protected grounds as being completely distinct from the persecution component. Under the *Fatin* and *Safaie* rationales, the claimant's lack of "conscientious opposition" (as determined by the court) plays a dual role.

On the one hand, it constitutes a failure to show prospective "persecution" in that claimant would not, according to the court's findings, undergo extreme suffering upon complying with the codes. On the other hand, the applicant's "lack of zeal" causes her not to qualify under the putative social group category through which she seeks international protection (women conscientiously opposed to gender-oriented oppressive social standards). As developed earlier, such analysis ignores the consequences (past and prospective) of a violation of the Islamic codes (including excessive punishment), and the human rights underpinnings of the

---

355 *See, e.g., U.S. Guidelines, supra* § I.5, note 61, at 11 (discussing principles of attribution based on overt manifestations of opinion).

356 Hathaway, *supra* § I.1, note 7, at 150.

claimant's position. Restraints imposed as the result of asserting a plausible human right will result in persecution if the State's reaction is disproportionate.[357] Moreover, a degree of commitment which would make of the asylum seeker a martyr is simply not required.[358]

### § V.5(b)(3). Claims Based on Serious Bodily Mutilation or Other Physical Harm

In *Annan* v. *M.C.I.*,[359] a female Christian from Ghana sought refugee status, alleging the possibility of undergoing "excision" (female circumcision). The "excision", claimant alleged, would result from the instigation of a Moslem man who wanted to marry her. Claimant sought protection alleging religion as a refugee ground. The Federal Court-Trial Division reversed the Refugee Division's denial of the claim.

The facts spelled out a pattern or practice of unconscionable conduct by private parties implicitly directed against a possible sub-group of Moslem women in Ghana who have converted to Catholicism. Before applicant's marriage, her mother had been forcibly subjected to excision, pursuant to Muslim custom. When the family required that excision be performed on the first child, she bled to death. The parents then converted to Christianity (Roman Catholicism), and fled to the south of Ghana in order to avoid having excision performed on their second daughter, the applicant. When the father later became a prosperous merchant, he was threatened with death if he did not convert back to Islam and have excision performed on the applicant. The father's complaints to the police went unheeded. In January of 1994, the son of a Kintampo police inspector harassed applicant to get her to marry him. Her rejection of his proposal led to her being kidnapped by the inspector's son and to applicant's being gang-raped by the son and his friends. The inspector's son then summoned a religious leader to determine whether excision had been performed and was advised that the operation would be conducted the next day to "purify" the claimant. The Federal Court-Trial Division noted:

> Clearly, the applicant fears returning to Ghana as she feels she may be forced to undergo excision by Muslim fanatics, especially as she cannot expect protection from the police since it is the inspector's son who is still pursuing

[357] *Cf.* Matter of A.-G.-, 19 I&N Dec. 502 (BIA 1987).

[358] Handbook, *supra* § I.1, note 30, ¶ 82.

[359] [1995] 3 F.C. 25 (T.D.).

> her in order to get her to marry him and force her to comply with Muslim customs.[360]

The court's analysis relies deeply on its determination that State protection would not be available. Ruling that it was obligated to analyze both Ghana's ability and willingness to protect the claimant, the tribunal concluded that the Ghanaian government had not yet realized its professed aim of making female circumcision illegal. Importantly, the court did not specifically address the question of whether claimant would be punished on account of "religion" as such.[361]

On the question of the serious harm feared, however, the *Anan* tribunal was unequivocal: Female circumcision is a "cruel and frightful practice," "frightful torture," and "atrocious mutilation".[362] Although the Federal Court-Trial Division indicates that the harm (excision) would be visited upon claimant "as a Roman Catholic", the court's broad characterization of female circumcision as a barbaric practice suggests strongly that it may be persecution *per se* when imposed on a resisting female. Implicitly, a heightened degree of religiously motivated opposition to the practice flowing from claimant's Catholicism is unessential to establishing either inclusion within the putative group (women who may be affected by the practice and do not wish to be), or to show that the harm to which the claimant stands exposed is persecution within the meaning of the refugee standard. With respect to "excision", the court determined:

> There is no doubt that the applicant is experiencing a subjective fear of being persecuted by Muslim fanatics who wish to impose on her, as a Roman Catholic, the cruel and barbaric practice of excision. Excision is a summary removal of the clitoris with whatever tools available, without sanitary precautions for the purpose of preventing the Muslim woman from experiencing any sexual enjoyment.[363]

The position of the Convention Refugee Determination Division appears to be that FGM constitutes "persecution" *per se* when imposed on a minor, i.e., with or without her consent. In this respect, the CRDD has recognized as a refugee under the social group ground a female minor who faced FGM in

---

[360] *Id.* at 28.

[361] *Id.* at 28 and 30. The case is discussed in Interpretation of the Convention Refugee Definition in the Case Law, *supra* § II.3, note 63, § 9.3.8.1.

[362] [1995] 3 F.C. 25, 28 (T.D.).

[363] *Id.* at 28-29. The question of whether opposition to the practice of Female Genital Mutilation (or FGM) is required for an asylum seeker is somewhat obscured in United States law, as the discussion which follows will illustrate.

Somalia if returned.[364] Serious harm was found in the resulting violations of Articles 37, 19 and 24 of the Convention on the Rights of the Child.[365] These provisions:

> (i) protect children from acts of torture;[366]
>
> (ii) provide for the establishment of programs to prevent acts of mental and physical abuse toward children;[367] and
>
> (iii) provide for the highest attainable standards of health for children.[368]

United States asylum law has now addressed the question of female genital circumcision or mutilation in an elaborate and articulate *en banc* opinion by the Board of Immigration Appeals. In *Matter of Kasinga*,[369] the asylum applicant was a native and citizen of Togo and a member of the Tchamba-Kunsuntu tribe who sought to avoid FGM which was about to be imposed on her. The Board reversed the decision of an immigration judge that the applicant had not made out a claim.

The facts are of interest. When applicant was 16 years old, applicant's father (who opposed the practice of FGM) died suddenly. Applicant was subsequently raised by her paternal aunt who advised applicant, in the summer of 1994, that she was to marry one Ibrahim Isaka thus becoming his fourth wife. As a condition of the marriage, applicant was to undergo FGM.[370] Applicant did marry Ibrahim Isaka, despite her objections, but she refused to execute the marriage certificate. Applicant was advised that she was to undergo FGM four days after the wedding ceremony. Two days prior to the scheduled mutilation, applicant, with the aid of her sisters, escaped from Ghana on an airplane bound for Germany. She later traveled to the United States where she was confined.[371]

The Board found that applicant feared persecution by virtue of her membership in a particular social group, which the Board defined as:

> Young women of the Tchamba-Kunsuntu Tribe who had not had FGM, as practiced by their tribe, and who opposed the practice.[372]

---

364 CRDD T-93-12198, T93-12199, **T93-12197**, May 10, 1994. (The decision is discussed with interest in Who is a Refugee?, *supra* § IV.5(a), note 325, at 190-191).

365 Convention on the Rights of the Child, *supra* § I.1, note 21.

366 *Id.*, *Art.* 37.

367 *Id.*, *Art.* 19.

368 *Id.*, *Art.* 24.

369 21 I&N Dec. 357 (BIA 1996).

370 *Id.* at 358-359.

371 *Id* at 359.

372 *Id.* at 365.

The definition thus offered by the Board adopts a combination of the first and second prongs of the *Acosta* test for determining particular social group membership.[373] In this respect, Ms. Kasinga's gender and tribal affiliation were attributes which she could not change; remaining in an unmutilated state, on the other hand, was a characteristic fundamental to applicant's identity or conscience which she should not be required to change.[374] Hence, the claimant's opposition to the practice of FGM remains an important element in establishing a claim.[375]

The immigration judge viewed the case as belonging to the same genre as Chinese population control claims where a norm of general applicability was not directed toward "punishing" the asylum seeker on account of one of the protected grounds but was aimed at some ulterior social, cultural or governmental policy objective. The Board was quick to dismiss the "intent to persecute" criterion in the instant case, ruling:

> [M]any of our past cases involved actors who had a subjective intent to punish their victims. However, the subjective "punitive" or "malignant" intent is not required for the harm to constitute persecution.[376]

Material to its consideration of the case was the Board's characterization of FGM. FGM was, in the Board's perception, a form of "sexual oppression" which had been historically utilized to "control women sexually". The clear purpose of FGM was to manipulate "women's sexuality in order to assure male dominance and exploitation".[377] The Board's findings are of significance. For perhaps the first time, a U.S. adjudicator is looking not simply at country conditions to determine whether an act can be deemed as persecutory with respect to a specific group. Rather, the Board identifies a universal framework within which to contextualize the practice of FGM. There can be no question but that the Board's willingness to portray FGM as aimed categorically at the oppression of women must be accounted for by

---

[373] Matter of Acosta, 19 I&N Dec. 211, 233 (BIA 1985).

[374] Matter of Kasinga, 21 I&N Dec. 357, 365-366 (BIA 1996).

[375] As discussed *infra*, Board member Lory Rosenberg reasoned in a concurring opinion that the claimant's reluctance to undergo FGM is not essential to identifying her as the member of a social group. The Rosenberg concurrence takes the view that non-consent goes to the issue of persecution—not to whether the claimant falls under a protected ground. *See id.* at 373-378.

[376] *Id.* at 365, *citing* Matter of Kulle, 19 I&N Dec. 318 (BIA 1985). It is significant that this rationale has now been adopted in the Ninth Circuit in a case involving a Russian woman threatened with "electric shock", in response to her Lesbian sexual orientation. *See* Pitcherskaia v. INS, 118 F.3d 641 (9th Cir. 1997).

[377] 21 I&N Dec. 365, 366-367 (BIA 1996). [Citations omitted].

advances made in general international law and (as will be discussed below) by the recent activities and pronouncements of the Committee on the Elimination of All Forms of Discrimination Against Women.

On the question of State protection, the Board ruled simply that (i) FGM was widely practiced in Togo; (ii) acts of violence against women were also tolerated by the police; (iii) most African women can expect little protection against FGM; and (iv) the government of Togo has a poor human rights record.[378] No effort was made in other words to show that the government acquiesced in the serious harm, or that government inaction was a requirement to finding that serious harm had been imposed on a protected ground.[379]

The question of the relationship between the applicant's objection to the practice of FGM and the existence of "persecution" on the one hand, and membership in a qualifying group on the other, was addressed in several concurring opinions.[380] Board member Lory Rosenberg dealt directly with the problem (at least insofar as it relates to applicant's qualifying under a protected ground), making clear her view that opposition to FGM is not essential to establishing membership in a particular social group.[381] Beginning with analysis of the recognized "reasons" for persecution, Board member Rosenberg found that the social group category resembles other

---

378 *Id.* at 367.

379 *Kasinga* was followed by the Second Circuit Court of Appeals in *Abankwa* v. *INS,* 185 F.3d 18 (2d Cir. 1999). The case involved a Ghanaian asylum seeker who feared the imposition of FGM in retribution for an extramarital relationship she had had earlier and which she believed would be discovered upon her becoming a tribal queen. While adding very little, if anything, which is new to the eligibility analysis made earlier by the Board in *Kasinga*, *Abankwa* does clarify that credible testimony standing alone can support a persecution claim based on FGM, and that such claimants should not be subjected to excessive corroboration requirements.

380 For instance, Board members Filppu and Heilman in a joint concurrence considered a proposed test submitted by the Immigration and Naturalization Service for deciding such cases which would have entailed a clear incorporation of "resistance" into the persecution requirement. Matter of Kasinga, 21 I&N Dec. 357, 368-373 (BIA 1996) (concurring opinion of Board members Filppu and Heilman). Such a requirement was essential in the Service's view since many Togolese and other women could now advance claims of past persecution who had already willingly had the circumcision performed. *Id.* at 370-371. The concurrence notes simply that the question is not presented by this case (Ms. Kasinga clearly was unwilling to undergo FGM), and that resolution of such issues must await future adjudications with appropriate facts. *Id.* at 371-373.

381 Matter of Kasinga, 21 I&N Dec. 357, 373-378 (BIA 1996) (concurring opinion of Board member Rosenberg). Board member Rosenberg's concurrence rests largely on the scholarly work of a leading commentator in the field of women's asylum claims. *Id., citing with approval* Pamela Goldberg, *Anyplace But Home: Asylum in the United States for Women Fleeing Intimate Violence*, 26 Cornell Int'l L. J. 565, 591-592 (1993).

refugee grounds which are based on status (race, nationality) rather than on belief (political opinion and religion). Specifically, the concurrence maintains:

> [S]uch requests [i.e., predicated upon the asylum seeker's status] involve a determination of whether the shared characteristics are those which motivate an agent of persecution to overcome or otherwise harm the individual. Consequently, while not inaccurate, it is surplusage to define the social group in this case by including as an element the applicant's opposition to the practice of female genital mutilation. [T]he applicant's political or social views [are relevant only] to whether the harm or abuse she faces constitutes persecution.[382]

Board member Rosenberg goes on to develop her argument, based on the foregoing general guideline, and concludes that the persecutor in this case sought to overcome not an opinion of the applicant, but rather a fixed characteristic which was an aspect of the particular social group to which she belonged: Ms Kasinga's "state of being non-mutilated and accordingly free from male dominated tribal control".[383]

The concurrence may help to establish a preferred doctrinal position under which the victim's consent is not required to establish a claim based on FGM and so bring U.S. asylum law into broad conformity with the policy objectives of CEDAW. In this respect, it must be noted that FGM, even if consented to, may occasion grave adverse health consequences. The practice itself, moreover, has received unqualified condemnation under emerging international law. The Committee on the Elimination of Discrimination Against Women has promulgated General Recommendation No. 14 to all States parties urging the latter to adopt specific measures with a view to eliminating FGM.[384] Specifically, the Committee calls upon States parties to seek eradication of FGM, primarily through disseminating information regarding the practice's health hazards.[385]

---

[382] *Id.* at 375-376 (concurring opinion of Board member Rosenberg ).

[383] *Id.* at 374.

[384] Committee on the Elimination of All Forms of Discrimination Against Women, General Recommendation No. 14, 9th Sess., 1990, U.N. Doc. A/45/38, 1 Int'l Hum. Rts. Rep. 21 (No. 1 1994).

[385] While the "recommendations" of the Committee cannot be considered as being coterminous with either conventional or customary international law, they must be viewed as important statements of policy by a norm-setting body. The actions of the Committee should therefore, be indicative of the responsibilities of States parties to CEDAW. Such recommendations should also, insofar as they are acceded to, constitute some evidence of the emerging state of customary international law. *See, e.g.*, Theodore Meron, Human Rights and Humanitarian Norms as Customary Law 25-36 (1989).

Emerging international human rights law, therefore, strongly suggests that imposition of female circumcision constitutes violation of a fundamental human right, even where the victim may unwittingly have conferred her consent. It would be consistent with this emerging normative standard, therefore, to characterize as persecution all acts of radical female circumcision, at least where the negative health consequences of the mutilation are dramatic.

The future course of refugee law may well follow Board member Rosenberg's methodology of interpreting the particular social group category. A jurisprudence along these lines is strongly supported (if not compelled) by the concerns of international public policy now being developed by the Committee on the Elimination of All Forms of Discrimination against Women. Affording protection in these circumstances is also in accordance with the clear mandate of the Universal Declaration of Human Rights that protected rights be enjoyed on an equal basis and without discrimination, particularly where discriminatory treatment leads to unconscionable suffering which is repugnant to the international community using any yardstick.[386]

### § V.5(b)(4). Claims Based on Serious Harm Inflicted in a Family Setting

The third line of cases examined here, and perhaps the most complex, involves violations of the claimant's rights in a family setting, including domestic violence situations. As noted earlier, these decisions tend to raise the greatest doubts about entitlement to refugee protection in that the context in which such claims arise appears, at first blush, to involve a purely private setting. It must be noted that the violence imposed in such instances is nearly always by non-governmental actors. What causes situations of household domestic violence to amount to a claim under the refugee definition? Why is this not an instance of purely personal violence which stands, as all purely personal harm stands, outside the refugee standard? Domestic violence decisions clearly constitute the defining parameters of refugee status based on membership in a particular social group.

As noted earlier, the viewpoint of leading feminists, as represented in the works of Catherine MacKinnon,[387] criticizes the modern structure of law, society and politics which is perceived as gender-oriented. As a result, the mistreatment of women by men is often characterized as "private" harm,

---

[386] UDHR, *supra* § I.1, note 12, Art. 2. *See also* McGoldrick, *supra* § I.3, note 45, at 269-300.

[387] *See generally* MacKinnon, *supra* § V.3, note 139, at 953.

while the mistreatment of men in a political context is called "torture" (or "public" harm). MacKinnon's viewpoint is gaining acceptance in modern refugee law.

It would appear, however, that treating women as a "particular social group" in domestic violence situations illustrates the futility of a "public/private" divide in determining who is a refugee. The imposition of serious harm on women by men which is accomplished pursuant to a pattern or practice of widespread social discrimination and a total absence of equal protection essentially raises old, not new concerns. The infliction of serious harm in this context is no more "private" than any practice of social discrimination against a group with fixed characteristics (e.g., race) is "private". Decisions in the United States and Canada illustrate that domestic violence situations can definitely raise concerns which are properly the subject of refugee jurisprudence.[388]

It is commonly maintained that such mistreatment becomes persecutory when there is an absence of State protection.[389] Examination of the case law, however, reveals that more than an absence of State protection is really involved in most cases. Rather, the greater part of the decisional law discussed in the following sections reflects a common situational analysis. Individual women bring themselves into conflict with discriminatory social and cultural norms by seeking to lead independent lives. When they express views or take positions which are at variance with the values espoused by their societies, they are confronted with violence for which there exists no adequate form of legal redress.

In the foregoing cases, the absence of State protection thus provides *an evidentiary basis* upon which to conclude that the harm feared or experi-

---

[388] *See, e.g., U.S. Gender Guidelines, supra* § I.5, note 61, at 2. The 1993 Declaration on the Elimination of Violence Against Women recognizes that violence against women in any form is a *per se* violation of fundamental human rights and operates as an obstruction to the realization by women of other basic human rights. Declaration on the Elimination of Violence Against Women, *adopted* 20 December 1993, G.A. Res. 48/104, UN Doc. A/48/29, *reprinted in* 33 ILM 1049 (1994).

[389] With respect to women facing harsh punishment as the result of failure to conform to social and/or religious codes, the comparative law commentary to the *U.S. Guidelines* has the following important annotation:

> This category includes women who, as the result of circumstances over which they have no control, are not able to comply with the expectations of their culture, religion or society, as well as those who make conscious choices that they cannot conform to those requirements. The treatment to which these women are subjected becomes persecutory when the state fails to provide protection from the abuse.

enced constitutes socially tolerated violence toward a specific group.[390] Under this analysis, household domestic violence can be seen to flow from a condition of widespread social discrimination in which arbitrary violence is imposed on the claimant in an environment of comparative impunity. Such violence is part of a more generalized pattern involving the subordination of women to men in the exercise of fundamental human rights. It takes place in an environment characterized by a total absence of equal protection within State and society. Hence, the resulting injury is non-personal in nature and the type of harm contemplated by the refugee standard.

Important evidence of widespread discrimination leading to persecution can often be found in distinctions maintained between the sexes in civil, political and social matters within the home State. The comparative law commentary to the *U.S. Guidelines* provides as follows:

> In assessing the severity of discrimination, the adjudicator should consider the position of women in applicant's country before the law, including their standing in court, their right to file a complaint and give evidence, their right to divorce and have custody of their children, and their right to own property.[391]

Such cases should be distinguished from those in which the State is "complicitous" in the harm and so may be itself a persecutor. These situations comprise circumstances in which (a) the State has engaged in structural discrimination by systematically refusing to provide relief to a specific class; or (b) the claimant has made repeated efforts to secure State protection and these have been rebuffed.[392] In the latter instance, the State's failure to provide protection may entail a failure of State responsibility and an act of persecution. Doctrinal support exists for the proposition that the State may itself engage in persecution by declining to act affirmatively in given instances. For instance, a State violates the social rights set out in ICESCR if it fails to respond to life-threatening economic needs despite a

---

*See* Kelley, Anker and Beasley, *supra* § III.3, note 26, at 819.

390 The absence of State protection is, in other words, evidential and not normative. The absence of institutions of State protection cannot qualify in any way the nature of the "persecution" which the claimant has experienced or fears from private agents. Similarly, a lack of State protection does not condition the existence of serious harm (violence amounting to physical or psychological abuse). nor the relationship of that harm to a statutory ground (advocacy of feminism or, in some cases, gender alone). *Cf.* Goodwin-Gill, *supra* § I.1, note 11, at 70-71.

391 *See* Kelley, Anker and Beasley, *supra* § III.3, note 26, at 820.

392 *But see* discussion of *Matter of R-A-*, Interim Decision 3403 (BIA 1996), *infra* this sub-section.

fiscal ability to do so or it withholds relief from a specific portion of the population.[393]

The initial Canadian decision specifically dealing with the question is *Mayers* v. *M.E.I.*[394] In *Mayers,* the Court of Appeal was presented with the situation of a woman who had been abused by her husband since her marriage at age 22 in 1971 until the time of her flight into Canada in 1986. The abuse was said to have included rape and involved mistreatment of the claimant's two children. Attempts to secure the assistance of the police had proven futile.[395] Under these circumstances, the Court of Appeal ruled that the CRDD had not erred as a matter of law in finding that claimant had a well-founded fear of persecution as the result of her membership in a particular social group which was defined as "Trinidadian women subject to wife abuse".[396]

The case was followed by the Refugee Division in granting refugee status to women who faced serious harm in the form of household domestic violence if returned to their country of nationality. In one case, the CRDD granted refugee status to a woman from Zimbabwe who was able to make out severe domestic abuse coupled with denial of protection by the government.[397] In another early decision, the CRDD compared household domestic violence to torture in granting the refugee claim of an Ecuadorian woman who sought protection from such serious harm.[398]

The Federal Court-Trial Division has now determined unambiguously that domestic violence can give rise to a claim of persecution based on a protected ground. In *Narvaez* v. *MCI*[399] the Trial Division dealt specifically with the question and found that "women subject to wife abuse in Ecuador" constituted a social group, holding that Ecuador is a patriarchal society and that Ecuadorian authorities are not interested in addressing domestic violence matters. The reasoning in *Narvaez* was specifically adopted in *Diluna* v. *M.E.I.*[400] where the Trial Division determined that the Convention Refugee Determination Division had erred in failing to find that "women subject to wife abuse in Brazil" were within the fourth ground of refugee protection.

---

393 *See, e.g.*, Hathaway, *supra* § I.1, note 7, at 111.

394 (1992), 150 N.R. 60 (F.C.A.).

395 *Id.* at 62.

396 *Id.* at 62-68.

397 CRDD U92-06668 (Feb.19, 1993).

398 CRDD U92-08714 (June 4, 1993).

399 [1995] 2 F.C. 55 (T.D).

400 (F.C.T.D., no. IMM-3201-94), March 14, 1995.

In *Vidhani* v. *M.C.I.*,[401] the Federal Court-Trial Division granted refugee status to a Moslem woman from Kenya on the ground, *inter alia*, that she would be forced under Kenyan law into a marriage which her father had arranged for her without her consent. As noted earlier, the court held that being forced into an involuntary marital union without more constitutes persecution.[402] However, the court also found the claimant to be within a protected social group by virtue of the serious harm which she would experience at the hands of (i) her father;[403] and (ii) her prospective spouse.[404]

Prior to June 1999, U.S. law appeared to be tracking Canadian case law, although U.S. decisions were not prolific or of precedential weight.[405] There were, in this respect, numerous adjudications by various immigration courts within the Executive Office for Immigration Review which helped develop the law to a considerable degree. This line of cases is examined in the paragraphs which follow. As will be discussed at greater length below, the doctrinal position developed by the immigration courts was called into severe question by a radical decision of the Board of Immigration Appeals in *Matter of R-A-*.[406] The Attorney General has vacated this decision, however, and new regulations have been proposed which are intended to address the concerns which *R-A-* spawned. These developments will presumably have the effect of restoring much of the pre-*R-A-* jurisprudence in this area.

Illustrative of this trend in the case law is *Matter of A- and Z-*,[407] decided on December 20, 1994. In that case, a Jordanian woman sought asylum based on abuse she had suffered at the hands of her husband, a prominent and successful businessman in Jordan.[408] Respondent showed that the abuse

---

[401] [1995] 3 F.C. 60 (T.D.).

[402] *Id.* at 65.

[403] *Id.*

[404] *Id.* at 66. *See also* Griffith v. M.C.I. (F.C.T.D., no. IMM-4543), July 14, 1999. There the Federal Court-Trial Division remanded to the CRDD the case of a native and citizen of St. Vincent who alleged that she would be exposed to domestic violence if she were returned there. The Trial Division ruled in effect that the CRRD had departed from the Canadian *Gender Guidelines* by disbelieving claimant without supplying any reasons for their conclusion.

[405] An excellent review of the U.S. cases appears in Karen Musalo, *The Developing Jurisprudence of Gender-Based Claims, in* Practicing Law Institute (eds.), 30th Annual Immigration and Naturalization Institute 513 (1997). *See also* Pamela Goldberg, *U.S. Law and Women Asylum Seekers: Where Are They and Where Are They Going?*, 73 Interpreter Releases 889 (July 8, 1996).

[406] Interim Decision 3403 (BIA 1999).

[407] A72 190 893, A72 793 219 (IJ Arlington, Va. Dec. 20, 1994) (Nejelski, IJ), *abstracted in* 72 Interpreter Releases 521 (April 17, 1995).

[408] *Id.* at 521.

had been continuing since her marriage in 1961. According to the findings, the husband often beat respondent in front of others, including periods when she was pregnant. Respondent's husband also isolated her from friends and family; restricted her travel; and exercised control and dominion over all aspects of her life. Respondent tolerated this mistreatment until May of 1990, when her husband threatened her with a gun. This prompted her exit from Jordan.[409]

The position of the Immigration and Naturalization Service at trial was that the abuse suffered flowed from a personal marital dispute and that asylum, therefore, was not appropriate. The immigration judge, however, determined that respondent had suffered on account of her membership in a particular social group and on account of her political opinion.[410] The applicant's political opinion, according to the adjudicator, was a "belief in Western values," while the social group consisted of:

> those women who espouse Western values and are unwilling to live their lives at the mercy of their husbands, their society, their government.[411]

The immigration judge quite clearly referred in his decision to the central concept underlying asylum claims based on gender, i.e., the absence of equal protection in the area of fundamental human rights.[412] An asylum seeker who predicates her entitlement to refugee-type relief on an overt manifestation of the right of women to enjoy human rights on an equal footing with men qualifies under both the political opinion and the social group grounds of refugee protection if she can demonstrate serious harm relative to such expression. The judge also referred unequivocally to the international public policy implications of equal protection as concerns the exercise of human rights and the relevance of those implications for the present decision. Specifically, the immigration judge held:

> The respondent is not willing to live in a harem completely protected by her husband, his society and his government. The emancipation of women is one of the most important world-wide political and social movements of this century. Precisely because of its importance, the freedom and equality of women is dangerous and threatening politics to her husband, his society, his government.
>
> The respondent's husband has beaten the respondent for three decades, but the respondent and her twelve-year-old son remain unbowed. They now seek protection in this country for political belief in the importance of individual

---

409 *Id.*

410 *Id.* at 521-522.

411 *Id.* at 522.

412 *Id.*

> freedom. Not just freedom for adult males but freedom for women and children too. They shall have the protection they seek under the asylum and withholding of deportation laws of the United States.[413]

A decision which is related (but not identical) is *Matter of M- and K-*.[414] *Matter of M- and K-* was the initial decision involving female genital mutilation as a basis for asylum. Respondent had been a native and citizen of Sierra Leone who had been involuntarily made the subject of FGM, which had been performed in highly unsanitary conditions. Apart from this mistreatment, however, respondent had also been beaten by her husband on the basis that she had been "mouthy". This had resulted in considerable physical wounds. Respondent refused to have any more children after the birth of her second child, and she joined the People's Democratic Party, a major opposition party in Sierra Leone, the PDP having been the object of frequent attacks by the government and by other opposition forces.

The immigration judge identified the particular social group in the case as a sub-group of women who had been forced to undergo forced female genital mutilation and those women who had been punished through physical abuse by their spouses for having asserted their individual autonomy. Specifically, the judge held:

> Where a law or mandatory societal custom targets women (or a subgroup of women, such as wives) either on its face or by application and imposes restrictions or requirements on women but not on men, and the penalty for such violation is serious, a claim of gender-based persecution will be recognized. In addition where serious offenses against women or wives—such as rapes, serious assaults and murder—are not punished or are lightly punished, or where women or wives are generally not granted protections accorded to men, the abuse will constitute gender-based persecution.[415]

In another decision of significance, *Matter of Sonia Sharmin*,[416] a Bangladeshi woman sought asylum based on physical spousal abuse resulting largely from claimant's efforts to define herself as an independent individual.[417] The respondent had been born in Bangladesh on May 13, 1967 and married on June 10, 1989. The marriage had been arranged. She arrived in the U.S. with a B-2 visitor's visa on April 30, 1995, her reason for leaving being that she was afraid of her husband. Respondent had been active in the

---

[413] *Id.*

[414] A72 374 558 (IJ Arlington, VA. August 9, 1995) (Nejelski, IJ), *abstracted in* 72 Interpreter Releases 1188 (September 1, 1995).

[415] *Id.* at 1189-1190.

[416] A73 556 033 (IJ New York, NY. Sept. 30, 1996) (Bukszpan, IJ).

[417] *Id.* at 3-7.

Jatyo Party which she supported by going to meetings and encouraging others to join the party by spreading its social message. Respondent also showed that she was a member of the women's wing of the Party, whose goals were the same as those of the main party except that it emphasized influencing women and encouraging them to join in the party's work. As a result of this work, respondent's husband, father-in-law and mother-in-law showered physical abuse upon applicant, sometimes beating her with a stick. This mistreatment eventually brought about her flight from Bangladesh to the United States.

The immigration judge found that the applicant qualified for asylum both under the political opinion ground and as the member of a particular social group. The thrust of respondent's claim, according to the opinion, was that:

> [A]s a young, Westernized, educated Muslim wife, voicing political opinion by both word and deed in her political party involvement and her de facto feminism, she was the target of persecution because of her membership in a particular social group and because of political opinion. [The actions of applicant's family members] *were sanctioned by and condoned by the government of Bangladesh and by the general society of the country and were inflicted upon her because she was perceived as a threat to the social order.*[418]

Like the immigration judge's decision previously cited, *Matter of A- and Z-*, the judge in *Sonia Sharmin* took official notice of the growing developments in international law affecting the human rights of women (including recent precedent by the Yugoslavian War Crimes Tribunal to the effect that rape is a crime against humanity under Article 6(c) of the Nuremberg Charter). As convincing evidence that women did not enjoy human rights on an equal basis with men in Bangladesh, and in fact had their human rights systematically and arbitrarily denied in that country, the judge cited numerous human rights reports relevant to current Bangladeshi country conditions demonstrating unequal treatment, on a pervasive and systematic basis, between women and men.

The strength of that opinion, however, and its clear basis for a grant of asylum can only be found in the court's thorough and painstaking analysis of the human rights background and general social conditions within Bangladesh. Not only is the absence of State protection for battered wives brought

---

418 *Id.* at 7. [Emphasis supplied]. The court specifically held, based on the country background evidence before it, that:

> Thus, Muslim married women are held to an inferior and unprotected position in Bangladesh, from which they cannot easily extricate themselves, and that the state sanctions this by deferring to religious laws in these matters.

*Id.* at 12.

out, but also the clear inability of Bangladesh to bring itself (despite apparent efforts) into conformity with the Convention on the Elimination of All Forms of Discrimination Against Women. This failure, human rights monitors have tended to agree, has resulted not merely from general ignorance of the law, but more importantly from the "social stigma" which obtains with respect to women's efforts to assert themselves on an independent basis.

Indeed the court sets out with exceptional clarity the analysis which must be made in determining whether a claimant has already suffered persecution on a protected ground in the context of household domestic violence. In this respect, the immigration judge examines the ongoing tension between the civil and criminal code of Bangladesh (applicable to Muslim and non-Muslim alike) and the religious family codes (applicable only to Muslims).[419] That tension has resulted in the temporary supremacy of the religious codes over secular efforts to control the former's discriminatory impact:

> Although a number of laws have been passed that specifically address the status and rights of women in Bangladesh, there are still many problems with the implementation of women's rights. One reason given for this situation is ignorance of the law, which is caused by a 'lack of social and political consciousness, low literacy, observation of seclusion and submission to husbands' wishes, lack of exposure to mass media, information, etc.'. *Although the civil law guaranteeing the legal rights of women may appear substantial, customs and traditions based primarily on Muslim personal or family law still take precedence in practice.*[420]

The analysis offered in *Sonia Sharmin* goes far to dispel any lingering notions that spousal abuse inflicted in a climate of widespread social discrimination is no more than a private matter, essentially outside the scope of the refugee definition. This is not to say that spousal abuse *per se* is a ground for refugee status irrespective of the country conditions wherein it is raised. However, where household domestic violence follows the asylum seeker's efforts to challenge discriminatory social norms, it is impossible to say that the applicant has not qualified under the prevailing criteria for refugee status.[421]

The reliance on State responsibility in the above cases leaves several questions unanswered. Specifically, is a mechanism of State protection (which does nothing to alleviate the claimant's plight) essential to make out a claim? What happens, for instance, where there is no State? Or where the

---

[419] *Id.* at 10, *citing* Immigration and Refugee Board, Documentation Center, *Women in Bangladesh* 3-4 (December 1993).

[420] *Id.* at 16, *citing* Immigration and Refugee Board, Documentation Center, *Women in Bangladesh* 12 (December 1993). [Emphasis supplied].

[421] *Id.* at 16.

State is paralyzed by social forces which it finds itself powerless to control? Does the absence of State institutions lead to the result that such a claim cannot be founded?

The analysis given in *Sonia Sharmin* strongly suggests that the adjudicator should follow a factual analysis in which the total situation controls. The capacity of private parties to inflict serious injury will thus be measured against the State's protective mechanisms and the State's capacity to offer an "adequate" remedy.[422] The country background materials are examined by the court in such a way as to make it clear that the discriminatory practices arising from Bangladeshi social and cultural norms have tended to dominate the comparatively weaker institutions of State protection. As a matter of evidentiary reality, however, it is clearly the practices arising from custom which have inflicted the discriminatory distress (the persecution) which State institutions have proven powerless to control.

In 1999, the Board issued a precedent decision, *Matter of R-A-*,[423] purporting to delimit if not to abrogate altogether this jurisprudence. *Matter of R-A-* has now been vacated by the Attorney General in an Order[424] which directs the Board to decide the case *de novo* once new asylum regulations, now pending in proposed form,[425] become final. Notwithstanding these recent developments, *R-A-* will be analyzed in substantial depth. In part, this analysis serves to highlight the human rights dimension to domestic violence cases by contrasting the result in *R-A-* with the more astutely reasoned outcomes in the United Kingdom and Canada. Finally, the proposed U.S. regulations are analyzed briefly, particularly with a view to showing how the rationale of *R-A-* might be modified through their provisions.

In *Matter of R-A-*, an immigration judge granted asylum to a Guatemalan woman who had been the victim of physical domestic violence by her husband, a former soldier. Her efforts to secure assistance from the police

---

422 On the "adequacy" of State protection under Canadian case law, *see, e.g.*, *Bobrik* v. *M.C.I.* (F.C.T.D., no. IMM-5519-93), September 16, 1994, at 4:

> [E]ven where the state is willing to protect its citizens, a claimant will meet the criteria for refugee status if the protection being offered is ineffective. A state must actually provide protection and not merely indicate a willingness to help. Where the evidence reveals that a claimant has experienced many incidents of harassment and/or discrimination without being effectively defended by the state, the presumption operates and it can be concluded that the state may be willing but unable to protect the claimant.

423 Interim Decision 3403 (BIA 1999).

424 *See, e.g.*, 78 Interpreter Releases 256 (January 22, 2001). *See also Reno Grants Asylum to Woman Who Fled Abuse in Guatemala*, The New York Times, January 20, 2001, at B3.

425 *See* 65 Fed. Reg. 76588, 76597 (December 7, 2000) (to be codified at 8 CFR § 208.15).

were unavailing as were her attempts to secure a divorce. The court determined that applicant had been punished because of her membership in a particular social group ("Guatemalan women who become involved intimately with Guatemalan men who believe in male domination [and] are targeted by their male companions ... when these men attempt to control them through violence") and political opinion (applicant's challenge to the husband's opinion that "women are to be subordinate to men"). Specifically, the immigration judge found:

> He [the husband] beat her [claimant] often, and at many occasions, inflicting severe injury. He dislocated her jaw, nearly pushed out her eye, tried to cut off her hands with his machete, kicked her in the abdomen and vagina, and tried to force her to abort when she was pregnant with her second child by severely kicking her in the spine. He would drag her by the hair, use her head to break windows and mirrors, whip her with pistols and electric cords, and threaten her with knives.... The sexual abuse severely injured [claimant] causing extensive hemorrhaging, excruciating abdominal pain and disease.[426]

Applicant's repeated pleas to the police for protection proved ineffective and a judge advised her that intervention would be futile. In addition, applicant submitted substantial evidence that spousal abuse in Guatemala is "common" to the point of being endemic and that there existed no realistic redress for such human rights violations.[427] Despite these glaring facts (and without really controverting them in any degree), the Board reversed.

The opinion rejected the immigration judge's conclusion that applicant had been persecuted on account of her membership in a particular social group, namely, "Guatemalan women who have been involved intimately with Guatemalan male companions who believe that women are to live under male domination".[428] The analysis here rests more on "nexus" than it does on the question of whether a protected ground has been made out. The Board began by declining to apply the same kind of analysis which it had in *Matter of Kasinga*[429] in which it had awarded asylum to a woman from Togo who feared FGM under the fourth Convention ground, concluding that "young women from the Tchamba-Kunsuntu tribe who had not had FGM as practiced by their tribe and who oppose the practice" constitute a particular social group. The analysis must be context dependent, the Board opined, and an operation which is formalized and specifically tailored to women is

---

426 *See* Matter of A-P-, A73 753 922 (IJ San Francisco Sept. 20, 1996) (Schooley Yam, IJ).

427 Matter of R-A-, Interim Decision 3403 (BIA 1999), at 5-6.

428 *Id.* at 17-18.

429 21 I&N Dec. 357 (BIA 1996).

generically different from physical abuse which is not, on its face, gender-specific.[430]

The Board's distinguishing its own precedent, it must be observed here, is disingenuous. In *Kasinga*, the Board had specifically rejected the notion that a "malignant" intent to punish was necessary to establish "persecution", finding that an intent on the part of the persecutor to "overcome" a characteristic or belief recognized by the law of refugee status would be sufficient. In the *Kasinga* decision, the Board concluded that the characteristic sought to be overcome by the social practice of FGM was the claimant's right to have "intact genitalia", i.e., to her state of unmutilated womanhood. A highly similar basis (the claimant's right to "independent womanhood") could easily have been used to support the conclusion that the applicant in *R-A-* was experiencing serious harm on account of the socially tolerated practice of domestic violence.

*Matter of R-A-* also rejected the methodology it had earlier adopted in civil war cases, namely, that systematic violations of human rights committed against a discernable group constitute evidence of persecutory intent. The Board opined that civil war claims arise in a "political" context which is largely lacking in domestic violence cases. Such an approach does disservice to the emerging notion of attributed characteristics and beliefs as applied to the social group ground. Framed simply, the Board's methodology in *Matter of R-A-* ignores the clear relevance to the asylum seeker's plight of serious harm taking place in a social context, particularly when that harm consists of systematic or widespread violations of human rights committed against a specific group with which claimant can be objectively identified.

The background material on Guatemala clearly reveals that the practice of spousal abuse is generalized and involves configurations of violence specifically directed against women. As was reflected in the *R-A-* decision itself, moreover, the resulting human rights violations often consist of acts of rape or torture. It is of moment to note that a parallel jurisprudence is developing with respect to "crimes against humanity" under international customary law which may ultimately encompass these cases. Recent jurisprudence establishes that where serious human rights violations (including rape and torture) are committed by individuals in a "systematic or widespread" manner, the agent of persecution may be held criminally accountable under the doctrine of universal jurisdiction.[431] These developments make clear that, under modern doctrine, core human rights may be asserted both

---

430 *Matter of R-A-*, Interim Decision 3403 (BIA 1999), at 21-22.

431 Theodor Meron, War Crimes Law Comes of Age 298-99 (1998), *citing* Prosecutor v. Tadic, No. IT-1-T (May 7, 1997).

vertically (i.e., against the State and its agents) and horizontally (i.e., against essentially "private" individuals and groups).

Criminal responsibility will vest, furthermore, irrespective of whether there is State involvement in the violation or whether the inhuman acts take place during armed conflict or in peacetime. No formal plan of execution is required so long as there is a course of conduct indicative of an implicit policy of discrimination. The requirement that the violations be "mass" or "systematized" signifies that there is no effective protection by the State and hence that the crime can appropriately be internationalized. Critically in this respect the new International Criminal Court Statute includes in its definition of "crimes against humanity" the following offenses when committed as part of a systematic or widespread "attack" against a civilian population: "rape, sexual slavery [...] or any form of sexual violence of comparable gravity". The new definition, intended to incorporate recent developments in modern international penal law, has obvious relevance to the *R-A-* decision and to the country background of prevalent spousal abuse in which it arose.[432]

The core notion of the case, however, and the aspect of it which brings it into such sharp contrast with Canadian and international jurisprudence, is in its treatment of State responsibility. The Board acknowledged that Guatemala had failed to relieve conditions of domestic abuse. But, the Board insisted, State inaction is "not a reliable indicator" with respect to the motivation of private parties.[433] And the Board virtually set down as a requirement that the State itself have some "malignant intent" in failing to offer protection. This was not a case, the Board reasoned, in which the Guatemalan government had encouraged its male citizens to abuse its female citizens or in which protection had unreasonably been withdrawn from a particular section of the population "with the expectation" that defenseless individuals would be subject to attack.[434]

The Board's treatment of the law of State responsibility is, perhaps, the most troubling aspect of its decision. The State's obligation to uphold human rights to an acceptable level under international law is not conditioned on whether the State has acted deliberately and with discriminatory malice in failing to provide protection.[435] State responsibility under prevailing international law standards is objective and a State which has the capacity to respond to human rights violations will be treated as responsible if it fails to

---

432 *See* U.N. Doc. A/CONF. 183/9, 17 July 1998, Art. 7(g).

433 Matter of R-A-, Interim Decision 3304 (BIA 1999), at 19.

434 *Id.*

435 *See, e.g.,* Anker 99, *supra* § I.2, note 32, at 193 and authorities cited therein.

act.[436] States are liable for acts of private parties where such acts are specifically covered by a treaty obligation (e.g., CEDAW) or where there is "State failure to exercise due diligence in the control of private actors".[437] Apart from these general observations concerning the law of State responsibility, the rationale of *R-A-* appears to directly conflict with the framework of decision recommended by UNHCR for adjudicating women's asylum cases based on domestic violence where the assistance of the State has been sought and rejected.

The United Nations High Commissioner for Refugees has now clarified its own view that the law of State responsibility plays a paramount role in establishing refugee claims.[438] In a recent essay by the Division of International Protection, UNHCR analyzes a case of Immigration and Refugee Board (CRDD) in which a Bulgarian woman was subject to periodic beatings and rapes by her husband throughout their seven-year marriage. Claimant had reported the event several times to the police, who had refused to take corrective action.[439] The IRB concluded that the acts were of sufficient severity to merit the characterization of torture within the meaning of the Convention against Torture.[440] The misconduct also violated claimant's right to personal integrity "enshrined" in Article 3 of UDHR. The deliberate failure to act on the part of the State's agents was at once a violation of the Torture Convention (in that a State official had clearly acquiesced in the claimant's mistreatment) and (so the IRB strongly implied) an act of persecution. As explained by the Division of International Protection:

> Sexual violence may often not emanate directly from the authorities. Nonetheless, as generally reflected in the UNHCR *Handbook on Procedures and Criteria for Determining Refugee Status,* this fact is no barrier to considering violence as persecution within the meaning of the Convention. The requirement of State protection against such actions needs to be addressed. When the State is unable or unwilling to protect, sexual violence, even at the hands of private actors, may be interpreted as persecution. The international instruments clearly establish State responsibility for safeguarding against such human rights violations. The Special Rapporteur on violence against women addressed the issue of private persons committing violence against women in her November 1994 report and concluded that States are legally responsible

---

[436] Ian Brownlie, Principles of Public International Law 437 (4th ed. 1990).

[437] *Preliminary report submitted by Special Rapporteur on violence against women, its causes and consequences, Ms. Radhika Coomaraswany, in accordance with Human Rights Resolution 1994/1995*, U.N. Doc. E/C.4/1995/42, 22 Nov. 1994, para. 102, at 24.

[438] UNHCR, Division of International Protection, *Gender-Related Persecution: An Analysis of Recent Trends*, Int'l J. Refugee L., 79, 87 (Special Issue: February 22-23, 1996).

[439] CRDD T-91-01497, November 1, 1994.

[440] Torture Convention, *supra* note 1104.

> for acts or omissions of private persons in certain circumstances, among which she includes instances where 'private acts are covered by provisions of a treaty obligation' and where 'there is State failure to exercise due diligence in the control of private actors'.[441]

Hence, the fact that States are responsible for enforcing human rights horizontally is of great probative significance for determining a claimant's refugee status when that responsibility is not met. In the case under discussion, the Bulgarian justice system had declined to prosecute the crime of domestic violence and so denied applicant a protected right under international law.[442]

A specific intent on the part of a "private" third party is not essential. The State has exposed to potential harm a discernable group for which it has responsibility. The State's failure to ensure that human rights are enjoyed "without discrimination" with regard to any kind of status (including gender) becomes a contributing cause of the persecution, and provides a nexus which may not be altogether manifest when purely private conduct is being examined. The relationship between lack of State protection and a refugee ground is provided by the invitation such lack of protection offers to third parties to act with impunity.[443]

The law of State responsibility, however, makes clear that, at some level, the failure of State agents to take corrective measures may well be attributed to the State and, in such an instance, a claim of persecution can be made on

---

441 UNHCR, Division of International Protection, *supra* this section, note 438, at 87.

442 *Id.*:

> [T]he failure of the justice system in Bulgaria to prosecute the claimant's husband for domestic violence denied her the protection which the international community recognizes as her right.

443 As indicated earlier, cases which involve a failure of State responsibility (as opposed to those where the State, despite its best efforts, is simply unable to control social forces subject to its jurisdiction) involve claims wherein the State may itself be responsible for the persecution threatened or imposed. As Deborah Anker has remarked, the test prevailing in international law should not be underestimated:

> A state's responsibility to respond to violations by non-State actors is relative. Evidence of a single violation or of a single investigation without meaningful results, does not establish State accountability. "Complicity must be demonstrated by establishing that the State condones a pattern of abuse through pervasive non-action". Under international law, the governing standard is that of due diligence; the test is whether the State undertakes its responsibilities of protection seriously. The pervasiveness of the violation may be indirect evidence of the state's complicity. Remedies provided by the laws of the state must be real and not mere formalities.

Anker 99, *supra* § I.2, note 32, at 196. [Citations omitted].

that basis. The question of State responsibility is thus coming to enjoy an enhanced role in refugee analysis. The failure of the State to uphold the horizontal enforcement of human rights may well be probative as to the conclusion that the serious harm feared or experienced is related to a protected ground. But events falling short of deliberate State inaction (as established by the conduct of its agents) can similarly meet the refugee definition where third parties are able to act in an environment of impunity. Even in the absence of tacit State complicity, an incapacitated State may well point toward the existence of unfettered patterns of social discrimination and so assist in making out a claim of persecution in the Convention sense.

The decision of the Board of Immigration Appeals (which essentially eschews any reliance on international human rights law) must be contrasted at this juncture with a March 1999 determination by the (U.K.) House of Lords which found eligible for asylum two Pakistani women who alleged essentially domestic violence as the basis for their claims.[444] The joint appeal involved separate but related cases:

> (i) a 43 year old applicant had left her home and had had a child in the U.K. Her fear was that her violent husband would accuse her of adultery and denounce her under Sharia law.
>
> (ii) a 45 year old applicant had, as a teacher, intervened in a quarrel among rival student factions with the result that the opposing faction accused claimant of infidelity. Her husband subsequently assaulted her, and applicant was required to proceed to hospital to recover from her injuries.

Each claimant set forth evidence establishing that there was a lack of State protection against acts of domestic violence. Both Lord Steyn's opinion[445] and that of Lord Hoffman[446] make clear the compelling nexus which exists between international human rights jurisprudence and refugee law as demonstrated by the Preamble to the 1951 Convention which affirms the obligation of States to uphold the principle that fundamental human rights be enjoyed without discrimination as to any status. Using the non-discrimination principle of modern human rights doctrine, Lord Steyn examines the situation in Pakistan discerning the ways in which women are systematically denied equal protection in civil, political and social matters.[447] On the related

---

[444] Islam (A.P.) v. Secretary of State for Home Dept., Regina v. Immigration Appeal Tribunal and Another Ex Parte Shah, 2 All ER 545 (House of Lords), *reprinted in* 11 Int'l J. Refugee L. 496 (1999).

[445] *Id.* at 496.

[446] *Id.* at 506.

[447] *Id.* at 505-506.

question of whether "women" are a particular social group so as to be within a refugee ground and a class deserving of protection under international law, Lord Steyn looks essentially to U.S. law on the "particular social group" category as formulated in the *Acosta* case.[448] As noted previously, *Acosta* recognized that groups similar to the other four grounds might satisfy the fourth Convention ground, and gender was certainly held together by an immutable characteristic within the meaning of the *Acosta* criteria. Again, human rights law and refugee doctrine were perceived as operating within a common framework of decision.

The most interesting opinion in the case is that of Lord Hoffman who examines the law of State protection (the issue with which the Board had the greatest difficulty). The critical element for Lord Hoffman (as for the Board) is whether the absence of State protection can be seen as an operative force in the persecution. Looking essentially at the example of the Nuremberg laws in Germany, Lord Hoffman clearly recognizes that the specific failure of the Nazi regime to protect Jews left them vulnerable to all kinds of attacks by third parties who themselves were not motivated by any kind of discrimination. (The example used is that of rival businessmen who attack a Jewish shopkeeper's store out of purely commercial incentives). The absence of a specific animus on the part of the third party is irrelevant, however: the State has failed to protect a specific class for which it has responsibility under international law and this has "caused" the persecution as effectively as if the State had committed the destructive act in question.[449]

The House of Lords thus adopts a correct view of causation and nexus which is based on the right/duty relationship. The State's obligation to enforce human rights provides an objective standard upon which specific classes can rely. Where the State's failure to observe its responsibilities has discriminatory effects, the resulting loss of protection is a breach of State responsibility towards adversely affected classes. The breach, in Lord Hoffman's analysis, is a contributing cause of the persecution, irrespective of either the intent of the State or the intent of the third parties engaged in the infliction of serious harm. The Board's position in *Matter of R-A-* is exactly the opposite: for the Board, it is not enough that either spousal abuse is systematically imposed or that there is a failure of State protection. Neither of these factors is sufficient if there is not some discernable evidence that either the State or the private party inflicting the suffering has acted with

---

[448] Matter of Acosta, 19 I&N Dec. 211 (BIA 1985).

[449] 11 Int'l. J. Refugee L. 496, 514 (1999).

specific malice toward the claimant and that malice is directly connected, in some way, with a protected ground.[450]

In the summer of 2000, the Board issued a precedent decision which constituted a small retreat from the preclusive ruling it had handed down in *R-A-*. *Matter of S-A-*[451] involved a native and citizen of Morocco who was afraid to return to her homeland because she had been beaten routinely by her father. The occasion of the beatings had been the respondent's refusal to dress conservatively and otherwise to conform to the father's ultra-orthodox Muslim beliefs. On one occasion, the asylum seeker had received a very short skirt from her aunt in the U.S. When her father caught her wearing this attire in public, he burned her thighs using a heated straight razor. On another occasion, the father beat applicant until she bled and confined her to the house because of her engaging in a conversation with a male stranger on the street. Respondent viewed mistreatment at the hands of her father as particularly pernicious since her two brothers escaped such punishment.

The Board concluded that there was an absence of State protection, acknowledging that the background material on Morocco indicated that any efforts to secure police or judicial intervention would be futile. In determining whether the harm could be linked to a protected ground, the Board found that the respondent had established a claim based on religion. In distinguishing the case from *R-A-* (and from other precedents holding that gender alone will not ground a claim), the Board concluded that respondent had undergone serious harm "on account of her religious beliefs as they differed with those of her father, concerning the proper role of women". The case illustrates that establishing a gender-based claim predicated on domestic abuse may be facilitated where the claimant is openly rejecting a gender-specific cultural code.[452]

---

[450] Importantly, the *Islam* and *Shah* consolidated appeals lend support to a doctrinal point previously insisted upon by Deborah Anker, that women *per se* constitute the social group for most gender-based asylum claims including those having domestic violence as their basis. As noted by Anker:

> [C]laims based upon domestic violence generally should be analyzed under the particular social group ground, with gender *per se* as the defining characteristic. Not to acknowledge that women constitute a particular social group creates analytical confusion, treats women fundamentally differently and holds them to a higher standard—treatment specifically rejected by the *INS Guidelines*.

Anker 99, *supra* § I.2, note 32, at 392.

[451] Interim Decision 3433 (BIA 2000).

[452] There have been a number of decisions handed down by immigration courts in the post-*R-A-* environment which raise interesting questions with respect to gender-based asylum cases. These issues include forced prostitution, gang rape, and honor killings. Practically

Finally, on December 7, 2000, the Immigration and Naturalization Service published for comment proposed regulations which purport to establish guidelines for deciding the parameters of the "social group" category and which were intended to address the problems generated by the *R-A-* decision. As noted earlier, in January 2001, the Attorney General directed the Board to reconsider *Matter of R-A-* in light of these new regulations when they become adopted in final form. As proposed, the new asylum rules would potentially serve to clarify a number of aspects of the case and to point in the direction of granting relief. The critical areas of analysis affected are: (i) State protection; (ii) nexus; and (iii) membership in a particular social group. The foregoing elements of the proposed regulations are analyzed below.

1. **State protection**. The proposed regulations indicate that, in considering whether the State is unwilling or unable to control the persecutor, the adjudicator should consider: (i) whether the government has taken steps to control the harm or suffering complained of; (ii) whether the claimant has reasonable access to protection which in fact exists. Included in these broad areas of inquiry are subsidiary criteria which must be considered, including:

> Government complicity with respect to the infliction of harm or suffering at issue; attempts by the applicant, if any, to obtain protection from government officials and the government's response to these attempts; official action which is perfunctory; a pattern of government unresponsiveness; general country conditions and the government's denial of services; the nature of the government's policies with respect to the harm or suffering at issue; and any steps the government has taken to prevent the infliction of the harm or suffering.[453]

2. **Nexus.** With regard to the critical question of whether serious harm can be connected in a significant way to a protected ground, the proposed regulations make clear that the test is a liberal one. The claimant is not obligated to establish that the persecutor's motivation is exclusively to overcome a ground of refugee protection. As proposed, however, the regulations require the claimant to show that the persecutor's incentive (to overcome a characteristic or belief) is "central." Evidence that the persecutor seeks to over-

---

all of the cases have resulted in denials by the immigration judge or grants which have been later reversed by the Board of Immigration Appeals in the light of *R-A-*. The cases are summarized in K. Musalo and S. Knight, *Gender-Based Asylum: An Analysis of Recent Trends*, 77 Interpreter Releases 1533 (Oct. 30, 2000). These cases will unquestionably be affected by the new developments which have been outlined herein in ways which are constructive from the point of view of women's human rights and which involve a rational application of the Convention refugee definition.

453 *See* 65 Fed. Reg. 76588, 76597 (December 7, 2000) (to be codified at 8 CFR § 208.15(a)).

come others with the characteristic or belief in question is highly relevant to the analysis.[454]

3. **Membership in a particular social group**. The rule's provision governing the fourth ground of refugee protection tracks the elements which have been developed in prior law, including: (a) immutable characteristics; and (b) associations which are so fundamental to the asylum seeker's identity or conscience that he/she should not be forced to relinquish them. Again, subsidiary criteria are to be considered in connection with this basic framework which serve as auxiliary considerations in determining whether the claimant has established her inclusion in a "social group": (i) close association among the members; (ii) common motive or interest; (iii) voluntary association among the group's participants; (iv) recognition of the group as a societal faction or as a distinct segment of the population; (v) the perception of the members themselves that they are bound together; and (vi) distinctions maintained by the society in question which indicate that the members of the group are in fact treated separately from members of society in general.[455]

The Board could unequivocally employ the foregoing criteria to overturn its prior holding in *R-A-*. The provisions on State protection, for instance, do not contain reference to any discriminatory motive on the State's part in withholding protection as was required in *R-A*. Rather, a critical inquiry must be made as to whether there is protection in fact, including an examination as to whether the claimant has reasonable access to such protection or whether efforts to obtain protection by the claimant would have proven fruitless. Such considerations would obviously have material bearing on the *R-A-* case in that, as made evident in the facts, applicant had made numerous efforts both to report her suffering to the police and had gone so far as to attempt to involve a judge, all of which had been unavailing.

The issue of nexus to a protected ground remains the core consideration to be resolved by the rules and it is here that the proposed regulations are most vague. The rule certainly accepts the "immutable characteristics" basis for social group formation put forward initially in *Acosta*. Presumably this reference constitutes regulatory approval of the case law developing the

---

[454] *See* 65 Fed. Reg. 76588, 76597 (December 7, 2000) (to be codified at 8 CFR § 208.15(b)). With respect to the issue of domestic violence, the prefatory materials to the proposed regulations reveal that this does not necessarily require a showing that persecuting husbands would be inclined to beat other men's wives. The analogy of slavery is made indicating that a slave owner could still persecute by beating his own slaves even though he was not inclined (or even able) to beat the slaves of other slave-owners. *See* 65 Fed. Reg. 76588, 76592-76593 (Supplementary Information) (December 7, 2000).

[455] *See* 65 Fed. Reg. 76588, 76597 (December 7, 2000) (to be codified at 8 CFR § 208.15(c)).

notion of women as a "social group" based on the unchangeable feature of their gender. More helpful are the provisions in the proposed regulation relating to group membership based on social perceptions. Important criteria pointing toward the existence of a social group can be found in (i) recognition of the group as a distinct aggregate within society or (ii) objective circumstances showing that the group is in fact treated separately from (and less favorably than) other members of the society in question.

The rule would thus open the door to an analysis based on attributed membership in a particular social group, or to one which takes into account a combination of immutable features and attributed characteristics or beliefs. As noted in the preface to the regulations, the treatment meted out in fact to women in Guatemala (including that domestic violence is viewed as a "family problem" and that R-A- herself received no protection when she sought police and judicial intervention) would play a substantial role in showing that women are viewed as occupying a discrete category of persons who are not entitled to the equal protection of the laws.[456]

This regulatory initiative signifies that the problems spawned by *R-A* are at least on their way to being resolved. While not specifically based upon the international law principles which were developed in the portion of this study critiquing *R-A-*, the new asylum regulations, even in proposed form, are a step forward in reaching results which are consistent with those principles. The new rules proposed by the Department of Justice are clearly necessary if U.S. jurisprudence is to experience the advances made in the case law of Canada and the United Kingdom. Such steps are absolutely essential if U.S. law is to adopt a framework of decision in domestic violence cases which is in conformity with the jurisprudence of human rights and non-discrimination.

## § V.5(c). International Protection and the New Humanitarian Order

The most troublesome of the restraints on the growth of the Convention refugee definition flows from the fundamental rubric that flight from general conditions of violence or of "natural" calamity do not satisfy the conditions of refugee status. Conversely, however, where such individuals have not crossed an international frontier, general international law has been more responsive.

The need to develop a body of principles which could successfully address the situation of individuals and groups victimized by general

---

[456] *See* 65 Fed. Reg. 76588, 76594 (December 7, 2000).

conditions of violence or famine has occasioned an increasing reliance on international humanitarian law and doctrine.[457] The "right" to humanitarian assistance to be provided by governmental and non-governmental agents is an outgrowth of the "right of initiative" under general international humanitarian law. The right of humanitarian assistance has been described in the following way by the *Commentary to the Geneva Convention I*:

> It is obvious that any organization can "offer its services" to the Parties to the conflict at any time, just as any individual can. To offer one's services costs nothing and, which is more important, in no way binds the recipient of the offer, since the offer need not be accepted. The International Committee of the Red Cross, for its part, has not failed to offer its services for humanitarian purposes during various civil wars, whenever it considered that this was in the interests of those suffering as a result of hostilities, just as it has offered them when any international conflict has broken out. The paragraph may therefore appear at first sight to be merely decorative without any real significance. Nevertheless, it is of great moral and practical value.[458]

Importantly, there is scholarly authority for the proposition that the "right" to offer humanitarian assistance may, in the development of general international law, be evolving into a "duty". This evolution is being forced upon the community of States by their close proximity to one another, by their growing interdependence, and by the developing ethic of international solidarity. Yves Sandoz writes:

> In the "global village" which the world has now become, States can be thought to have not only a right to open their eyes but also a duty to do so. The Charter of the United Nations does in fact lay down certain principles of governing action by the Organization "and its Members" in pursuit of the United Nations' objectives. [T]he influx of aliens in a number of countries is compelling States to examine the situation in the countries where those persons come from since their *refoulement* or their admission as refugees depends on that situation.

* * *

---

457 For a general discussion, *see* International Institute of Humanitarian Law (San Remo), *Guiding Principles on the Right to Humanitarian Assistance*, (Extract from *International Review of the Red Cross*, November-December 1993) [hereinafter *Guiding Principles on the Right to Humanitarian Assistance*], at 519-525. *See also* Maurice Torrelli, *From Humanitarian Assistance to "Intervention on Humanitarian Grounds"?*, (Extract from *International Review of the Red Cross*, May-June 1992), at 228-248.

458 Commentary to Geneva Convention I, *supra* § I.2, note 40, at 57-58.

> In short, it can be concluded from the ever-increasing interdependence of all States, the development of human rights and the emergence of the principle of solidarity that States today are no longer allowed a "right of indifference".[459]

On the other hand, Jovica Patrnogic has referred to the growing cooperation among States acting within the UN system to achieve practical results in disaster relief actions.[460] A framework of protection is proposed which would be available to civilians and others during relief actions based on specific provisions in international humanitarian law which apply by analogy. Existing humanitarian instruments come into play here and are supported by the "values" of the international community, including its concerns with respect to realization of the broad objectives set out in the Universal Declaration of Human Rights. It is this confluence of law, policy and international "values" which has come to be characterized as the "new humanitarian order":

> By "humanitarian order" the Jordanian Government clearly understood this term in a broad sense to mean in this context the human values applicable to the entire international order, whether found in the moral conscience or the law, or underlying the institution of international organizational arrangements. As such, the call for a new international humanitarian order amounts to a call for review of the entire international system of law and organization in the light and the re-affirmation of humanitarian values and in response to contemporary needs.[461]

This section analyses the development of humanitarian law and human rights principles relative to those who are affected by generalized conditions of violence or by natural calamity such as draught or famine. Those whose plight can be traced to a violation of those principles may qualify for refugee status if they manage to cross an international frontier.

International humanitarian law has progressively constricted the unilateral discretion of sovereign States with respect to the treatment of their own citizens in the area of internal armed conflict.[462] The Geneva Conven-

---

[459] Yves Sandoz, "Droit" *or* "Devoir d'Ingérence" *and the Right to Assistance: the Issues Involved*, (Extract from *International Review of the Red Cross*, May-June 1992), at 215-227.

[460] *See generally* Jovica Patrnogic, *Some Reflections on Humanitarian Principles Applicable in Relief Actions, in* Studies and Essays on International Humanitarian Law and Red Cross Principles in Honour of Jean Pictet 925 (Christophe Swinarski ed. 1984).

[461] *Id.* at 929.

[462] For a summary of international humanitarian law provisions governing the activity of belligerents in international and internal armed conflict, *see especially* the Geneva Conventions of August 12, 1949 and Protocols I and II thereto, *supra* § I.1, note 17. As concerns the relevance of international humanitarian law to internally displaced persons, *see generally* Jean-Philippe Lavoyer, *Refugees and Internally Displaced Persons: Inter-*

tions of August 12, 1949, as well as Protocols I and II thereto clearly impose upon States "elementary dictates of humanity" and non-derogable duties as concerns those who are *hors de combat*. These responsibilities entail the obligation to refrain from starvation as a method of warfare.[463]

Accordingly, Article 18(2) of Protocol II sets forth the responsibility of both States and insurgents to allow free passage of international relief consignments during internal conflicts where the civilian population is suffering from a lack of provisions (such as foodstuffs and medical supplies) which are essential for its survival.[464] Although that Article conditions acceptance of such humanitarian relief on the consent of the High Contracting Party concerned, the *Commentary* explains:

> The fact that consent is required does not mean that the decision is left to the discretion of the parties. If the survival of the population is threatened and a humanitarian organization fulfilling the required conditions of impartiality and non-discrimination is able to remedy the situation, relief actions must take place. In fact they are the only way of combating starvation when local resources have been exhausted.[465]

The inclusion of humanitarian relief provisions within the law of war relative to internal combat has its origins in the Geneva Conventions and Protocols as these are applicable to wars having an international character.[466] For instance, the mandatory passage of relief consignments to populations which are not occupied but are under the control of an adverse party to the conflict is provided for in Article 70 of Protocol I.[467] Under Article 55 of the Fourth Convention, moreover, an occupying power is obliged to ensure that the

---

*national Humanitarian Law and the Role of the ICRC,* (Extract from the *International Review of the Red Cross*, March-April 1995), at 162-180.

463 *See, e.g.*, Protocol II, *supra* § I.1, note 17, Art.14:

> Starvation of civilians as a method of combat is prohibited. It is therefore prohibited to attack, destroy, remove or render useless, for that purpose, objects indispensable to the survival of the civilian population, such as foodstuffs, agricultural areas for the production of foodstuffs, crops, livestock, drinking water installations and supplies and irrigation works.

464 *Id.*, Art. 18(2):

> If the civilian population is suffering undue hardship owing to a lack of the supplies essential for its survival, such as foodstuffs and medical supplies, relief actions for the civilian population which are of an exclusively humanitarian and impartial nature and which are conducted without any adverse distinction shall be undertaken subject to the consent of the High Contracting Party concerned.

465 *See, e.g., Commentary to Protocol II, supra* § I.2, note 36, at 1479.

466 *See, e.g., id* at 1476-1478.

467 Protocol I, *supra* § I.1, note 17, Art. 70.

population in an occupied territory possesses the necessary means of survival, and, to that end, to accept humanitarian relief consignments.[468]

The *Commentary to Geneva Convention IV* (relative to Article 55) articulates the fundamental nature of the policy considerations underlying these rules, and offers clarifying insights into their application. The *Commentary* indicates that Article 55 seeks to restore the traditional idea that armed conflict is limited in scope, being directed toward enemy belligerents and not at individuals who are *hors de combat*.[469] Accordingly, the following principles of construction obtain:

> (i) The supplies which the occupying power is required to ensure include all articles necessary to support life.
>
> (ii) If the resources of the occupying power prove inadequate, the necessary life-sustaining articles must be imported into the occupied territory.
>
> (iii) It is irrelevant where the food (or other provision) comes from or the means utilized to import it. The occupying power may even be obligated to tax the resources of its own citizens or to seek aid from an enemy State—so long as its absolute obligations under Article 55 are met.[470]

---

[468] Geneva Convention III, *supra* § I.1, note 17, Art. 55.

[469] Commentary: Geneva Convention IV Relative to the Protection of Civilian Persons in Time of War 309 (Jean Pictet ed. 1958).

[470] *Id.* at 309-310. Specifically, the *Commentary* sets forth:

> During recent conflicts thousands of human beings suffered from starvation during the occupation of the country ... The absence of food and medical supplies and unhygienic conditions encouraged the spreading of epidemics. The spirit behind Article 55 represents a happy return to the traditional idea of the law of war, according to which belligerents sought to destroy the power of the enemy State, and not individuals.
>
> * * *
>
> Supplies for the population are not limited to food, but include medical supplies and any article necessary to support life.
>
> The term "population" is general; it is not confined to civilians but will on occasion include members of the armed forces detained in the occupied territory.
>
> The duty of ensuring supplies is reinforced by an obligation to bring in the necessary articles when the resources of the occupied territory are inadequate. It should be noted that the Convention does not lay down the method by which this is to be done. The occupying authorities retain complete freedom of action in regard to this, and are thus in a position to take circumstances of the moment into account.
>
> What is essential is that the Occupying Power should in good time and with the means available to it, take measures to procure the necessary food for the population in the occupied territory....

The requirement not to divert humanitarian relief consignments during both internal and interstitial wars is thus well-established.[471] There can thus be no question but that some famine is man-made and results in part from the refusal by State authorities to accept relief consignments during civil and interstitial conflicts. Where that is the case, the classes who have been denied assistance should in principle be entitled to Convention refugee status when they seek escape from the conditions of famine thus created. It is evident, in any case, that where deliberately created famine affects a defined group, persecution by reason of a protected ground may be the appropriate characterization, rather than viewing those affected as victims of natural calamity or widespread conditions of violence.

The affirmative responsibility of belligerents under the Geneva Conventions and Protocols to provide humanitarian aid within occupied territories and to permit the passage of relief consignments with respect to other populations under their control has important implications for the further growth of refugee law. These implications flow from the growing convergence of the concept of "persecution" with human rights and humanitarian law violations. Conditions of mass starvation may, upon closer examination, not be the product of indiscriminate violence, but rather result from a warring power's diversion of humanitarian aid. Where this is the case, refugee status should be recognized in those fleeing such conditions. As Maureen Graves has written:

> Other disasters, including some partially "natural" in origin, involve similar government strategies. For instance, denial of famine relief to anti-government areas is not merely "generalized oppression", it is as "focused" as—and likely more effective than—more individualized attacks on residents. The "social group" eligibility criterion was designed to protect people facing persecution because of some collective identity. That groups to be persecuted may be large or that their elevated risk may occur in the context of general oppression or war are not disqualifying.[472]

---

Similar protections cover those whose liberty has been restricted in internal armed conflict under Protocol II, *supra* § I.1, note 17, Art. 5(1)(b) and (c).

471 Indeed, violation of the preclusion will give rise to criminal responsibility. *See generally Final Report of the Commission of Experts for Yugoslavia*, *supra* § IV.4(a), note 247, at 19.

472 *See generally* Maureen Graves, *From Definition to Exploration: Social Groups and Political Asylum Eligibility*, 26 San Diego L. Rev. 740, 814-815 (1989). The Graves article was cited with apparent approval by the [Canadian] Court of Appeal in *Chan* v. *M.E.I.* (1993), 156 N.R. 279, 297 (F. C.A.):

> Torture, beating, rape are prime examples of "persecution" but there are, presumably, a great many others. It has been suggested, for instance, that the denial of

An issue is raised as to whether these basic principles applicable in armed conflict can be extended to analogous situations, i.e., to drought, famine or general conditions of economic depression which occasion mass displacements or human exodus. The conclusion that individuals fleeing such situations may well now be Convention refugees is strongly suggested by developments in general international law and by the growing State acceptance of the "right of humanitarian initiative"[473] both by individual States, by non-governmental organizations [NGOs], most notably the International Committee of the Red Cross [ICRC] and finally by international governmental organizations [IGOs], again most notably the United Nations High Commissioner for Refugees [UNHCR].

The area of disaster relief actions, in other words, is one in which principles developed in international humanitarian law are coming to apply largely by analogy. The evolution of international humanitarian norms to cover situations of "public emergencies" (as opposed to exclusively armed conflict) is discussed in the Forward to *Guiding Principles on the Right to Humanitarian Assistance*:

> The[se] considerations bring into relief the variety of factors which can exist in situations calling for international humanitarian aid under circumstances which developed international law has not yet had occasion to address or to formulate legal concepts to meet these new contingencies. It is one of the aims of the International Institute of Humanitarian Law to promote the development of international humanitarian law to meet these and other new situations.[474]

The strengthening of the United Nations' role in the provision of humanitarian relief in General Assembly Resolution 46/182[475] makes humanitarian doctrine applicable, at least by analogy, to situations of natural disaster and other "emergencies". Violation of the rules outlined above may well, therefore, have a direct bearing on the question of who is a refugee, at least in situations where the diversion of humanitarian relief has the effect of jeopardizing the life and welfare of specific groups which have already been marginalized by the State and society in question.

Under General Assembly Resolution 46/182, States are urged to facilitate the work of NGOs and IGOs in making humanitarian assistance available, as

---

famine relief in anti-government areas [citation to Graves article] may come within the definition.

[473] *See, e.g.*, Protocol II, *supra* § I.1, note 17, Art. 18.

[474] *Guiding Principles on the Right to Humanitarian Assistance, supra* this section, note 457, at 520.

[475] UNGA Res. 46/182, U.N. Doc. A/46/L.55 (Dec. 17, 1991).

are neighboring States. The Resolution contains as an Annex guidelines which "derive directly from ICRC doctrine".[476] Representative of ICRC principles is the *Code of Conduct* prepared by the ICRC relating to disaster relief.[477] The *Code* contains the following broad statement of policy:

> The right to humanitarian assistance, and to offer it, is a fundamental humanitarian principle which should be enjoyed by all citizens of all countries. As members of the international community, we recognize our obligations to provide humanitarian assistance wherever it is needed. Hence the need for unimpeded access to affected populations, which is of fundamental importance in exercising that responsibility.[478]

The *Code of Conduct* also reflects that humanitarian aid is to be provided on a non-discriminatory basis, i.e., "regardless of the race, creed or nationality of the victim". The only priority recognized will be that of "proportionality" i.e., that aid will be prioritized according to the comparative need of the victim alone.[479] Correspondingly, the *Guiding Principles* prepared by the ICRC provide for a right to request and receive humanitarian assistance from competent national and international organizations.[480] Such assistance may be provided to "ensure respect for the human rights to life, health, protection against cruel and degrading treatment and other rights which are essential to survival, well-being and protection in public emergencies."[481]

The most recent foray of international law and policy into the rights of those in need of humanitarian assistance by virtue of conditions of upheaval can be found in the principles for internally displaced persons prepared by the Representative of the UN Secretary-General, Francis Deng.[482] Critically,

---

476 Goodwin-Gill, *supra* § I.1, note 11, at 223, n. 96.

477 International Committee of the Red Cross and International Federation of Red Cross and Red Crescent Societies, *The Code of Conduct: Principles of Conduct for the International Red Cross and Red Crescent Movement and NGOs in Disaster Response Programmes, in* International Committee of the Red Cross and International Federation of Red Cross and Red Crescent Societies, Handbook of the International Red Cross and Red Crescent Movement 824 (13th ed. 1994).

478 *Id.*, Principle 1.

479 *Id.*, Principle 2. The rule of proportionality referred to here is the broad doctrine that aid will be supplied on the basis of need alone and to the degree that the need in question requires to be addressed.

480 *Guiding Principles on the Right to Humanitarian Assistance*, *supra* this section, note 457, Principle 2.

481 *Id.*, Principle 1.

482 See *Further Promotion and Encouragement of Human Rights and Fundamental Freedoms, Including the Question of the Programme and Methods of Work of the Commission of Human Rights, Mass Exoduses and Displaced Persons. Report of the Representative of the Secretary General, Mr. Francis Deng, Submitted pursuant to Commission resolution*

the *Guiding Principles*, following the broad criteria set forth in certain regional instruments with regard to refugee protection, define "displaced persons" as:

> persons or groups of persons who have been forced or obliged to flee or to leave their homes or places of habitual residence, in particular as a result of or in order to avoid the effects of armed conflict, situations of generalized violence, violations of human rights or natural or human made disasters, and who have not crossed an internationally recognized State border.[483]

The *Guiding Principles* constitute a broad fusion of international human rights, humanitarian law and refugee principles and formulate a regime of protection governing those who are caught up in internal calamity. Under the *Guiding Principles*, displaced persons are protected against murder of all kinds, including genocide, summary executions and enforced disappearances.[484] They are also not to be subjected to indiscriminate attacks, starvation as a method of warfare, being used as military shields, attacks against their camps or settlements, or the use of anti-personal landmines.[485] The property of civilians is subject to broad protections against acts of violence.[486] Rape and mutilation are prohibited as are torture and cruel and inhuman treatment. The *Principles on Internal Displacement* also bar acts of gender-specific violence, and acts which impose slavery (including sale into marriage, sexual exploitation, or forced child labor).[487]

Elementary freedoms are guaranteed such as freedom from arbitrary arrest and detention[488] and the freedom of internal and external movement.[489] Displaced persons have certain education rights, at least through the primary level. Families are given the right to know the fate of missing relatives, and

---

*1997/39 (Addendum)*, U.N. Doc. E/CN.4/1998/53/Add.2, 54th Sess., Annex (1998), *reprinted in* 18(1) *Refugee Survey Quarterly* 163 (1999) [hereinafter *Guiding Principles on Internal Displacement*].

483 *Id.*, Introduction, Scope and Purpose. This definition has not always been universally accepted. For a essay critical of Deng's definition and suggesting an alternative which would limit the scope of the "internally displaced" definition to those who are the victims of deliberate human rights violations, *see* Nils Geissler, *The International Protection of Internally Displaced Persons*, 11 Int'l J. Refugee L. 451, 455 (1999).

484 *Guiding Principles on Internal Displacement*, *supra* this section, note 482. Principle 10(1).

485 *Id.*, Principle 10(2).

486 *Id.*, Principle 21.

487 *Id.*, Principle 11.

488 *Id.*, Principle 12.

489 *Id.*, Principles 14 and 15.

family members are to be reunited as quickly as possible.[490] Freedom of thought, conscience and religion are included as are the freedom of association and certain political participation rights.[491]

The core of the *Principles on Internal Displacement*, however, is the broad body of social rights upon which survival of the displaced depends and the corresponding provisions relating to "humanitarian initiative." Those struggling to secure their own survival must be seen as the chief object of solicitude for international public policy. Included within these social rights are: (i) the right to essential food and potable water; (ii) basic shelter and housing; (iii) appropriate clothing; and (iv) essential medical services and sanitation.[492] To secure these latter rights, the *Principles* make clear that the national authorities have principal responsibility.[493] Failing a remedy at the national level, however, the *Principles* continue to provide for a "right" of international initiative (the "right" to confer international humanitarian aid) which has its provenance in the customary law of war.[494] Consent to such aid being provided to those in need of it "shall not be arbitrarily withheld, particularly when the authorities concerned are unable or unwilling to provide the required humanitarian assistance.[495]

The questions arising for both humanitarian and refugee law by reason of these emerging developments are of the utmost concern. Primary among these is the scope of the State's discretion to decline international relief consignments affecting its citizens in situations which involve, for instance, violent upheaval or conditions of mass starvation. The application of humanitarian principle as a matter of law in such instances is extremely difficult to assess.[496]

Resolution 46/182, for instance, indicates that introducing relief consignments is dependent upon the "permission" of the host State. Richard Plender has argued, however, in connection with ensuing Resolution 48/116 em-

---

490 *Id.*, Principles 16.

491 *Id.*, Principles 22.

492 *Id.*, Principle 18.

493 *Id.*, Principle 25(1).

494 *Id.*, Principle 25(2).

495 *Id.* With respect to norms governing the right to return, there are two essential principles: (i) the right to return in safety and dignity with the assistance of the responsible authorities (Principle 28); and (ii) the right not to be discriminated against once the formerly "displaced person" has returned (Principle 29).

496 *But see, Guiding Principles on the Right to Humanitarian Assistance, supra* this section, note 457, Principle 7.

powering the UNHCR to extend, on a case-by-case basis, protection and assistance to the internally displaced, that:

> [A]n arbitrary refusal to permit the administration of humanitarian relief to internally displaced persons, in violation of human rights, may constitute an *abus de droit* which cannot prevent the United Nations Organization from discharging the tasks conferred upon it by the Charter.[497]

As shown above, this broad principle has now been adopted in the *Guiding Principles on Internal Displacement* prepared by Francis Deng.[498] The conclusion that the State's discretion is subject to a "rule of reason" in this area is also supported by the *Guiding Principles on the Right to Humanitarian Assistance* prepared by the ICRC. The latter provide that United Nations organs may resort to coercion where a sovereign's decision to reject international relief consignments has been unjustifiably refused:

> The competent United Nations organs and regional organizations may undertake necessary measures, including coercion, in accordance with their respective mandates, in the event of severe, prolonged and mass suffering of populations, which could be alleviated by humanitarian assistance. These measures may be resorted to when an offer has been refused without justification, or when the provision of humanitarian assistance encounters serious difficulties.[499]

The State's refusal to permit international relief consignments directed toward a specific group introduces into general conditions of upheaval the necessary element of a "deliberate moral agency" required to establish Convention refugee status. Affected groups, in such instances, are not victims of drought, famine or severe economic depression; rather the injury to them flows from violation of an emerging human right under international

---

[497] Richard Plender, *The Legal Basis of International Jurisdiction to Act with Regard to the Internally Displaced*, 6 Int'l J. Refugee L. 345, 356 (1994). The classic case of humanitarian intervention for the purposes of distributing humanitarian assistance is that of Somalia. For an extensive discussion examining the *droit d'ingérence* in the case of Somalia, *see* Marie-Dominique Perrot (ed.), *Dérives Humanitaires: Etats d'Urgence et Droit d'Ingérence* (1994). Somalia as precedent for the "right" to intervene for purely humanitarian reasons has been seriously questioned, however, on the ground that Somalia was not a State at the time of the intervention. *See, e.g.*, G. Plender, *supra* this note, at 354-355.

[498] *Guiding Principles on Internal Displacement, supra* this section, note 482, Principle 25(2).

[499] *Guiding Principles on the Right to Humanitarian Assistance, supra* this section, note 457, Principle 7.

law, the right to receive humanitarian assistance, which has been tendered in the circumstances, but unjustifiably refused.[500]

Those groups (identified as Internally Displaced Persons or "IDPs" while in the State of origin) have been displaced by virtue of human-made or natural calamity. However, their situation has been aggravated by the sovereign's misconduct. Accordingly, individuals comprising such groups ought in principle to have no difficulty in showing that the harm they fear or experience is "by reason of" a protected ground if they manage to cross an international frontier. The situation of the internally displaced is a case in point in which international institutions (including the UNHCR and the ICRC) have clearly designated a specific class as being in need of special protection. The failure to observe a defined duty towards a human aggregate which is the designated beneficiary of a treaty or customary norm both constitutes persecution and establishes a "social group" for refugee definition purposes.[501]

It is clear, in this respect, that the characteristic of being displaced is one which the victims are powerless to alter. Like situations arising out of internal armed conflict in which humanitarian law violations can constitute evidence of persecutory motive, injury which flows from a breach of duty toward a human aggregate gives rise to a presumption that serious harm has been imposed on account of a protected ground, especially when no rational explanation for refusing humanitarian aid is presented by the sovereign. Objective criteria can be looked to in such instances to determine whether the group affected was already marginalized, or the victim of political and/or social repression. The breach alone, however, of an affirmative duty by the State toward a defined group which emerging international law and policy has determined worthy of special protection, may well be representative of the type of case in which the criteria for social group persecution is satisfied by evidence of the violation itself, without more.

---

500 The obligation of the sovereign itself to relieve such conditions is beyond question, and the right to "international" assistance becomes operative only when domestic "remedies" have been exhausted. *See, e.g., Guiding Principles on the Right to Humanitarian Assistance, supra* This section, note 457, Principle 3(b), indicating that international measures become triggered when:

> all local possibilities and domestic procedures have been exhausted within a reasonable time, and vital needs are not satisfied or are not fully satisfied, so that there is no other possibility to ensure the present provision of supplies and services essential for the persons affected.

501 For a clear example of the emerging methodology *see, e.g.*, CRDD T93-12198, T93-12199, **T93-12197**, May 10, 1994.

General principles of human rights law, applied by analogy, support this result. In this respect, the Human Rights Committee has now interpreted Article 7 of the International Covenant on Civil and Political Rights to prohibit extradition, expulsion or refoulement of individuals which would result in the latter being exposed to torture, or to cruel, inhuman or degrading treatment.[502] The Committee has also determined that individuals should not be forcibly returned where their right to life would be threatened.[503] Where that right is threatened by conditions of starvation which can be traced to the State's inaction, the resulting harm will constitute "inhuman treatment" under Article 7.

For the refugee definition to be met, a showing must be made that serious harm is connected to a protected ground. The failure to accept (and to distribute to those in need) relief consignments can establish such "nexus" for refugee purposes based on principles of non-discrimination. The Committee on Economic, Social and Cultural Rights has, for instance, given an affirmative (or "social") interpretation to equal protection under the Covenant on Economic, Social and Cultural Rights to the effect that, as concerns the right to housing:

> States parties must give due priority to those social groups living in unfavorable conditions by giving them particular consideration.[504]

These developments are of moment for a variety of reasons. The adoption by the General Assembly of humanitarian doctrine in connection with disaster relief actions clearly brings to practical fruition the ongoing incorporation of the law and policy of Geneva into the broad institutional objectives of the United Nations. In addition, it informs international refugee law with a "social dimension" which protects the right to life by recognizing the principle of humanitarian aid.[505] Failure to cooperate with the protective

---

[502] *See* General Comments adopted by the Human Rights Committee, No. 20, ¶ 3, *in* General Comments adopted by the Human Rights Committee, Nos. 1-23, *reprinted in* Note by Secretariat, Compilation of General Comments and General Recommendations adopted by Human Rights Treaty Bodies, UN Doc. No. HR1/GEN/1/Rev. 1 (July 29, 1994).

[503] *Id.*, ¶¶ 14.1 and 15.3. For a discussion, *see* Walter Kalin, *Legal Protection of Internally Displaced Persons: Protection in International Human Rights Law, in* Internally Displaced Persons 15, 20 (International Committee of the Red Cross eds. 1995).

[504] General Comment No. 4, (1991), UN ESCOR, Supp. (No. 3), Annex III, at 117, ¶ 9, UN Doc. E/1992/23 (1992).

[505] The provision of humanitarian relief (and the very special status of the parties who are in need of it) must be seen as an outgrowth of the "social morality" of the Geneva Conventions and Protocols. For an explanation of the relationship between the provision of humanitarian aid and the principles of the Red Cross, *see* Jean Pictet, Red Cross Principles 48 (1956):

machinery established through UN Resolutions and other instruments by the host State should give rise to a claim under the 1951 Convention for those whose lives or freedom are threatened as a result. Such recognition "completes the circle" of protection by assuring that those whose right to life is compromised by the sovereign's refusal to comply with the emerging right to humanitarian assistance will receive surrogate protection under the law of refugee status.

---

On reflection, one sees that distributive justice is profoundly different from charity. It has been represented as a woman holding scales and blindfolded. It is true that this symbol could, in a sense, represent charity. Charity, like justice, knows man only as only as a human being, the label attached to him being without importance. Like justice, it holds the balance evenly between one man and another. Like justice again, it bestows its gifts on a recipient whom it has selected for valid reasons. But there the analogy ends. For while justice gives to each according to his rights, charity apportions its gifts on the basis of suffering endured in each case. To judge, is to distinguish the good from the wicked, the just from the unjust; it means assessing individual responsibility. Charity has nothing to do with that form of justice. It refuses to weigh the merits and faults of the individual. It goes much further than that; rising above the contrast between good and evil, it attains complete serenity and wisdom; it is then the very image of mercy, of boundless kindness.

# VI. CONCLUSION: HUMAN RIGHTS, HUMANITARIAN NORMS AND THE SCOPE OF THE PROTECTED GROUNDS

## § VI.1. Human Rights and Humanitarian Norms in the Continuing Expansion of the Convention Refugee Definition

The essential theme of this study has been that the five grounds of refugee protection should continue to be shaped by prevailing standards of non-discrimination and equal protection. This ongoing evolution, however, is not taking place at random, but rather within what can be termed a social and political morality. The framework for this morality must be seen in the broad principles of international human rights and humanitarian norms which provide broad points of reference for refugee jurisprudence.

It is now widely recognized that the three essential pillars of modern international public order are human rights law, international humanitarian law and the law of refugee status.[1] In the past, convergence between human rights law and humanitarian law was advocated by Jean Pictet, the leading commentator on the laws and customs applicable in armed conflict, who himself designated the new body of jurisprudence "human law".[2] Recent scholarly work has recommended a broad fusion of all three subject matter areas, arguing that only such a consolidation can bring about the kinds of protections which modern policy requires. A recent article concludes, for instance:

> In most conflicts, international human rights, humanitarian and refugee law are widely unknown, ignored or willfully disrespected. Almost every abuse of the civilian population or attack on humanitarian personnel is a breach of international law, representing a threat to security and peace. The challenge we are facing today is to bridge this gap and to strengthen the protection of

---

1 *See generally* O. Hieronymi, *Human Rights, Refugee Protection and Humanitarian Action*, 18 Refugee Survey Quarterly 1 (1999):

> International Humanitarian Law and Action, the protection of refugees and the victims of all forms of forced migration, and international human rights obligations are the three main pillars of the international system of defending the human person.

*Id.* at 1.

2 J. Pictet, *supra* § I.1, note 18, at 63-68.

> civilians in armed conflict, including vulnerable groups such as refugees and internally displaced persons whose situation is often compounded through the loss of vital needs for survival such as security, shelter, medical care and access to food and water.[3]

By proposing an interpretation of the law of refugee status which looks to international human rights and humanitarian law for definitional guidance, this study seeks to forward such a convergence and to close possible gaps in refugee protection.

This approach also appears supported by historical considerations. The framers' unambiguous reference in the Preamble of the 1951 Convention to the Universal Declaration of Human Rights indicates a desire for the refugee definition to evolve in tandem with human rights principles. A similar role for modern law of war flows from the latter's long-established function of protecting basic human rights during armed conflict. Accordingly, a teleological interpretation of the refugee definition would allow the grounds of refugee protection to evolve commensurately with developments in human rights and humanitarian law.

## § VI.2. Practical Examples of Human Rights Violations in Relation to the Refugee Definition

1. **Protection from Generalized Conditions of Upheaval.** The plight of individuals and groups caught up in mass migrations which have been occasioned by systematic human rights violations is an area of growing concern. Representative of this trend have been the recent influxes of Salvadoran and Haitian asylum seekers into North America which have been provoked by massive international humanitarian law violations (in the case of El Salvador) and (in the case of Haiti) by the overt social persecution of the poor wrought by a kleptocratic dictatorship.[4]

In a similar way, the basic pattern of humanitarian law violations taking place in the former Yugoslavia reveals that they were clearly directed along ethnic lines. Serious harm was transparently being imposed on a mass scale, and that harm was related to a ground protected under the law of refugee status (ethnicity or race). These violations have included: (i) mass killings, tortures and rapes; (ii) mass forcible deportation of civilians; (iii) arbitrary arrest, confinement and molestation of civilians; (iv) deliberate attacks on

---

[3] M. Robinson, *Human Rights, Refugee Protection and Humanitarian Action: Convergence and Cooperation*, 18(3) Refugee Survey Quarterly 11, 14 (1999).

[4] *See, e.g.*, Note, *Political Legitimacy in the Law of Political Asylum,* 99 Harvard L. Rev. 450, 465 (1985).

ambulances and hospitals; (v) obstruction of the delivery of food and medical supplies to the civilian population; and (vi) wanton destruction of religious and cultural property, to name a few.[5] Group determination (or prima facie determinations, subject to review) would appear appropriate in such instances.

In these instances, the pattern of migration has an overtly collective feature since harm or suffering has been directly inflicted on individuals because of their inclusion in targeted human aggregates. The notion that the refugee definition automatically excludes such claimants because of the Convention's individualized requirements is misplaced. It is a recognized matter of record that many forced migrations are directed against defined groups, and are accompanied by deliberate and grave violations of human rights.[6]

The situation of forced collective migrations, however, is representative of a wider analytic problem. Adjudicators are too inclined to examine mass flight superficially by looking only at general conditions, and to ignore more particularized aspects of the claim, including the human dimension. Study of the underlying situation may well reveal that a deliberate human agency has either created those general conditions or, at least, played a material role in rendering their effects more harmful as to specific classes. The State's failure to permit humanitarian relief consignments to marginalized groups during a natural famine is only one example among many of how consequences which are general in nature can be transformed into persecution by human intervention or inaction.[7]

2. **Protection Against Sovereign Acts of "Lawful" Prosecutions**. There have also been lesser migratory flows caused by discrete violations of human rights obtaining with respect to more limited classes. Young Yugoslavian men who refused to bear arms in the recent war of 1991-94, and who were threatened with prosecution for declining to become involved in

---

5 *See generally Final Report of the Commission of Experts for Yugoslavia, supra* § IV.4(a), note 247.

6 For an overview of humanitarian law principles and their application to forced mass migrations, *see generally* Beyani, *supra* § IV.4(b), note 245. For eligibility criteria in general, *see* Matter of S-P-, 21 I&N Dec. 486 (BIA 1996); *Canadian Civil War Guidelines, supra* § III.3, note 39.

7 As discussed earlier, while "common victimization" cannot constitute a *reason* motivating persecution, it can serve as significant *evidence* that the serious harm the claimant fears flows from an implicit policy of discrimination which affects the claimant and others with whom the claimant is inexorably linked in the perception of the persecutor.

internationally condemned atrocities, provide one example.[8] Also relevant to this category of claimants are the Chinese nationals whose right to procreative autonomy was denied by draconian invasions of their physical integrity, including compulsory sterilization and forced abortion.[9] A sizeable influx of refugees was also brought about by the flight of individuals fearing punishment for having lent support to the mujahidin (the Islamic fundamentalist group opposed to the Najibulah government) during the Afghan civil war. The basis for such claims was armed resistance to a regime which foreclosed all access to orderly democratic change through the instrument of State administered terror.[10] These three instances are representative of significant migrations involving highly individualized claims which are based on the asylum seeker's decision to disobey the law.

In the case of those fleeing from prosecution (Yugoslavian draft evaders, Chinese avoiding coercive family planning policies and Afghans fearing punishment for acts of insurgency) the fear has been inspired by a general pattern of repression which has triggered widespread acts of civil disobedience and consequent flight. Relief in such instances, however, must be seen as something more than simply protection against such abuses. In granting asylum, there is the implicit recognition that individuals who seek to overturn totalitarian regimes, refuse to bear arms on behalf of humanitarian law violators, or assert their procreative autonomy should be protected on public policy grounds since their actions enhance respect for human rights.

Such a response on the part of the international community is entirely appropriate for the world order which came into being at the conclusion of World War II and which has as its principal constituent documents the United Nations Charter and the Universal Declaration of Human Rights. As Ronald Dworkin has written:

> Both conservatives and liberals suppose that in a society which is generally decent, everyone has a duty to obey the law, whatever it is. That is the source of the 'general duty' clause in the orthodox position, and though liberals

---

8 U.S. Department of State, *Profile on Asylum Claims for the Former Yugoslavia* (1996). With regard to eligibility criteria for those resisting induction generally, *see* , *e.g.*, Matter of Salim, 18 I&N Dec. 211 (BIA 1982); Matter of A.-G.-, 19 I&N Dec. 502 (BIA 1987), *rev'd sub nom.* M.A. v. INS (I), 858 F.2d 210 (4th Cir. 1988), *vacated,* M.A. A26 851 062 v. INS (II), 899 F.2d 304 (1990); Barraza-Rivera v. INS, 913 F.2d 1443 (9th Cir. 1990); Zolfagharkhani v. M.E.I. (1993), 155 N.R. 311 (F.C.A.); Ciric v. M.E.I. [1994] 2 F.C. 65 (T.D.).

9 *See, e.g.*, Cheung v. M.E.I. (1993), 153 N.R. 145 (F.C.A.). Matter of C-Y-Z-, 21 I&N Dec. 915 (BIA 1997).

10 Matter of Izatula, 20 I&N Dec. 149 (BIA 1990). Gil v. M.C.I., (1994), 174 N.R. 292 (F.C.A.).

> believe that this duty can sometimes be 'overridden', even they suppose, as the orthodox position maintains, that the duty of obedience remains in some submerged form, so that a man does well to accept punishment in recognition of that duty. *But this general duty is almost incoherent in a society that recognizes rights.* If a man believes he has to demonstrate, then he must believe that it would be wrong for the Government to stop him, with or without benefit of a law. If he is entitled to believe that, then it is silly to speak of a duty to obey the law as such or of a duty to accept the punishment that the State has no right to give.[11]

Cases in which the claimant is asserting a fundamental human right and faces punishment under a law of general application focus attention on the centrality which human rights occupy in the modern system. The plight of asylum seekers who voluntarily face prosecution for engaging in acts of conscience illustrates the extraordinary weight which human rights enjoy both in connection with the refugee definition and with respect to the broader system of political and social morality within which that definition is evolving.

3. **Protection Against "Personal" Forms of Harm**. Parallel concerns apply to adjudications in which vulnerable groups seek asylum from conditions of serious harm in the home State, especially where such groups enjoy a high level of protection under international law and policy. Preeminent examples are women fleeing FGM,[12] and women suffering from abusive husbands in legal and social environments which effectively deny the claimant State protection.[13] Here again the "social interpretation" of human rights has been incorporated, to some degree, into refugee jurisprudence. The State's failure to intervene affirmatively in such circumstances gives rise to surrogate international human rights protection in the asylum State. Such claimants are being recognized based upon the adverse equal protection implications and objective marginalization which their accounts of persecution raise.

## § VI.3. Enhancing International Human Rights and Humanitarian Law as a Goal of Refugee Protection

The international community has an interest in upholding the normative content of contemporary human rights instruments, including the standards

---

11 Dworkin, *supra* § I.3, note 49, at 192-193. [Emphasis supplied].

12 Matter of Kasinga, 21 I&N Dec. 357 (BIA 1996); Annan v. M.C.I., [1995] 3 F.C. 25 (T.D.).

13 Vidhani v. M.C.I. [1995] 3 F.C> 60 (T.D.); Narvaez v. M.C.I., [1995] 2 F.C. 55 (T.D.); Matter of A- and Z-, A72 793 219 (IJ Arlington VA Dec. 20, 1994) (Nejelski, IJ); Matter of Sonia Sharmin, A73 556 033 (IJ New York, NY Sept. 30, 1996) (Bukszpan, IJ).

set forth in CEDAW and the Declaration on Violence Against Women.[14] Human rights compliance by States is the logical converse of refugee protection in that it helps to eliminate the "root causes" of refugee flows.[15] It is only appropriate in light of such a goal that refugee jurisprudence should look to equal protection standards in determining the scope of the Convention's coverage and to confer surrogate human rights relief where those with common status or shared beliefs have been effectively marginalized pursuant to an explicit or implicit policy of discrimination. A decision which grants refugee status, while recognizing the enhanced protection of vulnerable classes, goes far toward advancing this quintessentially humanitarian objective.

The most salient parallel to this role of refugee law is, perhaps, common Article 1 of the Geneva Conventions of August 12, 1949 which enjoins States parties to respect, and to ensure respect for, the core obligations of the Conventions "in all circumstances".[16] The Commentary to common Article 1 explains the universal scope of the rights protected and the *erga omnes* character of the undertakings by States parties in terms of an "imperative call to civilization". As set forth in the Commentary to Geneva Convention I:

> The motive of the Convention is such a lofty one, so universally recognized as an imperative call to civilization, that one feels the need for its assertion, as much because of the respect one has for it oneself as because of the respect for it which one expects from one's opponent, and perhaps even more for the former reason than for the latter.[17]

At the core of humanitarian law's universal claims lies respect for the dignity and worth of the human personality which operates as the philosophical mainstay of the Conventions and Protocols and provides the law of war with its core sustaining principle. The irreducible ethical character of the principles underlying the Geneva Conventions and their clear relationship to the protection of fundamental human rights can be glimpsed in a discarded

---

[14] United Nations High Commissioner for Refugees, *Conclusion and Decision on International Protection*, U.N. Doc. A/AC.96/911 (Oct. 12, 1998), ¶ 21, *reprinted in* 11 Int'l J. Refugee L. 227 (1999).

[15] United Nations High Commissioner for Refugees, *Managing Migration in a Wider Europe* (Council of Europe Seminar on Managing Migration in the Wider Europe, Strasbourg, Oct. 12-13, 1998), ¶ 18, *reprinted in* 17 Refugee Survey Quarterly 45 (1999).

[16] Common Article 1 of the Geneva Conventions of August 12, 1949 provides:

> The High Contracting Parties undertake to respect and to ensure respect for the present Convention in all circumstances.

Geneva Convention I, *supra* § I.1, note 17, Art. 1.

[17] Commentary to Geneva Convention I, *supra* § I.2, note 40, at 25. [Emphasis supplied].

Preamble to the Conventions recommended by the ICRC to the following effect:

> Respect for the personality and the dignity of human beings constitutes a universal principle which is binding even in the absence of contractual undertaking.
>
> Such a principle demands that, in time of war, all those not actively engaged in the hostilities and all those placed *hors de combat* by reason of sickness, wounds, capture, or any other circumstance, shall be given due respect and have protection from the effects of war, and that those among them who are in suffering shall be succoured and tended without distinction of race, nationality, religious belief, political opinion or any other quality....[18]

The Convention refugee definition thus enjoys a teleological relationship to human rights and humanitarian norms. Promoting the international morality represented by the United Nations Charter and related constituent documents must be seen as a parallel objective to the treaty's core goal of refugee protection. Conversely stated, an essential function of the law of refugee status is to further the growth of human rights and humanitarian law.

The Refugee Convention is an indispensable element of the modern international order. That order's governing instrument, the United Nations Charter, must be understood as a constituent document which is evolving in conformity with its fundamental purposes. Chief among these is the broadening and deepening of human rights. As Ian Brownlie has remarked:

> The clauses concerning human rights in the Charter provide a foundation for, and an impetus to further improvement in the protection of human rights. In the preamble the members 'reaffirm faith in fundamental human rights, in the equal rights of men and women...'. Article 1 defines the purposes of the United Nations to include cooperation 'in promoting and encouraging respect for human rights and for fundamental freedoms for all without distinction as to race, sex, language or religion'. Of key importance is Article 55, which states that 'the United Nations shall promote: (a) higher standards of living, full employment, and conditions, and conditions of economic and social progress and development... (c) universal respect for, and observance of, human rights and fundamental freedoms for all...'. Article 56 provides: 'All Members pledge themselves to take joint and separate action in cooperation with the Organization for the achievement of the purposes set forth in Article 55.'[19]

---

18 *Remarks and Proposals submitted by the International Committee of the Red Cross:* Documents for consideration of governments by the Swiss Federal Council to attend the Diplomatic Conference of Geneva (April 21, 1949), Geneva, February 1949, at 8, *quoted in* Commentary to Geneva Convention I, *supra* § I.2, note 40, at 21.

19 *See, e.g.*, Ian Brownlie, Principles of Public International Law 569 (1990).

On the other hand, it is similarly clear that the development and implementation of international humanitarian law equally form an aspect of United Nations objectives, despite the fact that these goals are not specifically mentioned in the Charter. The essential function of modern international humanitarian law (to protect human rights in armed conflict) assumes central importance in this regard.[20] Moreover, as noted in the Commentary to Protocol I: "Acting for the protection of man, also in time of armed conflict, accords with the aims of the United Nations no less than does the maintenance of international peace and security".[21]

The 1951 Convention on the Status of Refugees is an evolving constitutional document. It should not be given a static interpretation or one which isolates it from the social and political goals of the United Nations and the realization of human rights for all without discrimination. Rather, the 1951 Convention must be understood in its historical context and in conformity with the objectives of the larger constitutional order of which it is a part.

---

20 *Respect for Human Rights in Armed Conflict,* Report of the Secretary General, U.N. Doc. A/7120 (1969).

21 *See, e.g., Commentary to Protocol II, supra* § I.2, note 36, at 1034.

# ACKNOWLEDGEMENTS

The following authors and publishers have been most generous in giving their permission to reproduce material already in print. The section and footnote in brackets indicate where the quotation is to be found.

Butterworths Canada, Ltd.: James Hathaway, The Law of Refugee Status, at 110-111 and 136. Butterworths Canada, Ltd. (1991). [§ I.2, note 33; § V.3, note 83]. Reprinted with permission of Butterworths Canada, Ltd.

Cornell International Law Journal: Maryellen Fullerton, *A Comparative Look at Refugee Status Based on Persecution Due to Membership in a Particular Social Group*, 26 Cornell Int'l L. J. 505, at 547 (1993). [§ V.3, note 79]. Reprinted with permission of Cornell International Law Journal.

Harvard University Press: Ronald Dworkin, Taking Rights Seriously, at 192-193. Cambridge, Massachusetts: Harvard University Press (1977). [§ VI.2, note 11]. Reprinted with permission of Ronald Dworkin.

Harvard Law Review: Note, *Political Legitimacy in the Law of Political Asylum* 99 Harv. L. Rev. 450, at 456 (1985). [§ V.3, note 152]. Reprinted with permission of the Harvard Law Review Association.

International Committee of the Red Cross: Commentary: Geneva Convention IV Relative to the Protection of Civilians in Time of War, at 309-310 (Pictet ed.). Geneva: International Committee of the Red Cross (1958). [§ V.5(c), note 470]. Reprinted with permission of the International Committee of the Red Cross.

Jean Pictet, Red Cross Principles, at 48. Geneva: International Committee of the Red Cross (1956). [§ V.5(c), note 505]. Reprinted with permission of the International Committee of the Red Cross.

Oxford University Press: Ian Brownlie. Principles of Public International Law, at 569. Oxford: Clarendon Press (1990). [§ VI.2, note 19]. Reprinted with permission of Oxford University Press.

Matthew Craven, The International Covenant on Economic, Social and Cultural Rights: A Perspective on its Development, at 166, 178. Oxford: Clarendon Press (1995). [§ V.3, note 157]. Reprinted with permission of Oxford University Press.

Guy S. Goodwin-Gill, The Refugee in International Law, at 47-48 and 360-361. Oxford: Clarendon Press (1996). [§ V.3, note 97; § V.4, note 160]. Reprinted with permission of Oxford University Press.

G. Goodwin-Gill, S. Timberlake and R. Steinhardt, *Canas-Segovia v. Immigration and Naturalization Service: Brief Amicus Curiae of the Office of of the High Commissioner for Refugees, reprinted in* 2 Int'l J. Refugee Law 390, at 401 and 407 (1990). [§ II.3, notes 102 and 104]. Reprinted with permission of Oxford University Press.

Audrey Macklin, *Canada (Attorney-General) v. Ward: A Review Essay*, 6 Int'l J. Refugee L. 362, at 375 (1994). [§V.5(a), note 265]. Reprinted with permission of Oxford University Press.

Dominic McGoldrick, The Human Rights Committee: Its Role in the Development of the International Covenant on Civil and Political Rights, at 275. Oxford: The Clarendon Press (1994). [§ V.4, note 215]. Reprinted with permission of Oxford University Press.

UNHCR, Division of International Protection, *Gender-Related Persecution: An Analysis of Recent Trends*, Int'l J. Refugee L. 79, at 87 (Special Issue: February 22-23, 1996). [§ V.5(b)(4), note 441]. Reprinted with permission of Oxford University Press.

Oxford University Press and United Nations High Commissioner for Refugees: Chaloka Beyani, *A Political and Legal Analysis of the Problem of the Return of Forcibly Transferred Populations*, 16(3) Refugee Survey Quarterly 1, at 2 (1997). [§ IV.4(b), note 245]. Reprinted with permission of Oxford University Press.

A.W. Sijthoff: Atle Grahl-Madsen, The Status of Refugees in International Law, Vol. 1, at 250. Leyden: A.W. Sijthoff 1966. [§ IV.3, note 55].

University of Pennsylvania Press: W. P. Alford, *Making a Goddess of Democracy from Loose Sand: Some Thoughts on Human Rights in the People's Republic of China, in* Human Rights in Cross-Cultural Perspectives: A Quest for Consensus 65, at 73-74 (Abdullahi Ahmed An-Naim ed. 1992). University of Pennsylvania Press, 1991. [§ V.5(a), note 249]. Reprinted with permission of the University of Pennsylvania Press.

# INDEX

# Refugees and Human Rights

1. P. Kourula: *Broadening the Edges.* Refugee Definition and International Protection Revisited. 1997 ISBN HB 90-411-0480-1 PB 90-411-0481-X
2. B. Ghosh: *Huddled Masses and Uncertain Shores.* Insights into Irregular Migration. 1998 ISBN 90-411-0531-X
3. I.C. Jackson: *The Refugee Concept in Group Situations.* 1999 ISBN 90-411-1228-6
4. A.F. Bayefski and J. Fitzpatrick (eds.): *Human Rights and Forced Displacement.* 2000 ISBN 90-411-1518-8
5. M.R. von Sternberg: *The Grounds of Refugee Protection in the Context of International Human Rights and Humanitarian Law.* Canadian and United States Case Law Compared. 2001 ISBN 90-411-1726-1

KLUWER LAW INTERNATIONAL – THE HAGUE / LONDON / BOSTON